Rethinking Norman Italy

Manchester University Press

artes liberales

Series Editors

*Carrie E. Beneš, T. J. H. McCarthy,
Stephen Mossman and Jochen Schenk*

Artes Liberales aims to promote the study of the Middle Ages – broadly defined in geography and chronology – from a perspective that transcends modern disciplinary divisions. It seeks to publish scholarship of the highest quality that is interdisciplinary in topic or approach, integrating elements such as history, art history, musicology, literature, religion, political thought, philosophy and science. The series particularly seeks to support research based on the study of original manuscripts and archival sources, and to provide a recognised venue for increased exposure for scholars at all career stages around the world.

Previously published
Writing the Welsh borderlands in Anglo-Saxon England
Lindy Brady

Justice and mercy: Moral theology and the exercise of law in twelfth-century England
Philippa Byrne

Emotional monasticism: Affective piety in the eleventh-century monastery of John of Fécamp
Lauren Mancia

In Conclusion: Serving with Purpose, Living in Fulfillment

The Serve is not just a phase; it's a way to live a purposeful life rooted in Christ. Embracing your mission leads to fulfillment that no earthly relationship can match. Trust that God is preparing your heart and guiding your steps for the right relationship when the time comes.

Ms. Right felt gratitude as she absorbed the Counselor's words.

The Counselor expressed pride in her transformation and encouraged her to serve wholeheartedly. She advised Ms. Right to reflect deeply on the manual throughout the remainder of the week, allowing the lessons to sink in.

"Use this time to align your thoughts and actions with your purpose," the Counselor said gently. "On Saturday, return with Mr. Right for our final review session. Together, we'll celebrate your growth and prepare for the next chapter of your journey."

As they closed in prayer, Ms. Right left that day feeling empowered and ready to embrace her purpose with renewed confidence and joy.

Saturday: The Grand Finale

On Saturday, Ms. Right and Mr. Right met the Counselor on her lovely patio to celebrate the collaboration of Ms. Right's journey.

Viewing the complete Virtual Liberating Marital Experience, Ms. Right was emotional as she saw the manual dedicated to her.

"It's incredible to see everything come full circle," she said, wiping her tears.

Mr. Right agreed, reflecting on the profound journey they had taken together.

The Counselor thanked Ms. Right for her courage, offering her a chance to earn generational wealth through the project, honoring her journey and allowing it to bless others. Ms. Right accepted with gratitude, excited to make an impact.

"The Happily Ever After"

In the following months, Ms. Right successfully sought shared custody of her daughter, transforming her relationship with her ex-husband through the lessons she had learned.
Mr. and Ms. Right continued growing together, and he proposed after nine months. Eleven months later, they married in a beautiful ceremony, confident in their God-ordained union.

Their journey was one of healing and deep faith, starting a new life together, blessed by God.

What's Next...

We sincerely appreciate your time and openness in reading this book, and we hope it has inspired and challenged you in meaningful ways. If you haven't already done so, we encourage you to take the next step by visiting the website: https://maritalinspirations.org to engage with The Virtual Liberating Marital Experience. This resource builds upon the themes in these pages, offering deeper insights and practical tools for living with intention and relational fulfillment. Transformation begins when you release the spirit of scarcity and fully embrace the abundant life that awaits you. Your journey doesn't end here—this is just the beginning. We look forward to walking with you into a future filled with purpose, joy, and lasting love.

Contents

List of figures ... vii
List of tables ... ix
List of contributors ... x
Acknowledgements ... xv
List of abbreviations ... xvi

1 Introduction: rethinking Norman Italy – Joanna H. Drell ... 1

Part I: Historiographies

2 Norman Italy and Sicily through the eyes of British historians, 1912–76 – David Abulafia ... 15
3 The Norman Empire between the eleventh and twelfth centuries with special reference to the Normans in southern Italy – Luigi Russo ... 29
4 Historiography in the making: a name-list of Sicilian Muslims from the Rollus Rubeus cartulary of Cefalù cathedral – Alex Metcalfe ... 46
5 A fiscal provision of Count Roger of Ariano: traces of redactional variants in the *Chronicon* of Falco of Benevento – Edoardo D'Angelo ... 93

Part II: Identities and communities

6 Crucible of faith: *fitna* in the *Travels* of Ibn Jubayr – Joshua C. Birk ... 113
7 *Bellum civile*: urban strife and conflict management in early twelfth-century Benevento – Markus Krumm ... 132

8 Norman rulers and Greek-speaking subjects: the *Vitae* of Italo-Greek saints (twelfth and thirteenth centuries) and the negotiation of local identities – Eleni Tounta   152
9 *Griffones* and the city of Messina: urban encounters with crusading – Paul Oldfield   171

Part III: Religion and the Church

10 The foundation of St Euphemia in Calabria: a 'Norman' church in southern Italy? – Benjamin Pohl   191
11 King Roger II's legislation on the celebration of marriage – Elisabeth van Houts   212
12 The battle against simony in Norman Italy: perceptions, interpretations, measures and consequences – Lioba Geis   227
13 Some reflections on the women's monasteries of southern Italy in the eighth to twelfth centuries – Jean-Marie Martin   245

Part IV: Conquering Norman Italy and beyond

14 The Norman siege of Bari, 1068–71 – Charles D. Stanton   265
15 The past, present and future of Norman rule in Apulia: Roger II's silver *ducalis* – Sarah Davis-Secord   284
16 From Alexandria to Tinnīs: the kingdom of Sicily, Egypt and the Holy Land, 1154–87 – Alan V. Murray   305

Bibliography   323
Index   357

Figures

0.1 Graham A. Loud. Photograph courtesy of
Katherine Fenton. — xviii
4.1 Palermo, Archivio di Stato di Palermo, Fondo
Miscellanea Archivistica Serie II, n. 5, fol. 9v, lines
1–16 (Latin) (reproduced with the kind permission
of the Archivio di Stato in Palermo and the Ministero
per i beni e per l'attività culturale e per il turismo). — 87
4.2 Palermo, Archivio di Stato di Palermo, Fondo
Miscellanea Archivistica Serie II, n. 5, fol. 9v,
lines 1–8 (name list) (reproduced with the kind
permission of the Archivio di Stato in Palermo
and the Ministero per i beni e per l'attività
culturale e per il turismo). — 87
4.3 Palermo, Archivio di Stato di Palermo, Fondo
Miscellanea Archivistica Serie II, n. 5, fol. 10r,
lines 9–42 (name list) (reproduced with the kind
permission of the Archivio di Stato in Palermo and
the Ministero per i beni e per l'attività culturale
e per il turismo). — 88
4.4 Palermo, Archivio di Stato di Palermo, Fondo
Miscellanea Archivistica Serie II, n. 5, fol. 10v,
lines 17–22 (Latin) (reproduced with the kind
permission of the Archivio di Stato in Palermo
and the Ministero per i beni e per l'attività culturale
e per il turismo). — 88
10.1 Paris, Bibliothèque nationale de France, MS Lat.
11055, fol. 15r, lines 2–9 (detail) (© Gallica.
Reproduced with the kind permission of the
Bibliothèque nationale de France). — 202

10.2 Paris, Bibliothèque nationale de France, MS Lat. 11055, fol. 15r, lines 12–15 (detail) (© Gallica. Reproduced with the kind permission of the Bibliothèque nationale de France). 202
10.3 Paris, Bibliothèque nationale de France, MS Lat. 11055, fol. 16v, lines 17–19 (detail) (© Gallica. Reproduced with the kind permission of the Bibliothèque nationale de France). 202
10.4 Paris, Bibliothèque nationale de France, MS Lat. 11055, fol. 16r, lines 20–7 (detail) (© Gallica. Reproduced with the kind permission of the Bibliothèque nationale de France). 202
14.1 Concept of the Norman siege of Bari in 1068, based upon the description of the Italo-Norman chronicler Geoffrey Malaterra. (Charles Stanton with Peter Judge, reprinted by permission of Boydell & Brewer Ltd, from C. D. Stanton, *Norman Naval Operations in the Mediterranean*, 9781843836247 (Boydell Press, 2011), p. 42). 274
15.1 *Ducalis* of Roger II, Palermo, minted from 1140. British Museum, Inv. C.2706. Obverse: +IC XC RG IN ÆTERN around nimbate bust of Christ holding Gospel book. Reverse: R DVX AP and R R SLS ('Rogerius Dux Apulie' and 'Rogerius Rex Sicilie') and AN R X ('Anno regni decimo,' or 1140) with King Roger in imperial dress and Duke Roger in military dress with sword in right hand, both grasping a long patriarchal cross. Image © Trustees of the British Museum. 287
15.2 *Histamenon* of Alexius I, Thessalonica, minted 1081–92. American Numismatic Society, Inv. 1944.100.81428. Obverse: + KE RO ALES IC XC around nimbate bust of Christ holding Gospel book. Reverse: D/M/I/T/ D/EC/P/ with St Demetrius, with nimbus and in military dress with sword to the left, presenting patriarchal cross to Alexius, in imperial dress. Image courtesy of the American Numismatic Society. 289

Tables

4.1 Index of reconstructed names 61
5.1 Synoptic table of correspondences, Falco of Benevento,
    Chronicon Beneventanum, 1137.14.1–14 97
10.1 Foundation charters of St Euphemia and St Évroult 200

Contributors

David Abulafia is Emeritus Professor of Mediterranean History at Cambridge University, where he is a Fellow of Gonville and Caius College. He has written extensively about medieval Italy, trying to look at Italy from a southern perspective. His books include *The Two Italies* (1977), *Frederick II* (1988) and, most recently, *The Great Sea: A Human History of the Mediterranean* (2011) and *The Boundless Sea: A Human History of the Oceans* (2019). He is a Fellow of the British Academy, a member of the Academia Europaea and a visiting professor at the College of Europe (Natolin) and at the newly founded University of Gibraltar.

Joshua C. Birk is Associate Professor in History at Smith College. His work focuses on political history and cultural history across religious boundaries in the medieval Mediterranean world. His first book, *The Norman Kings of Sicily and the Rise of the Anti-Muslim Critique: Baptized Sultans*, explored the connections between the Christian kings of Sicily and their Muslim subjects. He is currently writing *Stupor Mundi: Frederick II and the Haute Cour of Jerusalem*, a pedagogical project designed to teach students about the legal and social history of the Kingdom of Jerusalem.

Edoardo D'Angelo is a PhD of the Université de la Sorbonne, Doctor Honoris Causa at the Université de Caen Normandie and Full Professor of Medieval Latin Philology at the Università di Napoli SOB. He has published over twenty-five monographs and more than 130 journal articles. Among his most recent publications are: *Radulphi Cadomensis Tancredus* (2011), *L'Epistolario di Pier della Vigna* (2014), *Pseudo Ugo Falcando Chronica* (2014), *Dall'Umbria al*

Mediterraneo all'Atlantico: l'Itineraria di Alessandro Geraldini (2017) and *Statutum Populi ciuitatis Ameliae a.D. 1346* (2019).

Sarah Davis-Secord is an historian of the multicultural world of the medieval Mediterranean basin, with a specific focus on Sicily and the central Mediterranean region. This research has been published in several articles and in the book *Where Three Worlds Met: Sicily in the Early Medieval Mediterranean* (2017). The book investigates the place of Sicily within the communications networks of the Mediterranean basin from the sixth to twelfth centuries. Her larger interests include Muslim–Christian interactions and the globalisation of trade and communication networks in the early medieval world. She is an associate professor in the Department of History at the University of New Mexico in Albuquerque.

Joanna H. Drell is Professor of History at the University of Richmond, specialising on medieval and renaissance Italy. Her research focuses on medieval southern Italy and Sicily, in particular the period of the Normans and Angevins. Recipient of numerous fellowships and grants, she has examined the Regno though the lenses of family and kinship, the crusades, textiles, migration and the works of Dante Alighieri. Her books include *Kinship and Conquest: Family Strategies in the Norman Principality of Salerno* (2002), and a co-edited volume of translations, *Medieval Italy-Texts in Translation* (with Frances Andrews and Katherine Jansen, 2009). She is currently studying perceptions of the Regno by northern Italians and peoples of the Continent, *Reimagining the Past: Perception and Representation of the Norman Kingdom of Southern Italy and Sicily*.

Lioba Geis received her PhD from RWTH Aachen University, Germany, with a thesis entitled 'Hofkapelle und Kapläne im Königreich Sizilien (1130–1266)'. In 2012, she was appointed as lecturer in Medieval History at the University of Cologne, Germany. Her postdoctoral research project 'Moral Economy and Ecclesiastical Office. Discourses about Simony in the Early Middle Ages (600–1050)' is concerned with a multidimensional analysis of the contemporary perception, interpretation and overcoming of simonistic actions. Since 2018 this project has been supported by the German Research Foundation (DFG) with the research grant 'Temporary Positions for Principal Investigators'.

Markus Krumm is Lecturer ('Akademischer Rat') in Medieval History at Ludwig-Maximilians-University Munich. He studied Medieval History, Eastern European History and German Language and Literature of the Middle Ages (German Medieval Studies) in Munich and Pisa. In 2017 he finished his dissertation on Alexander of Telese and Falco of Benevento, which has been published in the 'Bibliothek des Deutschen Historischen Instituts in Rom' series. His fields of research include the history of medieval southern Italy, history writing in the Middle Ages, the papacy and the prosecution of heretics.

Jean-Marie Martin (†), Professor, was a former director of research at the Centre national des recherches scientifiques, and a research associate of the École française de Rome and of the Centre de recherche d'histoire et civilisations de Byzance at Paris. He published numerous articles, co-edited volumes, and books, most notably *La Pouille du VIe au XIIe siècle* (1993), on medieval southern Italy in the Byzantine, Norman and Staufen periods. He also produced a number of critical editions of collected documents and other materials from south Italian archival collections.

Alex Metcalfe is currently Senior Lecturer in History at Lancaster University. His research focuses on the medieval Mediterranean, and includes several publications on Islamic and Norman Sicily such as *The Society of Norman Italy* (ed. with Graham A. Loud, 2002), *Muslims and Christians in Norman Sicily* (2003) and *The Muslims of Medieval Italy* (2009), an updated edition of which was published in Italian as *I musulmani dell'Italia medievale* (2019).

Alan V. Murray is Senior Lecturer in Medieval Studies at the University of Leeds and Director of the *International Medieval Bibliography*. His research interests include the crusades to the Holy Land and the principalities of Outremer, the Baltic crusades, and medieval warfare and chivalry. His books include *The Crusader Kingdom of Jerusalem: A Dynastic History, 1099–1125* (2000), *The Franks in Outremer: Studies in the Latin Principalities of Syria* and *Palestine, 1099–1187* (2015) and the edited reference work *The Crusades: An Encyclopedia*, 4 vols (2006). He is currently working on a biography of King Baldwin II of Jerusalem.

Paul Oldfield is Senior Lecturer in Medieval History at the University of Manchester. His research concentrates on medieval southern Italy and urban culture. He has published numerous articles, a co-edited volume and three monographs (*City and Community in Norman Italy* (2009), *Sanctity and Pilgrimage in Medieval Southern Italy, 1000–1200* (2014) and *Urban Panegyric and the Transformation of the Medieval City, 1100–1300* (2019)). He has held Fellowships from the AHRC and British Academy and is currently working on a project on memory and documentary culture in medieval Puglia with the support of a Leverhulme Trust Research Fellowship.

Benjamin Pohl is Senior Lecturer in Medieval History at the University of Bristol. His research focuses on medieval European history and historiography, codicology, palaeography and manuscript studies. He is the author of numerous journal articles and several books, including the monograph *Dudo of St. Quentin's Historia Normannorum: Tradition, Innovation and Memory* (2015) and the edited volume *A Companion to the Abbey of Le Bec in the Central Middle Ages (11th–13th Centuries)* (2017). He is currently writing his new monograph *Medieval Abbots and the Writing of History* and editing *The Cambridge Companion to the Age of William the Conqueror* (both forthcoming).

Luigi Russo is Associate Professor in Medieval History at the European University of Rome and Deputy Coordinator of the Degree Course in Science of Primary Education. His main research interests include the history of the Crusading movement and the history of the Normans in Italy and the Latin East. He is a member of the Board of Administration of CESN (Centro Europeo di Studi Normanni, Ariano Irpino), Fellow of OUEN (Office universitaire d'Etudes normandes, Caen), Scientific Committee Member of the Carnet Mondes normands médiévaux (http://mnm.hypotheses.org/a-propss/equipe), and editor of *Dizionario Biografico degli Italiani*. His most recent book is *I crociati in Terrasanta. Una nuova storia (1095–1291)* (2018).

Charles D. Stanton, a retired naval officer and airline pilot, is an independent scholar who earned a doctorate in history at Cambridge under David Abulafia, Fellow of the British Academy and author of *The Great Sea*. A winner of the Dennis Bethell Prize, Dr Stanton has written extensively on maritime warfare in the medieval Mediterranean, especially concerning the Norman conquest of southern Italy. His body of work includes numerous essays published in respected scholarly journals and three well-received monographs: *Norman Naval Operations in the Mediterranean* (2011), *Medieval Maritime Warfare* (2015) and *Roger of Lauria (c. 1250–1305), 'Admiral of Admirals'* (2019).

Eleni Tounta is Associate Professor in Medieval History at the Aristotle University of Thessaloniki. Her research interests focus on medieval political thought, medieval historiography, identities and power relations, and social history, especially in the Western Empire and southern Italy in the High and Late Middle Ages. Her publications include: *The Western* sacrum imperium *and the Byzantine Empire: Ideological Conflicts and Mutual Influences in the European Political Scene of the 12th Century (1135–1177)* (2008) [in Greek] and *Medieval Mirrors of Power: Historians and Narratives in Norman Southern Italy* (2012) [in Greek]. She also co-edited *Usurping Rituals* (2010).

Elisabeth van Houts is a Fellow and College Lecturer in Medieval History of Emmanuel College and Emeritus Honorary Professor of European Medieval History at the University of Cambridge. She has written widely on medieval Anglo-Norman history, gender and memory. Her most recent book is *Married Life in the Middle Ages, 900–1300* (2019).

Acknowledgements

We would like to thank all the contributors for their hard work and support. It is, however, with great sadness that we acknowledge the passing of Professor Jean-Marie Martin while this volume was in the final stage of production. His legacy is reflected in so many of the contributions here, he was a giant in the field, and ever supportive to his fellow historians. We also want to thank the editoral team at Manchester University Press, especially Meredith Carroll, and the peer reviewer for very helpful and encouraging comments. We are grateful for vital funding provided by the Tout Fund from the History Department at the University of Manchester and from the School of Arts and Sciences at the University of Richmond. A huge thank you to David Routt for his translations and meticulous copy-editing. Finally, while this volume is itself a thank you to Graham A. Loud, no acknowledgements could be complete without expressing our deep gratitude for the years of support, wise counsel and friendship which he has offered us and so many others. Graham is truly a pioneer of Norman Italy studies, and it is a pleasure to offer this small token of our appreciation and affection in return.

Abbreviations

ANS	*Anglo-Norman Studies*
BHG	*Bibliotheca hagiographica graeca*
Caracausi	G. Caracausi, *Dizionario onomastico*
DOdS	*della Sicilia: repertorio storico-etimologico di nomi di famiglia e di luogo*, 2 vols (Palermo, 1994)
Cattedrale di Benevento	*Le più antiche carte del capitol della cattedrale di Benevento (688–1200)*, ed. A Ciarelli, V. de Donato and V. Matera (Rome, 2002)
CDL, IV-2	*Codice diplomatico longobardo*, IV-2: *I diplomi dei duchi di Benevento*, ed. H. Zielinski (Rome, 2003)
ChBen	Falco of Benevento, *Chronicon Beneventanum*, ed. E. D'Angelo (Florence, 1998)
CMC	*Chronica monasterii Casinensis*, ed. H. Hoffmann (Rome, 1980)
CSS	*Chronicon Sanctae Sophiae (cod. Vat. lat. 4949)*, ed. J.-M. Martin (Rome, 2000)
CV	*Il Chronicon Vulturnense del Monaco Giovanni*, ed. V. Federici (Rome, 1925–40).
EHR	*English Historical Review*
Falcandus	*The History of the Tyrants of Sicily by 'Hugo Falcandus', 1153–69*, trans. G. A. Loud and T. E. J. Wiedemann (Manchester, 1998)
FSI	*Fonti per la storia d'Italia*
FSS	Benevento, Museo del Sannio, Fondo S. Sofia
Historia	*La Historia o Liber de Regno Sicilie e la Epistola ad Petrum Panormitane Ecclesie Thesaurium di Ugo Falcando*, ed. G. B. Siragusa, FSI 22 (Rome, 1897)

IP, Nicholson	*Chronicle of the Third Crusade: A Translation of the Itinerarium Peregrinorum et gesta regis Ricardi*, trans. H. J. Nicholson (Aldershot, 1997)
IP, Stubbs	*Itinerarium Peregrinorum et gesta regis Ricardi*, ed. W. Stubbs, in *Chronicles and Memorials of the Reign of Richard I*, Rolls Series 38, vol. 1 (London, 1864)
JL	*Regesta Pontificum Romanorum*, P. Jaffé *et al.* (eds), 2 vols, 2nd edn (Leipzig, 1885–88)
JMH	*Journal of Medieval History*
MEC	P. Grierson and L. Travaini, *Medieval European Coinage Vol. 14: South Italy, Sicily, Sardinia* (Cambridge, 1998)
MGH SS	Monumenta Germaniae Historica Scriptores
Mirto	*Rollus rubeus: Privilegia ecclesie Cephaleditane, a diversis regibus et imperatoribus concessa, recollecta et in hoc volumine scripta*, ed. C. Mirto (Palermo, 1972)
Monti	'Le Assise del Cod. Vaticano con il testo del Cod. Cassinese e quello delle costituzioni relative di Federico II' in G. M. Monti (ed.), *Lo Stato Normanno Svevo. Lineamenti e ricerche* (Trani, 1945)
PL	*Patrologia Latina*, ed. J. P. Migne, 221 vols (Paris, 1844–64)
QF	*Quellen und Forschungen aus italienischen Archiven und Bibliotheken*
RIS	Rerum Italicarum Scriptores
Roger II	*Roger II and the Creation of the Kingdom of Sicily*, trans. G. A. Loud (Manchester, 2012)
RPD	*Registrum Petri Diaconi (Montecassino, archivio dell'abbazia Reg.). Editione e commento*, ed. J.-M. Martin *et al.* (Rome, 2015)
Spata	*Le pergamene greche esistenti nel Grande Archivio di Palermo*, ed. G. Spata (Palermo, 1862)
WT	*Willelmi Tyrensis Archiepiscopi Chronicon*, ed. R. B. C. Huygens, Corpus Christianorum Continuatio Mediaevalis 63–63A (Turnhout, 1986)

Figure 0.1 Graham A. Loud. Photograph courtesy of Katherine Fenton.

1

Introduction: rethinking Norman Italy

Joanna H. Drell

Graham A. Loud has been a pioneering scholar, indefatigable researcher and forceful presence in the field of Norman Italy (*c.* 1000–*c.* 1200) since the late 1970s and remains one of its most active contributors. His many publications and his dedicated mentorship of students have resulted in the burgeoning of the study of medieval southern Italy and Sicily. This pluralistic society where Christian, Muslim, Jew, Greek, Latin, Lombard and Norman commingled is now a fixture at academic meetings and in classrooms, journals and other publications in the UK, the US, the Continent and elsewhere. It spans a range of scholarly interests: a Mediterranean society, an economic crossroads, an innovator in lay and ecclesiastical governance, and a multicultural frontier. Norman Italy has moved from the wings to centre stage in medieval studies and is in fruitful interplay with other popular corners of medieval interest: the crusading movement, medieval Spain and the putative home of modernity, northern Italy.[1] Thanks to Loud's efforts, references to Norman Italy as 'the other conquest' have waned.[2]

This volume brings together a number of Graham Loud's colleagues – some of them his former students – to celebrate his extraordinary career and his seminal contribution to the study of Norman Italy. Loud's groundbreaking research is not only the common influence underpinning this collection of chapters by some of the field's leading scholars but it also continues to inspire the traversing of scholarly frontiers and the re-evaluation of the relationship between Norman Italy and the broader medieval world, enquiries fruitfully in progress.

From the outset it is important to delineate the geographical and chronological boundaries of this volume. What is meant by 'Norman Italy' and what period is addressed here? To be sure, some chapters focus on southern Italy and others on Sicily while yet others reference the kingdom of Sicily. This is not uncommon in scholarship on the region. Depending on context, 'medieval southern Italy' refers to the territory from the Abruzzi down to Sicily or simply the peninsula south of Rome but excluding Sicily. The varying definitions are all legitimate. While it is generally agreed that Norman Italy 'begins' with the arrival of the first Norman mercenaries and pilgrims around the turn of the millennium, as recounted by William of Apulia in *The Deeds of Robert Guiscard* and Amatus of Montecassino in *The History of the Normans*, the period's close cannot be so precisely located.[3] Some scholars strictly mark the passing of the Norman period with the end of King Tancred's reign in 1194. Upon Tancred's death the throne entered into the orbit of the House of Hohenstaufen (also referred to as 'the Staufen') through Tancred's aunt, Constance – daughter of Roger II, wife of Holy Roman Emperor Henry VI and mother of future Emperor Frederick II, the next king of southern Italy and Sicily. Others, however, consider the same Frederick II a ruler of 'Norman Italy' owing to his descent from Roger II and consequently they extend Italy's 'Norman' era through his death in 1250.

There is also scholarly disagreement regarding when Norman Italy ceased to be 'Norman' because of the extent of Norman intermarriage and intermingling with the local populace and the petering out of Norman immigration into the south. Moreover, scholars often conflate 'Norman' with 'French', which further muddies the waters regarding Norman influence.[4] Loud himself made what many deem the definitive argument on this topic in his 1981 article, 'How "Norman" was the Norman conquest of southern Italy?'[5] As prosopographical work on charters and other evidence continues, we may gain further clarity regarding the contours of Italy's 'Normanness' in the future. In this volume we acknowledge the mutability of 'Norman Italy' not only as a concept but also as a discrete chronological period.

Also by means of introduction, in a volume that honours Graham Loud it is appropriate to reflect on Loud's contributions to the field.[6] While he was not the first scholar to explore the fertile research ground of medieval southern Italy, he has done much over his career to introduce Norman Italy to a broader anglophone audience.[7] His publications range so widely in genre and subject that this introduction cannot possibly touch upon them all. However, several themes and priorities in his scholarship stand out. First of all, his key monographs (thus far) largely though not exclusively explore Norman Italy's political and ecclesiastical history: *Church and Society in the Norman Principality of Capua, 1058–1197* (1985), *The Age of Robert Guiscard: Southern Italy and Norman Conquest* (2000) and *The Latin Church in Norman Italy* (2007).

In addition to the themes that fuel Loud's historical enquiries, a signal feature of his work is how much of his output has contributed to the creation of a research field virtually from the ground up and in effect has blazed the path for others to follow. As Abulafia's chapter in this volume suggests, the scholars working on Norman Italy in any language were not numerous before Loud. For Loud, as for many of us working in the closing decades of the twentieth century, basic information about Norman Italy was not easy to uncover. Graham helped to create a base of knowledge for the field not only with his major monographs but also with dozens of articles, studies fanning out in manifold scholarly directions.[8] He, moreover, has written encyclopedic and synthetic accounts of the Norman period flowing from his unrivalled knowledge of original sources.[9] Beyond his trailblazing original scholarship, among Loud's most enduring legacies are his meticulous and readable translations of the principal southern Italian chronicles, among them the works of Alexander of Telese, Romuald of Salerno, Falco of Benevento and 'Hugo Falcandus', as well as other major texts.[10] These translations have made the field accessible to a new group of anglophone researchers and students. And it is now possible to teach medieval southern Italian history in the classroom, to bring the field more clearly into the orbit of medieval Italian history and to integrate it into the narrative of the broader medieval world.[11]

By the time this volume appears, it is likely that Loud will have neared completion of his next major project, *The Social World of the Abbey of Cava, c.1020–1300*. It plumbs the vast archive of the Benedictine monastery of the Holy Trinity at Cava de' Tirreni as a springboard for a social and economic history of the principality of Salerno. In undertaking this research project on the abbey and its social world in the central Middle Ages, Loud acknowledges the influence of *Annaliste* historians – among them Jean-Marie Martin, whose work appears in this volume – who explored fundamental cultural, geographic, environmental, economic and social structures.[12] Loud's familiarity with the Cava materials makes him uniquely well suited to pursue this project. Indeed, it was Loud who introduced a number of us to the documentary riches contained in this monastic archive in the small town south-east of Naples, just outside Salerno.

Finally, the breadth of Loud's impact on the field is reflected in the international assemblage of scholars eager to participate in this volume. It is no coincidence that this collection's non-anglophone contributors remark upon Loud's membership in the European community of scholars, especially scholars in southern Italy and Germany.[13] The embracing of Loud by these academic circles has in turn enabled him to make the international corpus of scholarship accessible to English-speaking scholars lacking the connections he has carefully forged and tended across his career.[14] Here, the internationally diverse contributors uncover fruitful interconnections within the ever-growing British, North American, Italian, French and German historiographies of Norman Italy, a testament to the field's fracturing of national and regional academic boundaries, one of Professor Loud's greatest legacies.

This collection offers a wide-ranging, holistic examination of Norman Italy's role in some of the medieval world's most important transitions, and, conversely, assesses how these currents of change made themselves manifest in Norman Italy. Until recently, there have been few volumes of essays dedicated to Norman Italy since Loud and Metcalfe's 2002 overview of the field.[15] Collections more commonly include contributions on Norman Italy but focus more broadly on the greater Norman world and largely conceive of Norman Italy within the old paradigm of frontier and periphery.[16] The contributions here emphasise the socio-cultural, religious and political histories of Norman Italy and then, either explicitly or implicitly, evaluate the region's place in much wider transitions.

The contributors, moreover, reassess and recast the paradigm by which Norman Italy has been conventionally understood. Within the scholarly field, Norman Italy's uniqueness has long rested on its geographic location on Latin Europe's periphery, an environment that intermixed Latin Christians with Byzantine Greeks and Muslims and fostered a vibrant multiculturalism. While elements of this characterisation remain valid, continuing scholarly exploration is sparking a rising awareness of cross-pollination between Norman Italy and the wider medieval world in the eleventh and twelfth centuries. This collection's studies underscore that Norman Italy was not just a parochial Norman nor Mediterranean entity but also an integral player in a number of medieval worlds. This volume consequently endeavours to move the field's emphasis beyond the frontier and to articulate both Norman Italy's contribution to broader historical currents and the impact in turn of these currents upon Norman Italy, an instance of reciprocal influence perhaps surpassing the sum of its parts. This focus has led the volume's scholars to explore many broader realms in which Norman Italy participated, including the secular and monastic Church, aristocratic networks, the papacy, crusading, urbanisation, Byzantium and Islam.

The volume clusters around four major strands in current scholarship about Norman Italy, themes that Loud himself pioneered:

1 Historiographies
2 Identities and communities
3 Religion and the Church
4 Conquering Norman Italy and beyond

(1) Historiographies: Abulafia and Russo address different aspects of the historiographical development of Norman Italy studies. Abulafia's focused exploration of British scholarship on Norman Italy from its inception through the early 1970s shows how the historiographical construction of the region has evolved and provides the context in which Loud's pioneering work emerged. Russo reassesses modern historiography with an eye to the rising interest since the mid-1970s in the Italian portion of the Norman experience, and he then revisits medieval writers of history to test how comfortably the framing of Norman expansion in Italy as part of an 'imperial' venture fits. D'Angelo offers a provocative rereading of an incident in the Regno's political life that is recounted by one of the major chroniclers, Falco of Benevento, and shows how our understanding both of the history of Norman Italy and of the Normans' own historiography remains a work in progress. Metcalfe edits, translates and contextualises a name-list of Sicilian Muslims subject to a Christian abbey at Cefalù, a document suggesting new historiographical pathways, especially for prosopography and socio-economic history.

(2) Identities and communities: Birk, Krumm, Tounta and Oldfield all speak to the formation of identity by individual communities in Norman Italy's multicultural environment. Birk examines the evolving impressions of a Muslim intellectual, Ibn Jubayr, regarding the vicissitudes of the Muslim experience as he visited far-flung Muslim communities not only under Muslim rule in the *Dār al-Islām* but also under Christian sway in the kingdoms of Jerusalem and Sicily. Krumm looks at the emergence of urban identity with its attendant civil strife through the filter of a single urban conflict in Benevento and uncovers not only the complex interplay between the papacy and the local Norman aristocracy but also the influence of local antagonisms and the nobility's conception of honour. Italo-Greek saintly *vitae* from Sicily and Calabria offer a prism through which Tounta discerns the adaptation of Italo-Greek identity to a new political reality following the Norman conquest of southern Italy and reveals plural identities forged by place and circumstance, identities subject to further evolution and decline with passage of time. A wintering by French and English crusading contingents in Sicily, en route to the Third Crusade, informs Oldfield's analysis of the convergence of Latin, Greek and urban identities when they came face to face with 'foreign', royal and crusading mentalities, an analysis enriched by Oldfield's interweaving of traditional Anglo-Norman narratives with local Sicilian evidence.

(3) Religion and the Church: Pohl, Van Houts, Geis and Martin each examine a facet of religion and ecclesiastical life in Norman Italy. Pohl, through a meticulous examination of charters, exposes the influence of a monastic house in the Norman Cotentin upon St Euphemia in Calabria, a later southern Italian foundation, and clarifies its position among other Norman-founded monastic houses. Van Houts examines Roger II's innovative marriage legislation, most particularly the king's efforts to establish royal control of legitimate marriage by making a priest's blessing in a church a prerequisite for the exchange of property negotiated in the marriage bond and situates this reform within the broader European context. Geis explores the Latin Church's efforts to combat simony against the backdrop of a reforming papacy endeavouring generally to expand its influence beyond Rome and trying specifically

to enforce canonical standards in a southern Italy where Norman rulers were in process of Latinising ecclesiastical structures in onetime Greek and Muslim areas. Nunneries in Campania present Martin a pathway to address the long-overlooked rise and evolution of female monasticism in pre-Norman Italy and its intimate bonds with aristocratic networks, the papacy and Campania's principal male houses, a development profoundly shaped by the dearth of urban development outside Naples and the gradual regularisation of the region's ecclesiastical structures.

(4) Conquering Norman Italy and beyond: Stanton, Davis-Secord and Murray address from a variety of perspectives the role of conquest in creating and expanding Norman Italy. Stanton analyses the conquering of strategically important Bari, a watershed campaign both in the application of naval military tactics and in the construction of Norman Italy through its breaking of Greek influence in the region, its quelling of Greek support for fractious Norman nobles, and its making Norman expansion across the Adriatic conceivable. Davis-Secord looks at Roger II's strategies to consolidate and expand his power on mainland southern Italy in the wake of the creation of the kingdom of Sicily and to legitimise both his own rule and that of his anticipated successor through numismatic images evoking a useful historical past. Murray offers a much-needed reassessment of a Norman king's attempt to exert influence well beyond his realm's borders with an analysis of the Sicilian expeditions to Egypt, a study that exposes the tensions between the king of Sicily and the king of Jerusalem and their disparate attitudes towards Byzantium as friend or foe in their projects.

In so far as the contributions here display the breadth and dynamism of Norman Italy as a scholarly field, they also inevitably reveal the range and richness of the evidence being brought to bear in the investigation of Norman Italy: documentary, historical, liturgical, hagiographic, legal, artefactual, prosopographical, topographical, narrative, material and numismatic. The collection offers freshly edited documents (Metcalfe, Pohl, Krumm) as well as rereadings of well-known primary texts (Russo, D'Angelo). Coins are used to reveal royal strategies (Davis-Secord) while naming data offers glimpses of the lower socio-economic strata (Metcalfe). Yet, a common thread woven throughout the contributions is the foundational work of Graham Loud as translator, 'archivophile' and scholar. In this important sense, the work presented here is inconceivable without Graham Loud.

To be sure, the chapters offer only a snapshot of the vibrant and multifaceted field of Norman Italy in the present moment. Noticeably absent from and beyond the scope of this collection – due to the limitations of space and time – are discussions of some of the impressive artistic and architectural legacy of southern Italy and Sicily. Noteworthy recent scholarship on southern Italian artefacts and other historical media – for example manuscripts, textiles and mosaics – include the cross-disciplinary research of Winkler *et al.* on Norman Sicily, Tronzo and Bruzelius on Naples, and Safran on the Salento.[17] Often drawing on new digital tools and methods, these scholars examine material and visual evidence – its creation, purpose and reception – to understand better the diverse societies of the medieval south.[18] These studies demonstrate not only that historical understanding evolves but also that a physical object's significance likewise may wax or wane according to viewer and time.

The field has progressed considerably from the early accounts of the pursuits of Robert Guiscard and his relations – the narrative foundations of the field – as outlined by Abulafia in the first chapter. How then does this volume meet the promise of its title and 'rethink' Norman Italy? The scholarship included here reflects the field's maturation and its movement in ever-richer and more complex directions. While Loud's extensive body of work inspired the broad categories around which the contributions are organised, many of the chapters share emphases that put them in dialogue with each other. For example, Van Houts, Davis-Secord, Murray and Stanton all touch on the political strategies of the Norman leaders, in no small part in their efforts to build and legitimise power. Both Oldfield and Metcalfe illuminate economic practices in the kingdom and cast light on the role of local conditions and non-elites on economic life. The easy movement of ideas and people across the region's porous boundaries is revealed by Martin, Birk and Murray. The fluidity of cultural identities and attitudes are underscored by Pohl, Birk and Tounta. Overall, the volume reveals how much of Norman Italy's 'underbelly' (to borrow from my co-editor Oldfield) gradually becomes better known to us: aristocratic (non-royal) networks, diverse voices, local practices, cultural memory. In the

Introduction 9

meantime, the influence of Norman Italy is reinforced through connections with the crusades (Oldfield), popular religion (Tounta) and Church reform (Geis).

Finally, in the introduction to their 2002 collection, Loud and Metcalfe observed that 'the student of Norman Italy and Sicily faces a challenging and often difficult field but one in which there are exciting possibilities for further research. There are many subjects still to be explored and many sources to be exploited'.[19] Almost two decades later this volume not only arose from an acceptance of the challenge posed by Loud and Metcalfe but also demonstrates that the challenge remains ongoing, nowhere nearly met because of the many areas still open to fruitful research. The chapters that follow offer a blueprint for how scholarship on this crucial region is likely to develop in coming decades, scholarship immeasurably indebted to the foundational research of Graham Loud.

Notes

1 There is too much literature to list here but some prominent and recent works include: On crusading, see for example the articles by Drell and Oldfield in K. Hurlock and P. Oldfield (eds), *Crusading and Pilgrimage in the Norman World* (Woodbridge, 2015); P. Chevedden, '"A crusade from the first": The Norman conquest of Islamic Sicily, 1060–1091', *Al-Masāq: Islam and the Medieval Mediterranean* 22 (2010), 191–225; P. Oldfield, *Sanctity and Pilgrimage in Medieval Southern Italy, 1000–1200* (Cambridge, 2014), ch. 5; S. C. Davis-Secord, 'Medieval Sicily and southern Italy in recent historiographic perspective', *History Compass* 8 (2010), 61–87. On medieval Spain, see P. Oldfield, 'The Iberian imprint on medieval southern Italy', *History* 93 (2008), 312–27. See also the articles in J.-M. Martin and R. Alaggio (eds), *'Quei Maledetti Normanni'. Studi offerti a Errico Cuozzo*, 2 vols (Ariano Irpino, 2016); S. Carocci, *Signorie di Mezzogiorno: società rurali, poteri aristocratici e monarcha (XII–XIII secolo)* (Rome, 2014), also now available in English as *Lordships of Southern Italy: Rural Societies, Aristocratic Powers, and Monarchy in the 12th and 13th Centuries*, trans. L. Byatt (Rome, 2018); A. Nef, *Conquérir et gouverner la Sicile islamique aux XIe et XIIe siècles* (Rome, 2011); D. M. Hayes, *Roger II of Sicily: Family, Faith, and Empire in the Medieval Mediterranean World* (Turnhout, 2020).

2 *The Other Conquest* was the title of John Julius Norwich's book about the Normans who travelled to and settled in southern Italy in the eleventh – and twelfth – centuries, published by Harper & Row in New York, 1967. That same year Longman released the book under the title *The Normans in the South*.
3 G. A. Loud, *The Age of Robert Guiscard: Southern Italy and the Norman Conquest* (Harlow, 2000), pp. 1–99, especially 60–6. For another example, see J. France, 'The occasion of the coming of the Normans to Italy', *JMH* 17 (1991), 185–205.
4 See especially L.-R. Ménager, 'Inventaire des familles normandes et franques émigrées en Italie méridionale et en Sicilie (xie–xiie siècles)', in *Roberto il Guiscardo e il suo tempo: Relazioni e commuicazioni nelle Prime Giornate Normanno-Sveve del Centro di studi normanno-svevi* (Rome, 1975), pp. 260–390.
5 G. A. Loud, 'How "Norman" was the Norman conquest of southern Italy?', *Nottingham Medieval Studies* 25 (1981), 13–24. Also, G. A. Loud, 'The "Gens Normannorum": Myth or reality?', *ANS* 4 (1982), 104–16, and his 'Continuity and change in Norman Italy: The Campania during the eleventh and twelfth centuries', *JMH* 22 (1996), 313–43. Also, J. Drell, 'Cultural syncretism and ethnic identity: The Norman "conquest" of southern Italy and Sicily', *JMH* 25 (1999), 187–202. Loud further addresses this topic in 'Norman traditions in southern Italy', in S. Burkhardt and T. Foerster (eds), *Norman Tradition and Transcultural Heritage: Exchange of Cultures in the 'Norman' Peripheries of Medieval Europe* (Farnham, 2013), pp. 35–56.
6 Several of Loud's seminal publications are included in the bibliography at the end of this volume.
7 Loud readily acknowledges his debts to John Cowdrey, Evelyn Jamison, Norbert Kamp and others whose work came before him.
8 Some of his dozens of articles were published in Ashgate collections in 1999 and 2000; his more recent scholarship has appeared in journals and edited volumes.
9 For examples, see his introduction to *The Age of Robert Guiscard* and his contributions to *The New Cambridge Medieval History*, vol. 4 (Cambridge, 2004).
10 See *The History of the Tyrants of Sicily by 'Hugo Falcandus' 1154–69*, trans. G. A. Loud and T. Wiedemann (Manchester, 1998) and *Roger II and the Creation of the Kingdom of Sicily*, trans. and ed. G. A. Loud (Manchester, 2012). Loud originally made these translations in typescripts for his students at the University of Leeds and then generously shared them with young doctoral students unable to have access even to imperfect Latin editions. I was fortunate to be one of

those students when Graham – very patiently – supervised my Brown University PhD thesis.
11 Greater interest in southern Italy inspired the editors of *Medieval Italy: Texts in Translation*, ed. K. L. Jansen, J. Drell and F. Andrews (Philadelphia, 2009) to devote one third of the volume to southern Italian primary texts.
12 Loud discusses the influence of Martin and the works of the French *Annales* school in his unpublished valedictory lecture upon his retirement from the University of Leeds, 16 October 2019. Loud shared the text of these remarks with me.
13 For example, Loud translated Hubert Houben's biography of Roger II of Sicily: H. Houben, *Roger II of Sicily: A Ruler between East and West*, trans. G. A. Loud and D. Milburn (Cambridge, 2002).
14 Along with his major project on the Cava archive, in recent years Loud has developed his research interest in Staufen medieval Germany. He has co-edited (with Jochen Schenk) a volume of essays, *The Origins of the German Principalities, 1100–1350: Essays by German Historians* (Abingdon, 2017), and has translated more Latin chronicles about Italy and Germany. See *The Crusade of Frederick Barbarossa: The History of the Expedition of the Emperor Frederick and Related Texts* (Abingdon, 2010) and *The Chronicle of Arnold of Lubeck* (Abingdon, 2019).
15 G. A. Loud and A. Metcalfe, *The Society of Norman Italy* (Leiden, 2002). See for example: T. Jäckh and M. Kirsch (eds), *Urban Dynamics and Transcultural Communication in Medieval Sicily* (Paderborn, 2017) and the edited volume from E. A. Winkler, L. Fitzgerald and A. Small which is focused thematically on the impact of material culture on the cultural narrative of Norman Italy: *Designing Norman Sicily: Material Culture and Society* (Woodbridge, 2020).
16 K. J. Stringer and A. Jotischky (eds), *Norman Expansion: Connections, Continuities, Contrasts* (Abingdon, 2013), and Burkhardt and Foerster (eds), *Norman Tradition*. See the recently published second volume: K. J. Stringer and A. Jotischky (eds), *The Normans and the 'Norman Edge': Peoples, Polities and Identities on the Frontiers of Medieval Europe* (London, 2019).
17 C. Bruzelius and W. Tronzo, *Medieval Naples: An Architectural and Urban History 400–1400* (New York, 2011); L. Safran, *The Medieval Salento: Art and Identity in Southern Italy* (Philadelphia, 2014).
18 Not included in this collection but uniquely medieval southern Italian are examinations of medicine, especially the work of Monica Green. See *The Trotula: A Medieval Compendium of Women's Medicine*, ed. and trans. M. H. Green (Philadelphia, 2001). See also F. E. Glaze's

'Salerno's Lombard prince: Johannes "Abbas de Curte" as medical practitioner', *Early Science and Medicine* 23 (2018), 177–216; and E. Kwakkel and F. Newton, with an introduction by E. Glaze, *Medicine at Monte Cassino: Constantine the African and the Oldest Manuscript of his Pantegni* (Turnhout, 2019).

19 Loud and Metcalfe, *The Society of Norman Italy*, p. 13.

Part I

Historiographies

2

Norman Italy and Sicily through the eyes of British historians, 1912–76

David Abulafia

Interest among British historians in Norman Italy and Sicily has been slow to develop. By the start of the twenty-first century the number of scholars with an interest in that part of the world in that period had grown to include not just Graham Loud but Jeremy Johns (for the Islamic dimension in particular), Alex Metcalfe (ditto), Paul Oldfield (for the south Italian mainland especially), not to mention a flow of doctoral dissertations produced in Leeds, Lancaster, Oxford, Cambridge and elsewhere. At the start of the twentieth century, by contrast, the major account in English of the arrival of the Normans in southern Italy and the career of Robert Guiscard was still that of Edward Gibbon, as it had been for over a century, 'the only connected narrative that we have in English of one of the most romantic periods in medieval history', to cite Edmund Curtis, writing in 1912.[1] What was written from 1912 onwards reveals a fascinating divergence between deep archival research, influenced by German medieval historiography, and persistent attempts to link the southern Normans to those of Normandy and England as part of a common process of transformative Norman expansion with repercussions across Europe and the Mediterranean. Whether this was expressed through certain racial features that made the Normans into superhumans, or derived from a common sense of their Norman (maybe even Viking) ancestry was a question that lingered right up to the 1970s. The terminal point for this chapter has been set at 1976, marking the publication of two books with contrasting views of 'Norman identity' and coinciding with the emergence of Graham Loud on the academic scene.

At the beginning of the twentieth century two historians, Evelyn Jamison from Oxford and Edmund Curtis, then a lecturer at the University of Sheffield, began to explore Norman Italy in very different ways. More will be said about Evelyn Jamison in a moment, but some points of comparison between the two historians need to be noted. Edmund Curtis was first to publish (though there is no evidence they were in competition with one another) and launched what became a successful academic career with his book *Roger of Sicily and the Normans in Lower Italy 1016–1154*.[2] Curtis, like Jamison, absorbed the work of German, French and Italian historians, including Heinemann, Caspar, Kehr, Amari and Chalandon – particularly Chalandon.[3] This was, after all, just the moment when German scholarship was engaging with the sources for south Italian and Sicilian medieval history in highly innovative ways, bringing the techniques of diplomatics to bear on scattered and sometimes dubious charter material from across the Norman realm. Evelyn Jamison understood the publication of Chalandon's great work to mean that other approaches to the history of Norman Italy than grand narrative were needed, leading her to delve into archives across the Mezzogiorno, picking up the baton of Kehr, Caspar and others.

Jamison remained loyal to her southern Normans throughout her very long career, but for Curtis Norman Italy provided a springboard to a career in the medieval history of Norman lands in the west, not the south. Edmund Curtis was born in Lancashire in 1881 (he died in 1943) and his childhood circumstances in no way suggested that he would eventually become Professor of Medieval History at one of the most venerable universities in the British Isles.[4] His father was an architectural draughtsman from County Donegal and his mother came from Belfast; they were members of the Protestant Church of Ireland. At first the Curtis family prospered, but following the early death of his mother he and his family ended up in Silvertown, in the London Docklands, with little work for his father and only one apparent option: Edmund Curtis left school at thirteen to earn some money for the family, working for a time in a rubber factory for ten and a half hours a day, and earning eight shillings (£0.40p) a week. But he was also a part-time poet, and within a couple of years his poetry was noticed by two benefactors, a schoolmaster clergyman and a Jewish philanthropist, who paid for his education at boarding schools in Devon and Cumberland. There, he developed a taste for history and won a scholarship to

Keble College, Oxford, followed by a first-class degree, and, a year later, he won appointment as Lecturer in History at Sheffield University, which had only come into existence in the past few months. Research demands on lecturers were rather less heavy than nowadays: it took seven years for *Roger of Sicily* to appear, although in the meantime he published two articles on medieval Ireland in the *English Historical Review* in 1908 and 1910. This subject, rather than Norman Italy, was to become his great passion; his Irish background and his election in 1914 to the Erasmus Smith chair of history at Trinity College Dublin diverted him for the rest of his career from Norman Italy. His *History of Medieval Ireland* (1923) remains one of the major attempts to map out the history of a land which, in his view, would have prospered far more under a native dynasty – so much for the Normans and their English successors.[5] Indeed, his otherwise complimentary obituarists criticised Curtis for occasional inaccuracies and for allowing arguments such as this one to influence his interpretation.

Roger of Sicily was not based on archival research, but he did travel in southern Italy in 1908, 'absorbing local colour and atmosphere', as one of his Irish obituarists was to write. His style would nowadays be regarded as somewhat pompous, but it was elegant and eloquent. The book is lightly footnoted, although what notes there are show attention to original sources such as Amatus of Monte Cassino and documentary materials; for the chroniclers he tended to rely on del Re's composite edition.[6] Curtis's book appeared in an Anglo-American series, *Heroes of the Nations*, edited by the medieval historian H. W. C. Davis of Oxford, whose extensive expertise included the Normans in England, and it was the most adventurous subject in a list of titles that is otherwise fairly predictable: Nelson, Julius Caesar, Charlemagne, and so on. How Curtis obtained the commission is unknown, but the book is very much a product of its time. It begins with the triumph of the 'Northern races' in southern Italy – the Goths, the Lombards and the Normans. He argued that the confusion of peoples (or, in his language, 'races') in southern Italy meant that no single group could hope to impose unity; that would have to be imposed by an outside conqueror such as the Norman invaders.[7] There is much material in the first chapter about the Lombard 'race', while Curtis also admitted that 'their distinctiveness as a Teutonic nation had indeed vanished ... they had become at once Catholic and Italian'; at the same time he laid emphasis on the survival of Lombard law, the Germanic titles of various office-holders and even some place-names.[8] But Curtis was also sensitive to the way Byzantine power operated in southern Italy, keeping direct interference to a minimum so long as the Apulians accepted Byzantine overlordship and paid their taxes; and this would even extend to accepting the use of Lombard rather than imperial law in some circumstances.[9] For Curtis, the south, not the north, of Italy was where 'the communal impulse' was first felt, in towns such as Gaeta and Amalfi and in some of the Apulian cities; after all, Bari rebelled against the Byzantines in 1009, setting off the cycle of events that saw the Normans establish themselves in the region.[10]

A similar obsession with racial origins is displayed in Curtis's descriptions of the Normans. They were 'now becoming Gallicised in blood, physique and culture, from their Norse ancestors'. Actually, their physique seems to have remained much the same, as he goes on to confess: Tancred, the father of Robert Guiscard and Roger I, was reputed to have possessed 'tremendous physical strength'.[11] Guiscard was, for Curtis, 'the true hero of the epic of the Norman conquest of Lower Italy', fully comparable to William the Conqueror – 'a far more picturesque figure than that other giant of Norman history'. Given his own background, it is no surprise that Curtis approved of the rags-to-riches way that Guiscard had risen to leadership of the Normans without 'sanction of birth, lineage, or hereditary right', unlike the duke of Normandy.[12]

Roger II only appears on page 102, and it goes without saying that once he moves from the narrative of conquest to discussion of major themes such as law-making, the administrative machinery of the kingdom, relations with the papacy, the treatment of subject populations, and so on, Curtis's work shows its age and has long been superseded. Yet at the time it was written the book did show some important insights: he was interested, for instance, in the constant problem medieval governments faced in 'connecting the local with the central government'. Like one historian of the Regno after another, he tried to make sense of the *duana de secretis* and its relationship with the *duana baronum*, seeing the distinction as that between an office supervising the royal domains and another supervising the king's vassals. To this question he devoted a technical appendix, trying to disentangle the views of Garufi, Amari and Chalandon, and agreeing in the end with Chalandon's French shrug: 'influence arabe, influence byzantine, influence normande … on ne peut dire quelle est celle qui l'a emportée'.[13] Another appendix engaged with the question of the legatine authority acquired by Roger I, the so-called 'Sicilian Monarchy', showing mastery of the German literature on this much-disputed question.[14] Sometimes the poet *manqué* returns to life, as when Curtis describes the love of King Roger for Palermo, 'with its groves of orange and almond filling all the beautiful valley of Conca d'Oro, and the cool winds blowing from Monte Pellegrino'.[15] Nonetheless, he paid due attention to the widest possible range of topics: the African campaigns, Roger's attempts at involvement in the Second Crusade, Idrisi's *Kitab Rujjar* (with the help of Jaubert's translation). Roger is an autocrat: 'the absolutism of a Roman Emperor of the sixth century is transferred bodily to the grandson of the poor knight of Hauteville'. His complex character is brought out quite well: 'he preferred to inspire fear rather than encourage familiarity'; he insisted on the exercise of justice, was hard-working but also capable of great cruelty, at least if Falco of Benevento, who made him worse than Nero, is to be believed; but he was also a man of the widest scientific interests and generous to the scholars he patronised.[16]

Curtis's book is substantial: 483 pages. By the time he had covered the early Normans and Roger II he had run out of space for detailed coverage of William I and II and the collapse of the Norman dynasty at the end of the twelfth century. All that, and the reigns of Frederick II and Manfred, were surveyed in a mere thirty pages. At least this ensured that his history of the Normans in southern Italy and Sicily finished on a high note, at the end of the remarkable reign of King Roger II. Overall, Curtis's book, which has tended to be pushed into the sidelines, should be treated with some respect. It was a thoughtful attempt to grapple with a difficult and – at that period – neglected area of medieval history at a popular level.

Evelyn Jamison (1877–1972) was the subject of a study I contributed to the Festschrift for Errico Cuozzo, and the comments here will concentrate instead on her aims at the start of her career.[17] These were set out in her classic monograph on the Norman administration of Apulia and Capua, based on research she conducted while she was funded by a research fellowship to which she had been elected by Somerville College, Oxford.[18] She dated her interest in Norman Italy to 1898, even before, she explained, the work of Heinemann, Kehr, Caspar and Chalandon had begun to focus attention on the neglected subject of the Normans in southern Italy and Sicily. What attracted her was not just the 'dramatic story of the Norman adventure in the South' but the constitutional and administrative arrangements that emerged in the Norman territories; 'the older writers stimulated rather than satisfied the spirit of inquiry'. Jamison had originally thought of comparing Norman institutions in southern Italy with those in Normandy and England, in the hope of recovering an *ur*-Norman system of government – as indeed the eminent American historian Charles Homer Haskins was beginning to do.[19] But the sheer quantity of material she identified in Italian archives rapidly distracted her from following that will-o'-the-wisp, as did the encouragement of south Italian archivists and historians such as Riccardo Filangieri in Naples.

When she was offered her fellowship she realised that this was too large a subject to be handled within the three years of freedom that the fellowship offered.[20] She would need to choose between the mainland and the island parts of the kingdom, and to concentrate on a particular stretch of time.[21] Rather than spending time in Oxford, she treated her research fellowship as an opportunity to travel, and set off for Italy. The director of the newly established British School at Rome, Thomas Ashby, suggested she should begin by basing herself in the Archivio di Stato at Naples, whose director he knew; and so she began her travels, often in horse and cart, around the archives of southern Italy.

Her identification of government officials, such as master captains and master chamberlains under William I, was the starting point for detailed research into one of the central questions concerning the Norman kingdom: how the king managed to impose his authority, bearing in mind the stiff resistance that Roger II had faced at the start of his royal career, and how William I managed to bounce back from the serious reverses the monarchy experienced after King Roger's death. Moreover, the invaluable archival material she collected (and left in her will to the Warburg Institute in London) was placed in the wider context of political developments within the kingdom, such as German and Byzantine attempts to displace Roger and the rebellion against Maio of Bari.

Although her attention occasionally turned in other directions, her interest in the administration of the Regno never abated amid the distractions of a successful academic career at Lady Margaret Hall, Oxford.[22] Her long-awaited edition of the *Catalogus Baronum* appeared just after her death – a document she had used in her first monograph, with the limited help of del Re's edition in his *Cronisti e scrittori*. Admittedly, by 1972 she had been sitting on the proofs for some years, with only the short preface still to be written when I met her the year before; and in the end the commentary volume had to be written by Errico Cuozzo.[23] An interest in art historical evidence enabled her to shed new light on the ecclesiastical history of the Regno.[24] Her book on Admiral Eugenius, also published by the British Academy, took a brave and controversial stance, insisting that he was the writer known under the misnomer 'Hugo Falcandus'. She did not convince most of her readers; but in the process of discussing the career of this Greek official at the Norman court she opened up many new perspectives, as she did with the last article she published in her lifetime, at the age of ninety-one, on *Judex Tarentinus*.[25] The depth of her understanding of how the government of Norman Sicily and Italy worked enabled her to apply a powerful imagination to her material, so that the reader even of her more technical studies is mentally conveyed deep into the Regno, observing from close quarters the in-fighting at the court of William I and II, or the activities of the royal judges in the south Italian provinces.

Enrico Mazzarese Fardella wrote in a tribute to her published by the Istituto Italiano per il Medio Evo: 'chiamati a dovere rispondere alla domanda: "che cosa devono a Evelyn Jamison gli studi sui normanni nell'Italia meridionale e in Sicilia?" rispondiamo istintivamente: "tutto" '.[26] Her discussion of the administration of southern Italy set off further debate from the 1960s onwards, first with Mario Caravale (whose work she was reading when I met her, and which she hoped to review) and with Enrico Mazzarese Fardella. After her death the eminent Japanese historian of the Regno Hiroshi Takayama and the English scholar of Islamic Sicily Jeremy Johns engaged once again with her arguments. The perennial problem of the relationship between the two *duana*s has continued to give rise to disagreement.[27]

Evelyn Jamison devoted much of her life to her college as well as to scholarship. But she did leave an important legacy in her pupils, of whom the most distinguished was Marjorie Chibnall, a scholar of Anglo-Norman rather than Siculo-Norman history, though her general book on the Normans extended to southern Italy as, naturally, did her research on Orderic Vitalis, the Norman chronicler who had so much to say about the faraway Normans engaged in conquering southern Italy.[28] Another pupil, Dione Clementi, kept the flag of Norman Sicilian studies flying while working on an edition of one of the most valuable sources for the history of the Regno, the chronicle of Alexander of Telese. Previously, she had made a signal contribution to the study of the last days of the Norman kingdom with her calendar of diplomas of Emperor Henry VI.[29]

Evelyn Jamison did not pursue the comparison with England once she embarked on her archival research at the start of the twentieth century, but Dione Clementi did contribute a short excursus to Vivian Galbraith's classic study of Domesday Book, comparing what little Sicilian evidence there was for estate registers or something similar with the evidence for the compilation of Domesday.[30] Rather, Miss Jamison considered links between England and Sicily from the perspective of late twelfth-century contacts between two kingdoms whose rulers were aware of an earlier Norman past. Assumptions about a past common history would help smooth the path when arranging marriage alliances, notably that between Joanna, daughter of King Henry II of England (who was not exactly a Norman anyway), and William II, King of Sicily. Artistic links can also be detected. Most famously, several officials at the Sicilian court hailed from England, such as Thomas Brown and Robert of Selby. These links were the subject of a remarkable Italian Lecture at the British Academy.[31] Did this add up to a sense of common identity? R. H. C. Davis (1918–81 – his father had been the editor of the series in which Curtis's book had appeared) thought most definitely not. In a brief but unrelenting challenge to those who tried to identify a common Norman achievement from the British Isles to Sicily, Spain and Antioch, he wrote: 'the Sicilian kings showed not the slightest desire to appear Norman'.[32] He considered that Evelyn

Jamison had been too willing to accept the view of common identity when she cited Orderic Vitalis as a champion of Norman-ness.[33] This was surely unfair, since Orderic was looking backwards from Normandy to an earlier heroic age, whereas the later Norman kings of Sicily coincided with Henry II of England and the Angevin ascendancy. For Davis, English officials and scholars at the Sicilian court were clever men in search of good patrons, able to fit in in all sorts of places, as much in the Latin kingdom of Jerusalem as in the Norman kingdom of Sicily.

The real target of Davis's wrath was those British historians who assumed that if one was competent to write about Normans in England, then it was easy to make the jump and claim expertise in Norman Italian history as well. The most prominent of those historians was D. C. Douglas (1898–1982), whose biography of William the Conqueror appeared to great acclaim in 1964.[34] His approach to Norman history in his next book, *The Norman Achievement*, involved not so much a powerful sense of common identity as extraordinary inherited abilities that enabled Normans, whether of the ducal line or more modest Hautevilles, to conquer vast realms and transform Europe – and not just Europe, because they also played such a significant role in the First Crusade, among them Bohemond of Taranto/Antioch and Tancred the future prince of Galilee. They were supermen. It was almost a racial quality.[35] Some of the connections Douglas found were feeble indeed, such as the coincidence between Guiscard's career in Italy taking off and William ending his minority, both in 1047.[36] Douglas was, however, persistent. A second – alas, rather inaccurate – book, *The Norman Fate*, appeared in 1976, taking the story up to the death of Roger II. Douglas was a star performer as a lecturer and enjoyed his attempts to paint across a broad canvas. His British Academy obituarist R. H. C. Davis described the 'relish' with which he set to work on these volumes and the 'gusto' with which he declared 'How the critics will go for it! How they will tear it to bits!' – and, as has been seen, one of those who most effectively tore his approach to bits was his future obituarist.[37] But Douglas's bold ideas did not penetrate very deeply. The paradox that emerges from his books is that, on the one hand, the Normans are presented as great state-builders and on the other hand they are shown to be very willing to assimilate the methods of their predecessors and neighbours – in southern Italy and Sicily, Lombards, Byzantines, Arabs. By the end of his books one might conclude that the 'genius' of his Normans consisted not in preserving but in losing whatever distinctive identity they had.[38]

One writer who responded with unbounded enthusiasm to the cultural mélange of medieval Sicily was the young ex-diplomat John Julius Cooper, second viscount Norwich (1929–2018) who had no pretensions to academic standing but who opened up the history of the Normans in southern Italy and Sicily to a wide audience in his highly readable pair of books based on the work of Chalandon, *The Normans in the South* and *The Kingdom in the Sun*. Yet he also took care to read the chronicles and to visit the monuments of Norman Sicily. In various incarnations they remain the most accessible popular histories of the southern Normans, although the characterisation of the great Norman leaders is sometime avowedly imaginative: writing of the breakdown in relations between Guiscard and Roger I he speculates about 'a new aspect of the Guiscard's character now appearing for the first time – jealousy of his brother, many years younger and possessed of ambitions and qualities in no way inferior to his own. Was there in fact room in Italy for both of them?'[39] William I of Sicily is a thoroughly bad sort who luxuriates in his palaces while letting his subjects suffer from earthquakes and other trials – or maybe he should be called William the Sad rather than William the Bad and was a deeply unhappy man on to whose shoulders had been loaded unexpected responsibilities (having expected an elder brother to succeed to the throne).[40] Such judgements are no worse than those offered by Steven Runciman in his *History of the Crusades* or *The Sicilian Vespers*, though Norwich's literary style was more ornate.

Viscount Norwich came upon the subject almost by chance. He was taking a holiday in Sicily with his wife in 1961 and had not expected to see the wonders that he found: 'here were cathedrals, churches and palaces which seemed to combine, without effort or strain, all that was loveliest in the art and architecture of the three leading civilisations of the time'.[41] Had there been a book on this subject in English (he disdained Curtis) he would not, he said, have needed to go ahead and write his own. And – as even academic reviewers had to admit – he had filled a notable gap in the historical literature. During his long writing career, he never really matched these two books, neither in his history of Venice nor his history of

Byzantium, largely because he found it easier to paint the portrait of the Hauteville rulers, and much more difficult to portray most of the faceless doges and poorly documented minor emperors who filled the pages of his books on Venice and Byzantium. At a time when professional historians are inclined to turn up their nose at those outside (and indeed inside) the universities who attempt to reach a wide audience, it is important to remember that there has also to be room for books such as these which can even open up areas scholars have neglected.[42]

As Davis was aware, the monarchy created by Roger II, with its Byzantine and Islamic ceremonial trappings (as displayed in Roger's mantle and the Martorana mosaic), was very far removed from anything practised in Norman England. A glimmer of awareness of common identity might be found in the supposed gift of a crown to his fellow-'Norseman' Roger by King Sigurð of Norway during his crusade to the Holy Land, but that story was related a century later in Iceland, and tells one nothing about how Normans in either Sicily or England saw themselves. But historians of Norman England would not let go of Sicily after Davis delivered his warnings. Donald Matthew's *Norman Kingdom of Sicily* (1992) was the work of an often provocative historian of Norman England, who was clearly much happier handling southern Italy, whose Latin character made it recognisable, than the island of Sicily. Its great virtue was the refusal to cut off the history of Norman Sicily once Henry VI of Hohenstaufen conquered the Regno, but to carry the discussion through to the defeat of Manfred in 1266.

Since 1976 there has been a growing recognition that the history of medieval Italy does not stop somewhere a little south of Rome. Moreover, there has been greater interest in the idea of looking at the peninsula as a whole and in thinking about some of the long-term continuities in the south, from the Lombards through the Normans and Hohenstaufen to the Angevins and Aragonese. Attention has focused on the towns as well as the monarchy and the feudal nobility, on Jews as well as Muslims and Greek Orthodox, as well of course as the Latin Church. The economic history of the Regno has attracted increasing attention, as have its material survivals – mosaics, ivory boxes, *muqarnas* decorations, ceramics. The question of Norman-ness has largely been set to one side. The study of the Regno is in a healthy condition, but its pioneers should not be forgotten.

Notes

1. E. Curtis, *Roger of Sicily and the Normans in Lower Italy 1016–1154* (New York, 1912), p. iii. See ch. 56 of Edward Gibbon's *History of the Decline and Fall of the Roman Empire*, 7 vols (London, 1853–55), vol. 6, pp. 301–40 [Robert Guiscard], and 340–57 [the Norman Kingdom of Sicily].
2. Curtis, *Roger of Sicily*.
3. F. Chalandon, *Histoire de la Domination normande en Italie et en Sicile*, 2 vols (Paris, 1907).
4. For what follows, see T. W. Moody, 'Edmund Curtis (1881–1943)', in the Trinity College Dublin publication *Hermathena* 63 (1944), 69–78; the memoir by 'J. H.' in *Analecta Hibernica* 16 (1946), 387–9, closely followed for his early career by P. Maume, 'Curtis, Edmund', *Dictionary of Irish Biography* (Cambridge, 2009), s.v.
5. E. Curtis, *A History of Medieval Ireland from 1110 to 1513* (Dublin, 1923; enlarged in 1938 to begin in 1086); for a full bibliography of his writings see T. W. Moody, 'The writings of Edmund Curtis', *Irish Historical Studies* 12 (1943), 393–400.
6. *Cronisti e scrittori sincroni napoletani* I, ed. G. del Re (Naples, 1845).
7. Curtis, *Roger of Sicily*, p. 15.
8. Curtis, *Roger of Sicily*, pp. 1, 8.
9. Curtis, *Roger of Sicily*, p. 22.
10. Curtis, *Roger of Sicily*, pp. 29–31.
11. Curtis, *Roger of Sicily*, p. 39.
12. Curtis, *Roger of Sicily*, p. 81.
13. Curtis, *Roger of Sicily*, pp. 339, 343, 469–72; Chalandon, *Histoire de la Domination*, vol. 2, pp. 652–3.
14. Curtis, *Roger of Sicily*, pp. 461–4.
15. Curtis, *Roger of Sicily*, p. 302.
16. Curtis, *Roger of Sicily*, pp. 297–301.
17. D. Abulafia, 'Evelyn Jamison, champion of Southern Italy, champion of women's education', in J.-M. Martin and R. Alaggio (eds), *'Quei Maledetti Normanni': Studi offerti a Errico Cuozzo*, 2 vols (Ariano Irpino, 2016), vol. 1, pp. 1–12; also C. V. Wedgwood, 'In memoriam: Evelyn Mary Jamison, 1877–1972', *The Brown Book: Lady Margaret Hall Oxford* (December, 1972), p. 35.
18. E. Jamison, 'The Norman administration of Apulia and Capua more especially under Roger II and William I 1127–1166', *Papers of the British School at Rome* 6 (1913), 211–481.
19. His thoughts on this were later summarised in C. H. Haskins, *The Normans in European History* (Boston, 1915).

20 These aspects of Miss Jamison's career are discussed in more detail in Abulafia, 'Evelyn Jamison', pp. 2, 4, 6, and 9, of which the following paragraphs are a partial summary.
21 Jamison, 'Norman administration', p. 219.
22 E. Jamison, *Studies on the History of Medieval Sicily and South Italy*, ed. D. Clementi and T. Kölzer (Aalen, 1992), contains all her articles but omits the two monographs on Norman administration and Admiral Eugenius.
23 *Catalogus Baronum*, ed. E. Jamison, FSI 101 (Rome, 1972); also 'Additional work by E. Jamison on the *Catalogus Baronum*', *Bullettino dell'Istituto Italiano per il Medio Evo* 83 (1971), 1–63; E. Cuozzo, *Catalogus baronum. Commentario*, FSI 101 (b) (Rome, 1984).
24 E. Jamison, 'Pisan churches on the Via Traiana', *Journal of the British Archaeological Association* n.s. 35 (1929–30), 163–88; 'Notes on Santa Maria della Strada at Matrice, its history and sculpture', *Papers of the British School at Rome* 14 (1938), 32–97.
25 E. Jamison, *Admiral Eugenius of Sicily: His Life and Work and the Authorship of the* Epistola ad Petrum *and the* Historia Hugonis Falcandi Siculi (London, 1957); E. Jamison, 'Judex Tarentinus', *Proceedings of the British Academy* 53 (1968), 289–344.
26 E. Mazzarese Fardella, 'Il contributo di Evelyn Jamison agli studi sui Normanni d'Italia e di Sicilia', *Bulletino dell'Istituto Italiano per il Medio Evo* 83 (1971), 65.
27 M. Caravale, *Il Regno Normanno di Sicilia* (Milan, 1966); E. Mazzarese Fardella, *Aspetti dell'organizzazione amministrativa nel Regno normanno e svevo* (Milan, 1966); H. Takayama, *The Administration of the Norman Kingdom of Sicily* (Leiden, 1993); J. Johns, *Arabic Administration in Norman Sicily: The Royal Dīwān* (Cambridge, 2002), and now Takayama's invaluable collected essays, *Sicily and the Mediterranean in the Middle Ages* (Abingdon, 2019).
28 M. Chibnall, *The Normans* (Oxford, 2000); see also her *The World of Orderic Vitalis* (Oxford, 1984) and her edition *The Ecclesiastical History of Orderic Vitalis*, 6 vols (Oxford, 1969–80); D. Greenway, 'Marjorie McCallum Chibnall, 1915–2012', *Biographical Memoirs of Fellows of the British Academy* 13 (2014), 43–62.
29 *Alexandri Telesini abbatis Ystoria Rogerii regis Sicilie, Calabrie atque Apulie*, ed. L. de Nava, commentary by D. Clementi, FSI 112 (Rome, 1991); also her 'Calendar of the diplomas of the Emperor Henry VI concerning the Kingdom of Sicily', *QF* 35 (1955), 86–225.
30 D. Clementi, 'Notes on Norman Sicilian surveys' in V. H. Galbraith (ed.), *The Making of Domesday Book* (Oxford, 1961), pp. 55–8.

31 E. Jamison, 'The Sicilian monarchy in the mind of Anglo-Norman contemporaries', *Proceedings of the British Academy* 24 (1938), 237–85; also 'The alliance of England and Sicily in the second half of the twelfth century', *Journal of the Warburg and Courtauld Institutes* 6 (1943), 20–32.
32 R. H. C. Davis, *The Normans and their Myth* (London, 1976), p. 86.
33 Davis, *Normans and their Myth*, p. 14.
34 D. C. Douglas, *William the Conqueror* (London, 1964).
35 D. C. Douglas, *The Norman Achievement, 1050–1100* (London, 1969).
36 Douglas, *Norman Achievement*, p. 5.
37 R. H. C. Davis, 'David Charles Douglas, 1898–1982', *Proceedings of the British Academy* 69 (1983), 513–42.
38 See now G. A. Loud, 'The "Gens Normannorum": Myth or reality?', *ANS* 4 (1982), 104–16.
39 J. J. Norwich, *The Normans in the South* (London, 1967) – citation from p. 113; *The Kingdom in the Sun* (London, 1970). Note that John Julius Cooper published under the name of John Julius Norwich.
40 Norwich, *Kingdom in the Sun*, pp. 242–5.
41 Norwich, *Normans in the South*, p. xi.
42 My own interest in Norman Italy was aroused by reading *The Normans in the South* as an undergraduate.

3

The Norman Empire between the eleventh and twelfth centuries with special reference to the Normans in southern Italy

Luigi Russo

Since the last quarter of the twentieth century the concept of 'empire' has had undoubted influence on the historiography of the Norman world when judged by contributions that appeared in the mid-1970s. It is enough to recall John Le Patourel's influential book, *The Norman Empire* (1976), which employed the term 'to describe the complex of dominion and lordship which William the Conqueror and Henry Beauclerc, with their vassals and ministers, built up on either side of English Channel', even while Le Patourel himself recognised that the title was 'provocative'.[1] In the same year, R. H. C. Davis published *The Normans and their Myth*. Davis's work is a great classic in Norman studies that, though brief, recognises the importance of discussing 'the Normans in the light of their myth in order to discover how they became Normans, how they changed their ideas of what a Norman was, and how eventually they lost their identity'.[2]

After all, the idea of an 'empire' as used for the Norman world was first proposed by Charles Homer Haskins, the famous American medievalist of the last century. At conferences in America in 1915, Haskins coined, not without triumphalism, a definition of the Norman Empire 'only in the broader and looser sense of the word, a great composite state, larger than a mere kingdom and imperial in extent if not in organization'.[3] This interpretation was developed further in the 1990s by Pierre Aubè in *Les Empires normandes d'Orient*. In his conclusions regarding the Norman subjugation of southern Italy, Aubè leaves no doubt about his triumphalist interpretation of the Norman conquest: 'Nul sortilège ne devait jamais entacher, dans la longue mémoire des hommes, cette aventure triomphale dans laquelle s'était incarné la génie des Normands'.[4]

However, some critics immediately detected discrepancies and incongruities in the expression 'cross-Channel world', recently revived by David Bates, editor of the documents of William the Conqueror and foremost authority on England's first Norman king.[5] These polemics have never reached a sufficiently meaningful definition – even if inaccurate – of the concept of a 'Norman Empire', a definition clear and understandable enough to address a general public outside Norman studies.[6] In fact, John Le Patourel's proposed definition was never presented as a final model but as a means to encourage a new approach to the role of the Normans in England's history.[7]

In any case, the last decade of twentieth century was very different from the 1970s. The 1990s were deeply influenced by the dissolution of the Soviet Union and the strong assertion of a European political construction. The Maastricht Treaty, signed in 1992, has been the crux of heated political discussion with strong historical overtones in the United Kingdom, especially the debate before and after the Brexit referendum (23 June 2016).[8] The vicissitudes of the Normans in historiography, irrespective of national events and viewed from a pan-European perspective, are perhaps best illustrated by a 1994 exhibition in Rome at the National Museum of the Palazzo di Venezia. The huge catalogue – roughly 600 pages – celebrates a gathering of the day's leading scholars of Norman history and reflects a clearly disproportionate scholarly interest in Normandy and southern Italy. England and the Holy Land remained in the background, and the contribution of the Nordic peoples to medieval Russia was omitted completely. Historians can now fill that gap with new interdisciplinary research about the relationship between the East and the West, research that inspired an excellent edited volume by a French-Russian team (CNRS and Russian Academy of Sciences)[9] published after the exposition 'Russie Vikings' at the Musée de Normandie of Caen in 2011.[10] In a programmatic essay in the catalogue for the Roman exhibition (*La coscienza normanna oggi*) Jean-Yves Marin definitely declared that 'nell'attuale sviluppo regionale che si conosce dell'Europa, le complicità lontane possono aiutarci ... a costruire un futuro di culture differenziate, testimoniando ognuna rispetto per l'altra'.[11] With this statement, the French scholar clarified the key role of academic research on Norman identity as a common element for the construction of the European politics at that time.[12] As many well know, those enthusiastic interpretations about European identity nowadays encounter many difficulties. At the same time, a keen sensitivity towards the problematic aspects of the elaboration of a common European identity has appeared in the historiography, a sign of greater awareness of the crisis emerging on the European continent since the 1970s.[13]

In any event, the last two decades have corresponded with a great international renewal of Norman studies.[14] Two books arising from meetings held at Cerisy-La-Salle in 1992 and 2011 demonstrate the historiographical refinement attained today, *Les Normands en Méditerranée dans le sillage des Tancrède* and *911–2011: Penser les mondes normands médiévaux*.[15] The chronological and geographical scope of Norman activities is apparent in the more recent book,[16] while the earlier one focuses on the victorious deeds of Norman knights in southern Italy.[17] *911–2011*, in particular, does not deal with an unique Norman identity, but encompasses the history of the full Norman diaspora, from Normandy to the Latin East.[18] The history of the origins of the duchy of Normandy now devotes more attention to both the continuities and the socio-political disruptions occurring in northern France during the tenth century, a fact today well understood thanks to Pierre Bauduin's research.[19] The concept is addressed again effectively in one of the most recent and broad syntheses of Norman history written by another University of Caen medievalist, François Neveux. According to him, 'au fond, la réussite normande, en Angleterre comme en Italie, est sans doute le fruit d'un metissage, beaucoup plus culturel que purement physique'.[20] After all, it is no accident that David Bates, one of the most influential scholars on the relations between the two shores of the English Channel, in a recent monograph considered it worthwhile to rethink the concept of 'empire'. Bates depicts this term as a 'rich tapestry of human agency operating around a complex, but ultimately definable, framework of norms, scripts and rules', a definition very far removed from those previously advanced and marking a rethinking of old historiographical paradigms.[21]

Furthermore, the Italian peninsula leads this renewal of Norman studies, especially due to the impetus provided initially by the Centro di Studi Normanno-Svevi in Bari and later by the Centro Europeo di Studi Normanni in Ariano Irpino. Indeed, these two research centres not only have organised influential conferences for reconsidering the impact of Norman studies in Italy but they also have continuously maintained links with research from the main European historical schools and promoted close relations between transalpine and Italian scholars.[22] It is, therefore, no coincidence that the contributions of Graham Loud are present in both series of studies published by these Italian research centres, a reflection of the leading position, universally recognised, of the scholar celebrated in this volume.[23]

This academic renewal has 'flowed' into works addressed to the general public: for example, in a recent synthesis for a German-speaking audience, immediately translated into Italian, Hubert Houben portrayed Norman history as a sequence of important changes. His focuses for attention were 'i processi di acculturazione e di integrazione, di stretta attualità in un mondo, come quello attuale, sempre più globalizzato e caratterizzato da migrazioni e contatti oltre che da conflitti fra religioni e culture differenti'.[24] A very similar line of inquiry was pursued by Keith Stringer and Andrew Jotischky in their collection of papers gathering the results of a research project promoted by Lancaster University, an investigation of the 'characteristics of Norman expansion on the peripheries of Christian Europe, in order to contribute to a re-evaluation of the contours and coordinates of *the Norman world or worlds* and, more generally to assess in novel ways the processes of medieval state-making and the construction (or reconstruction) of *identities*'.[25] Here we stress the plural approach adopted by the editors: they preferred to talk about 'worlds' and 'identities', a clear sign of the broad movement of academic research and the main trends of actual investigations.

The foregoing can be summarised with the words of Marc Bloch in his last, unfinished, work on historical methodology: 'Le passé est, par définition, un donné que rien ne modifiera plus. Mais la connaissance du passé est une chose en progrès, qui sans cesse se transforme et se perfectionne'.[26] What better evidence of this can there be than the scholarly opinions summarised here from the century-long dialogue regarding the meaning of the Norman conquests of the central Middle Ages? Surely, we agree with the statement by leading medievalist Raoul Manselli in 1968: 'i Normanni ... non sono più un mito, ma continuano a stupirci'.[27] The study of the Normans, moreover, represents an excellent field of investigation for verifying the characteristics of European expansion in the Middle Ages, provided that there is an awareness of the many historiographical strands that intersect in the study of the different Norman worlds. In this field, two of Graham Loud's books – *The Age of Robert Guiscard* and *The Latin Church in Norman Italy*[28] – are among the most significant contributions to a historiography whose key moments have been retraced in this introduction, which does not pretend to address exhaustively the vibrant, continuing intellectual debate, a debate evident in the recent proceedings of the Ventunesime Giornate Normanno-Sveve of Bari.[29]

Here we will restrict our analysis to southern Italy, with particular attention to the relationships between centres of power and historiographic writings in Norman Italy in the eleventh and twelfth centuries. The main features of Anglo-Norman historiography have already been deeply examined by many scholars, starting with the influential analysis by Italian medievalist Ovidio Capitani forty years ago: the emphasis on Norman victories, the craftiness of Norman leaders, the audacity of their territorial ambitions represented on the basis of strongly secular interpretative categories.[30] These elements contributed to the identification of a peculiarity of Norman historiography in the medieval age. Upon arrival in Italy around the early eleventh century, the northern knights – coming from a broad swathe of transalpine Europe, not just Normandy, as shown by Léon-Robert Ménager[31] – successfully gained an autonomous political space through their political reconstruction of southern Italy at the expense of the Byzantine and German empires. The Normans' ascension culminated with the royal coronation of Roger of Hauteville as King Roger II in Palermo on Christmas Day 1130.[32]

The Norman knights were represented as the main beneficiaries of the two empires' woes during the years in which the Hauteville dynasty gained a foothold in southern Italy, a political area that – even if central geopolitically – had previously been characterised by extreme political and cultural fragmentation.[33] All this unleashed caustic accusations of tyranny directed at Roger II from many quarters, critiques that spurred a debate that deeply engaged the principal exponents of Christianity in the second quarter of the twelfth century.[34]

The key aspect of the forging of Norman rule in southern Italy was the Norman ability to build new political and institutional balances. During the central centuries of the medieval era, Normans were established as a true political novelty; for this reason they had to fill a gap in legitimacy in the eyes of their age's other players. That is why, *inter alia*, they commissioned historical works. This seems obvious when we read the different prologues of these histories, such as that in the *Gesta Roberti Wiscardi* by William of Apulia, addressed to Roger Borsa, Guiscard's son and heir (as well as Pope Urban II),[35] or that in *De rebus gestis Rogerii* by Geoffrey Malaterra, to be scrutinised below.

Let us now read the double dedicatory epistle that acts as a prologue to the *De rebus gestis Rogerii*. Although it is not addressed to Roger I but instead to Ansger, bishop of Catania,[36] Geoffrey makes it clear that he received orders directly from the Norman count to write a 'clear and easy to understand' text (*planum ... et facilem ad intelligendum*). The same subject was chosen by Roger, who ordered (*injunxit*) the chronicler to narrate the victories won in Calabria and Sicily.[37] What is more interesting is the awareness shining through the two epistles of the significance of transmitting the memory of the past, a perspective shared by all the stakeholders. Geoffrey, first of all, dwells on the ancient tradition of the need that 'the deeds of brave men should be recorded in writing and transmitted to posterity. This prevents actions which ought to be remembered, and those who have performed them, being consigned to oblivion; and, even more, it enables those deeds which have been entrusted to writing and are read about and known by future generations, to make those who did them seem to live on through the memory of their lives'.[38] This imperative likewise seemed clear to Geoffrey's patron, Roger I, an interested listener of the ancient stories, who wanted his deeds to be immortalised through a history that bestowed legitimacy on him and his heirs. This viewpoint was shared by the men closest to the Norman count, those who supported the initiative and who probably suggested Geoffrey as the chronicler of the *De rebus gestis Rogerii*.[39] Beyond the grandiose expressions in the double dedicatory epistle of the imperative to preserve deeds for posterity, a glimpse of a clear-cut policy of memory shared by the whole Sicilian court and Count Roger appears in Malaterra's ending of his work with a transcription of Urban II's bull *Quia propter prudentiam tuam* (5 July 1098), the so-called Apostolic Legacy which sealed the Normans' conquests.[40] The time had come to write a history, even better *the official story* of the actions of the victorious Normans in southern Italy. Above all, the text was needed to celebrate the triumphs of Roger I, who had come as a *juvenis* into Italy around forty years earlier, and to memorialise an age for which memory was disappearing.[41] Therefore, Geoffrey does not exclude defects in the memories of his informants who helped him to collect the happenings of events preceding his arrival, when he was still in France.[42]

I linger on the prologue of *De rebus gestis Rogerii* because, in my opinion, it represents a perfect example of the Norman court's desire to obtain legitimation at the end of an age of military conquest and of a far-sighted marriage policy with the leading local aristocratic clans.[43] This legitimation was even more necessary given the still unfinished political unification of southern Italy under the leadership of the Hauteville clan at the end of the eleventh century.[44]

After all, there is a close link between the writing of history and the centres of power: the main three chroniclers in the mainstream of the Norman historiography (Amatus of Montecassino, William of Apulia and Geoffrey Malaterra) all wrote during the last twenty years of the eleventh century and all expressed an overall rethinking of the arrival of Normans on the Italian scene, emphasising in retrospect the role of the Hauteville clan.[45] All these writers came from circles, either directly or indirectly, linked to the winners: Amatus dedicated his work to Desiderius, abbot of Montecassino, and acknowledged the great advantages that Richard of Capua and Robert Guiscard had given his monastery.[46] William underlined that his work had been requested by Roger Borsa, son and heir of Robert Guiscard,[47] while Malaterra wrote his book because Roger I and his court insisted upon it.[48] Therefore, presenting the history of Italo-Normans in the eleventh century amounted to the complete expression of the achievements of the warriors who had arrived from northern lands, a history that lurks in germ in Geoffrey Malaterra's first book where he proposed an extensive reconstruction of the feats of Norman warriors from Normandy to southern Italy.[49]

To sum up, we have seen that the concept of 'empire', even though a well-established historiographical tradition, does not find adequate support in the sources for the Normans in Italy. When this concept was employed as an analytical tool to make sense of the quick success of the Norman expansionism, it was too broad and imprecise to be applied without qualification in every land affected by the Norman diaspora. Despite the concept's limitations, it should be emphasised that the legitimating discourse of the Norman conquests in Italy presumed a self-affirmation that reflected a strong desire for domination broadly linked to the notion of *imperium*.[50] Nevertheless, it is important to underscore that the military conquests of the Normans in southern Italy were strongly supported ideologically by historiographical works, works that demonstrated a marked inclination to celebrate their successes, particularly those achieved by the Hauteville clan, even though the fragility of the manuscript tradition casts doubt on the sharing of these ideas outside the Norman court.[51] To this fragility we must add the absence of an autonomous Norman documentary tradition that led the Normans to adopt the Byzantine documentary practices operating in southern Italy, yet another example of the conquerors' pragmatic reliance upon subjugated ethnic groups.[52] This documentation must therefore be treated with the utmost caution in the historical assessment of the characteristics of the Norman conquest of southern Italy briefly recalled here.

The emphasis on the legitimacy of the Norman conquests of Italy is closely linked to the Hauteville clan, a family who saw its rise as confirmation of its own historical providence and did not conceal any unscrupulous conduct in this ascent regardless of the potential for complaints from ecclesiastics of their age.[53] This new Hauteville power, with its assumption of the royal title in 1130, proposed a new synthesis of the traditions of government, a pattern of governance so discontinuous with the past as to cause a heated debate in twelfth-century Europe, but this is a story on which I do not dwell here.[54]

Notes

This chapter is a revised and expanded version of my article 'The Norman Empire nella medievistica del XX secolo: una definizione problematica', *Schede Medievali* 54 (2016), 159–73.

1 J. Le Patourel, *The Norman Empire* (Oxford, 1976), p. 354; the affirmation that 'the title is provocative' is at p. vi. See also p. 325: 'The Norman kings were more than kings. In addition to their kingdom, and to a duchy in which they were scarcely less than kings, they were overlords of other kings. For such a complex as they ruled, a word that describes a political structure of higher status than a kingdom seems not inappropriate ... if the word "empire" is used in its more modern sense, and is associated with the implication of its derivatives "imperialism" or "empire-building", it appears all the more fitting, for these implications extend the notion of hegemony to exploitation, which is not hard to find in the Norman lands'. See D. S. Spear, 'The Norman empire and the secular clergy, 1066–1204', *Journal of British Studies* 21 (1982), 1–10.

2 R. H. C. Davis, *The Normans and their Myth* (London, 1976), p. 16.

3 C. H. Haskins, *The Normans in European History* (Boston, 1915), p. 87. But see also p. 23: 'The Anglo-Norman empire of the twelfth century was the marvel of its day'. See also p. 85: 'The Norman empire is the outstanding feature of the twelfth century, as the conquest of England was of the eleventh'.

4 P. Aubé, *Les Empires normands d'Orient* (Paris, 1991), p. 298. 'No spell should ever have sullied, in the long memory of men, this trimphal adventure in which the spirit of the Normans became incarnate' (trans. D. Routt).

5 For further details see D. Bates, *The Normans and Empire* (Oxford, 2013), pp. 1–2 and footnotes. See also *Regesta regum Anglo-Normannorum: The Acta of William I, 1066–1087*, ed. D. Bates (Oxford, 1998); and D. Bates, *William the Conqueror* (London, 2018).

6 Although it comes to different conclusions, J. Green, 'Unity and disunity in the Anglo-Norman state', *Historical Research* 63 (1989), 115–34, especially p. 116, has underlined the strong influence of Le Patourel's monograph.

7 As noted by M. Chibnall, *The Debate on the Norman Conquest* (Manchester, 1999), pp. 115–17.

8 For the controversy see the *Financial Times* article by G. Rachman, 'Rival historians trade blows over Brexit' (13 May 2016).

9 P. Bauduin and A. E. Musin (eds), *Vers l'Orient et vers l'Occident: Regards croisés sur les dynamiques et les transferts*

culturels des Vikings à la Rous ancienne (Caen, 2014). See also V. I. Petrukhin, 'The Normans and the Khazars in the south of Rus (the formation of the "Russian land" in the Middle Dnepr area)', *Russian History* 19 (1992), 393–400, which criticises Russian historiography of the second half of the twentieth century aimed at explaining every historical phenomenon on a national basis in order to omit any foreign influence.

10 See www.officiel-galeries-musees.com/musee/musee-de-normandie/exposition/russie-viking-vers-une-autre-normandie (accessed 17 January 2019).

11 M. D'Onofrio (ed.), *I Normanni popolo d'Europa, 1030–1200* (Venice, 1994), p. 373. 'In the current regional development that one is familiar with from Europe, distant complicities can help us … to build a future of different cultures by bearing witness to respect of each one for the other' (trans. D. Routt).

12 See D. J. A. Matthew, *L'Europa normanna* (Rome, 1987), a series of lectures given by the author at the University of Venice in 1986.

13 See the preface by M. Vagnoni to I. Baumgärtner, M. Vagnoni and M. Welton (eds), *Representations of Power at the Mediterranean Borders of Europe (12th–14th Centuries)* (Florence, 2014), p. vii, which argues for a 'reconsideration of the concept of Europe, its borders, and its cultural identity'.

14 The situation of medieval studies on the Mezzogiorno has been tackled by D. Abulafia, 'Il Contesto mediterraneo e il primo disegno delle Due Italie', in G. Galasso (ed.), *Alle origini del dualismo italiano. Regno di Sicilia e Italia centro-settentrionale dagli Altavilla agli Angiò (1100–1350)* (Soveria Mannelli, 2014), pp. 11–28, especially pp. 11–15.

15 Respectively, P. Bouet and F. Neveux (eds), *Les Normands en Méditerranée dans le sillage des Tancrède* (Caen, 1994, 2001) and D. Bates and P. Bauduin (eds), *911–2011: Penser les mondes normands médiévaux* (Caen, 2016).

16 See www.unicaen.fr/craham/spip.php?article574&lang=fr (accessed 17 January 2019): 'Les thèmes abordés seront envisagés sur une longue période (IXe–XIIIe siècle) et sur un espace couvrant l'Europe du Nord-Ouest (Normandie, Angleterre, Ecosse, Pays de Galles, Irlande), l'Europe septentrionale et orientale (Scandinavie, littoral de la Baltique, Russie), le bassin méditerranéen (Italie du Sud, Proche-Orient, Byzance)' ['The themes approached will be considered over a long period (ninth to thirteenth centuries) and across a space covering northwestern Europe (Normandy, England, Scotland, Wales, Ireland), northern and eastern Europe (Scandinavia, the Baltic coast, Russia), the Mediterranean (southern Italy, the Near East, Byzantium)'] (trans. D. Routt).

17 See in particular P. Bouet, '1000–1100: La conquête', in Bouet and Neveux (eds), *Les Normands en Méditerranée*, pp. 11–23 (we quote from the first edition).
18 It is not by chance that the term diaspora is used in the recent book of J. Jesch, *The Viking Diaspora* (London, 2015), pp. 68–81. On the historiographic concept of diaspora, further details are found in L. Abrams, 'Diaspora and identity in the Viking age', *Early Medieval Europe* 20 (2012), 17–38, especially p. 17, n. 1. For a broad analysis, see R. Cohen, *Global Diasporas: An Introduction* (London, 2008).
19 P. Bauduin, *La première Normandie (Xe–XIe siècles). Sur les frontières de la haute Normandie: Identité et construction d'une principauté* (Caen, 2004); P. Bauduin, *Le monde franc et les Vikings, VIIIe–Xe siècle* (Paris, 2009).
20 F. Neveux, *L'Aventure des Normands (VIIIe–XIIIe siècle)* (Paris, 2006), p. 192. 'After all, the Norman success, in England as in Italy, is without doubt the fruit of an interbreeding, much more cultural than purely physical' (trans. D. Routt).
21 Bates, *The Normans and Empire*, p. 186.
22 Respectively, R. Licinio and F. Violante (eds), *I caratteri originari della conquista normanna. Diversità e identità nel Mezzogiorno (1030–1130)* (Bari, 2006); R. Licinio and F. Violante (eds), *Nascita di un regno. Poteri signorili, istituzioni feudali e strutture sociali nel Mezzogiorno normanno (1130–1194)* (Bari, 2008); P. Cordasco and M. A. Siciliani (eds), *Il Mezzogiorno normanno-svevo fra storia e storiografia* (Bari, 2014); E. D'Angelo and C. Leonardi (eds), *Il Papato e i Normanni: Temporale e spirituale in età normanna* (Florence, 2011); Galasso (ed.), *Alle origini del dualismo italiano*.
23 We refer to 'Politics, piety and ecclesiastical patronage in twelfth-century Benevento', in E. Cuozzo and J.-M. Martin (eds), *Cavalieri alla conquista del Sud. Studi sull'Italia normanna in memoria di Léon-Robert Ménager* (Rome, 1997), pp. 283–312; G. A. Loud, 'Il regno normanno-svevo visto dal regno d'Inghilterra', in G. Musca (ed.), *Il Mezzogiorno normanno-svevo visto dall'Europa e dal mondo mediterraneo* (Bari, 1999), pp. 175–95.
24 H. Houben, *I Normanni*, Italian trans. (Bologna, 2013; orig. edn Munich, 2012), p. 9. 'The processes of acculturation and of integration, of strict reality in a world, like that present world, always more globalised and characterised by migrations and contacts as well as by conflicts between different religions and cultures' (trans. D. Routt).
25 K. J. Stringer and A. Jotischky (eds), *Norman Expansion: Connections, Continuities and Contrasts* (Abingdon, 2013), p. 1 (italics are mine). A second volume from this project has recently appeared: K. J.

Stringer and A. Jotischky (eds), *The Normans and the 'Norman Edge': Peoples, Polities and Identities on the Frontiers of Medieval Europe* (London, 2019).
26 M. Bloch, *Apologie pour l'histoire ou Métier d'historien*, 2nd edn (Paris, 1974), p. 58. 'The past is, by definition, a datum which nothing in the future will change. But the knowledge of the past is something progressive which is constantly transforming and perfecting itself' (trans. M. Bloch, *The Historian's Craft*, trans. P. Putnam (New York, 1963), p. 58).
27 R. Manselli, 'Epilogo', in *I Normanni e la loro espansione in Europa nell'Alto Medioevo*, Settimane di Studio del Centro Italiano di Studi sull'Alto Medioevo 16 (Spoleto, 1969), p. 804. 'The Normans ... are no more a myth, but they continue to amaze us' (trans. D. Routt).
28 G. A. Loud, *The Age of Robert Guiscard: Southern Italy and the Norman Conquest* (Harlow, 2000); and *The Latin Church in Norman Italy* (Cambridge, 2007).
29 M. Boccuzzi and P. Cordasco (eds), *Civiltà a contatto nel Mezzogiorno normanno-svevo: economia società istituzioni* (Bari, 2018).
30 See the classic contribution of O. Capitani, 'Specific motivations and continuing themes of the Norman chronicles of southern Italy: Eleventh and twelfth centuries', in *The Normans in Sicily and Southern Italy: The Lincei Lectures 1974* (Oxford, 1977), pp. 1–46; G. A. Loud, 'The "Gens Normannorum": Myth or reality?', *ANS* 4 (1982), 104–16 and 205–9; K. B. Wolf, *Making History: The Normans and their Historians in Eleventh-Century Italy* (Philadelphia, 1995); S. Tramontana, 'I luoghi della produzione storiografica', in G. Musca (ed.), *Centri della produzione della cultura nel Mezzogiorno normanno-svevo* (Bari, 1997), pp. 21–40; E. Albu, *The Normans in their Histories: Propaganda, Myth and Subversion* (Woodbridge, 2001), pp. 134–5; lastly L. Russo, 'Oblio e memoria di Boemondo d'Altavilla nella storiografia normanna', *Bullettino dell'Istituto Storico per il Medio Evo* 106 (2004), 137–65 (now reprinted in an updated version in L. Russo, *I Normanni del Mezzogiorno e il movimento crociato* (Bari, 2014), pp. 37–64).
31 L.-R. Ménager, 'Inventaire des familles normandes et franques emigrées en Italie méridionale et en Sicile (XIe–XIIe siécles)', in *Roberto il Guiscardo e il suo tempo* (Rome, 1975), pp. 279–410 [= L. R. Ménager, *Hommes et institutions de l'Italie normande* (London, 1981), updated by some *Additions*]. Supplementary discussion is provided by A. Varvaro, 'Les Normands en Sicile aux XIe et XIIe siècles. Présence effective dans l'île des hommes d'origine normande ou gallo-romane', *Cahiers de Civilisation Médiévale* 23 (1980), 199–213.

32 Worth mentioning is H. Houben, *Ruggero II di Sicilia. Un sovrano tra Oriente e Occidente*, Italian trans. (Rome, 1999; orig. edn Darmstadt, 1997), pp. 66–77. Recently: G. M. Cantarella, *Ruggero II* (Rome, 2020), pp. 87–95.

33 The geopolitical centrality of Sicily and southern Italy is underlined by C. D. Stanton, *Norman Naval Operations in the Mediterranean* (Woodbridge, 2011), pp. 1–8; on relations between the papacy and the Normans see G. M. Cantarella, 'Liaisons dangereuses: il papato e i Normanni', in D'Angelo and Leonardi (eds), *Il Papato e i Normanni*, pp. 45–58. Interesting insights on the change of perspective of the Norman society in Italy are now in J. Drell, 'From lemons to legislation: Welcoming foreigners in the medieval Regno', in J.-M. Martin and R. Alaggio (eds), *'Quei maledetti Normanni'. Studi offerti a Errico Cuozzo*, 2 vols (Ariano Irpino, 2016), vol. 1, pp. 371–84.

34 See the very important discussion by H. Wieruszowski, 'Roger II of Sicily, *Rex-Tyrannus*, in twelfth-century political thought', *Speculum* 38 (1963), 46–78.

35 *Guillaume de Pouille, La Geste de Robert Guiscard*, ed. and trans. M. Mathieu (Palermo, 1961), *Prologus*, p. 98: 'Parce tuo vati pro viribus alta canenti/ Clara, Rogere, ducis Roberti dignaque proles,/ Imperio cuius parere parata voluntas/ Me facit audacem: quia vires quas labor artis/ Ingenium negat, devotio pura ministrat./ Et patris Urbani reverenda petitio segnem/ Esse vetat; quia plus timeo peccare negando/ Tanti pontificis quam iussa beningna sequendo' ['Pardon your poet who sings of these great deeds as best he can, illustrious Roger, worthy son of Duke Robert; it is my wish to serve your rule which makes me audacious, since pure devotion provides the skill which [natural] talent and art denies. The request of the reverend father Urban forbids me to be slothful, since I fear that I shall sin more by refusing so great a pontiff than by following his benevolent instructions']. The English translation of William of Apulia by G. A. Loud is available at: https://ims.leeds.ac.uk/wp-content/uploads/sites/29/2019/02/William-of-Apulia.pdf. Further details in A. Bisanti, 'Composizione, stile e tendenze dei *Gesta Roberti Wiscardi* di Guglielmo il Pugliese', *Archivio normanno-svevo* 1 (2008), 87–132.

36 About Ansger, abbot of Santa Eufemia and Bishop of Catania, see G. T. Beech, 'The remarkable life of Ansger, a Breton monk and poet from the Loire Valley who became bishop of Catania in Sicily 1091–1124', *Viator* 45 (2014), 149–74.

37 Geoffrey Malaterra, *Histoire du Grand Comte Roger et de son frère Robert Guiscard, Vol. 1: Livres I & II*, ed. M.-A. Lucas-Avenel (Caen, 2016), *Epistula secunda*, p. 123: 'laboriosos et non sine magno discrimine triumphos suos, qualiter videlicet primo Calabriam, dehinc

vero Siciliam armata manu subjugaverit' ['his victories, won in the face of great difficulties and dangers, namely his conquest through force of arms first of Calabria and then of Sicily']. The new critical edition of this text is today incomplete. Only books I and II have been finished, so I have used the earlier edition when quoting from books III and IV.

38 Geoffrey Malaterra, *Histoire du Grande Comte Roger*, p. 123: 'fortium facta virorum … ad posteros transmittere, ne facta memoranda cum ipsis a quibus fiunt silentio depereant, sed potius ita litteris commendata et a futuris lecta vel cognita ipsos a quibus facta sunt, quadam vita memoriae, quodammodo vivere faciant'. Further details in G. M. Cantarella, 'La fondazione della storia nel regno normanno di Sicilia', in *L'Europa dei secoli XI e XII fra novità e tradizione: sviluppi di una cultura*. Atti della decima Settimana internazionale di studio della Mendola (Milan, 1989), pp. 171–4; L. Shopkow, *History and Community: Norman Historical Writing in the Eleventh and Twelfth Centuries* (Washington, DC, 1997), pp. 193–6; inspiring reflections about twelfth century historiography are in L. B. Mortensen, 'The glorious past: Entertainment, example or history? Levels of twelfth-century historical culture', *Culture and History* 13 (1994), 69–71.

39 Geoffrey Malaterra, *Histoire du Grand Comte Roger*, p. 123. Tramontana, 'I luoghi della produzione storiografica', p. 25, underlines the importance of the passage as confirmation of the birth around Roger I of 'un gruppo di intellettuali intenti a consolidare la nascente struttura statale normanna' ['a group of intellectuals intent on consolidating the nascent Norman state structure'] (trans. D. Routt).

40 *De rebus gestis Rogerii Calabriae et Siciliae comitis et Roberti Guiscardi ducis fratris eius auctore Gaufredo Malaterra*, ed. E. Pontieri, RIS 2nd ser. 5:1 (Bologna, 1925–28), bk IV, ch. 29, pp. 107–8 (the original text has been lost); *Regesta Pontificum Romanorum*, ed. P. Jaffé et al., 2 vols, 2nd edn (Leipzig, 1885–88), vol. 1, no. 5706 (5 July 1098). S. Fodale, 'Il Gran Conte e la Sede apostolica', in *Ruggero il Gran Conte e l'inizio dello Stato normanno* (Rome, 1977), pp. 25–42, especially pp. 37–40 (reprinted and enlarged in S. Fodale, *L'Apostolica Legazia e altri studi su Stato e Chiesa* (Messina, 1991), pp. 51–117).

41 Geoffrey Malaterra, *Histoire du Grand Comte Roger*, bk I, ch. 19, p. 193; Amatus of Montecassino, *Ystoire de li Normant. Édition du manuscript BnFfr. 688*, ed. M. Guéret-Laferté (Paris, 2011), bk III, ch. 43, p. 335. Houben, *Ruggero II di Sicilia*, p. 13, n. 1, leans towards the testimony of Amatus that dates the arrival of Roger in Italy after Civitate (1053), unlike Malaterra who postpones it until after the death of Humphrey (1057), dating accepted by Loud, *The Age of Robert Guiscard*, p. 123.

42 Geoffrey Malaterra, *Histoire du Grand Comte Roger, Epistula prima*, p. 119. On the provenance of Geoffrey see the close scrutiny of H. Houben, 'Adelaide "del Vasto" nella storia del regno normanno di Sicilia', in H. Houben, *Mezzogiorno normanno-svevo: Monasteri e castelli, ebrei e musulmani* (Naples, 1996), pp. 82–3 and n. 10: 'Sicuro è soltanto che egli apparteneva alla comunità monastica benedettina di S. Agata di Catania e che, prima di entrare in questo monastero, era stato in *Apulia*; ciò vuol dire, nel linguaggio di Malaterra, nel Mezzogiorno continentale ad esclusione della Calabria' (p. 83) ['It is certain only that he belonged to the Benedictine monastic community of St Agata of Catania and that, before entering into this monastery, he had been in *Apulia*, which means, in the language of Malaterra, in the continental Mezzogiorno to the exclusion of Calabria'] (trans. D. Routt).

43 In this regard see M.-A. Lucas-Avenel, 'Le récit de Geoffroi Malaterra ou la légitimation de Roger, Grand Comte de Sicile', *ANS* 34 (2012), 169–92. For a careful reconstruction of the Norman settlement see E. Cuozzo, 'L'unificazione normanna e il regno normanno-svevo', in G. Galasso and R. Romeo (eds), *Storia del Mezzogiorno*, II/2, Il medioevo (Rome, 1989), pp. 597–608. See also Loud, *The Age of Robert Guiscard*, pp. 92–185. Cf. J. Drell, 'Cultural syncretism and ethnic identity: The Norman "conquest" of southern Italy and Sicily', *JMH* 25 (1999), p. 189: 'The Normans eventually insinuated themselves into the highest levels of Southern Italian society through *military prowess and clever intermarriage*' (italics are mine).

44 G. A. Loud, 'How "Norman" was the Norman conquest of southern Italy?', *Nottingham Medieval Studies* 25 (1981), p. 30: 'Historians have been too ready to see the Norman invasion as the inevitable prelude to south Italian unification, without considering that its chief effect was to add further elements to an already disunited land'.

45 A fresh analysis by a pupil of Prof. Loud provides valuable insights into a broader reconsideration of the family dynamics of the Hauteville kin group in the context of the conquest of southern Italy: see F. Petrizzo, 'Band of brothers: Kin dynamics of the Hautevilles and other Normans in southern Italy and Syria, c.1030–c.1140' (PhD dissertation, University of Leeds, 2018), especially pp. 228–32.

46 See Amatus of Montecassino, *Ystoire de li Normant*, p. 236: 'Et autresi me recorda que ces grans homes (*scil.* i Normanni) sont tant liberal et devot a notre monastier, et por la merite que par aucun de lo monastier le fait lor par perpetuel mémoire soit escrit'. About Amatus see J. Kujawiński, '*Ystoire de li Normant*, una testimonianza del secolo XI?', in G. M. Cantarella and A. Calzona (eds), *La Reliquia del Sangue*

di Cristo: Mantova, l'Italia e l'Europa al tempo di Leone IX (Mantua, 2012), pp. 359–71; M. Guéret-Laferté, 'L'identité normande dans l'Ystoire de li Normant d'Aimé du Mont-Cassin', in M. Guéret-Laferté and N. Lenoir (eds), La Fabrique de la Normandie (CÉRÉdI, 2013), http://ceredi.labos.univ-rouen.fr/public/?l-identite-normande-dans-l-ystoire.html (accessed 17 January 2019).

47 *Guillaume de Pouille, La Geste de Robert Guiscard*, bk V, p. 258: 'Nostra, Rogere, tibi, cognoscis carmina scribi./ Mente *tibi* laeta *studuit parere* poeta' ['You know, Roger, that I have written this song for you. The poet has joyfully done his best to fulfil your instructions']. Italics are mine.

48 See also G. M. Cantarella, *Principi e corti: L'Europa del XII secolo* (Turin, 1997), p. 241. Further details are in P. Garbini, 'Lo stile della storia in Goffredo Malaterra', in F. Delle Donne (ed.), *In presenza dell'autore. L'autorappresentazione come evoluzione della storiografia professionale tra Basso Medioevo e Umanesimo* (Naples, 2018), pp. 13–34, especially p. 22: 'Risulta ben chiaro insomma il circuito cortese dell'impresa storiografica di Goffredo' ['The courtly circle in short emerges very clearly from Geoffrey's historiographical work'] (trans. D. Routt).

49 Further details are in R. Canosa, *Etnogenesi normanne e identità variabili. Il retroterra culturale dei Normanni d'Italia fra Scandinavia e Normandia* (Turin, 2009), pp. 64–76. See Geoffrey Malaterra, *Histoire du Grand Comte Roger*, bk I, chs 1–3, pp. 135–9.

50 See also A. Nef, 'Imaginaire impérial, empire et oecuménisme religieux: quelques réflexions depuis la Sicile des Hauteville', *Cahiers de recherches médiévales et humanistes* 24 (2012), 227–49.

51 An aspect well underlined in M. Zabbia, 'La cultura storiografica dell'Italia normanna riflessa nel *Chronicon* di Romualdo Salernitano', in I. Bonincontro (ed.), *Progetti di ricerca della Scuola storica nazionale: Contributi alla IV settimana di studi medievali* (Rome, 2009), pp. 5–16.

52 Fundamental is G. Breccia, 'Il *sigillion* nella prima età normanna. Documento pubblico e semipubblico nel Mezzogiorno ellenofono (1070–1127)', *QF* 79 (1999), 1–27, especially p. 8.

53 Further details are in G. A. Loud, 'Churches and churchmen in an age of conquest: Southern Italy, 1030–1130', *The Haskins Society Journal* 4 (1992), 37–53.

54 More specifics about Norman kingship are in M. Vagnoni, *Le rappresentazioni del potere. La sacralità regia dei Normanni di Sicilia: un mito?* (Bari, 2012); G. M. Cantarella, *La Sicilia e i Normanni. Le fonti del mito* (Bologna, 1988), pp. 155–85; and lastly A. Peters-Custot, ' "Byzantine" versus "Imperial" kingdom: How "Byzantine" was the Hauteville king of Sicily?', in F. Daim *et al.* (eds), *Menschen, Bilder, Sprache, Dinge. Wege der Kommunikation zwischen Byzanz und dem Westen, 2. Menschen und Worte* (Mainz, 2018), pp. 235–48, with reference to all previous bibliography.

4

Historiography in the making: a name-list of Sicilian Muslims from the Rollus Rubeus cartulary of Cefalù cathedral

Alex Metcalfe

This chapter examines three folios from the 'Rollus Rubeus' cartulary of Cefalù in Sicily, held in the Archivio di Stato at Palermo.[1] The 120-page volume was compiled in Latin between 1329 and 1330 by Roger of Mistretta, a scribe from the cathedral church of St Saviour and SS. Peter and Paul, at the request of its new bishop, Thomas of Butera.[2] The three folios include a list of eighty-three 'men' given to the church by its founder, King Roger II (r. 1130–54).[3] In royal Sicilian contexts, most extant name-lists were confirmations of Muslim *villani* made during 1144 and 1145, which were mainly composed from older records written out in Greek and Arabic. As for the in-house records of Latin-rite churches, typically drawn up in Latin. In some cases, the Latin was a translation, or else the scribe had transliterated or transcribed pertinent data into Latin characters.

The Rollus Rubeus name-list not only informs us of the church's record-keeping practices, but it also makes rare reference to the Muslims' response of flight, fight or conversion towards the end of their long-running revolts between 1189 and 1246. As a fourteenth-century record of a twelfth-century grant that also refers to calamitous, poorly remembered events in the thirteenth, this in-house recollection is a germane example of historiography in the making. Furthermore, the name-list is unique in that it refers to services due, and it also reckons the tax liabilities of each *villanus* in gold *tari* as a unit of account. To find this quality and quantity of tax-assessment evidence in Norman Italy is exceptional, so it is surprising that the name-list has made only cameo appearances in discussions of Sicilian villeinage, seigneurial revenues, comparative fiscal burdens or the conditions of Muslims living on the lands of Latin-rite churches.[4] It is less surprising that the list has been edited.[5] Unfortunately, all three editions are riddled with mistakes caused by the difficulty of deciphering the Latinate versions of the villeins' original Arabic names. The reconstruction of those names, which is key to unlocking historical data within the list, is one of the primary aims of this chapter.

Internal characteristics of the text and its dating

Unlike the rest of the cartulary, the dark brown ink of the name-list is now so faint as to be barely legible without an ultra-violet reading lamp. The images reproduced in this chapter have been darkened in order to see the text at all. In total, the text comprises sixty-four lines of which the *arenga*, *promulgatio* and *narratio* occupy sixteen lines; the name-list, which is divided into two faintly ruled columns of forty-two lines each, spans two folios, each measuring twenty-four by thirty-six centimetres. A dating clause, including references to the church's revenue-collection, concludes the text. Two hands can be detected in the composition: one was a neatly written (but not always grammatically correct) Latin hand. The other was Greek, and can be seen in the addition of initial letters resembling *litterae nobiliores* – in this case, spatially and stylistically distinct characters made before each name in a thin-nibbed quill.[6] The letters *alpha* and *sigma* can be seen in twenty-one instances, and may perhaps be taken as evidence of collaboration between Latin and Greek scribes to transform the name-list into Latin characters.[7]

The dating of the list cannot be determined with certainty, but the argument can be broken down into two parts. The first concerns the period that the name-list and additional information became incorporated into the church's own records. The second concerns the date when the villeins were granted to the church. An appended *datatio* clause in lines 17–18 states that taxes and services were due from the start of August of the Second Indiction, which corresponds to the years 1140, 1155, 1170, 1185, 1200, 1215, 1230 and 1245. Given the long political strife during Muslim uprisings in western Sicily, which may account for the reference to the chaotic condition of the church's records in lines 6–12, Garufi suggested a composition date of 1244. While this may have been the date when the church had taken stock of its records and villeins, it is certainly not the date of the original concession. For this, we are told that the 'villeins' were granted to the church during Roger II's reign – that is to say, between 1130 and February 1154. When matched with the Indiction date, this would suggest that the concession had been made in 1140.[8] Interpreting the *datatio* clause is, however, obfuscated by the claim in line 15 that the name-list had been compiled from old records, thus raising the distinct possibility that it was drawn up from multiple sources, and cannot be assigned a single composition date.

With regard to the use of older records, we possess other similar Rogerian grants of men to Cefalù, which may shed some light on the composition process, and thus the dating. In 1136, the monks possessed Latin lists of men from Collesano and Rocella. They had been given to the church by Abbot David of Holy Trinity at Mileto in January of that year. In February 1145, these were incorporated into a long royal Arabic–Greek *plateia* or *jarīdat al-rijāl* ('register of men') that confirmed the names of 225 *villani* whom Roger II had granted the church.[9] The 1145 list refers to data retrieved from an older, now lost, record from 1132. So, by 1145, Cefalù had records of all its villeins who were known to the church and/or to the crown by name, and who had been granted by Roger II. Of importance for the dating argument are close resemblances between three names that appear on both the 1145 list and the Rollus Rubeus: the shaykh ʿAbd al-Mawlá and *abdelmula ben rays*;[10] ʿAbd al-Raḥmān bin al-Ḥanash[11] and *abderrahamen hanes*; ʿUmar bin Muhīb[12] and *omor ben meib*. In addition, the 1145 list recorded a number of familial names echoed in the Rollus Rubeus, suggesting a continued presence of relatives in the area.[13]

Although this does not provide an exact date, it narrows down the possibilities by corroborating the idea that the villeins on both the Cefalù and Rollus Rubeus name-lists were most likely alive within a generation of one another. As most villeins in the Rollus Rubeus were not included in the 1145 list, it is fair to infer that the Rollus Rubeus post-dated Roger's royal confirmation of 1145. Thus, it most likely recorded a younger generation of villeins, for example those who had formed new, and therefore taxable family units that had not existed at the time of the 1145 confirmation, or those who had not previously been registered. Support for the notion that these were 'unregistered' villeins are two oblique references in the text itself. The first is that some of the villeins had become *clerici in eadem ecclesiam*. However, in the Constitutions of Melfi (1231), a law said to date to the time of William II forbade 'registered' (*adscriptitii*) villeins from becoming clerics.[14] Second, the *datatio* clause contains a cryptic reference to them as *villani exteri*, which recalls the twelfth-century terminology of 'unregistered' villein categories.[15]

The final clause, which contains the *datatio*, offers a series of puzzling claims that have provoked more discussion than any other aspect of the name-list. In terms of textual cohesion, the first three lines of the clause correspond to the preceding name-list with little controversy. Thus, we find references to 'the aforesaid villeins', and we learn the extent of their labour services. The *datatio* follows, and the total of taxes reckoned in *tarì* is slightly miscalculated as 630, not 623. In the final two lines, we first encounter a curious category distinction between villeins; the eighty-three *villani exteri* in juxtaposition to 3,088 unnamed *villani civitatenses* or 'townsfolk villeins' – a previously unattested term.[16] Whoever these people were, their overall tax burden was ambivalent: the church used to receive double – but double of what? Double the amount the other villeins paid? Or double their total number, such that each of them paid two *tarì* per head? Or did they give twice the amount of labour services? If that were not confusing enough, the final line contains an incomprehensible reference to some form of substitution involving Jews 'as stated'. Nothing points to an explanation in the text. While it is not impossible to imagine that it refers to the transfer of North African Jews to Sicily to work in agriculture following the deportation of Muslims to Lucera, this is guesswork.[17] It is quite plausible that the references to Jews and *villani civitatenses* are afterthoughts with no bearing on the preceding name-list. In any event, it is clear that the named villeins not only rendered tax reckoned in cash, but they also provided labour services. Given that most of those on the name-list were probably Muslims, then this qualifies the notion that the Sicilian Muslims' tax burden was calculated in cash only by payment of the *jizya* or religious capitation tax in addition to a land tax. In practice, taxes may have been commuted into labour services but, on the lands of Cefalù, Muslim villeins were specifically registered as providing both tax and labour to the church.

Before presenting a reconstruction of the Latin version of the original Arabic names, the Latin text and an English translation follow.

Latin text

1 Quam[a] vis abrogata lex in utilitate[m] eccl[es]ie fuerit primit[us]
2 p[ro]mulgata nimis t[ame]n e[st] ei[us] notitia necessaría [et] salubris
3 nec e[st] utile. ut eradat[ur] de librís. Immo penit[us] [co]ns[er]va[n]da
4 ut quanta fuerit pia devotio[b] statuentis ab in ea studentib[us]
5 dec[er]nat[ur]. Quam ob re[m]. Cum s[anc]te memoríe Rog[erius] Rex.[c] Sicilíe.
6 no[n] solu[m] ceph[alude]nssem eccl[esi]a[m] largiflue reb[us] dotaverít. Immo
7 etia[m] [et] víllanis qui ob p[re]lator[um] neglige[n]tiam. [et] potentior[um] usur-
8 patione[m] sac[ri]legam [et] mutatione[m] dominii n[ec] no[n] guerrar[um]
9 discrimína su[n]t lib[er]tate[m] adepti qua[m]vís de eís aliqui. Qua-
10 dam lib[er]tatem[d] usurpata, cleríci f[ac]ti su[n]t in eadem eccl[esi]am.[e] Aliqui
11 arma militaría usurpatíve su[m]persu[n]t igitur(?) [sunt?][f] alibi ita q[uod] villano-
12 rum memoría ipsius eccl[es]ie. nulla v[e]l modica aliqualit[er] ha[bea]t[ur].
13 Nichilomín[us] originalíu[m] villanor[um] no[m]i[n]a. ut qua[n]ta fu[er]it p[re]-
14 dicti Regis donatio. Qua[n]tus honor eccl[esi]e p[re]dicte a posterís
15 recolatur ad re[m] futura[m] memoria[m] rep[er]ta in scriptis antiq[ui]s
16 pr[e]senti op[er]e renov[en]t[ur]. Quor[um] hec no[m]i[n]a sunt.

[a] In the left-hand margin there is a two-line note (in an early modern, possibly sixteenth-century hand) in light brown ink: *Collecta villanorum ep[iscop]atus / cephaludensis.*
[b] Here and elsewhere, Spata preferred to transcribe the Latin letter 't' as 'c', hence his renditions of *devocio, negligenciam, potenciorum, nuntacionem* and *donacio.*
[c] Here and elsewhere, I have maintained the original manuscript's punctuation.
[d] *Sic* for the ablative absolute, *libertate.*
[e] *Sic* for locative ablative, *ecclesia.*
[f] The manuscript reading is unclear. No word appears to be missing, although *igitur* is a tentative suggestion. Spata reads: *susceperunt in regno.*

		-A-[a]		-B-	
			t[á]r[enos][b] xl[c]	[et]	dietas
1	α	b derrahame[n] hanes	t[á]r[enos] viii	l	oseph bichi	t[á]r[enos] viii
2	h	amet[d] lupus	t[á]r[enos] viii	b	ulays	t[á]r[enos] viii
3	α	b d[e]rrahame[n] be[n] antar[e]	t[á]r[enos] viii	σ	idika[g] elba[n] baca[h]	t[á]r[enos] viii
4	h	amet[f] fr[ater] antar	t[á]r[enos] vi	α	btelkefi[j] fab[er].	t[á]r[enos] viii
5	α	ntar[i] ben fellac	t[á]r[enos] viii	m	ohumet ben sidehelu[k]	t[á]r[enos] viii
6	h	Isahamel				

[a] Fol. 9v contains names from columns A and B, rows 1–8. Rows 9–42 are contained on fol. 10r.
[b] Spata reads *ti* throughout, presumably for *t[aren]i*, although there is no justification for this contraction from the text since the letters 't' and 'r' were written consistently and clearly. Mirto reads *tarenos* throughout, which is correct in the accusative; cf. the objective case of *t[á]r[enos]* and *dietas*.
[c] Spata, *Pergamene greche*, reads xi. Mirto, *Rollus rubeus*, reads XL. The letter 'l' is clearly taller than the preceding 'x', suggesting that it cannot be the letter-numeral 'i'. Indeed, the numeral 'i' never exceeded the height of the letter before it.
[d] Spata reads *amec*.
[e] Spata reads *ucar*.
[f] Mirto reads *Amet*.
[g] Spata reads *idilza*; Mirto reads *Sidilza*.
[h] Mirto reads *el Bambaca*.
[i] Mirto reads *Ucar*.
[j] Spata reads *bdelhefi*; Mirto reads *Abdellzefi*.
[k] Spata reads *sidehebn*; Mirto reads *Sidehelu*.

(*continued*)

7	h	asen ben nema[a]	t[á]r[enos] xii	b	uzikir[b] tecalas[c]	t[á]r[enos] vi
8	b	ugínia[d] ben móyb.	t[á]r[enos] viii	α	bd[e]sseid ca[r]pe[n]t[ar]ius[e]	t[á]r[enos] vii
9	l	oh[anne]s ria[f]	t[á]r[enos] xvi	o	mor[g] chaulin[h]	t[á]r[enos] vi
10	h	asen zarcka[i]	t[á]r[enos] vi	o	mor[i] laapsi	t[á]r[enos] iiii
11	σ	olimen bundau	t[á]r[enos] vi	σ	idika[k] bouac	t[á]r[enos] iiii
12	α	ly bucacte.[l]	t[á]r[enos] vi	m	eheres[m]	t[á]r[enos] vi
13	h	amut bugatas	t[á]r[enos] viii	e	lýas	t[á]r[enos] vii

[a] Spata reads *beinnema*.
[b] Spata reads *uzilzir*; Mirto reads *Buzilzir*.
[c] Spata reads *de calas*. Mirto is possibly correct to read *De Calas* but conjoined as *decalas*.
[d] Spata reads *ugima*.
[e] Mirto reads *Carpenterius*.
[f] Spata reads *ohmes* and *riaz*; Mirto reads *Riaz*. The final letter bears a Latin abbreviation mark. The *a* is a correction and has overwritten another, now illegible, letter.
[g] Spata reads *monc*.
[h] Spata reads *haulin*.
[i] Spata reads *zarcha*; Mirto reads *Zarka*.
[j] Spata reads *mor*.
[k] Spata reads *sidilza bovak*; Mirto reads *Sidilza Bovac*.
[l] Spata reads *libuate*.
[m] Spata reads *cheres*.

14	h	useín elfil	t[á]r[enos] xii	n	icol[aus][a] coccarell[us][b]	t[á]r[enos] vii
15	α	btella far[c]	t[á]r[enos] x	i	oseph elmabéy	t[á]r[enos] vi
16	b	ulkaír[d] be[n] mohuluf	t[á]r[enos] vi	i	oseph be[n] hanes	t[á]r[enos] viii
17	σ	olimen be[n] haamar	t[á]r[enos] viii	l	oseph be[n] elgidir	t[á]r[enos] vi
18	h	ise sandialu[e]	t[á]r[enos] viii	σ	olimen be[n] bulkasen	t[á]r[enos] vi
19	m	aymon be[n] mohuluf	t[á]r[enos] viii	r	anda maálla	t[á]r[enos] vi
20	α	bd[e]lganý bugatas	t[á]r[enos] xiii	f	ilipp[us] curviserius[f]	t[á]r[enos] vii
21	b	oabdillís boazar[g]	t[á]r[enos] x	o	thime[n][h] ben paýs[i]	t[á]r[enos] viii
22	n	eem nikír[j]	t[á]r[enos] iiii	h	amet ben maadile	t[á]r[enos] vi

[a] Spata reads *icotus*.
[b] Tentative reading due to the close similarity and physical proximity of the written letters.
[c] Mirto reads *Abdella Sar*.
[d] Spata reads *ulzair*.
[e] Tentative reading. The scribe has initially written *Sandulu* as both Spata and Mirto read. However, a short bar also appears through the first *u*, which separates the letter into *ia*. After this, a short apostrophe mark has been made.
[f] Spata reads *philippus curvuriserius*.
[g] A tentative reading that could also be *luazar*. Spata reads *tuazar*.
[h] Mirto reads *Ethimen*.
[i] A clear reading. Spata reads *rays*.
[j] Spata reads *nlzir*; Mirto reads *Nilzir*. The first letter 'l' has a small cross above it, possibly because it was originally an acute accent cancelled by a similar stroke made the other way at a right-angle to it.

(*continued*)

23	α	b d[e]sseid bulbul	t[á]r[enos] viii	σ	idika[a] be[n] antar	t[á]r[enos] vi
24	o	sein elgidiR[b]	t[á]r[enos] x	o	thime[n] be[n] mila[c]	t[á]r[enos] vi
25	m	ule furnari[us]	t[á]r[enos] vii	u	ucher be[n] rays	t[á]r[enos] vi
26	b	ulcasen carpi[n]teri[us]	t[á]r[enos] xx[d]	α	lbelcalaca be[n] amar	t[á]r[enos] vi
27	α	ly ta[n]bur[e]	t[á]r[enos] viii	h	asem cauchet	t[á]r[enos] vi
28	h	asem ben hcleyR[f]	t[á]r[enos] viii	c	asm[us][g] be[n] muge	t[á]r[enos] vi
29	α	bd[e]lmula[h] be[n] rayś[i]	t[á]r[enos] vi	α	bd[e]lmíse ben gund[i][j]	t[á]r[enos] vi
30	m	òhumet osbernu	t[á]r[enos] viii	o	mor[k] ben meib	t[á]r[enos] vi
31	o	thime[n] lascaR[l]	t[á]r[enos] vi	o	thime[n] maltí	t[á]r[enos] viii

[a] Spata reads *idilza*; Mirto reads *Sidilza*.
[b] Spata reads *elgidik*.
[c] Could also be *nule* or miscopied for *Mule*. Spata and Mirto read *Mila*.
[d] Mirto reads XI.
[e] Spata reads *tambur*; Mirto reads *Tambur*.
[f] Spata reads *heleyi*; Mirto reads *Heleyr*. The scribe may have transposed the letters in *belceyr*; cf. Arabic *al-khayr*.
[g] Spata reads *asinus*.
[h] The final letter appears to have been a *u* originally, but then altered to form an *a*. Mirto reads *Abdelmula*.
[i] Spata reads *burays*.
[j] Mirto reads *Gunder*.
[k] Spata reads *moz*; Mirto reads *Omoz*.
[l] Spata reads *lascak*.

32	o	Beid	t[á]r[enos] iiii	c	asmol[s][a] be[n] elgidir	t[á]r[enos] vi
33	h	amet elgurab	t[á]r[enos] iiii	u	lahe[n][b] be[n] bulkasen	t[á]r[enos] vi
34	a	bd[e]lgani[c] turus	t[á]r[enos] iiii	m	ohumet elauir[us][d]	t[á]r[enos] vi
35	u	uscinen[e]	t[á]r[enos] vi	m	ohumet barisari[us][f]	t[á]r[enos] vi
36	c	asm[us][g] ben raýs	t[á]r[enos] viii	f	icien	t[á]r[enos] vi
37	h	ise cognat[us] hanes	t[á]r[enos] iiii	m	use turus	t[á]r[enos] vi
38	α	bd[e]lla ben eylel	t[á]r[enos] vi	o	seín marahe[n]	t[á]r[enos] iiii
39	r	ays Romor[h]	t[á]r[enos] xii	u	ulufe	t[á]r[enos] vi
40	α	bd[e]llaac. raýs	t[á]r[enos] viii	h	asen be[n] muse	t[á]r[enos] viii
41	m	òhaluf[i] fr[ater] ei[us]	t[á]r[enos] viii	b	erbeb	t[á]r[enos] vi
42	m	ellec[j]	t[á]r[enos] vi	y	smaèl mudib[er/us][k]	t[á]r[enos] vi

[a] Spata reads *asinus*; Mirto reads *Casmus*.
[b] Spate reads *iaben*; Mirto reads *Ilaben*.
[c] Spata reads *bdelganus*.
[d] Spata reads *elavikus*.
[e] The letters *ci* are tentative. Originally, it appears to have been either *u* or *ci*. Mirto also reads *Buscinen*.
[f] Spata reads *barisanus*.
[g] Spata reads *asinus*.
[h] Spata reads *komor*. Initial letter struck through with a cross in the same ink as the main text.
[i] Spata reads *obaluf*.
[j] Spata reads *ellet*; Mirto reads *Mellet*. The final letter is unclear; it could be *t*.
[k] Spata reads *mudibus*; Mirto reads *Mudiber*.

17 Un[us] ᵃ quisq[ue] v[ero] dictor[um] villanor[um] dabat dietas viginti q[ua]-
18 tuor. In angariís [et] collectis a k[a]l[e]ndis aug[us]ti se[cun]de indict[i] o[n]is
19 v[e]l aliar[um] indictionu[m]. In su[m]ma t[a]r[e]nos sexcentos trigi[n]ta.
20 De villanis exterís.ᵇ De villanis civitate[n]ssib[us] qui fue-
21 runt tria milia octuaginta octo Recipiebat eccl[es]ia in
22 dupplum. p[ro] quib[us] villanís [c]o[m]pensati su[n]t iudei ut ibi di[citur]ᶜ

English translation

Although a law, which would have been originally issued for the benefit of the church, has lapsed, knowledge of it is nonetheless absolutely necessary and valuable – it is pointless to erase it from the [record] books. On the contrary, it is to be comprehensively maintained so that as great as the pious devotion of the lawgiver was, it might be reckoned by those who devote their attention to such things. For this reason, King Roger of Sicily, of holy memory, not only endowed the church of Cefalù lavishly with possessions, but also with men (*villani*). Some of them attained their freedom due to the neglect of high-ranking clergy, the unlawful violation of lords, or the change of rule as well as through crises of wars. Some of them, having illegally gained their liberty, were made monks in this very church; others unlawfully took up military arms and so are elsewhere, with the result that the record of this church's men was either nothing or otherwise very little. Nevertheless, let the names of the original men found in the old documents be repeated in this present work, so that as great as the grant of the aforesaid king was, and how great its esteem to the said church, a record may be recalled in posterity by future generations. These are their names:

ᵃ Fol. 10v.
ᵇ Spata reads *esteris*.
ᶜ In the left-hand margin, a three-line note has been made in same hand and ink as the marginal note above. It reads: *tra[n]sumptu[m] privilegii Regis R- / ogerii de dote et hono[r]e qua[m] / fecit ecclesie cephaludensis.*

	-A-		-B-	
1	ʿAbd al-Raḥmān al-Ḥanāsh	tarì 40	and services	
2	Aḥmad al-Diʾb(?)	tarì 8	Yūsuf (bichi)	tarì 8
3	ʿAbd al-Raḥmān ibn ʿAntar	tarì 8	Abū l-Aysh/ʿIs(?)	tarì 8
4	Aḥmad akhū ʿAntar	tarì 8	Ṣadaqa al-Bambāq	tarì 8
5	ʿAntar ibn Fallāḥ(?)	tarì 6	ʿAbd al-Kāfi al-Ḥaddād(?)	tarì 8
6	Ismāʿīl	tarì 8	Muḥammad ibn Sayyid Ahlihi	tarì 8
7	Ḥasan ibn Niʿma	tarì 12	Abū l-Dhikr ibn Khalāṣ(?)	tarì 6
8	Abū l-Jināya/Jany(?) ibn Muhib	tarì 8	ʿAbd al-Sayyid al-Najjār	tarì 7
9	Yaḥyá (Ria)	tarì 16	ʿUmar (chaulin)	tarì 6
10	Ḥasan al-Zarqāʾ	tarì 6	ʿUmar al-(laapsi)	tarì 4
11	Sulaymān (bundau)	tarì 6	Ṣadaqa al-Bawwāq	tarì 4
12	ʿAlī (bucacte)	tarì 6	Mukhriz	tarì 6
13	Ḥammūd (bugatas)	tarì 8	Ilyās	tarì 7
14	Ḥusayn al-Fīl	tarì 12	Niqūla al-Qalānisī(?)	tarì 7
15	ʿAbd Allāh al-Fār	tarì 10	Yūsuf al-(mabey)	tarì 6
16	Abū l-Khayr ibn Makhlūf	tarì 6	Yūsuf ibn al-Ḥanāsh	tarì 8

(continued)

17	Sulaymān ibn al-Ḥammār(?)	tarí 8	Yūsuf ibn al-Jadr	tarí 6
18	ʿIsá (sandialu)	tarí 8	Sulaymān ibn Abī l-Qāsim	tarí 6
19	Maymūn ibn Maklūf	tarí 8	Randa(?) (maálla)	tarí 6
20	ʿAbd al-Ghani (bugatas)	tarí 13	Filīb al-Kharrāz(?)	tarí 7
21	Abū ʿAbd Allāh Abū ʿAzr(?)	tarí 10	ʿUthmān ibn al-(pays)	tarí 8
22	Niʿma al-Naqīr(?)	tarí 4	Aḥmad ibn Muʿadila	tarí 6
23	ʿAbd al-Sayyid al-Bulbul	tarí 8	Ṣadaqa ibn ʿAntar	tarí 6
24	Ḥusayn al-Jadr	tarí 10	ʿUthmān ibn Mila(?)	tarí 6
25	Māwlá al-Khabbāz	tarí 7	Abū Bakr ibn al-Raʾīs	tarí 6
26	Abū l-Ḥasan al-Najjār	tarí 11	(Albelcalaca) ibn ʿAmmār	tarí 6
27	ʿAlī al-Ṭunbūr	tarí 8	Ḥasan (cauchet)	tarí 6
28	Ḥasan ibn al-Khayr	tarí 8	Qāsim ibn Mūsá(?)	tarí 6
29	ʿAbd al-Mawlá ibn al-Raʾīs	tarí 6	ʿAbd al-Masīḥ(?) ibn al-Jundī	tarí 6
30	Muḥammad (osberru)	tarí 8	ʿUmar ibn Muhib	tarí 6
31	ʿUthmān al-ʿAskar/ʿAshqar	tarí 6	ʿUthmān al-Māliṭī	tarí 8
32	ʿUbayd	tarí 4	Qāsim ibn al-Jadr	tarí 6
33	Aḥmad al-Ghurāb	tarí 4	Abū l-(aben) ibn Abī l-Qāsim	tarí 6

34	ʿAbd al-Ghanī al-Ṭurūsh	tarì 4	Muḥammad al-Aʿwar(?)	tarì 6
35	Abū Shanaʾān(?)	tarì 6	Muḥammad (barisarius)	tarì 6
36	Qāsim ibn al-Raʾīs	tarì 8	Fityān	tarì 6
37	ʿĪsā ibn akhī l-Ḥanāsh	tarì 4	Mūsā al-Ṭurūsh	tarì 6
38	ʿAbd Allāh ibn (eylel)	tarì 6	Ḥusayn (maraben)	tarì 4
39	al-Raʾīs ʿUmar	tarì 12	Abū l-ʿAfw(?)	tarì 6
40	ʿAbd al-Ḥaqq al-Raʾīs	tarì 8	Ḥasan ibn Mūsá	tarì 8
41	Makhlūf akhūhu	tarì 8	Barbar(?)/rabīb(?)	tarì 6
42	Mālik / Mallāḥ	tarì 6	Ismāʿīl al-Muʾaddib	tarì 6

Indeed, each one of the said men used to give twenty-four days' work in labour (*angariis*) and services (*collecta*) from the first day of August of the Second Indiction and of other Indictions. In total, 630 *tarì* from 'outside' men (*de villanis exteris*). From the 'townsfolk' men (*de villanis civitatenssibus*) who were 3,088 [in number], the church received double. For those men whom Jews had substituted, it is there as stated.

Onomastics and internal prosopography

A dozen names were rendered in Latinate or francophone forms.[18] Indeed, the example of *carpentarìus* from the Old French term *charpentier* ('carpenter') may provide a clue about the scribe's linguistic background. Such versions were unlikely to have reproduced the actual names by which the villeins referred to themselves and probably resulted from the Latin scribe's decision to translate an Arabic term.[19] Of note is that the names Nicolas and Philip (Niqūla and Filīb) were well attested in Sicily among Arabicised Christians – a reminder not to assume automatically that everyone on the list was Muslim. The decision to translate tended to apply to second names, especially those that implied an occupation or trade. Moreover, given that almost a quarter of those listed had such names, we should not fall into the trap of imagining that these 'villeins' were simply peasants tilling the land. In terms of their tax liabilities, those with 'professional' names paid more or less the same on average as the others listed.[20]

The Latin transcription almost certainly affected the original Arabic names by producing bipartite forms in line with long-term, north-to-south naming trends across the medieval Latin West. The formal registration practices of Latin notaries working within municipal, regional and royal administrations during the Normano-Staufen periods accelerated this movement within which southern Italy, and Sicily in particular with its mixed population and widely disparate naming practices, had been slow to harmonise with an emerging norm of bipartite names found elsewhere to the north. One consequence of this for Arab-Muslims, both in Sicily and in al-Andalus where we witness a similar trend, was the contraction of customary naming strings. Patronymic *kunya*s (Abū, 'father

Table 4.1 Index of reconstructed names

Rollus Rubeus	Reference	Arabic	Notes
abdelgani	[34A]	ʿAbd al-Ghanī	Common masculine personal name (p.n.) and theophore, 'slave of the All-Sufficient One' (Qurʾān 3:97, 39:7, 47:38, 57:24).
abdelgany	[20A], see abdelgani above	ʿAbd al-Ghanī	
abdelkefi	[5B]	ʿAbd al-Kāfī	Common masc. p.n. and theophore, 'slave of the Sufficient'; not attested in the Qurʾān as a name of God.
abdella	[15A], [38A]	ʿAbd Allāh	Common masc. p.n. and theophore, 'slave of God'; epithet of the Biblical and Quranic prophet Jesus (Qurʾān 19:30).
abdellaac	[40A]	ʿAbd al-Ḥaqq	Common masc. p.n. and theophore 'slave of the Truth' (Qurʾān 6:62, 22:6, 23:116, 24:25).
abdelmise	[29B]	ʿAbd al-Muḥsin or ʿAbd al-Masīḥ	The former a common masc. p.n. and theophore, 'slave of the Beneficent'; not attested as a name of God in the Qurʾān; attested half-a-dozen times among Muslims of Sicily, but phonetically some way short of *abdelmise*. The latter, 'slave of the Messiah', strongly suggestive of a Christian; cf. palace eunuch of the same name whom Ibn Jubayr met in 1184.[a] Not otherwise attested in Sicily.

[a] On the palace eunuch, ʿAbd al-Masīḥ, see Ibn Jubayr, *Riḥla*, 2nd rev. edn, ed. M. J. de Goeje and W. Wright (Leiden, 1907), pp. 324–7, trans. in Johns, *Arabic Administration*, pp. 213–15; see also G. Mandalà, 'La sottoscrizione araba di ʿAbd al-Masīḥ (Palermo, 15 ottobre 1201)', *Quaderni di studi arabi* 3 (2008), 153–64.

(*continued*)

Table 4.1 (Cont.)

Rollus Rubeus	Reference	Arabic	Notes
abdelmula	[29A]	ʿAbd al-Mawlá	Common masc. p.n. and theophore, 'slave of the Lord'; not attested in Qurʾān.
abderrahamen	[3A]	ʿAbd al-Raḥmān	Common masc. p.n. and theophore, 'slave of the Merciful'; attested throughout the Qurʾān.
abdesseid	[8B], [23A]	ʿAbd al-Sayyid	Common masc. p.n. and pseudo-theophore, 'slave of the Master'; attested in Qurʾān as epithet of Prophet Muḥammad (Qurʾān 3:39).
abterrahamen	[1A], see abderrahamen above	ʿAbd al-Raḥmān	
albelcalaca	[26B]	ʿAbd al-Khāliq(?), Abū l-Kalkha(?), Abū Qalāqis(?)	Highly problematic reconstruction of the garbled first name. ʿAbd al-Khāliq is a masc. theophore, 'Slave of the Creator', attested in Sicily only twice.[a] However, if the interpretation of *albel-* is Abū l-, there are several possibilities, only one of which is attested in Norman Sicily, i.e. Mūsá l-Kalkha (> Μοὐσες κέλχα, where *kalkha* may refer to 'a giant fennel'.[b] Other, even remoter, possibilities include variations around q-l-q ('being uneasy, agitated') and k-l-k-ʿ ('bone fragments') in Arabic. The Greek p.n. diminutive Καλάκης should not be entirely discounted.

[a] For ʿAbd al-Khāliq, see Cusa, *I diplomi*, pp. 572a and 577b in the Catania *jarīda* of 1145, renewed from 1095.
[b] For Mūsá l-Kalkha, see Cusa, *I diplomi*, p. 278b; for *kalkha*, see H. Wehr and J. M. Cowan (eds), *A Dictionary of Modern Written Arabic: Arabic-English*, 3rd ed. (Wiesbaden, 1961; repr. Beirut, 1980), p. 836. This dictionary is only cited here for well-known terms in Arabic. See also F. Corriente, *Dictionary of Andalusi Arabic* (Leiden, 1997), p. 465.

aly	[12A], [27A]	'Alī	Common masc. p.n., 'high, exalted, sublime'; name of the cousin and son-in-law of Prophet Muhammad, fourth Sunnī Orthodox Caliph, first of the line of Shī'a Imams. 'Alī a highly popular name among Sicilian Muslims; not uncommon as a Christian name. Frequently attested in Sicilian Greek as ἄλις; possibly related to the modern surname, Alì, attested in southern Italy and Greece.[a]
amar	[26B]	'Ammār	Common masc. p.n. formed from the verb '-m-r, 'to live long, thrive, prosper, flourish'.[b]
antar	[3A], [4A], [5A], [23B]	'Antar	Masc. p.n., 'to display heroism';[c] 'Antar was the well-known hero of the Arabic *Romance of 'Antar*. Not a common personal name in either Arabic nomenclature or in Sicily, where it was attested only once as 'Antar bin al-Qawsarī.[d]
barisarius	[35B]	?	This vaguely recalls the names Barisanus of Trani, and Barisan of Ibelin, which are ethnonyms of Bari (cf. mod. surname Varisano); or possibly derived from French *vairre*, 'furrier', or from the ancient Greek and Byzantine name, Belisarios. The original Arabic possibly started with Abū l-.

(*continued*)

---

[a] On the modern surname Alì, see G. Caracausi, *Dizionario onomastico della Sicilia: repertorio storico-etimologico di nomi di famiglia e di luogo*, 2 vols (Palermo, 1994), vol. 1, p. 36. Henceforth, Caracausi, *DOdS*.
[b] Wehr and Cowan, *Arabic*, p. 643a.
[c] Wehr and Cowan, *Arabic*, p. 648a.
[d] For 'Antar bin al-Qawsarī, see Cusa, *I diplomi*, p. 277a.

Table 4.1 (Cont.)

Rollus Rubeus	Reference	Arabic	Notes
ben	[3A], [5A], [6B], [7A], [8A], [16A], [16B], [17A], [17B], [18B], [19A], [21B], [22B], [23B], [24B], [25B], [26B], [28A], [28B], [29A], [29B], [30B], [32B], [33B], [36A], [38A], [40B]	bin	Latin transliteration of Arabic *ibn* or *bin*, 'son of', 'kin group of', 'clan of'.
berbeb	[41B]	Barbar(?), *rabib*(?)	Possibly an ethnonymic *nisba* meaning 'Berber'.[a] The term *rabib* ('stepson') was frequently found in name-lists, although it is not clear to what/who it might refer to here.
bichi	[2B]	?	
boabdillis	[21A]	Abū ʿAbd Allāh	Common moniker in the form of a teknonym (*kunya*) used as a common masc. p.n. (*ism*); lit. 'the father of ʿAbd Allāh'; also used as a *kunya* of Prophet Muḥammad.

[a] 'Berber' was not normally used as a given name (*ism*). The closest example is a 'man' listed only as al-Barbarī. See Cusa, *I diplomi*, p. 139a.

boazar [21A]	Abū l-ʿIzz(?) or Abū ʿAzr(?)	Abū ʿAzr, masc. figurative *kunya*, lit. 'father of the reprimand'. Not attested in Sicily. More likely a garbled version of a common moniker, Abū l-ʿIzz (*laqab-kunya*), used as a common masc. p.n., lit. 'father of the might, power, honour, force'.[a]
bouac [11B]	al-Bawwāq	'Horn-player', 'piper' from *al-būq*, 'hornpipe'; cf. Spanish *albogue*, Basque *alboka*; attested in the Cefalù *jarīda* of 1145.[b]
bucacte [12A]	Abū l-Qaʿda(?)	The Latin is so garbled that restoration of original Arabic is impossible. Unattested suggestion of Abū l-Qaʿda, lit. 'father of the seat or buttocks' as a nickname is one of many guesses.
bugatas [13A], [20A]	?	Very large number of equally implausible possibilities, compounded by the final 's' that is possibly a Latinate addition. Abū l-Jaʿda as a masc. figurative *kunya*, lit. 'father of the curl, wrinkle' is an otherwise unattested possibility.
buginia [8A]	Abū l-Jināya(?)	Abū l-Jināya or Abū l-Jany, masc. figurative *kunya*, 'father of the harvest'. Alternatively, a *laqab* or nickname, such as 'father of the crime', 'criminal'. Not otherwise attested in Sicily.

[a] Wehr and Cowan, *Arabic*, p. 609.
[b] For *būq* 'a kind of pastoral flute', ultimately derived from the Greek βῶκα, see Corriente, *Andalusi Arabic*, p. 71; for Maymūn bin al-Bawwāq in the Cefalù *jarīda*, see Cusa, *I diplomi*, p. 477b.

(*continued*)

Table 4.1 (Cont.)

Rollus Rubeus	Reference	Arabic	Notes
bulays	[3B]	Abū l-ʿAysh(?), Abū l-ʿĪs(?)	Abū l-ʿAysh or Abū l-ʿĪs.[a] Reconstruction hampered by the difficulty of establishing the intended reading when the Arabic was written without vowels. Thus, although this form is attested, it is unclear which of the two forms was meant.[b]
bulbul	[23A]	Bulbul	Arabic for 'nightingale', occasionally used in naming strings. Distinctive second name closely associated with the Cefalù jarīda of 1145.[c]
bulcasen	[26A], see bulkasen below	Abū l-Qāsim, Abū l-Qāsim or Abū l-Ḥasan	
bulkair	[16A]	Abū l-Khayr	Moniker (laqab-kunya) used as a common masc. p.n. among both Sicilian Muslims and Christians in the form of an honorific; lit. 'father of the good'; 'generous, charitable, beneficent, kind';[d] masc. p.n. kunya, lit. 'father of the Good'.

[a] For aʿyās pl. ʿīs as 'camels of good stock', see Wehr and Cowan, Arabic, p. 661.
[b] Cf. the examples in Cusa, I diplomi, pp. 252b, 264b, 565b and 581b.
[c] See Bū Hajar Bulbul and Bulbul's wife in Cusa, I diplomi, pp. 474b and 477b.
[d] Wehr and Cowan, Arabic, p. 267a.

bulkasen	[18B], [33B]	Abū l-Qāsim, Abū l-Qāsim or Abū l-Ḥasan	First two options are monikers in the form of a teknonym (*kunya*) used as a common masc. p.n.; lit. 'father of the divider';[a] also the *kunya* of the Prophet Muḥammad. Alternatively, *bulkasen* a teknonym (*kunya*), 'the father of al-Ḥasan', sometimes used as masc. p.n. (ism); also used as moniker for imam and caliph ʿAlī (d.661), the father of al-Ḥasan (d.670). In the estate of Bū Kināna in western Sicily, we find a kin-group name Ibn Abī l-Ḥasan.[b]
bundau	[11A]	Abū l-Dāwʾ or Abū l-Dawāʾ	Abū l-Dawāʾ, masc. figurative *kunya*, 'father of medicine/remedy'; cf. Ibn Dawāʾ (ἐπὶν δέουὲ), and modern Sicilian surname 'Buddua', to which it may be related, or Abū l-Dāwʾ, masc. p.n. *kunya*, lit. 'father of brightness'.[c] Also the name of early twelfth-century poet and Norman Sicilian administrator.[d] Nasalisation, required in both alternatives, was a shared characteristic of Norman Sicilian dialects.[e]

[a] Wehr and Cowan, *Arabic*, p. 763b.
[b] Cusa, *I diplomi*, p. 158a and 158b.
[c] Ibn Dawāʾ among villeins' names, see Cusa, *I diplomi*, pp. 276a, 577b and 578b; see also discussion in Caracausi, *DOdS*, i, p. 207.
[d] On Abū l-Ḍawʾ Sirāj Ibn Rajāʾ (fl. c. 1112–c. 1145), the Arab-Sicilian poet and Muslim official of Roger II, see Johns, *Arabic Administration*, pp. 88–90.
[e] On nasalisation across medieval Sicilian dialects, see Metcalfe, *Muslims and Christians*, pp. 171–2.

(*continued*)

Table 4.1 (Cont.)

Rollus Rubeus	Reference	Arabic	Notes
buscinen	[35A]	Abū l-S.nān, Abū l-Asnān, Abū Ushnān or Abū Shana'ān.	The Latin consonants -sc- suggests an attempt at reproducing Arabic letter *shīn*, hence the suggestions of *Abū Ushnān*, masc. figurative *kunya*, 'One who deals with potash or saltwort'; *Abū Shana'ān*, masc. figurative *kunya*, 'father of hate'. Semantically, however, neither are likely. *Abū l-Asnān*, masc. figurative *kunya*, 'father of the teeth' is more fitting in that respect, but none of the above is attested in Sicily. A certain Salām Abū l-Sinān, masc. figurative *kunya*, lit. 'father of the spearhead', attested at least in Sicily, given in Greek as πουσινέν.[a]
buzikir	[7B]	Abū l-Dhikr	Common masc. p.n. (*ism*) in form of a moniker (*kunya/laqab*); lit. 'father of remembrance', i.e. of God.[b]
carpentarius	[8B]	Latin: *carpentarius*	Norman French *carpentier*, 'carter, carpenter'. The modern surnames Carpentiere and Carpentieri are more closely associated with Campania than Sicily.[c] The Arabic equivalent, *al-najjār*, is well attested among *villani*.[d]

[a] For the name Salām Abū l-Sinān, see Cusa, *I diplomi*, p. 279.
[b] A. de Biberstein Kazimirsky, *Dictionnaire arabe-français*, 2 vols (Paris, 1860), vol. 1, p. 776. Henceforth, Kazimirsky, *Dictionnaire arabe-français*.
[c] Caracausi, *DOdS*, vol. 1, pp. 313–14.
[d] For *al-najjār* ('carpenter'), see Cusa, *I diplomi*, pp. 153a, 156a, 160b, 173b, 178b, 250b, 257b, 270b, 514a, 582b, 592a; at Cefalù, see p. 474a for Aḥmad and Ṣadaqa, sons of al-Najjār.

carpinterius	[26A], see carpentarius above	Latin: carpentarius	
casmos	[32B], see casmus below	Qāsim	
casmus	[28B], [36A]	Qāsim	Common masc. p.n., lit. 'divider', 'distributor'.[a]
cauchet	[53B]	Qajīd(?)	Unusual name in Arabic; attested in western Sicily as Sayyid Ahlihi bin Q.jīd, presumably a kin-group or professional name; cf. Andalusi Arabic *qujita lišabbāt*, 'shoe lace'; *mālem al-gugitit*, 'maker or seller of laces'.[b]
chaulin	[9B]	?	
coccarellus	[14B]	Latin: *cocca* or *cuculla*	Possibly from Late Latin *cocca*, 'conch', 'shell';[c] or *cuculla* (monk's cowl, which in Arabic was well attested in Sicily as *al-qalānisī*.[d]
cognatus	[37A]	Latin: 'in-law'	

(continued)

[a] Wehr and Cowan, *Arabic*, p. 763b.
[b] For the problematic name Ibn Q.jīd, see Cusa, *I diplomi*, p. 248a; see also Corriente, *Andalusi Arabic*, p. 415.
[c] For a plausible derivation of *coccarellus*, see G. Souillet, 'Bécherel, Cocherel et Choisel', *Annales de Bretagne* 65 (1958), 547–50.
[d] For the name *al-qalānisī* among 'villeins', see Cusa, *I diplomi*, pp. 173b, 283a, 566a, 566b, 575b, and 576b.

Table 4.1 (Cont.)

Rollus Rubeus	Reference	Arabic	Notes
curviserius	[20B]	Latin: *cor(de) visarius*	Latin *cordevisarius* > *corvesarius* > *curvisarius*, 'shoemaker', but also more generally, 'leather-worker'. Ultimately derived from *cordevisus*, 'a goatskin prepared after the Córdoban fashion', attested as early as ninth century.[a] The Arabic equivalent, *al-kharrāz*, was well attested.[b]
eius	[41A]	Latin: 'his'	
elauirus	[34B]	al-A'war(?)	Common descriptive epithet in Arabic; lit. 'one-eyed';[c] attested once elsewhere in Sicily.[d]
elbanbaca	[4B]	al-Banbaq	From Greek and Latin *bombax*, 'cotton';[e] cf. Ibrāhīm al-Banbaq in the Cefalù *jarīda*.[f]
elfil	[14A]	al-Fīl	Lit. 'the elephant'. Also cf. *Madīnat al-Fīl*, an Arabic name for Catania, but *al-Fīl* was not usually a reference to someone from there. Not otherwise attested in Sicily.

[a] J. F. Niermeyer (ed.), *Mediae Latinitatis Lexicon minus* (Leiden, 2001), p. 273.
[b] For the name *al-kharrāz* ('leather-worker', 'shoemaker'), see Cusa, *I diplomi*, pp. 141b, 145b, 253b, and possibly also 572b, 573a, and 576b from the Catania name-list.
[c] Wehr and Cowan, *Arabic*, p. 656b.
[d] See Cusa, *I diplomi*, p. 164a for 'Abd al-'Azīz al-A'war.
[e] On *bombax*, see Niermeyer, *Medieval Latin*, p. 101.
[f] For Ibrāhīm al-Banbaq, see Cusa, *I diplomi*, p. 475a.

elgidir	[17B], [24A], [32B]	al-Jadr	Lit. 'the wall', but used figuratively as occupational name; attested in Cefalù *jarīda*.[a]
elgurab	[33A]	al-Ghurāb	Probably from Arabic for 'the crow', 'raven' (and also the name of a boat), but not attested as personal names or place-names in Sicily. NB also kin-group name of Banū l-Ghurābī.[b] *Ghurābī* can also refer to a *rhinoptera adspersa* or Rough Cownose Ray.
elmabey	[15B]	?	
elyas	[13B]	Elias. Arabic: Ilyās	Common Biblical name widely diffused around the Mediterranean across all communities, and well known in Sicily from Elias Cartomensis, a convert and prominent knight in the Norman conquest army. It survives as a modern surname 'Elia'.
eylel	[38A]	al-Layl(?) or al-ʿAlīl(?);	Ibn al-Layl, masc. nickname 'Son of the Night'. Only Abū l-Layl, lit. 'father of the night', attested in Sicily (Yūsuf bin Bū l-Layl and Barq al-Layl, both from western Sicily).[c] Ibn al-ʿAlīl, 'the sick person, soft, gentle, pleasant', also possible but not attested in Sicily.

[a] Cusa, *I diplomi*, p. 170; see p. 476 for Ḥasan al-Jadr from Cefalù.
[b] For ʿAlī bin al-Ghurābiya of Calatrasi, see Cusa, *I diplomi*, p. 172b.
[c] Cusa, *I diplomi*, p. 248a.

(*continued*)

Table 4.1 (Cont.)

Rollus Rubeus	Reference	Arabic	Notes
faber	[5B]	al-Ḥaddād	Reconstruction assumes that the Latin scribe translated the widely attested Arabic occupational name *al-ḥaddād* as *faber*, 'smith' or 'blacksmith'.[a]
far	[15A]	al-Fār	Form *al-fār* ('the mouse, rat') preferred to *al-fārr* ('the fugitive') since animals (for example, snakes *ḥanāsh*; bear, *al-dubb*; chicken, *al-dajāj*; rooster, *al-dīk*; nightingale, *bulbul*; goldfinch, *ḥassūn*; falcon, *al-bāz*; crow, *al-ghurāb*; pig (Abū) *khinzīr*; foal, *al-flūv*; small birds, *al-furfūr*; rat, *al-jurdhān*) were included in the repertoire of twelfth-century Sicilian personal names.[b]

[a] For occurrences for *al-ḥaddād* ('smith') in western Sicily, see Cusa, *I diplomi*, pp. 142b, 150b, 152b, 153b, 160b, 160b, 172b, 178b, and 259b (who was the only 'unregistered' man); in the Catania name-lists, see pp. 566b, 567a, 567b, 569b, 572a, 572b, 575b, 576a, 576a, 576b, 582a, 584a, and 585a.
[b] For *al-Fār* or *al-Fa'r*, see Cusa, *I diplomi*, pp. 137a and 141b.

| (ben) fellac | [5A] | al-Falaq | Name or nickname of unclear connotation; Arabic *falaq* means 'dawn';[a] 'sky, celestial sphere', 'wheel';[b] also *falq*, 'crack, split, crevice'; 'plait of esparto grass'; 'natte, tresse de jonc pour les nattes'.[c] Given the existence of masc. p.n. such as *fajr* ('dawn') in Arabic, the most likely vocalisation *falaq*, not *falq*;[d] cf. also 'Uthmān al-Falqa, nickname implying occupation of woodcutter; *falqa*, 'splinter or firewood';[e] cf. also *falaqa*, 'one half of a split thing'; 'éclat de bois; laize d'étoffe; *falaqa*: est un instrument composé d'un morceau de bois, aux deux extrémités duquel une corde est attachée de manière à former un arc'.[f] Al-*fallāh*, 'peasant farmer', is theoretically possible, but exceptional in Sicily. Given Arabic names of his apparent relatives (*abderrahamen ben antar*, *hamet frater antar* and *sidika ben antar*), this man's names are unlikely to be related to Latinate forms *Antero* or *Falco*. |

(*continued*)

[a] Wehr and Cowan, *Arabic*, p. 727a, for 'dawn, crack, split, crevice'.
[b] Corriente, *Andalusi Arabic*, pp. 405–6, for *falaq* as 'sky, celestial sphere, wheel'.
[c] R. P. A. Dozy, *Supplément aux dictionnaires arabes*, 3rd ed., 2 vols (Leiden, 1877; Beirut, 1991), vol. 2, p. 288, for 'natte, tresse de jonc pour les nattes'; Corriente, *Andalusi Arabic*, p. 406, for 'plait of esparto grass'.
[d] See Cusa, *I diplomi*, p. 176b, for 'Abd al-Wahhāb Fal.q.
[e] Corriente, *Andalusi Arabic*, p. 405.
[f] Dozy, *Supplément*, ii, p. 288, and Cusa, *I diplomi*, p. 570a for Hilāl bin Fal.q.

Table 4.1 (Cont.)

Rollus Rubeus	Reference	Arabic	Notes
ficien	[36B]	Fityān	Fityān; lit. 'youths' (pl. of *fatā*), often referring to eunuchs or high-ranking slaves in service of ruling household.[a] However, the term can also refer to eunuchs or soldiers. In Sicily, this peculiar plural form was apparently used as p.n.[b]
filippus	[20B]	Philip. Arabic: Filīb	Greek name, but also frequently used by 'Arab-Christians' in Sicily.
frater	[4A], [41A]	Latin 'brother'	
furnarius	[25A]	al-Furnānī	Cf. al-Furnānī ʿAlī from Calatrasi, nickname suggesting occupation of 'oven-owner'; loan word from Greek φουρνᾶρος, of analogous form to βουρδονάνι/βουρδονάρι and φερνένι.[c] Latinised version here shows that term understood across all three languages.

[a] See E. Lévi-Provençal, 'fatā', in *Encyclopaedia of Islam*, 2nd ed., 13 vols (Leiden, 1986), vol. 2, p. 837.

[b] For the curious name of Fityān as a personal or kin-group name, see Cusa, *I diplomi*, p. 132b (Fityān bin ʿUthmān al-Thūmī); p. 166b ('his brother Fityān); p. 252a (Fityān brother of Hilāl); p. 258a (Jawhar bin Fityān); p. 268a (ʿAbd al-Rajāʾ nephew of Fityān); p. 249b (Fityān Ibn Baraka) (brother of ʿUthmān, Ḥasan, and Khilfa); p. 265b (Qāsim cousin of Fityān); p. 277b (Fityān al-Ḥajjām); p. 281a (Fityān al-Barmīlī); p. 284a (Fityān al-Khayyāṭ). All were attested in western Sicily. For reasons that I cannot explain, only one of them was registered on the list as being 'of the men'; the other 90 per cent were unregistered 'smooth men' or *min al-maḥallāt* ('from the camps'). For the use of Fityān as a fictive kin-group name among eunuchs of the royal palaces, see Johns, *Arabic Administration*, pp. 213, 228 and 251.

[c] For al-Furnānī ʿAlī, see Cusa, *I diplomi*, p. 169b. G. Caracausi, *Lessico greco della Sicilia e dell'Italia meridionale (secoli X-XIV)* (Palermo, 1990), pp. 118, 596 and 605.

(ben) gunde	[29B]	al-Jundi	'Soldier', cf. Bu l-Ḥusayn bin Jundiya from Dasīsa.[a]
(ben) baamar	[17A]	Ibn al-Ḥammār	Well-attested occupational nickname, 'donkey driver'.[b]
hamet	[2A], [4A], [22B], [33A]	Aḥmad	Most likely a Maghribi/Sicilian Arabic pronunciation of Aḥmad, very common masc. p.n., 'the most praised', or possibly Ḥammād, less common masc. p.n., lit. 'a man who praises things much'.[c]
hamut	[13A]	Ḥammūd	Common masc. p.n., lit. 'highly praised'.
hanes	[1A], [16B], [37A]	al-Ḥanāsh	Lit. 'snakes', probably a Sicilian Arabic version of ḥanash, pl. aḥnāsh, recalling an important kin-group around Cefalù.[d]
hasem	[53B]	Hāshim(?)	Common masc. p.n., lit. 'destroyer'; also name of famous ancient Arab tribe, and name of great-grandfather of Prophet Muḥammad.
hasen	[7A], [10A], [28A], [40B]	Ḥasan	Common masc. p.n., lit. 'handsome'. Al-Ḥasan was son of the fourth Orthodox Caliph ʿAlī and second in the line of Shīʿa Imams.

[a] For Bu (sic) l-Ḥusayn bin Jundiya, see Cusa, I diplomi, p. 258a. The name seems to refer to a (fictive?) kin-group of the Banū Jundī.
[b] Wehr and Cowan, Arabic, p. 205a; see Cusa, I diplomi, pp. 160b, 264a, 152a, 285a, for Ḥusayn al-Ḥammār, Yaḥyā bin al-Ḥammār, Abū Faḍl al-Ḥammār and Salām al-Ḥammār from western Sicily, and pp. 577b and 581b for ʿAlī al-Ḥammār and Muhib al-Ḥammār from the Catania list.
[c] E. W. Lane, An Arabic–English Lexicon, 8 parts (London, 1863), part 2, p. 640.
[d] Wehr and Cowan, Arabic, p. 210a; Cusa, I diplomi, p. 474a.

(continued)

Table 4.1 (Cont.)

Rollus Rubeus	Reference	Arabic	Notes
hcleyr	[28A]	al-Khayr(?). See *buḫair* above.	
hisahamel	[6A]	Ishmael. Arabic: Ismāʿīl	Common masc. p.n. shared by the Quranic and Biblical prophet Ishmael.
hise	[18A], [37A]	ʿĪsá	Common masc. p.n. and Arabic version of name of Biblical Jesus, and Quranic prophet of Sūrat Maryām (Qurʾān 19:30).
husein	[14A]	Ḥusayn	Common masc. p.n.; diminutive form of al-Ḥasan, 'the handsome one'. Al-Ḥusayn, son of fourth Orthodox Caliph ʿAlī and Fāṭima (Prophet Muḥammad's daughter), and third in line of Shīʿa Imams. In Sicily, the Kalbid dynasty was also referred to as Banū Abī l-Ḥusayn.
Iohannes	[9A]	Arabic: Yaḥyá	Common masc. p.n. shared by Biblical John the Baptist, son of Zakarīyā (Qurʾān 6:85).
Ioseph	[2B], [15B], [16B], [17B]	Arabic: Yūsuf	Common masc. p.n. from Biblical and Quranic prophet Joseph (Qurʾān 12), son of Yaʿqūb (Qurʾān 6:84), son of Isḥāq, son of Ibrāhīm.
laapsi	[10B]	?	

lascar	[31A]	al-Ashqar or al-ʿAskar or al-ʿAskarī	*Ashqar*, 'light-skinned, fair-haired', well attested among Sicilian villeins generally, including Cefalù area.[a] Alternatively, derived from *al-ʿAskar*, 'the army', or *al-ʿAskarī* 'the soldier', less well attested although not rare. Both sometimes written with agglutinated definite article in Greek as well as in Latin, making them indistinguishable and disguising their provenance. Given the predominance of Arab-Muslim names in this list, an Arabic derivation preferred to Greek name Λάσκαρης.[b] NB nearby toponym and modern surname 'Làscari'.
lupus	[2A]	Lupus or al-Lubb	Lupus (< Latin 'wolf') or al-Lubb (< Arabic 'kernals'). Problematic name with possible derivation from Latin or more likely via the translation of an Arabic word or a transliteration that has migrated to the nearest recognisable Latin term. Same difficulty regarding toponym *khandaq al-lubb* > *vallonis luporum*;[c] cf. also the modern surname 'Lupo' (and numerous toponyms) attested across Sicily and southern Italy.[d]

[a] For *al-ashqar*, see Cusa, *I diplomi*, p. 479a (Cefalù); pp. 575a and 576b (Catania), and pp. 153a, 165a, 166b, 252a and 258b (Monreale).

[b] Caracausi, *DOdS*, vol. 2, p. 840, who seems to prefer a Greek derivation.

[c] For the translation of *khandaq al-lubb* as *vallonem lupi*, see Cusa, *I diplomi*, pp. 205 and 181; cf. also pp. 195 and 231 for *kudyat al-lubbūb* which became *monticulus luporum* in Latin.

[d] Caracausi, *DOdS*, vol. 2, p. 889.

(*continued*)

Table 4.1 (Cont.)

Rollus Rubeus	Reference	Arabic	Notes
(ben) maadile	[22B]	Muʿadila	Kin-group name of the Banū Muʿadila. The name Muʿadila, 'justice, équité';[a] *muʿaddil*, 'average' 'middle', attested three times among villeins, once in the Cefalù *jarīda*.[b]
maàlla	[19B]	?	Possibly a name such as Mann Allāh ('the grace of God').[c]
maltí	[31B]	al-Maltī	Locative *nisba*, 'the Maltese'.[d]
marahen	[38B]	?	
maymon	[19A]	Maymūn	Common masc. p.n., lit. 'fortunate, lucky, blessed'.[e]
meheres	[12B]	Muḥriz	Common masc. p.n., lit. 'obtainer, winner, possessor'; frequently attested in Ifrīqiya where Muḥriz b. Khalaf (d. 1022) was a revered holy man and teacher whose *zāwiya* is in Tūnis.[f]
(ben) meib	[30B]	Muḥib	Common masc. p.n., 'awe-inspiring, awesome, venerable, grave, solemn, dignified'.[g]

[a] Kazimirsky, *Dictionnaire arabe-français*, vol. 2, p. 192.
[b] For ʿĪsá bin Muʿadila in the Cefalù *jarīda* of 1145, see Cusa, *I diplomi*, p. 478a; two other 'men' (Baraka and Ibrāhīm) of the Banū Muʿadila are found at Qalʿat al-Trāzī (Calatrasi) in western Sicily; see Cusa, *I diplomi*, pp. 176b and 178b.
[c] Cusa, *I diplomi*, pp. 68a and 576b; for Mann Allāh bin al-Dalīl and his three sons, see Cusa, *I diplomi*, pp. 136b, 139a, 141a, 142a.
[d] Wehr and Cowan, *Arabic*, p. 889a.
[e] Wehr and Cowan, *Arabic*, p. 1109b.
[f] Wehr and Cowan, *Arabic*, p. 167.
[g] Wehr and Cowan, *Arabic*, p. 1042a.

mellec	[42A]	Malik or possibly Malik, Mallāḥ or Mallāk	Common masc. p.n., literally, 'owner, proprietor; landowner, landholder, landed proprietor'.[a]
(ben) mila	[24B]	Mila(?)	Possibly from Mīla or a kin group from Mīla in western Ifrīqiya (modern Algeria).
mòhaluf	[41A], see mohuluf below	Makhlūf	
mohuluf	[16A], [19A],	Makhlūf	Common masc. p.n., lit. 'that which can be replaced or paid for', 'compensation', but also synonym of *khalaf*, 'successor'.[b]
mohumet	[6B], [30A], [34B], [35B]	Muḥammad	Common masc. p.n. and name of the final prophet in Islam. Lit. 'he who is praised, commendable, laudable'.
moyb	[8A]	Muhib	Common masc. p.n., 'awe-inspiring, awesome, venerable, grave, solemn, dignified'.[c]
mudiber	[42B]	al-Muʾaddib(?)	Epithet implying an occupation; *muʾaddib*, 'educator'; teacher in a Quranic school'; cf. also *muʾaddab*, 'well bred, well mannered civil, urbane'.[d]

(*continued*)

[a] Wehr and Cowan, *Arabic*, p. 923b.
[b] Corriente, *Andalusi Arabic*, p. 164.
[c] Wehr and Cowan, *Arabic*, p. 1042a.
[d] Wehr and Cowan, *Arabic*, p. 10a.

Table 4.1 (Cont.)

Rollus Rubeus	Reference	Arabic	Notes
muge	[28B]	Mūsá(?). See *muse* below	
mule	[25A]	Mawlá	Common masc. p.n., 'lord'.[a]
muse	[37B], [40B]	Mūsá	Common masc. p. n. and name of the Biblical and Quranic prophet Moses.
neem	[22A]	Ni'ma. See *nema* below	
nema	[7A]	Ni'ma	Common masc. (and fem.) p.n., 'benefit, blessing, boon, benefaction, favor, grace, kindness'.[b]
nicolaus	[14B]	Nicholaus. Arabic: Niqūla	Common masc. p.n. used by both Greek and Arabic-speaking Christians in Sicily; a Latinised version of the common Greek masc. p.n. Νικόλαος, also well attested in Arabic as Niqūla among Sicilian Christians.

[a] Oddly, the name *Mawlá* is not known among Sicilian *villani* from western Sicily or Catania. The closest is *Mawlāt*, a female equivalent; see Cusa, *I diplomi*, p. 580b. It was, however, attested among villeins from Calabria (p. 27) and was well known among a variety of Christians in the Val Démone (e.g. p. 535, and especially Garufi, 'Censimento e catasto', pp. 90–2, where we find *Mules calotos*, *Mules*, *Mules ios cali*, *Mules tu geruneri*, *Mules tuchabuani* and *Mules turomeu* in merely a handful of villages). The name may have had a Christian connotation, and thus enjoyed wider currency among Arabic-speaking Christian communities, e.g. ὁ ἱερεὺς μωλέ καὶ πρωτοπαπᾶς in Cusa, *I diplomi*, p. 685, line 2.
[b] Wehr and Cowan, *Arabic*, p. 980b.

nikír	[22A]	al-Naqīr(?)	Unusual term from root of n-q-r with several diverse connotations, including 'wooded pail' (*naqīr*); name also attested in Cefalù *jarīda*.[a]
obeid	[32A]	ʿUbayd	Common masc. p.n.; diminutive of ʿAbd, 'slave or servant'.[b]
omor	[10B], [30B], [39A]	ʿUmar	Common masc. p.n. shared by the famous Orthodox caliph, ʿUmar ibn al-Khaṭṭāb (d. 644).
omur	[9B], see *omor* above	ʿUmar	
osbernu	[30A]	?	
osein	[24A], [38B]	Ḥusayn	Common masc. p.n.; diminutive form of al-Ḥasan, 'the handsome one'. Al-Ḥusayn son of fourth Orthodox Caliph ʿAlī and Fāṭima (Prophet Muḥammad's daughter), and third in line of Shīʿa Imams.
othimen	[21B], [24B], [31A], [31B]	ʿUthmān	Common masc. p.n. shared by the famous Orthodox caliph, ʿUthmān ibn al-ʿAffān (d. 656).
pays	[21B]	al-Raʾīs(?). See *rays* below	

(*continued*)

[a] Corriente, *Andalusi Arabic*, p. 537; for Muḥammad al-Naqīr from Cefalù, see Cusa, *I diplomi*, p. 477a.
[b] Wehr and Cowan, *Arabic*, p. 586b.

Table 4.1 (Cont.)

Rollus Rubeus	Reference	Arabic	Notes
randa	[19B]	Randa(?)	Arabic *randa*, 'laurel' (cf. mod. Sicilian *rannu*, 'bay tree').[a] Not attested as a given name (*ism*). Al-Randa was an estate in western Sicily with defined limits (*divisa rande*); possibly derived from an eponymous kin group, cf. *ḥiṣṣat* ('the allotment of') *Ibn al-Randi*.[b]
rays	[25B], [29A], [36A], [39A], [40A]	al-Raʾīs	Lit. 'the head', 'chief'.[c] In Sicily, possibly also reference to coordinator of the *mattanza* or tuna-cull; the term is well attested in Sicilian dialects from thirteenth century to present.
ria	[9A]	?	
sandialu	[18A]	?	
sidebelu	[6B]	Sayyid Ahlihi	Nickname used as masc. p.n., lit. 'leader of his people/family'. Commonly used in Sicily as masc. p.n.; see also Ibn Hishām: 'When the Prophet arrived at Medina, ʿAbd Allāh was the leader of its people' (*wa-sayyid ahlihā ʿAbd Allāh*).[d]

[a] Kazimirsky, *Dictionnaire arabe-français*, vol. 1, pp. 923–3; Corriente, *Andalusi Arabic*, p. 219; cf. also G. Piccitto, *Vocabolario Siciliano*, 5 vols (Catania–Palermo, 1977–2002), vol. 4, p. 10, and vol. 1, p. 230, for *arānmilu*, 'oleander'.
[b] See Cusa, *I diplomi*, p. 193 (*divisa rande*), p. 203 (*al-Randa*) and p. 228 (*hadd al-Randa*, 'the boundary of al-Randa'); cf. p. 216 (*ḥadd Ḥiṣṣat Ibn al-Randī*, 'the boundary of the allotment of Ibn al-Randi) and p. 187 translated as *ad fines cultura filii randi*.
[c] Wehr and Cowan, *Arabic*, p. 318a.
[d] ʿAbd al-Malik Ibn Hishām, *al-Sīra al-nabawiya*, ed. M. al-Saqqā, 2 vols (Cairo, 1955), vol. 2, pp. 234–5.

sidika	[4B], [11B], [23B]	Ṣadaqa	Common masc. p.n., 'alms, charity'.[a]
solimen	[11A], [17A], [18B]	Sulaymān	Common masc. p.n. shared by the Biblical Solomon and Quranic prophet (Qurʾān 27:15–17).
tanbur	[27A]	al-Ṭunbūr	A *ṭunbūr*, a 'long-necked musical instrument resembling the mandolin' and *tunbūrī*, a player of the instrument.[b] Although unattested in either form in medieval Sicily, 'Tamburo' is a modern surname from same origin.[c]
tecalas	[7B]	ibn(?) Khalaṣ(?)	*Khalāṣ*, 'liberation, deliverance, salvation'; masc. p.n., 'liberation, salvation';[d] or in Christian thought 'redemption', attested among Sicilian villeins on five occasions. Given the Arab-Muslim first name of Abū l-Dhikr, and the general absence of villeins with Greek names in list, the well-attested Greek personal name Καλάς as a source seems less likely.
turrus	[34A], [37B]	al-Ṭurrus(?)	Most probably derived from Sicilian toponym *Turrus*, in turn most likely derived from Latin *turris*, 'tower'. Arabic *al-aṭrash* ('the deaf one') also possible.
vlaben	[33B]	?	

[a] Wehr and Cowan, *Arabic*, p. 509a.
[b] Wehr and Cowan, *Arabic*, p. 570.
[c] For the modern surname of Tamburo, see Caracausi, *DOdS*, vol. 2, p. 1597.
[d] Wehr and Cowan, *Arabic*, p. 254b.

(*continued*)

Table 4.1 (Cont.)

Rollus Rubeus	Reference	Arabic	Notes
vucher	[25B]	Abū Bakr	Common masc. p.n. (*ism*) in form of moniker (*kunya*/*laqab*); lit. 'father of the young camel', but well known as name of Orthodox caliph Abū Bakr al-Ṣiddīq (d.634); cf. the possible origins of the surname Buccheri.[a]
vulufe	[39B]	Abū l-ʿAfāʾ(?)	Abū l-ʿAfāʾ or Abū l-Lūf. Abū l-ʿAfāʾ, masc. figurative kunya, 'father of ruin, obliteration'. Abū l-Lūf, masc. figurative nickname or professional name 'father of the loofa'. Neither attested in Sicily.
Ysmaèl	[42B]	Ishmael Arabic: Ismāʿīl	Common masc. p.n. shared by the Quranic and Biblical prophet Ishmael.
zarcka	[10A]	al-Zarqāʾ(?)	Lit. 'the blue one'. Not otherwise attested in Sicily, except in diminutive form *zurayqa*, a nickname (*laqab-kunya*) of uncertain meaning; possibly a diminutive of *zarqa*, 'coup de lance',[b] or *zurqa*, 'blue' or 'a certain bead for the purpose of fascination';[c] possibly also related to a type of snake called a *zurayq* (*echis carinata*).[d] Here, apparently part of kin-group name; e.g. the Banū Zurayqa in western Sicily.[e]

[a] For the modern surname Buccheri, see Caracausi, *DOdS*, vol. 1, p. 206.
[b] On the Arabic root z-r-q, see Dozy, *Supplément*, vol. 1, p. 587; Kazimirsky, *Dictionnaire arabe-français*, vol. 1, pp. 923–3; Cusa, *I diplomi*, p. 203.
[c] Lane, *Arabic–English Lexicon, part 3*, p. 1227; Kazimirsky, *Dictionnaire arabe-français*, vol. 1, pp. 987–8.
[d] Dozy, *Supplément*, vol. 1, p. 588.
[e] For the Banū Zurayqa, see Cusa, *I diplomi*, pp. 148b and 160a.

Historiography in the making 85

of'), teknonymics *nasab*s (ibn, 'son of', 'clan of') as well as ethnic identifiers, 'tribal' names and locatives (*nisba*s) gave way to 'X son of Y', and hence simple 'XY' combinations in which the Y element tended to reflect occupations, nicknames and Arabic first names (*ism*s).[21] In this respect, the Rollus Rubeus list is an important trend-marker and provides early evidence for the development of Sicilian surnames derived from Arabic, some of which have survived into the present day.

Fiscal considerations and internal prosopography

First, we can elicit some basic factual information from the text in which we find a total of eighty-three villeins represented by a total of 149 names. Of their tax burden, calculated in *tarì*, neither the name nor the type of tax is stated. Given that one or two of the villeins had names suggestive of Christians, we should not assume that the tax was the *jizya* or religious head tax, payable in two instalments per year. We should show similar caution about assuming the tax had been levied solely on land or produce since many of the villeins seem to be engaged in crafts or trades with no direct connection to the land. They may, of course, have been minor landlords with men in their service, but we are not told this explicitly. On safer grounds, we know from the subtotals of *tarì* that they were due to pay a total of 623 *tarì*. This gives an average tax burden per capita of 7.5 *tarì*. There were significant disparities between the highest taxpayer ('Abd al-Raḥmān Ḥanāsh), at forty *tarì*, and the lowest – eight men who paid only four *tarì* each.[22] About 88 per cent (seventy-three of eighty-three) paid eight *tarì* or less. The median and mode were both six *tarì*, with basic increments usually of two *tarì*. Only seven out of the eighty-three villeins (8.5 per cent) paid an odd amount (one man paid thirteen, another eleven, and five seven *tarì* each). Thus, while differences in the tax burden across households probably reflected disparities in material wealth, most of these differences were minor.

While this is not the place to discuss the purchasing power of the *tarì* in twelfth-century Sicily, a few rough indicators may be helpful. For instance, a house in Cefalù in 1191, which was located near the tower of the city gate, was rented to a Latin notary for sixteen *tarì* per annum.²³ If such comparisons have merit, then the closest relevant fiscal data derives from a handful of sources. In 1095, ninety-five named Muslims from western Sicily paid 750 *tarì* twice a year in addition to 300 *modia* of wheat and barley.²⁴ A late eleventh- or twelfth-century name-list from mainly Christian villages recorded that, at Naso, 102 *villani* returned 140 [*salmas*] *frumenti*; at Fitalie, 111 *villani* owed 322 *tarì* and an unknown amount of their harvest; at Librizzi fifty-nine men gave 256 *tarì*.²⁵ At Librizzi in 1117, a delegation of *villani* successfully negotiated terms of service with their abbot.²⁶ They were to give one week of labour in every four, plus forty days of labour for sowing, a day at harvest and three at the *vendemmia*. No dues reckoned in cash terms were mentioned. At Mezzoiuso in western Sicily around 1177, the tax burden of three Muslim *villani* was specified as thirty *tarì* in *jizya* payments and a land-tax of twenty *modia* of wheat and ten of barley.²⁷

In the Rollus Rubeus list, higher rates were paid by those listed in Column A. There, the highest taxpayer appears at the top of that column, which reveals something of the registration process and highlights a rough socio-economic difference between those at the top and those towards the bottom. Where two or more people appear to be related, sons usually paid less than fathers, revealing a sliding scale of returns with lower amounts due from younger taxpayers. Overall, the average *tarì* payable for those with 'ibn' ('son of') in their names was below average at 6.83. Thus, from among the clearest examples of familial relations and tax burden, Ḥusayn al-Jadr paid ten *tarì*, while his sons, Qāsim and Yūsuf, paid six *tarì* each. ʿAbd al-Raḥmān al-Ḥanāsh paid forty *tarì*, his son Yūsuf paid eight and his nephew ʿĪsā four. Al-Raʾīs ʿUmar paid twelve *tarì*; one son Qāsim paid eight, and two others (Abū Bakr and ʿAbd l-Mawlá) paid six each. However, not all the fiscal–familial data was so consistent. While ʿAntar ibn Fallāḥ paid six *tarì*, his brother Aḥmad/Ḥamīd paid eight; one son, ʿAbd al-Raḥmān, also paid eight, and another son, Ṣadaqa, six. Of note is that one such younger-generation *villanus* paid twelve *tarì*, showing that there was always room for variation. Similarly, there were inconsistencies within occupations: one Carpentarìus paid eleven *tarì*, another seven.

Historiography in the making

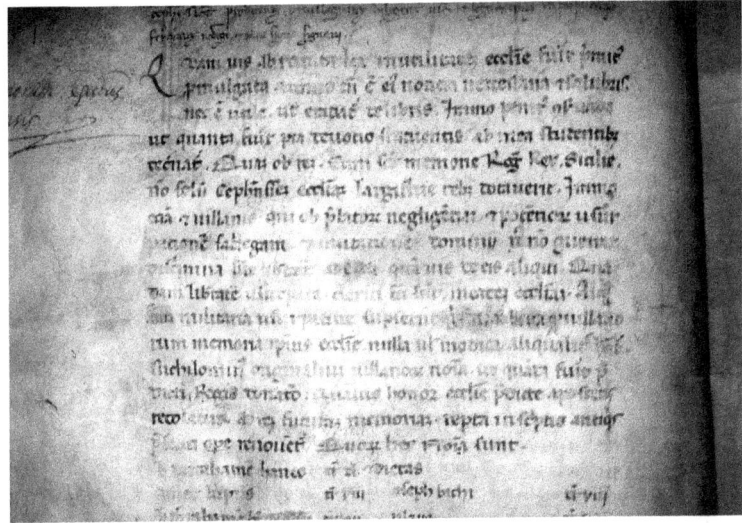

Figure 4.1 Palermo, Archivio di Stato di Palermo, Fondo Miscellanea Archivistica Serie II, n. 5, fol. 9v, lines 1–16 (Latin).

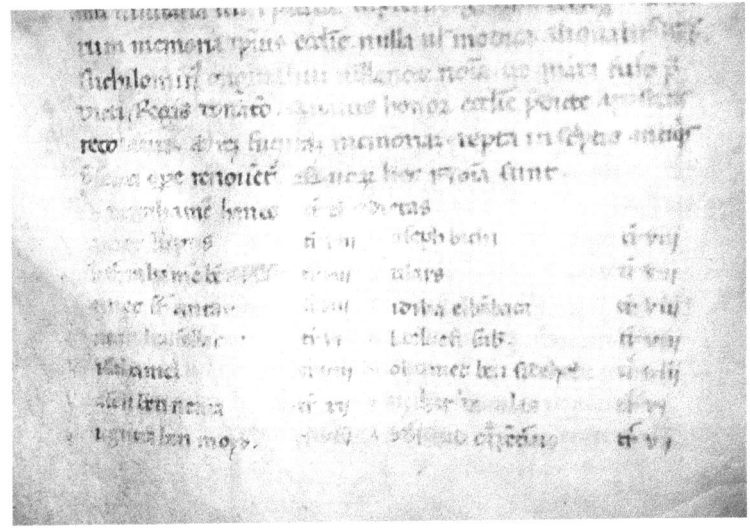

Figure 4.2 Palermo, Archivio di Stato di Palermo, Fondo Miscellanea Archivistica Serie II, n. 5, fol. 9v, lines 1–8 (name list).

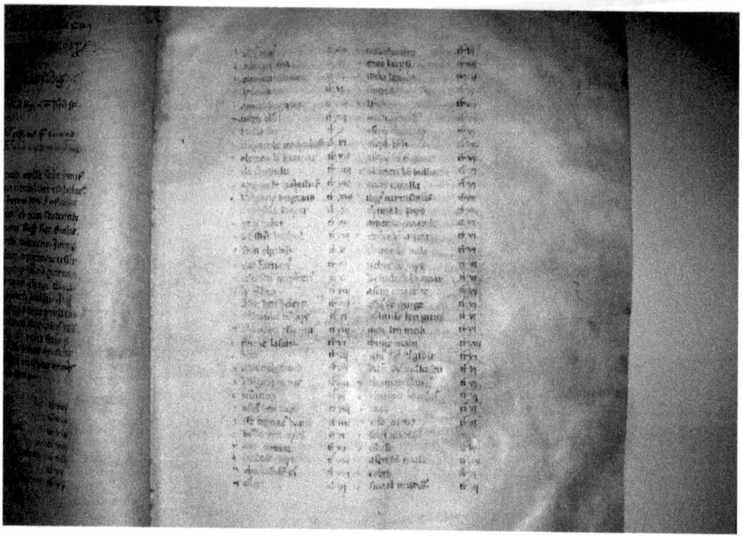

88   Historiographies

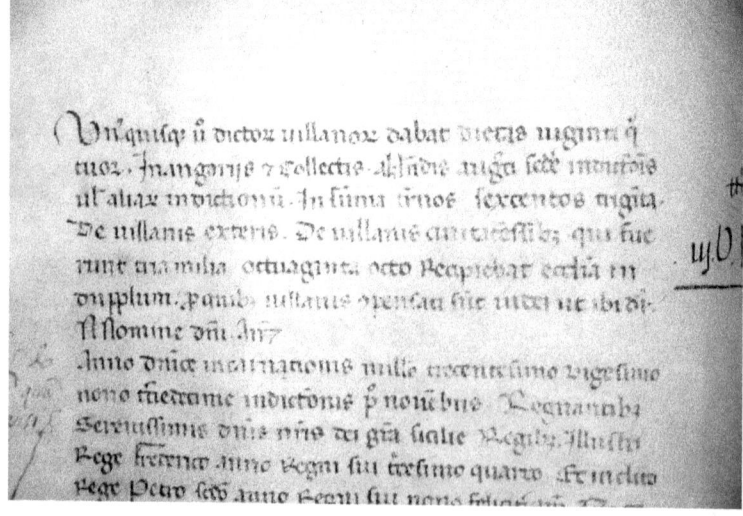

Figure 4.3 Palermo, Archivio di Stato di Palermo, Fondo Miscellanea Archivistica Serie II, n. 5, fol. 10r, lines 9–42 (name list).

Figure 4.4 Palermo, Archivio di Stato di Palermo, Fondo Miscellanea Archivistica Serie II, n. 5, fol. 10v, lines 17–22 (Latin).

Much can be done with this evidence that cannot be undertaken in this chapter. Limited as this may be, it is hoped that it will afford a clearer view of naming, identity, prosopography, community, occupations and tax obligations, data at the very heart of medieval history and historiography as viewed through a church cartulary of King Roger II's own foundation, rather than through narratives or charter evidence with which it can be profitably used in tandem.

Notes

1 Palermo, Archivio di Stato di Palermo, Fondo Miscellanea Archivistica Serie II, n. 5, fols 9^r–10^r. The images from the Rollus Rubeus in this article are reproduced with the kind permission of the Archivio di Stato in Palermo and the Ministero per i beni e per l'attività culturale e per il turismo.

2 *Rollus rubeus: Privilegia ecclesie Cephaleditane, a diversis regibus et imperatoribus concessa, recollecta et in hoc volumine scripta*, ed. C. Mirto (Palermo, 1972). Henceforth: Mirto.

3 The bishopric of Cefalù was founded in September 1131, for its relations with the Sicilian crown, see G. A. Loud, *The Latin Church in Norman Italy* (Cambridge, 2007), pp. 324–9; for a survey of the church's holdings in the Norman period, see L. T. White Jr, *Latin Monasticism in Norman Sicily* (Cambridge, MA, 1938), pp. 189–201.

4 To date, the most detailed discussion of the name-list is found in J. Johns, *Arabic Administration in Norman Sicily: The Royal Dīwān* (Cambridge, 2002), pp. 61–2; see also I. Peri, *Villani e cavalieri nella Sicilia medievale* (Bari, 1993), p. 80; in the wider context of southern Italian villeinage, see P. Corrao, 'Il servo', in G. Musca (ed.), *Condizione umana e ruoli sociali nel Mezzogiorno normanno-svevo. Atti delle none giornate normanno-sveve, Bari, 17–20 ottobre, 1989* (Bari, 1992), pp. 61–78; F. Panero, *Schiavi, servi, e villani nell'Italia medievale* (Turin, 1999), pp. 295–304 and 324–30; S. Carocci, 'Le libertà dei servi. Reinterpretate il villanaggio medievale', *Storica* 37 (2007), 51–94.

5 *Le pergamene greche esistenti nel Grande Archivio di Palermo*, ed. G. Spata (Palermo, 1862), pp. 421–2. Henceforth: Spata; C.-A. Garufi, 'Censimento e catasto della popolazione servile: nuovi studi e ricerche sull'ordinamento amministrativo dei Normanni in Sicilia nei secoli 11 e 12', *Archivio storico siciliano* n.s. 49 (1928), 1–104 (at pp. 97–100); Mirto, pp. 39–41.

6 The initial letters of each name are omitted in Spata's edition.
7 The Latinate forms such as *Abdesseid* and *Abderrahaman* (for 'Abd al-Sayyid and 'Abd al-Raḥmān), in which the Arabic definite article *al-* has been assimilated, follow the sound of the Arabic rather than rendering it letter by letter.
8 See also the discussion of dating in Johns, *Arabic Administration*, p. 62. The dating argument given by Carocci, 'Le libertà dei servi', p. 92, n. 107, is blighted by several errors of detail.
9 In the 1145 list from Cefalù, the Arabic rubric states that 'And there came Jocelm (J.tsālim), the bishop of Cefalù; Guascin (W.skīn), and Bernard (B.rnārd), and you brought a list ... date of which was twelve years ago in which there was that which was granted to the great cathedral church at Cefalù.' After the name-list, we are told that 'they also brought a list written in Latin by the abbot and monks belonging to the monastery of St Angelus in Mileto', *I diplomi greci ed arabi di Sicilia pubblicati nel testo originale, tradotti ed illustrate*, ed. S. Cusa (Palermo, 1868–82, repr. Cologne–Vienna, 1983), pp. 472–80, at p. 473 and p. 479. For a full translation and discussion, see Johns, *Arabic Administration*, pp. 123–7. We can infer that the royal administration had relied on data supplied by the church itself, an indication of a high degree of interdependency between Church and state record-keeping. For discussion and comparison of the name-lists, see A. Metcalfe, *Muslims and Christians in Norman Sicily: Arabic Speakers and the End of Islam* (London, 2003), pp. 71–3 and 146–8.
10 For al-Shaykh 'Abd al-Mawlá on the Cefalù list from 1145, see Cusa, *I diplomi*, p. 473b. This example assumes that *al-shaykh* and *al-ra'īs* < 'rays' ('chief', 'head') are effectively synonyms. In the Rollus Rubeus, the syntax of *rays omor* confirms the use of *ra'īs* as an honorific appellation.
11 For 'Abd al-Raḥmān bin al-Ḥanash in the Cefalù *jarīda* of 1145, see Cusa, *I diplomi*, p. 474a. The attested presence of the Banū l-Ḥanash in the area shows that they were an important kin-group. As such, the Arabic term *ibn* here probably means 'kin-group of', not 'son of'.
12 For 'Umar bin Muhīb on the Cefalù list, see Cusa, *I diplomi*, p. 478a. Both 'Umar and Muhīb are Arabic personal names (*ism*s), so *ibn* here means 'son of', not 'kin-group of'.
13 For *ioseph ben hanes* and *hise cognatus hanes*, cf. 'Alī al-Ḥanash in Cusa, *I diplomi*, p. 476a; for *sidika elbanbaca*, cf. Ibrāhīm al-Banbaq (p. 475a); for *hamet ben maadile*, cf. 'Īsá and his brother Abū Juma'a, the sons of Mu'adila (p. 478a); for *abdesseid bulbul*, cf. Bū Ḥajar Bulbul (p. 474b) and Bulbul's wife (p. 477b); for *othimen malti*, cf. 'Alī al-Mālṭī (p. 475a); for *osein el gidir*, *casmus ben elgidir* and *ioseph*

ben elgidir, cf. Ḥasan al-Jadr (p. 476a); for *sidika bouac*, cf. Maymūn bin al-Bawwāq (p. 477b); for *othimen lascar*, cf. Ḥusayn al-Ashqar (p. 479a).

14 On 'registered' (*adscriptitii*) villeins being barred from the clergy, see Johns, *Arabic Administration*, p. 149.

15 In Norman Sicily, 'unregistered' men were called *al-muls*, *exografoi* or *inscriptitii*, while 'outsiders' and 'newcomers' were referred to as *ghurabā'*, *xénoi* or *advenae*. Neither category was considered 'registered'. On distinctions among villeins, see Johns, *Arabic Administration*, pp. 144–67, and A. Nef, *Conquérir et gouverner la Sicile islamique aux XIe et XIIe siècles* (Rome, 2011), pp. 482–507, both with full bibliographies. The latter work, surprisingly, contains no reference to the Rollus Rubeus except in the bibliography.

16 On this debate, see also Johns, *Arabic Administration*, p. 62.

17 *Constitutiones regni Siciliae: ristampa anastatica dell'edizione di Napoli del 1786*, ed. G. Carcani (Messina, 1992), pp. 290–1; see discussion in D. Abulafia, 'Ethnic variety and its implications: Frederick II's relations with Jews and Muslims', in W. Tronzo (ed.), *Intellectual Life and the Court of Frederick II Hohenstaufen* (Washington, DC, 1994), pp. 213–24, at p. 218.

18 The Latinate renditions in the list are Filippus, Iohannes, Ioseph, Nicolaus, Ysmael, Barisarius, Carpentarìus, Carpintarìus, Coccarellus, Curvisarius, Faber and Furnarius.

19 On the tendency of non-Arab scribes to translate Arabic terms in personal names, add Latinate or Greek terminations, omit the Arabic definite article and so on, see Metcalfe, *Muslims and Christians*, pp. 127–73.

20 Occupations and tax due in *tarì* (shown in brackets): Abū l-Ḥasan al-Najjār (eleven); Ḥusayn al-Jadr (ten); ʿAbd al-Ḥaqq al-Raʾīs (eight); ʿAbd l-Kāfī al-Ḥaddād (eight); Qāsim ibn al-Raʾīs (eight); Ṣadaqa al-Bambāq (eight); Sulaymān ibn al-Ḥammār (eight); ʿAbd l-Sayyid al-Najjār (seven); Filippus Curviserius (seven); Nicolaus Coccarellus (seven); Mawlā al-Furnū/Khabbāz (seven); ʿAbd al-Mawlá ibn al-Raʾīs (six); Abū Bakr ibn al-Raʾīs (six); Abū l-ʿAfw (six); ʿAntar ibn Fallāḥ (six); Ibn al-Jundī (six); Qāsim ibn al-Jadr (six); Yūsuf ibn al-Jadr (six); Ṣadaqa al-Bawwāq (four).

21 For similar observations in a Sicilian context, see K. Korhonen, 'The role of onomastics for diachronic sociolinguistics: A case study on language shift in late medieval Sicily', *Journal of Historical Linguistics* 1/2 (2011), 147–74. For identity issues arising from onomastics, see A. Metcalfe, 'Before the Normans: Identity and societal formation in Muslim Sicily', in D. Booms and P. Higgs (eds), *Sicily, Heritage of the World* (London, 2019), pp. 102–19.

22 If the forty *tarì* of 'Abd al-Raḥmān Ḥanāsh were to be excluded from the total, then the per capita average falls slightly from 7.5 *tarì* to 7.1 *tarì*.

23 *Documenti inediti dell'epoca normanni in Sicilia*, ed. C.-A. Garufi (Palermo, 1899), pp. 244–6; White, *Latin Monasticism*, p. 200.

24 Cusa, *I diplomi*, p. 1. Consideration of the examples cited can be found in A. Nef, 'Conquêtes et reconquêtes médiévales: la Sicile normande est-elle une terre de réduction en servitude généralisée?', *Mélanges de l'École française de Rome, Moyen-Âge* 112/2 (2000), pp. 579–607, especially pp. 593–9. For caveats and exampla concerning revenue calculations, see S. Carocci, *Lordships of Southern Italy: Rural Societies, Aristocratic Powers and Monarchy in the 12th and 13th Centuries*, trans. L. Byatt (Rome, 2018), pp. 416–25.

25 Garufi, 'Censimento e catasto', pp. 92–5. These readings are tentative due to poor preservation of the manuscript, and the less-than-reliable edition.

26 Cusa, *I diplomi*, pp. 512–13.

27 On this, and questions surrounding the taxation of Muslim villeins, see J. Johns, 'The boys from Mezzoiuso: Muslim *jizya*-payers in Christian Sicily', in R. Hoyland and P. Kennedy (eds), *Islamic Reflections, Arabic Musings: Studies in Honor of Professor Alan Jones* (Cambridge, 2004), pp. 243–55.

5

A fiscal provision of Count Roger of Ariano: traces of redactional variants in the *Chronicon* of Falco of Benevento

Edoardo D'Angelo

The *Chronicon Beneventanum* (= *ChBen*) of notary and judge Falco of Benevento[1] is known to us from a relatively late tradition. The Samnite protophysician Giulio del Sindico around 1530 drew a copy from the archetype. Falco's twelfth-century manuscript in Beneventan script, which was missing at least one folio both at its beginning and end, is now lost, as is del Sindico's transcription of it. Del Sindico's lost copy, nonetheless, was the source either directly or indirectly for the three most important manuscript versions of the *ChBen* now extant:[2] Codex San Martino 66 of the Biblioteca Nazionale in Naples (seventeenth century) contains the longest text to have come to us (the years 1102–40); Vatican Barb. lat. 2330 (sixteenth century) contains a text for 1112–40; and Vatican Barb. lat. 2345 (sixteenth–seventeenth centuries), derived from a later copy (it too having disappeared) of del Sindico's exemplar, contains the transcription only for 1137. The first printed edition (the *editio princeps*), produced by Antonio Caracciolo in 1626, has retained a certain importance in the Falconian tradition. Caracciolo likely drew it from another lost copy of the Beneventan protophysician's transcription.[3]

The portions of Falco's chronicle lost to us because of missing folios – the very beginning and end of it – can be reconstructed along broad lines through the thirteenth-century chronicle of St Mary of Ferraria.[4] The author of this later chronicle, an anonymous Cistercian monk, indeed used a manuscript of the *ChBen* in which the *incipit*[5] and the final part must have been still there to be read when he prepared the early portion of his own chronicle. In particular, according to a first reconstruction by Paul Fridolin Kehr and a later one by the undersigned, the Ferrariense monk would have had to draw from the *ChBen* not only for the years 1102–40 but also for 1099–1101 and 1141–44.[6]

Falco's text, even with the characteristics of the manuscript tradition described above, does not pose particularly weighty problems of textual transmission. It seems reasonable to believe that, if there had been incongruities or complexities in the original, they were normalised in del Sindico's humanist-era copy, notwithstanding the Beneventan physician's declarations of absolute fidelity and adherence to the text he was transcribing.[7]

There exists, however, a textual situation in the chronicle that makes one ponder the possibility of a double redaction by Falco of an important episode in his narrative.

The year was 1137. Roger II of Hauteville was consolidating his conquest of the continental Mezzogiorno despite the formation of a league of the most important southern lords against him, a league led spiritually by Pope Innocent II and militarily by Roger's brother-in-law Rainulf of Alife and Prince Robert of Capua. The war against Roger was perhaps at its most dramatic moment: The emperor of Germany, Lothar III, had descended into Italy. Roger was in retreat on several fronts.

The administrators of Benevento took advantage of this circumstance to entreat Pope Innocent, at this moment in the city, to ask the emperor to free Benevento from the fiscal exactions for which it was beholden to the district's Norman barons, in particular to the count of Ariano and his subfeudatories. The pope dispatched the patriarch of Aquileia[8] and Cardinal Gerard of Santa Croce[9] to Lothar, encamped just outside the city, to request that he appeal to the count of Ariano, Roger Drengot,[10] on behalf of the Beneventans for an exemption.

The emperor accepted the request and summoned the count. Roger Drengot consented to the oath of renunciation of feudal rights on behalf of his vassals, but he declined to render it personally since he had already done it in the time of the Beneventan constableship of Rolpoto of Sant'Eustasio (therefore, between c. 15 November 1132 and 30 June 1134).[11] The count summoned some of his vassals for the oath. Falco, in paragraphs 1137.14.7–9, furnishes the oath's precise text. At that point, Roger of Ariano summoned his other

barons, those of Montefusco.[12] At the end, on 6 September 1137, Cardinal Gerard reported all to Pope Innocent.
This is Falco's account (the year was, as said, 1137):

[14.1] His ita peractis, iudices et sapientes civitatis eundem dominum papam precantur, quatenus apud imperatorem intercederet, ut de antiqua afflictione, quam civitas longe lateque perpessa est, imperator ipse Beneventanos liberaret: videlicet de vinearum fidantiis, et angariis, terratico et de omnibus reditionibus, quas Normandis redere soliti sunt: [14.2] 'Quoniam quidem nos et patres nostri, avi et proavi Deum oravimus, ut imperatoris adventum partibus istis largiri dignaretur, per cuius adventum libertatis vigorem, et securitatis, consequeremur, nunc vero, pater sanctissime, et quia voluntas et potestas concessa est bene nobis faciendi, lacrimis oramus, ut de tanto periculo tributorum civitatem beati Petri eripias.' [14.3] Apostolicus itaque pietate divina correptus super civitatis longa afflictione condolens, patriarcam Aquileiae, aliosque cardinales et Girardum specialiter cardinalem suum presbiterum, virum valde venerabilem et discretum, ad imperatorem direxit, qui foras in prefato loco castrametatus erat, expostulans, ut comiti Rogerio de Ariano preciperet eiusque baronibus, ut fidantias et omnes redditus, quos de hereditatibus Beneventanorum habere solitus erat, quietas dimitteret. [14.4] Imperator itaque, precibus Apostolici acceptis, nec mora, vocari fecit prefatum comitem, ut cum baronibus suis veniret, et sacramento interveniente, petitionibus Apostolici obtemperaret. [14.5] Comes itaque adveniens coram imperatore confessus est, se hoc iuravisse et confirmavisse tempore comestabuli Rolpotonis, qui pro civitate hoc petierat. [14.6] Denique barones, quos secum duxit, iurare coegit sicut Apostolicus exigebat: in primis Alferius Draco, et Robertus de la Marca, et Bartholomeus de Petra Pulcina, et Tadeus de la Greca, et Girardus de Lanzulino, et Sarolus de lo Tufo, et sic iuraverunt: [14.7] 'Iuro et promitto, quod ab hac hora in antea non queram nec queri permittam de cunctis hereditatibus Beneventanorum fidantias, angarias, terraticum, olivas, vinum, salutes, nec ullam dationem, scilicet de vineis, terris aspris, silvis, castaneetis, et ecclesiis. [14.8] Et liberam facultatem tribuo in hereditatibus Beneventanorum venandi, aucupandi, et in eis et de eis quodcumque voluerint faciendi, et per hoc mercatum civitati non disturbabo nec disturbari consentio. [14.9] Haec omnia attendam bona fide sine fraude.' [14.10] Et taliter eis iurantibus, precepit imperator, ut alios suos barones Montis Fusci vocaret ad iddem sacramentum faciendum. [14.11] Quibus actis, prefatus Girardus cardinalis cum sapientibus civitatis omnia haec domino papae retulerunt: hoc sacramentum factum est sexto die intrante mensis Septembris.[13]

Immediately after these words, the story continues thus:

[14.12] Altera autem die idem Girardus cardinalis cum iudicibus ad imperatorem tetendit, ut ab ipso comite et suis baronibus sacramentum huiusmodi acciperet. [14.13] Comes vero Rogerius sacramentum illud facere noluit, confitens se tempore preterito illud fecisse; suos vero barones de Monte Fusco iurare precepit: videlicet Raonem de lo Tufo, Accardum, Gemundum, Eternum, Onfridum ceterosque, qui circa Beneventum fidantias accipiebant. [14.14] Et his taliter actis, salvatori Deo et Innocentio papae gratias egimus, cuius virtute et gratia tantam consecuti sumus libertatem.[14]

As is evident, the matter of the appeal for the oath and then the rendering of it, which seemed definitive and closed with paragraph 14.11, is unexpectedly taken up again, with the narration, expressed what is more in a more or less similar manner, of a sequence of events for all practical purposes already recounted. In both paragraphs 14.3 and 14.12 Cardinal Gerard went to the emperor to make him ask the Norman barons for the renunciation of the tributes. In the same way, the contents of paragraph 14.13 correspond to paragraph 14.5 and also recapitulate paragraph 14.10: Roger of Ariano again declined to pronounce the oath personally but agreed to impose it on his own vassals. The correspondence between the contents of paragraphs 14.14 and 14.11 is also obvious: Both are, evidently, the narrative closing of the question of the oath of renunciation of the tributes. Table 5.1 is a synoptic table of these correspondences.

The duplication of information is explicable by thinking of the presence of a double redaction. Paragraphs 14.12–14 appear absolutely redundant (and partly contradictory in meaning) with respect to much of what precedes them. From a logical point of view, the transition between paragraphs 14.11 and 14.12 is revealed as unjustifiable; in 14.11, it is all finished, Cardinal Gerard could make his report to the pope, and Falco by recording the date closed the account of the negotiation officially and definitively. But precisely immediately afterward, the same Cardinal Gerard would go to the emperor in order that he might convince the Arianese to swear.

A fiscal provision of Count Roger of Ariano

Table 5.1 Synoptic table of correspondences, Falco of Benevento, *Chronicon Beneventanum*, 1137.14.1–14

[14.1] the judges of the city of Benevento go to Pope Innocent II to pray to him to intercede with Emperor Lothar, so that he may promote for them a fiscal exemption	
[14.2] request directed by the Beneventans to the Pope	[14.12] Cardinal Gerard goes to the emperor in order that the latter may ask from the Norman lords the oath of renunciation of the tributes
[14.3] the Pope sends the Patriarch of Aquileia and Cardinal Gerard to the emperor, in order that the latter may ask the count of Ariano to renounce the tributes he collects from the Beneventans	
[14.4] the emperor summons the count of Ariano and his vassals	
[14.5] the count of Ariano goes to the emperor and maintains to have already carried out that oath at the time of the constableship of Rolpoto, who had already asked it of him	[14.13] the count of Ariano declines to give that oath, maintaining to have already carried it out sometime ago
[14.6] then the count of Ariano makes his vassals swear: Alferius Draco, Robert de la Marca, Bartholomew of Pietrelcina, Tadeus de la Greca, Gerard de Lanzulino, Sarolus de lo Tufo	
[14.7–9] text of the oath	
[14.10] after this oath, the emperor orders the count to make his barons of Montefusco render one identical to it	[14.13] … but he makes his barons of Montefusco swear: Rao de lo Tufo, Accardus, Gemondus, Eternus, Humphrey and the others who received tributes in the vicinity of Benevento
[14.11] after this, Cardinal Gerard makes a report to the Pope; the oath is held on 6 September	[14.14] after this, the Beneventans render thanks to the Lord and to Pope Innocent, who helped them to obtain that benefit

It therefore is hypothesised that blocks 14.1–11 and 14.12–14 represent two redactions of the same episode. But why two redactions? And if it is so, what was the chronological order of their drafting?

The story conveyed in 14.12–14 is a sort of *mise-en-abîme* of the longer and more detailed story in the preceding paragraphs. It relates the same events but with extreme concision. Paragraphs 14.1–11, conversely, are an extended account that plunges into detail regarding the issue of exemption from feudal tributes:

1 The text of the speech is quoted in which the Beneventans pray to the pope to intercede with the emperor.
2 The names of the pope's two envoys to the emperor are reported in 14.3 while in 14.12 the patriarch of Aquileia is not mentioned and the Beneventan judges are part of the delegation.
3 The count of Ariano agrees to force the vassals to make the oath but refuses to render it personally and maintains he had made it already in the time of the constableship of Rolpoto of Sant'Eustasio; 14.13 lacks this chronological annotation.
4 The names of the barons who swear are different: in 14.6 they are Alferius Draco, Robert de la Marca, Bartholomew di Pietrelcina, Tadeus de la Greca, Gerard de Lanzulino and Sarolus de lo Tufo; in 14.13, *the barons of Montefusco* swear: Rao de lo Tufo, Accardus, Gemondus, Humphrey, Eternus, 'and others who received "guarantees" in the neighbourhood of Benevento'.
5 The precise text of oath rendered by the Normans is quoted (14.7).
6 In 14.11 the date of the oath is supplied (6 September); 14.14 lacks this chronological notation.

It seems, therefore, reasonable to hypothesise that the first draft of the episode encompasses paragraphs 14.1 and 14.12–14. It is necessary to suppose that 14.1 served as an introductory paragraph for paragraphs 14.12–14; otherwise, the expression *sacramentum huiusmodi* in paragraph 14.12 would not make sense. Very terse, this account provides the essential details of the event. The date can be inferred by combining a date given in the chronicle's preceding chapter (1137.13.4: *quinto die videlicet intrantis mensis Septembris*) with the phrase that opens paragraph 14.11, *his ita peractis*. At a later point, Falco decided to modify this account.

He particularly intended to render the representation of the episode more solemn, official and, above all, documented, so he enlarged it by inserting the fictitious speech of the Beneventans to the pope, the annotations concerning the presence of the patriarch of Aquileia, the chronological detail on Roger of Ariano's first oath of renunciation, the names of a series of important barons of Val Fortore, the precise text of the oath, the date.

It is not difficult to establish, in broad outline, the motivations for such an intervention. Falco was always very attentive not only to political but also to legal and fiscal data relevant to his city, and a measure like Emperor Lothar's on the tributes owed to the district's Norman feudatories was truly very important, so the notary-chronicler drove himself to underscore it with all the rhetorical and technico-historiographical devices at his disposal. However, it can be less simple to single out a contingent and precise events-based motivation for the editorial revision.

First hypothesis: after 1143

A first hypothesis would lead one to think that the chronological block from October to December 1137 could have been written by Falco after 1143.

That is to say, it would be possible to tie the revision to the episode of the 'theft' by Roger's chancellor, Robert of Selby, of the document confirming the exemption established by Lothar, a confirmation the Norman king granted in the first days of November 1137 and that was quoted by Falco in its entirety (1137.22.1-7); however, this transcription has been proven by Carlrichard Brühl on the basis of its diplomatic profile to have been a forgery.[15] For the singular episode we do not possess Falco's account but only the summary made by the Unknown Cistercian Monk of St Mary of Ferraria:[16]

> [Rogerius rex] rupit libertatem, quam eis fecerat tempore Anacleti et tempore Innocentii de exactionibus reddituum et angariarum, quibus Beneventani subpositi fuerant a Normannis, et per barones adiacentes Beneventanis illos plurimum infestabat. Mictunt itaque Beneventani ad regem supplicantes et exorantes, ut concessam libertatem eis conservaret. Mictit rex cancellarium suum Robertum

videre privilegium in Beneventum; quod videns tenuit, nec reddidit priusquam illud rescribat et regi ostendat. E[g]reditur igitur de Benevento cancellarius cum privilegio inlicentiatus. Beneventani infenstantur, affliguntur, et extra egredi metuunt. Capitur Beneventanus archiepiscopus in itinere a Thoma de Fenuculo ire volens ad summum pontificem. Fiunt note Apostolico molestie, quibus Beneventanus populus cotidie infestatur et affligitur.[17]

This was among the most terrible moments for Benevento. With a genuine surprise attack, the kingdom's chancellor, the Englishman Robert of Selby,[18] seized possession of the document through a pretext and fled the city. The Beneventans were left exposed to the reprisals of the neighbourhood's Norman barons, who did not hesitate to behave cruelly. Thomas of Fenucolo immediately had Archbishop Gregory arrested while he was going to Celestine II to draw the pope's attention to the complaints of the faithful Beneventan subjects.

After 1140 (the assembly of Silva Marca, near Ariano), the policy of Roger II was one of pacification, normalisation and reorganisation (political and administrative) of the newborn *Regnum*, both towards the cities and towards the feudal domains. The Hauteville was strongly committed to defining his own domination over the *Terra Beneventana* and over its chief town: regarding the first, by eliminating hostile feudatories and substituting for them others in his confidence; regarding the second – the genuine papal enclave in his *Regnum* – by endeavouring to reorganise Benevento's *libertates* and autonomy,[19] along with the fraudulent removal of the *privilegium* he himself had conceded: here, therefore, the captivity for life in Sicily of Roger Drengot and his wife and the subsequent suppression of the same county (with the consequent creation of the new county of Buonalbergo, secure from 1150, entrusted to Robert of Medania),[20] which, following a brilliant intuition of Errico Cuozzo, was truly Italy's first Norman county.[21] Inside this county, numerous fees had indeed been already assigned in 1139–40 to Thomas of Fenucolo, also named justiciar.[22]

This might be the political circumstance that pushed Falco to reinforce the story of the oath of fiscal renunciation. Around 1143 the situation in the Arianese county was particularly tangled: With the incumbent and his wife having disappeared, the *barones* remained on the field, especially those of Val Fortore and the valley of the Ufita.[23] In the first redaction, the notary-chronicler had treated the episode with relative conciseness. He had highlighted the count and mentioned only a few minor vassals, the *barones de Monte Fusco*. But things were considerably changed six years later: The *Regnum Siciliae* was by this time a political reality and was becoming an administrative one. Benevento was going through a very delicate moment of passage while its condition as extraterritorial city under papal dominion was being defined; moreover, from the moment at which the new and definitive Hauteville leadership needed to reorganise the feudal *contado* according to its own needs and requirements, so too was Benevento's relationship with the *contado* being redrawn.

Falco's urban chronicle, like the cartulary-chronicles of the great south-central monasteries, was the repository of the city's legal memory. The 1137 provision of fiscal exemption was important, even vital: And at that moment neither was a thorough account of it given, nor, above all, was the text quoted in the same manner as Falco did with the Rogerian document that confirmed it (the only document transcribed verbatim by Falco!) and that had now vanished because of the royal chancellor's dishonourable blitz.

Graham Loud, in a brief but acute intervention, has outlined a composite stratigraphy for the *ChBen* by ascertaining that it 'was thus written in stages, and not as a continuous whole'.[24] On the basis of considerations concerning Falco's attitude towards Roger II, it is Loud's opinion that the chronicle's account of the final months of 1137 was written 'soon after the events in question or after the peace between the king and Innocent II in the summer of 1139'.[25] According to Carlrichard Brühl, the part of the chronicle that presents the transcription of the privilege of confirmation conceded by Roger (1137.22: November 1137) was composed roughly between 1141 and 1142.[26] Loud deems 'inconceivable' the hypothesis that the idea both of including this transcription and of inserting a new redaction of the oath of the Arianese came to Falco after the autumn of 1143, since in that case the notary-chronicler would not have wasted the opportunity to insert 'some of his choicest invective to denouncing the fraudulence and untrustworthiness of the King'.[27] In truth such an objection does not seem insurmountable: Why should Falco have spoken badly of

Roger at the moment in which – albeit *a posteriori* – the sovereign conceded to the Beneventans what they had requested?

Second hypothesis: December 1137

There is, however, a second possible hypothesis regarding the chronological positioning of the second redaction of the episode of the renunciation of tributes.

With respect to 6 September 1137, the date of the oath, the geopolitical status of the Sannio was already starting to change at the beginning of October. The counteroffensive launched by Roger against the papal-imperial league was formidable; he violently seized Capua, then a good part of Alta Irpinia and the *Terra Beneventana*, including the lands of the count of Ariano. Naples[28] and Benevento then submitted to him (1137.17.2), 'not paying attention at all to fidelity to Pope Innocent'. But on 30 October Roger was harshly defeated by the allied troops led by his brother-in-law Rainulf of Alife at Rignano Garganica; the king took refuge in Salerno. It was at this point that the pro-Rogerian archbishop of Benevento, Rossemanus, asked the Hauteville to renew, in favour of the city of the Calore, the privileges that *supradictus imperator concesserat* (1137.21.2).

But at the end of November Rainulf reconquered the county of Ariano and again also subjugated its vassals, who were mentioned thus by Falco (1137.24.3): Alferius Draco, Robert de la Marca, Robert of Pietramaggiore, Robert of Potofranco *aliosque barones*. In the meantime, however, Benevento remained under Rogerian obedience. This might have been the circumstance that pushed Falco to reinforce the account of the oath of fiscal exemption: Benevento had changed party, but, given that in Ariano the anti-Rogerian standards waved again, the city intended to underline and to remember the concession on the part of the emperor of the exemptive measure. One observes how the first two of the barons named in 1137.24.3 correspond to the first two of the 'second' draft of the episode of the oath; both the lists, moreover, contain feudatories from Val Fortore (except, probably, Sarolus del Tufo). The feudatories *in servitio*[29] listed in the 'first' redaction of the episode instead were all barons of Montefusco who, with the exception of Rao de lo Tufo and Eternus, were named only that one time in the chronicle.[30] We have already emphasised then how, in the 'second' redaction, the oath of the Arianese vassals developed in two tranches: The six most important vassals of Val Fortore swore first, then, without being mentioned personally, the *barones Montis Fusci* (1137.14.10). Robert de la Marca and Bartholomew of Pietrelcina figured among the vassals of Val Fortore: It is a matter of two feudatories of fair importance, whom Falco had singled out previously for their one bold anti-Rogerian oath (1132.16.1). In the same manner, the presence in the 'first' draft of the episode of Gerard de Lanzulino and of Sarolus de lo Tufo is probably accounted for by the fact that these two died in the battle of Rignano (1137.20.6), so around two months after the oath of renunciation of tributes.[31]

In proper summary, the list of the oath-takers in the 'second' draft of the episode is composed from the count of Ariano's most important feudatories personally, territorially and politically, compared to the five barons of Montefusco mentioned in the 'first' draft (1137.14.13). The return of the Arianese vassals to the anti-Rogerian league through Rainulf's conquest at the end of November may have induced Falco to stress how they were also present at the performance of the oath asked of them by Emperor Lothar (Alferius Draco and Roberto de la Marca), including two individuals at that moment deceased (Gerard de Lanzulino and Sarolus de lo Tufo). A *terminus post quem* for the editorial variant – paragraphs 1137.14.2–11 – can be therefore identified at the end of November of 1137, the moment of the reconquest of the county of Ariano by the anti-Rogerian league.[32]

Apart from, however, the precise determination of the time of the draft, the ascertainment of the existence of a double redaction by the author for the episode of the oath of renunciation of tributes by the Arianese barons constitutes a further element of proof for two recent findings of Falconian criticism: (a) the chronicle was composed at very different moments temporally; and (b) even with this, it did not arise out of anti-Norman or anti-Rogerian aims, but as true and proper civic, urban, 'communal' historiography, much nearer to the genetic characteristics and to the purposes of the contemporaneous historiographical output of the cities of northern Italy than to the dialectics and to the ethnic or political trajectories of the 'Norman' historiography of southern Italy.[33]

Notes

This chapter was translated from the Italian by D. Routt.

1 Cited from this edition: Falco of Benevento, *Chronicon Beneventanum*, ed. E. D'Angelo (Florence, 1998).
2 A fourth manuscript example of the Falconian text is Biblioteca Nazionale, Naples, San Martino 364, paper, eighteenth century, copied (*descriptus*) from San Martino 66. A further manuscript copy is contained in the Biblioteca Nazionale, Rome, Fondo Gesuitico 404, paper, seventeenth century, the text of which was taken up again at the press of Caracciolo (see the following note).
3 On the manuscript tradition of the *ChBen*, see E. D'Angelo, 'Studi sulla tradizione di Falcone Beneventano', *Filologia Mediolatina* 1 (1994), 129–81, and *ChBen*, ed. D'Angelo, pp. lxxii–lxxviii. The *editio princeps* is found in *Antiqui chronologi quattuor*, ed. A. Caracciolo (Naples, 1626), pp. 178–343.
4 *Ignoti Monachi Cisterciensis Chronica Romanorum pontificum et imperatorum ac de rebus in Apulia gestis (ab an. 781 ad an. 1228)*, ed. A. Gaudenzi (Naples, 1888).
5 That some sort of prologue must have preceded the *ChBen* seems likely from the following assertion of Falco (1133.3.3): 'cumque predictus Girardus cardinalis rector preesset civitatis ... Falconem notarium, scribam Sacri palatii, istius opusculi factorem, sicut in principio legitur, iudicem civitatis ordinavit' ['And while this said Cardinal Gerard was acting as rector of the city he ... appointed the notary Falco, scribe of the Sacred Palace and the author of this little work, as one can read at its beginning, to be a city judge']. Trans., *Roger II*, p. 203.
6 See P. F. Kehr, 'Ergänzungen zu Falco von Benevent', *Neues Archiv der Gesellschaft für ältere deutsche Geschichtskunde* 27 (1902), pp. 445–68; D'Angelo, 'Studi', pp. 175–80.
7 D'Angelo, 'Studi', pp. 134–5.
8 The patriarchs of Aquileia were often of German nationality and in relationships of alliance with the emperors of Germany; so too the one mentioned here in Lothar's retinue, Pellegrinus I of Ourtenberg, patriarch from *c.* 1130 to 1161.
9 Gerard Caccianimici, Cardinal-Priest of Santa Croce in Jerusalem, who would then be Pope Lucius III from March 1144 to February 1145, formerly rector of Benevento in 1132–33, was papal legate in the same city. For the individual, see O. Vehse, 'Benevent als Territorium des Kirchenstaates bis zum Beginn der avignonesischen Epoche. I', *QF* 22 (1930–31), 87–160, here p. 137; D. Girgensohn, 'Documenti beneventani inediti del secolo XII', *Samnium* 40 (1967), 262–317, here p. 295.

10 Roger was the son of Jordan, count of Ariano, dead in 1127. He was, as all the Drengots, a bold adversary of Roger of Hauteville. For the individual, see E. Cuozzo, *Normanni: Feudi e feudatari* (Salerno, 1996), pp. 189–90.

11 Rolpoto of Sant'Eustasio – the surname would possibly refer to today's locality of Sant'Eustachio, a hamlet of the town of Montoro Superiore, sixteen kilometres south of Avellino; see *ChBen*, p. 259 – was head of the sworn association (commune) that took power in Benevento after the assassination of the papal rector William in 1128. He was later named constable by Pope Innocent II, when the city returned, for a certain period, into the hands of that party (see *ChBen*, 1132.15.3), given the mortal hatred Rolpoto harboured for the Anacletian rector Crescenzius. He went into exile to Naples together with Falco on 1 July 1134 and died a few days afterward in a shipwreck, together with his one son, when he attempted to emigrate to Pisa (*ChBen*, 1134.6.1–3).

12 Montefusco (a commune twenty-one kilometres south of Benevento) was the fee of the county of Ariano; see Cuozzo, *Normanni*, pp. 112–13.

13 'After this the judges and wise men of the city begged the lord pope that he intercede with the emperor that the latter free the Beneventans from an old affliction from which the city had suffered greatly and for a long time, namely the *fidantiae* from the vines, the *angariae, terraticum*, and all the other dues which the Normans had been accustomed to exact. "For we, our fathers, grandfathers and great-grandfathers have prayed to God that he deign to grant the coming of an emperor to these parts, through whose arrival we might secure freedom and security. Now indeed, most holy Father, since the opportunity and power to benefit us has been granted to you, tearfully we all pray that you release the city of St Peter from these burdensome tributes". Moved by Divine piety and sympathising with the city's long affliction the pope sent the Patriarch of Aquileia and other cardinals, and particularly his Cardinal priest Gerard, a venerable and discreet man, to the emperor, who was camped outside the city in the place mentioned above, requesting that he instruct Count Roger of Ariano and his barons freely to remit the *fidantiae* and all the other dues which they were accustomed to exact from the hereditary properties of the Beneventans. The emperor acceded to the prayers of the pope and without delay had the count summoned, that he come to him with his barons and grant, on oath, the pope's petition. Coming before the emperor the count confessed that he had [already] sworn to and confirmed what was requested on behalf of the city in the time of the Constable Rolpoto. Then he made the barons whom he had brought with him swear what the pope required. These were Alferius Draco, Robert de la Marca, Bartholomew of Pietrilcina, Tadeus de la Greca, Gerard de Lanzulino and Sarolus de lo Tufo, and

they swore thus: "I swear and promise that from this hour forward I shall not seek nor shall I allow to be sought from any hereditary property of the Beneventans *fidantiae, angaria, terraticum*, olive tax, wine tax, *salutes*, nor any *dazio*, whether from vines, uncultivated ground, woods, chestnut trees or churches, and I concede liberty for hunting and fowling in the hereditary properties of the Beneventans and to do with them whatever they want, and I shall not disturb the city market nor shall I allow it to be disturbed. I shall observe all this in good faith and without fraud". After they had thus sworn the emperor ordered that his other barons from Montefusco be summoned to take this same oath. Once this had been done Cardinal Gerard and the elders of the city recounted all this to the lord pope. This oath was taken on 6th September.' Trans., *Roger II*, pp. 224–5.

14 'The next day Cardinal Gerard and the judges went to the emperor to receive a like oath from the count and his [other] barons. Count Roger was unwilling to take the oath, saying that he had already previously taken it, but he ordered his barons of Montefusco to swear it, namely Rao de lo Tufo, Accardus, Gemundus, Eternus, Humphrey, and the others who had received *fidantiae* from Benevento. For these actions we gave thanks to God the Saviour and Pope Innocent, through whose virtue and grace we had been granted so important an exemption.' Trans., *Roger II*, p. 225.

15 Cf. *Rogerii II Regis Diplomata Latina*, ed. C.-R. Brühl, Codex Diplomaticus Regni Siciliae, Ser. I.ii(1) (Cologne, 1987), pp. 101–9. 'Con l'ipotesi della Falschung si spiegherebbe poi, secondo lo studioso tedesco, anche l'ambiguo comportamento dei Beneventani, otto anni dopo, nei confronti del cancelliere regio Roberto di Selby: questi, inviato in città dal re per controllare il documento, lo sottrae, lasciando repentinamente la città, senza però che nessuno dei Beneventani osi fermarlo o, in seguito, protestare presso Ruggero. Tale ricostruzione è convincente ma non fornisce prove certe di una "volontà" falsificatrice da parte di Falcone: non si può escludere, che egli fosse in buona fede all'atto di trascrivere *quella* versione; oppure ancora, se essa è opera diretta del cronista, è possibile che egli l'abbia effettuata senza poter disporre direttamente, sotto i suoi occhi, del testo originale'; *ChBen*, p. xxviii. 'With the hypothesis of Falschung would also be explained then, according to the German scholar, the ambiguous behaviour of the Beneventans eight years later toward the royal chancellor Robert of Selby: The latter, sent into the city by the king to check the document, takes it away and suddenly leaves the city, without, however, any of the Beneventans daring to stop him or, later on, to protest to Roger. Such a reconstruction is convincing but it does not provide proof certain of

a falsifying "will" on Falco's part: It cannot be ruled out that he was in good faith in the act of transcribing *that* version; or else yet, if it is the direct word of the chronicler, it is possible that he carried it out without being able to have at his disposal directly, under his own eyes, the original text.' Translation from Italian by D. Routt.

16 *Ignoti Monachi Cisterciensis Chronica*, p. 27.

17 '[King Roger] violated the freedom that he had made for them in the time of Anacletus and the time of Innocent from the tributes of revenues and forced services to which the Beneventans had been subjected by the Normans, and, through the barons neighbouring to the Beneventans, he attacked them many times. And so the Beneventans sent word to the king, supplicating and moving that he might preserve the liberty conceded to them. The king sent his Chancellor Robert to view the privilege in Benevento; seeing which, he kept it and he did not return it before he wrote back and disclosed it to the king. The chancellor therefore left from Benevento with the privilege without having obtained permission. The Beneventans were attacked, were injured and were afraid to venture out. The Beneventan archbishop, wanting to go to the high pontiff, was seized on the way by Thomas of Fenucolo. The troubles by which the Beneventan people daily were attacked and injured were made known to the Apostolic One.' Trans. D. Routt.

18 On this individual, see E. Caspar, *Ruggero II e la fondazione della monarchia normanna di Sicilia*, Ital. trans. (with an introductory essay from O. Zecchino) (Rome, 1999), pp. 187–8, and, on the episode, pp. 311–12.

19 See, for all, E. Jamison, 'The Norman administration of Apulia and Capua especially under Roger II. and William I., 1127–1166', *Papers of the British School at Rome* 6 (1913), 211–481, here pp. 257–8; E. Mazzarese Fardella, 'Problemi preliminari allo studio del ruolo delle contee nel regno di Sicilia', in *Società, potere e popolo nell'età di Ruggero II* (Bari, 1979), pp. 41–54; E. Cuozzo, '*Quei maledetti Normanni'. Cavalieri e organizzazione militare nel Mezzogiorno normanno* (Naples, 1989), pp. 105–13.

20 See Cuozzo, '*Quei maledetti Normanni'*, pp. 123–5; Cuozzo, *Normanni*, p. 97.

21 See E. Cuozzo, 'Intorno alla prima contea normanna nell'Italia meridionale', in E. Cuozzo and J.-M. Martin (eds), *Cavalieri alla conquista del Sud: Studi sull'Italia normanna in memoria di L.-R. Ménager* (Rome, 1998), pp. 171–93.

22 Thomas of Fenuculo – *Fenuculum* is a castle, today ruined, that rose on a rocky hill on the bank of the river Calore near the today's locality

of Ponte Finocchio, about ten kilometres north of Benevento; cf. E. Cuozzo, *Catalogus baronum. Commentario*, FSI 101 (b) (Rome, 1984), p. 74; *ChBen*, p. lviii – son of Hugh of Castelpoto (known also as Hugh Infante senior), and brother of Hugh Infante junior, was baron of the *Terra Beneventana*; see Cuozzo, *Catalogus*, pp. 278–9; G. A. Loud, 'Monarchy and monastery in the Mezzogiorno: The abbey of St. Sophia, Benevento and the Staufen', *Papers of the British School at Rome* 49 (1991), pp. 287–8. For his loyalty to Roger, at the end of the hostilities, various possessions *in capite de domino rege* were recognised to him: Finocchio, Torrecuso, Castelpoto, Apollosa, Torre Palazzo, plus various fees *in servitio*.

23 Apart from those mentioned by Falco, remembered above all were the counts of Greci, descendants of the Gerard attested in the *ChBen* in 1121, probably the brother of Jordan of Ariano. See E. Jamison, 'The Abbess Bethlem of S. Maria di Porta Somma and the barons of the Terra Beneventana', in *Oxford Essays in Medieval History Presented to Herbert Edward Salter* (Oxford, 1934), pp. 33–67 [reprinted in E. Jamison, *Studies on the History of Medieval Sicily and South Italy*, ed. D. Clementi and T. Kölzer (Aalen, 1992), pp. 123–57].

24 G. A. Loud, 'The genesis and the context of the Chronicle of Falco of Benevento', *ANS* 15 (1993), 177–98, here p. 189.

25 Loud, 'Genesis', p. 188.

26 See *Rogerii II Regis Diplomata Latina*, pp. 131–3.

27 Loud, 'Genesis', p. 189.

28 See *ChBen*, 1137.16.1–17.2.

29 For this definition, see, for example, Cuozzo, '*Quei maledetti Normanni*', pp. 53–61.

30 Doubt remains whether the Eternus of the *ChBen*, 1137.14.15, may be identified with the knight captured by Jordan of Ariano in one of his encounters with the Beneventan constable Landulf della Greca in 1119 (see *ChBen*, 1119.2.11).

31 And of importance is the presence in the group of those taking oaths of Alferius Draco and Robert de la Marca: They are two of the vassals of the count of Ariano who at the end of November are resubjugated by the anti-Rogerian coalition, which appears in the lands of the county under the livery of the knights led by Rainulf of Alife (*ChBen*, 1137.24.3).

32 Such a reconstruction would coincide also with the idea of Loud, 'Genesis', p. 191: 'most of the long 1137 section was probably written during the autumn of that year, though it seems that the last part, dealing with the royal privilege to Benevento and the negotiations at

Salerno, was written separately and rather later ... When this last part of the 1137 section was written must depend on when the forged text of the royal charter was compiled, but at the latest this was before 1143, and might have been some time earlier.'

33 See *ChBen*, pp. xlvi–xlviii, and E. D'Angelo, *Storiografi e cronologi latini del Mezzogiorno normanno-svevo* (Naples, 2003), pp. 36–8.

Part II

Identities and communities

6

Crucible of faith: *fitna* in the *Travels* of Ibn Jubayr

Joshua C. Birk

In 1183 Ibn Jubayr, a Muslim bureaucrat from Granada, undertook a two-year pilgrimage to Mecca. He recorded the journey in a text known as his 'Travels' (or *Riḥla*), which both depicts the Almohads as the rightful rulers of the Islamic world and argues that Islam is properly practised only in their territories. During the rest of his journey, he describes a chaotic, fractured political world in which devout Muslims frequently suffer abuse. Throughout his *Riḥla*, he communicates this disorder by frequently using the word *fitna*. Scholars who have examined the use of *fitna* in the *Riḥla* have asserted that for Ibn Jubayr it meant both 'civil strife' and 'temptation'. Netton argues that *fitna* was central to the alienation that Ibn Jubayr experienced in Christian territories. He observes that the author's use of the word 'often signals, or reinforces, a certain sense of the strange, the alien or the exotic' that threatened to cause Muslims to deviate from their faith.[1] Davis-Secord expands the importance of *fitna* further. She argues that Ibn Jubayr sees it as 'the primary cause of disunity in the world'.[2] Granara stresses that Ibn Jubayr uses *fitna* to describe the 'attraction to the "other" and the crossing of religious, social, legal, and linguistic boundaries'.[3]

A focused exploration of the term allows us to see shifts in both the frequency and meaning of *fitna* throughout the text and to divide Ibn Jubayr's use of it into three phases. In the first phase, when Ibn Jubayr travels through polities governed by Muslims – the *Dār al-Islām* – *fitna* describes wars and skirmishes within the Muslim community or characterises Muslims whose deluded misbelief has created a zealous fanaticism threatening the whole community. Ibn Jubayr's use of *fitna* increases dramatically in the second phase, when he travels through the kingdom of Jerusalem.

He applies *fitna* to conflicts between Christian and Muslim leaders, and, more importantly, he uses it to describe the legal protections, physical security and material comforts that Christian overlordship offers Muslim subjects. These protections and comforts have lulled Muslims into complacency whereby Christian rule is tolerated and ultimately their religious devotion threatened. At the same time, he pairs these uses of *fitna* with Quranic verses that invoke the idea of divine testing in which God inflicts hardships on the devout to evaluate the strength of their religious conviction. In this usage, *fitna* is not an exclusively negative concept threatening Muslim unity. It instead is the moment in which God tests the faith of Muslim communities in ways that ultimately reaffirm their religious devotion. In the third phase, Ibn Jubayr describes Sicily, where he encounters William II, a Christian king who has adopted, at least superficially, cultural practices of an Islamic court and has surrounded himself with Muslim administrators and servants. In Sicily the clear cultural markers between Christian and Muslim observed in the rest of Ibn Jubayr's journey collapse, which initially leaves him positively disposed to Sicily's Christian king. However, Ibn Jubayr became increasingly critical of Sicilian Christians over the duration of his stay. He adapts *fitna* to refer both to the allure of the Sicilian ruler's wealth and power and to acts of toleration and kindness extended by Sicily's Christians to Muslims, both of which threatened to pull Muslims away from their faith. Ibn Jubayr uses *fitna* not to critique the devotion of Sicily's Muslims but to extol their adherence to the faith in the face of these divine trials.

Ibn Jubayr and the *Riḥla*

Ibn Jubayr reveals little about himself in the *Riḥla*. Most of what we do know about him comes from the fourteenth-century writings of Lisān al-Dīn ibn al-Khaṭīb[4] and Ahmed ibn Mohammed al-Makkari, a seventeenth-century elaborator on al-Khatib's work.[5] Ibn Jubayr undertook a pilgrimage to Mecca in 1183; his detailed account of the journey established his reputation as an intellectual and a skilled writer while demonstrating his deep conviction and devout religious faith. His remarks about his motivations for the journey are oblique; he mentions only a desire to fulfil his obligation for pilgrimage.[6] Netton argues that the text demonstrates that *kaffāra* (expiation of sin) provided the primary motivation, though Ibn Jubayr revelled in the acquisition of *ilm* (knowledge).[7] Philips argues that Almohad rulers sent Ibn Jubayr to gather information about the eastern Mediterranean in the wake of Saladin's victory over the Fatimid caliphate and that Ibn Jubayr crafted his account to demonstrate his pious learning and elevate his own reputation.[8] Dejugnat asserts that his *Riḥla* was a piece of Almohad propaganda, a foreshadowing of an Almohad *jihād* that would liberate Sicily's Muslims before sweeping into Egypt and finally Damascus.[9] After his return from the *hajj*, Ibn Jubayr became a pious scholar specialising in interpretation of hadith. At his death in 1217, he had a reputation for piety and erudition that seems to have come primarily from his account of these initial pilgrimages, *The Travels (Riḥla) of Ibn Jubayr*. This text served as a template for other works in the emergent Arabic genre of travel literature, most notably the *Riḥla* of Ibn Baṭṭūṭa.[10]

Ibn Jubayr's *Riḥla* documents more than two years of journeying that took him from Granada to Mecca and back. Embarking in February 1183, he took a Genoese ship from Iberia to Alexandria, then south along the Nile, before crossing the Red Sea and arriving in Mecca. He spent almost two-thirds of a year at Mecca and participated in a host of rituals. On his return trip he travelled to Baghdad, Damascus and the kingdom of Jerusalem, before securing transport on a Genoese vessel to cross the Mediterranean. In October 1184, his vessel sank in the strait of Messina, and Ibn Jubayr escaped the shipwreck primarily due to the generosity of the Sicilian king. After recovering in Sicily, he travelled overland across the island's northern coast, eventually chartered a vessel to Granada and reached home in March 1185, just over two years after he had set forth.

Ibn Jubayr's account of this journey provides a wealth of invaluable information about Muslim communities along the pilgrimage route from Iberia to Mecca. He kept a detailed diary, and these initial writings provided the material of the *Riḥla*.[11] Rather than crafting a cohesive image of his travels, he offers insight into his impressions of specific moments. This allows us to see how the author's views evolve over the course of his travels. This clarifies why Ibn Jubayr gives a positive initial description of William II and the Islamic cultural influences within his court, only to depict William's adoption of the trappings of Islamic rulers as something sinister by the end of his stay in Sicily. It elucidates the seeming contradiction between his blanket condemnation of Muslims living under Christian rule in the kingdom of Jerusalem, only later to praise the piety of Sicilian crypto-Muslims, ostensible converts to Christianity under pressure from a Christian king.

Meaning of *fitna* and *Riḥla*

Fitna, commonly translated as 'temptation', 'discord' or 'civil strife', has a wide range of connotations, which make it challenging to understand the ways in which Ibn Jubayr uses the term.[12] The word's root refers to smelting, the application of heat to ore to remove impurities from metals.[13] In the Qur'ān, *fitna* usually alludes to divine testing in which 'all individuals will be put to a test according to God's Will'.[14] God inflicts hardship on humans as a way to discern their faith and separate the pious from the impious. However, the term can also refer to divine punishment, and this conflation of punishment and testing makes the term difficult to interpret. In addition, even within the Quranic text, *fitna* several times evokes not divine testing but discord within the Muslim community.[15]

Fitna took on a different meaning in the years shortly after the prophet Muḥammad's death. The murder of the third caliph 'Uthmān sparked an internal crisis of succession that threatened to tear apart the newly formed Muslim community. Inside the Sunnī community, this vicious internal conflict became known as the first *fitna*, and the word assumed an increasingly political dimension, a signal of a collapse of harmony among Muslims that threatened to fracture the community.[16] The word also acquired increasingly negative connotations expressed in political and legal theories condemning participation in any sort of revolution.[17] Ibn Jubayr's contemporary Ibn al-Athīr argued that the word had taken on an entirely different negative meaning, not evocative of a trial of faith and instead referring to war, internal conflict and disbelief.[18] In modern political discourse, *fitna* is entirely divorced from the notion of divine testing and is associated with manipulation

Crucible of faith 117

and conspiracy that lead to the underdevelopment and military weakness of Arab polities.[19]

The genre of the *riḥla* – Islamic travel literature – focuses both on the author's pursuit for knowledge and the writer's account of wonders found on the journey.[20] The genre emerged as a response to the problem of *fitna*, intense political divisions within the Muslim world.[21] The Malikite jurist Abū Bakr ibn al-'Arabī (d. 1147–48) observed a Muslim world in which the caliphate's authority had collapsed and factionalism had riven the unity of the *umma*. However, he imagined *riḥla* as a way to reveal the common centre of the Islamic world and heal the rifts created by *fitna*. Ibn Jubayr expanded on Abū Bakr ibn al-'Arabī's template for *riḥla*: he wrote an account of the *hajj* in an attempt to establish both the pilgrimage itself and the sacred space of Mecca as a unifying centre for Islam, while simultaneously establishing the legitimacy of the Almohad caliphs as the answer to the political divisions plaguing the Muslim community.

Fitna in the *Dār al-Islām*

The theme of religious discord among Muslims features prominently throughout the *Riḥla*. Exploring how Ibn Jubayr centres these conflicts is necessary to understanding his conceptualisation of *fitna*. His travels through the *Dār al-Islām* comprise roughly four-fifths of the manuscript. Throughout this portion of his *Riḥla*, *fitna* describes violent battles and skirmishes or misguided religious beliefs that threaten the Muslim community's unity. He bemoans the sectarian divisions that inhibit Muslim unity and particularly notes the poor treatment of pilgrims to Mecca by their fellow Muslims.

Ibn Jubayr's outrage becomes most acute when he reaches the Hejaz, the western portion of the Arabian Peninsula containing the holy sites that should unify the Muslim community.[22] Instead, the region's Muslims 'are schismatics and partisans who have no religion and have splintered into diverse ideologies'[23] and rob and abuse Muslim travellers. Pilgrims receive worse treatment from their co-religionists than do the region's Jews and Christians. In the face of these abuses, Ibn Jubayr asserts that only violent conquest by the Almohads, his patrons, can heal these rifts.[24] He links the legitimacy of Almohad political rule with the correctness of religious practice in his homeland: 'There is no Islam except in the territories of the Maghreb,' a region spared the sectarian divisions plaguing the Hejaz.[25] These divisions undermine the integrity of the community of believers. This disunity manifests itself in financial abuses Muslims suffer at the hands of co-religionists in the Hejaz. The seizure of their wealth undermines unity, overturns religious hierarchy and reduces Muslims to the status of Christians and Jews, 'as if they were a part of the population of *dhimmah*'.[26]

When Ibn Jubayr travels through lands governed by Muslim rulers, he uses *fitna* in one of two ways, both reinforcing this issue of the internal division among Muslims. First, the term describes violent internal strife among Muslims, ranging from civil wars to smaller-scale conflicts among Muslim travellers. When travelling through Egypt, he comments on the burned-out husks of buildings damaged in 1168/69 and uses them to reference 'the *fitna* at the end of the Fatimid dynasty'.[27] Here, Ibn Jubayr alludes to attempts by the Fatimid vizier Shāwar to resist the Frankish invasion of Amalric of Jerusalem in late 1168. Shāwar set fire to large parts of Fusṭāṭ in an effort to halt the advance of Amalric's forces and deny the city to his opponents.[28] Shāwar would eventually pay Amalric 100,000 dinars to end his offensive but was himself executed when Shīrkūh, Saladin's uncle, took control of Egypt in 1169.[29] *Fitna* here conflates the destruction caused by the Fatimid attempts to stave off Frankish invasion with the disruption caused when one Muslim dynasty seized control of Egypt from another.

When he reaches Mosul, he first describes the city's fortifications and praises its walls and tower that secured it against 'incidents of *fitna*'.[30] *Fitna* here refers obliquely to Saladin's unsuccessful siege of the city in 1182, just a year before Ibn Jubayr's pilgrimage. In both cases, Ibn Jubayr employs *fitna* when making observations on civic architecture, an opportunity to evoke memories of the recent conflict between Muslim polities. Throughout the text, Ibn Jubayr explicitly praises Saladin, the singular exception to the division and misrule he observes elsewhere in Muslim lands during his pilgrimage.[31] Saladin's protection of pilgrims in his territory and safeguarding of them while travelling in Arabia elevate the legitimacy of his rule in Ibn Jubayr's eyes. When he encounters political misbehaviour or religious malpractice while traversing Saladin's territories, he frequently excuses the sultan of responsibility for these vices. These couched references to *fitna* fit within Ibn Jubayr's larger pattern of absolving Saladin of culpability for political conflict between Muslim powers. He acknowledges the physical structures that testify to the violent conflict between Muslims rulers but refers to the *fitna* itself in an oblique fashion that does not assign blame or even identify the parties involved in the conflicts.

He also describes smaller skirmishes between Muslim ethnic groups as *fitna*. When travelling through Yemen, at the spring of Dinquash, the crush of travellers sparked animosity between the Oghuz – a local Turkman tribe – and Arab caravan masters from the Qudah'ah tribe. Fortunately, the dispute never escalated to violence. 'This almost became a *fitna*, but God prevented it.'[32] Similarly, while in the markets of Mina east of Mecca, he observed the beginnings of an armed brawl between Mecca's black (*sūdān*) inhabitants and visiting Turks from Iraq, but 'God offered protection from the evil of this *fitna*' and quickly pacified the hostilities. In both cases, Ibn Jubayr witnesses the beginnings of conflicts or near-hostilities and thanks God for preventing a *fitna* from escalating into more widespread internal conflicts.

The second way Ibn Jubayr uses *fitna* when travelling through Muslim lands is to characterise those consumed by religious misbeliefs threatening to Muslim unity. When leaving Aleppo he sees the mountains of Lebanon and reflects on the castles belonging to the Nizari Isma'īlīs, whom he condemns as heretics. He stresses how their leader, Rashīd ad-Dīn Sinān, deluded his followers, 'deceived them with idle words and phantasms', 'bewitched them with his artifice'[33] and misled them into accepting his divinity and obeying his every command. Ibn Jubayr appeals to God and offers 'praise to Him from whom we take refuge from the *fitna* in religion'. *Fitna* here describes those enraptured with fanatical misbelief inimical to the Muslim community.

Ibn Jubayr uses *fitna* similarly to characterise the behaviour of a deluded mob of worshippers at a sacred well near Mecca. Ibn Jubayr relates a false rumour believed by pilgrims: that the well's water had risen miraculously.[34] Ibn Jubayr's companions disproved this rumour, but kept this information to themselves for fear that they would be assailed by the mob for debunking the miracle. When describing the initial spread of these rumours, Ibn Jubayr adds 'God protect us from this *fitna*'. Enraptured by their misbelief, devout pilgrims are transformed into a zealous mob capable of attacking fellow Muslims. Like with the Nizari Ismaʿīlīs, *fitna* here describes a state of deep delusion potentially leading to violence and conflict among Muslims.

Fitna and the Crusader States

Ibn Jubayr's use of *fitna* shifts dramatically when he moves towards lands ruled by Christians. The concept becomes the centrepiece of his writing. He uses *fitna* in the roughly twenty pages describing his journeys through the kingdom of Jerusalem as many times as in the previous 250. While *fitna* initially defined the state of conflict between Muslim leaders, the term begins to describe the war between Muslims and Christians as well. Ibn Jubayr centres his definition on the material conditions that lead Muslims to tolerate Christian rule. At the same time, he references Qur'anic verses that urge Muslims to see the material benefits of Christian lordship as a divine test of the strength of their faith.

As he enters the kingdom of Jerusalem, he takes note of 'The fire of *fitna* that flares up between the two parties of Christians and Muslims'[35] and 'The *fitna* occurring between Muslim emirs and their [Christian] kings'.[36] Notably, Ibn Jubayr envisions an interreligious conflict that does not have the disruptive effect that he observed in *fitna* between Muslims. This new form of *fitna* occurs only between elites, with no visible effect on the inhabitants of these territories. 'The warriors test themselves at war, while the masses are in good health, and the earth belongs to the victor.'[37] Ibn Jubayr's picture of a conflict that only affects the elites belies the nature of the conflict between Saladin and the Crusader States in the period. After the kingdom of Jerusalem's armies were defeated by Saladin in 1179, they adopted a Fabian strategy of harassing Saladin's forces and degrading his ability to remain in the field while avoiding pitched, open-field battles.[38] In response, Saladin's forces devastated cultivated landholdings in an attempt to provoke the kingdom's armies into a direct attack. Ibn Jubayr jubilantly reports Saladin's victories in his 1184 campaign.[39] While travel and trade between Damascus on one side and Acre and Tyre on the other continued despite these conflicts, Ibn Jubayr must have seen the disruption in the lives of agrarian labourers, since he travelled across the territory where the battles were waged. As with his description of Mosul's walls, Ibn Jubayr obfuscates the impact of Saladin's campaigns against his co-religionists who lived under Christian dominion.

Initially, Ibn Jubayr pairs this new vision of elite *fitna* restricted to rulers and the military castes with praise for generosity and fairness that Christians extend to Muslims and he lauds their support for Muslim hermits at Mount Lebanon.[40] He presents Christian behaviour positively, primarily as a device for extending his critique of Muslim disunity and the abuse by Muslim elites of their co-religionists. His observations regarding Christian support of Muslim holy men remind the reader of abuse of Muslim pilgrims on the Hajj by rapacious Muslims controlling the route to Mecca; however, he never frames Christian generosity as a threat to the region's Muslims, as he would do in his description of Sicily.

When he enters territory directly ruled by Christians, Ibn Jubayr alters his use of *fitna* yet again by applying it both to positive treatment of Muslims by Christians and to the sexual temptation presented by Christian women. Ibn Jubayr unambiguously condemns the existence of Christian polities in lands once ruled by Muslims and continually appeals to God for their destruction. He bemoans how Muslim agrarian labourers tolerate Christian overlordship, but he initially blames this not on these Muslims themselves but on abusive Muslim lords whose unjust exactions from their peasants drive them to seek Christian overlordship. 'The group of Muslims complains about oppression from landowners of their faith, and they praise the behaviour of their adversary and their enemy, the Frankish landowner, and expect justice from him.'[41]

When observing the acquiescence of these Muslim communities to Frankish rule, Ibn Jubayr notes that '*fitna* has filled their hearts' and makes an appeal: 'May God protect us from this *fitna*.'[42] Here, the term invokes a 'captivation' that has pulled Muslims into error, but unlike the active ensorcellment ensnaring the Nizari Ismaʿīlīs, these Muslim farmers have succumbed to the placid toleration of Christian misrule because it offers them protection from abusive Muslim rulers.

However, at this moment, after using *fitna* with an exclusively negative connotation throughout the text, Ibn Jubayr cites a Qur'anic verse which turns the word's meaning on its head. He appeals to Muslims who struggle under the unjust exactions of Muslim lords to turn to God rather than yearn for improved conditions under Christian rulers: 'This is not but Your trial (*fitna*) by which You send astray whom You will and guide whom You will.'[43] The verse conveys the classic Qur'anic sense of *fitna* as a divine trial of faith dividing the pious from the impious.[44] In the Qur'ān, it is Moses who invokes this idea of divine testing shortly after condemning the Israelites for constructing the Golden calf in his absence and then suffering through an earthquake. Moses emphasises that God could have destroyed the Children of Israel for their transgression. Instead, he offered mercy for those who had believed in falsehoods but now repent. These penitents should see the hardship as a test of faith and put their trust in God for both forgiveness and protection. On the surface, this quote suggests that Muslims should see harsh treatment from Muslim lords as a test of faith rather than long for better circumstances from their religious enemies, but the verse's context widens its applicability. It stresses that God offers the opportunity for forgiveness and reconciliation to all who have ignorantly strayed into error, including the Muslims who have placidly accepted the temporal benefits of Christian rule.

While Ibn Jubayr initially presents a conciliatory image of Muslims living in the kingdom of Jerusalem and blames their acceptance of Christian rule on the abusive behaviour of Muslim lords, his views of these Muslims harden as he enters Tyre. This shift reminds us that Ibn Jubayr's writings reflect his notes and observations made as he travelled. His writings do not present axiomatic principles but instead capture his evolving impressions and reactions over the course of the journey. As he moves from a countryside of Muslim villages into the urban space of Tyre and Acre, he confronts signs of Christian domination that incense and infuriate him.[45] He sees these cities, with mosques converted into churches, as defiled space and links their physical debasement with the presence of the cross and impiety.

In his account of Tyre, Ibn Jubayr's description of a sumptuous Christian wedding ceremony expands his definition of *fitna* to include the material and sexual allures that might tempt Muslims to tolerate dwelling in Christian space. After describing the bride, he implores 'God [to] protect us from the *fitna* of this sight' and then recounts the wedding procession, with particular emphasis on the participation of Christian women.[46] Though Ibn Jubayr's use of *fitna* to underscore the earthly temptation presented by Christian women and the allure of a dominant Christian culture seems new, it reinforces the impermissibility of Muslim cohabitation in Christian space. He follows his description of the ceremony with an oral account of Muslims who fled Acre and Tyre when Christians captured it but later returned. Ibn Jubayr offers a brief Quranic verse, 'And God is predominant over His affair',[47] whose context, again, provides a metaphor for understanding the plight of Muslims living among unbelievers. Ibn Jubayr quotes a passage describing Joseph after his enslavement and sale to al-'Azīz in Egypt. Al-'Azīz elevates Joseph to an esteemed position within his household, while al-'Azīz's wife continuously attempts to seduce Joseph. He parallels the plight of devout Muslims of Acre to Joseph, subject both to the sexual temptations of his master's wife and to the material allure of al-'Azīz's wealth. Muslim observers of the Christian wedding ceremony, like Joseph, were challenged to maintain their religious devotion in the face of the sumptuous luxury and sexual allure of the dominant culture. This verse frames the *fitna* of Christian society not simply as a temptation or source of captivation but as a trial of faith. It is a vehicle for Ibn Jubayr to call on Muslims to retain their commitment to God when confronted by the rich material worlds and tantalising fascinations offered by nonbelievers.

Ibn Jubayr no sooner offers this sympathetic depiction of Muslims under Christian rule than he retracts it. He rejects the permissibility of such actions: 'There is no forgiveness in the eyes of God for any Muslim to remain in communities within the country of the infidel … they will suffer hardships and horrors in [the infidel's] country.'[48] While this assertion falls in line with contemporary legal doctrine,[49] this explicit prohibition contrasts sharply with his more generous portrait of Muslim agrarian workers labouring under Christian rule and his later treatment of the Muslim population of the kingdom of Sicily. Ibn Jubayr's encounters with the teeming Christian masses who dominated Acre provoked this condemnation. Ibn Jubayr had grown increasingly frustrated with Muslims who tolerated Christian defilement of the city that Muslims once ruled. He cites both insults against the prophet Muḥammad and the uncleanliness of Christians, embodied by their mixing with swine, as the most egregious examples of the contamination endured by Acre's Muslims.

Fitna and the journey to Sicily

In Sicily, Ibn Jubayr entered a world that challenged his assumptions about the cultural markers dividing Muslims and Christians.[50] The clear boundaries between the respective faithful apparent thus far on his journey collapsed as he encountered Christians who adopted elements of Islamic culture and Muslims who practised their faith in secret while feigning adherence to Christianity. Initially, the lack of overt hostility to Islam and the adoption of Islamic culture positively disposed Ibn Jubayr to Sicilian Christians and their king, but he became increasingly critical of them as he came to understand the Sicilian milieu. Ibn Jubayr once again repeatedly uses *fitna* to describe Sicily but here the term describes the allure of Christians who adopted the cultural trappings of the Islamic world and acted magnanimously towards Muslims. Though this *fitna* threatened to subvert the faith of the island's Muslims, Ibn Jubayr ultimately chooses to depict the robust and enduring conviction of Sicilian Muslims, who remain devoted despite daunting tests of faith.

Ibn Jubayr's experiences in the Crusader States shaped his initial perceptions of Sicily. Fierce storms disrupted his return journey and left his vessel shipwrecked off the coast of Messina in December 1184. Ibn Jubayr escaped possible death or enslavement, in part, through the intervention of William II, king of Sicily. William's hospitality to Ibn Jubayr after the shipwreck created a positive impression, as did the Sicilian king's wealth. The ways in which William and Christians in Sicily treated Muslims stood in stark contrast with the abuses and attacks on his faith that Ibn Jubayr endured in the kingdom of Jerusalem. However, as he travelled across Sicily and conversed with the island's Muslims, Ibn Jubayr became increasingly critical of this Christian culture. Over his four-month stay, he came to see the munificence of Sicily's Christian king as a threat to the Muslim faith.

Fitna figures prominently in Ibn Jubayr's account of the island. He abandons any usage that hints at overt civil strife. Instead, he expresses curiosity about a Christian culture that adopted superficial Islamic trappings and he uses *fitna* to express horror at the potential for Christian generosity and benevolence to lure Muslims into a weakening or even rejection of their faith. At the same time, Ibn Jubayr does not repeat his earlier harsh criticism of Muslims living under Christian rule in the kingdom of Jerusalem. *Fitna* here highlights the trials that Sicily's Muslims endure in adhering to their faith as they faced these challenges.

Ibn Jubayr initially praises William II, a stark contrast with his insulting of Baldwin IV of Jerusalem, whom he compared to a pig. He presents William as a just king who heeds the recommendations of his Muslim advisers and surrounds himself with beautiful palaces. Ibn Jubayr bestows the greatest compliment he could offer a Christian king, that he resembles a Muslim ruler: 'In [William's] immersion in the amenities of the kingdom, in the arrangement of his laws, in the development of his procedures, in the division of the ranks of his men, in the magnificent pageantry of the sovereign, in showing his finery, he resembles Muslim kings.' After lauding the splendour of William's court, Ibn Jubayr subverts the meaning of William's wealth by depicting his vast resources and cultural sophistication as *fitna* that tests the convictions of highly educated Muslims: 'He has doctors and astrologers, who he vehemently covets and takes great care of, to such an extent that when he becomes aware of a doctor or astrologer travelling through his land, he orders their detention and grants him such a lavish livelihood that he forgets his home. May God by his grace protect Muslims from such *fitna*.'[51] Unlike the Muslim agrarian labourers who tolerated Christian overlordship because it protected them from abuse by Muslim landlords, Ibn Jubayr depicts Sicily's wealth as *fitna* that tempts scholars to abandon their Muslim homeland.

Ibn Jubayr uses encounters with converts to Christianity to show the disconnect between outward behaviour and an interior truth that permeates his account of Sicily. He paints a sympathetic picture of elite Sicilian Muslims who nominally converted to Christianity but maintained an interior Islamic faith and continued to express their devotion. The eunuchs who served in the Sicilian court embodied the disconnect that Ibn Jubayr observed between outward conduct and interior truth.⁵² These eunuchs were taken from Muslim territories as children and enslaved by the Sicilian king. They converted to Christianity and were raised and trained at the Sicilian court, but Ibn Jubayr insists that they retained their Islamic faith and observed Islamic rituals despite these trials.⁵³ These eunuchs may have been following the practice of *taqīya*, an Islamic legal concept allowing Muslims to conceal their true religious convictions in times of duress.⁵⁴ Ibn Jubayr not only praises the faith and charitable acts of 'Abd al-Masīḥ and other court eunuchs but also their interest in and hospitality towards Muslim pilgrims. Through their support of Muslim pilgrims, the crypto-Muslim eunuchs in the Sicilian court are the obverse of the predatory Muslim lords who exploited pilgrims around Mecca. Ibn Jubayr stresses that God bestows miraculous protection upon these eunuchs: 'They sometimes [pray] in a place where the eye of their king might fall upon them, but mighty and sublime God veils them. They do not cease their intentions and secret advice to Muslims in their ceaseless struggle of faith (*jihād*).'⁵⁵ Far from his previous assertion that Muslims could not live under Christian rule, Ibn Jubayr praises the way Sicilian eunuchs covertly persisted in their faith and argues that such actions support the larger Muslim community.

Ibn Jubayr applies the notion that surface acts of benevolence were *fitna* that could lure Muslims away from their faith not only to William II and the royal court but also to the Christian population of Sicily as a whole. In Palermo, Ibn Jubayr saw that Muslims could not publicly practise all elements of their religion and lived apart from their Christian neighbours, the result of violent anti-Muslim riots in the 1150s and 1160s.⁵⁶ But as he traversed the island he encountered Christian communities tolerant of public celebration of Islam and he writes about hearing the call of the muezzin at Castello di Solanto and registers his amazement upon observing Christian toleration of processions and feasts at the conclusion of Ramadan in Trapani.⁵⁷ These public expressions of faith were a vast departure from what he had seen in the Crusader States, but he frames Christian acceptance of these displays not as tolerance or kindness and instead, much like the actions of William II, as *fitna* testing the religious conviction of Muslims. He mentions that groups of Christians regularly greeted him and treated his party with kindness but for him these salutations had a 'pliant intent towards Muslims which could cause *fitna* to bring low ignorant souls'. He calls on Allāh to 'safeguard the people of Muḥammad ... from *fitna*'.[58]

Ibn Jubayr stresses apostasy as the greatest threat to Sicily's Muslims, but he uses *fitna* as a way to praise Muslims who maintained their faith in spite of this enticement.[59] He views 'ignorant souls', particularly women and children, as prone to apostatising from Islam.[60] Ibn Jubayr cites Quranic verses to stress the piety of these crypto-Muslims, just as he used similar verses to portray Muslims in the kingdom of Jerusalem sympathetically. He recounts the story of a prominent jurist, Ibn Zur'ah, a Sicilian *qāḍi* coerced by William II into converting to Christianity.[61] Despite the fact that conversion seems to have elevated Ibn Zur'ah's standing in the royal administration, Ibn Jubayr stresses that he was compelled to convert and did not do so to advance his career. Ibn Jubayr insists that Ibn Zur'ah secretly maintained his Muslim faith and presents a Quranic verse to defend him: 'Except for one who is forced [to renounce his religion] while his heart is secure in his faith.'[62] Rather than offer Ibn Zur'ah as an example of how cultural pressures erode the devotion of Sicilian Muslims, Ibn Jubayr uses him to illustrate how these Muslims triumph over these tests of faith and adhere to Islam even when tempted by the wealth and power offered by court service.

The idea of *fitna* permeates Ibn Jubayr's *Riḥla*, yet the multifaceted ways which he deploys the term resist simple classification. Initially, *fitna* has an entirely negative connotation. It illustrates internal conflicts and fascination with religious beliefs that divide the Muslims and provide the justification for Almohad dominion over the whole of the *Dār al-Islām*. In the Crusader States, *fitna* comes to refer to the placid toleration of Muslims who live under Christian dominion and are subject to the allure of the dominant Christian culture. Ibn Jubayr moves away from the negative meaning of *fitna* and stresses the idea of *fitna* as a test of faith. This idea of divine testing becomes more prevalent in Ibn Jubayr's account of Sicily, where a Christian ruler and populace co-opted elements of Islamic culture and exhibited a surface-level generosity towards Muslims. Ibn Jubayr used this final instance of *fitna* to praise the devotion and piety of Sicilian Muslims, even those who had publicly renounced their faith.

Notes

1. I. R. Netton, 'Basic structures and signs of alienation in the "Riḥla of Ibn Jubayr"', *Journal of Arabic Literature* 22 (1991), p. 36.
2. S. Davis-Secord, 'Bearers of Islam: Muslim women between assimilation and resistance in Christian Sicily', in M. Moore (ed.), *Gender in the Premodern Mediterranean* (Tempe, 2019), pp. 63–95.
3. W. Granara, *Narrating Muslim Sicily: War and Peace in the Medieval Mediterranean World* (London, 2019).
4. Ibn al-Khaṭīb, *Al-Iḥāṭa fī akhbār Gharnaṭa*, ed. M. 'Abd Allāh 'Inān, 4 vols (Cairo, 1973), vol. 1, p. 218. A. Kynsh, 'Ibn-Al Khaṭīb', in M. R. Menocal, R. P. Scheindlin and M. Sells (eds), *The Literature of Al-Andalus* (New York, 2000), pp. 358–71.
5. Ahmed ibn Mohammed al-Makkari, *The History of the Mohammedan Dynasties in Spain*, trans. P. de Gayangos, 2 vols (New York, 1964), vol. 2, pp. 400–1.
6. The narrative that Ibn Jubayr undertook his pilgrimage in recompense for being forced to consume alcohol stems from al-Makkari.
7. Netton, 'Basic structures and signs of alienation', p. 22.
8. J. Phillips, 'The travels of Ibn Jubayr and his view of Saladin', in K. V. Jensen, K. Salonen and H. Voght (eds), *Cultural Encounters During the Crusades* (Odense, 2013), pp. 77–8.
9. Y. Dejugnat, 'Ibn Jubayr', in K. Fleet *et al.* (eds), *Encyclopedia of Islam*, 3rd edn (Leiden, 2017), pp. 130–2.
10. J. N. Mattock, 'Ibn Baṭṭūṭa's use of Ibn Jubayr's *Riḥla*', in R. Peters (ed.), *Proceedings of the Ninth Congress of the Union Européenne des Arabisants et Islamisants* (Leiden, 1981), pp. 209–18. G. Calasso, 'Les tâches du voyageur: décrire, mesurer, compter, chez Ibn Jubayr, Nāṣer-e Khosrow et Ibn Baṭṭūṭ'a', *Rivista degli Studi Orientali* 73 (1999), 69–104.
11. E. Webber, 'Construction of identity in twelfth-century Andalusia: The case of travel writing', *The Journal of North African Studies* 5 (2000), 1–8, and Netton, 'Basic structures and signs of alienation', p. 25.
12. For a full lexigraphy see E. W. Lane, *An Arabic-English Lexicon* (Edinburgh, 1877), part 6, pp. 2335–6.
13. L. Gadet, 'Fitna', in B. Lewis *et al.* (eds), *Encyclopedia of Islam*, 2nd edn (Leiden, 1991), vol. 2, pp. 930–1.
14. N. Rouzati, *Trial and Tribulation in the Qur'an: A Mystical Theodicy* (Berlin, 2015), p. 30.
15. H. J. Fisher, 'Text-centered research: *Fitna* as a case study and a way forward for guests in the house of African historiography', *Sudanic Africa* 5 (1994), pp. 233–4.

16 J. Wansbrough, *The Sectarian Milieu: Content and Composition of Islamic Salvation History* (New York, 1978), pp. 119–29.
17 A. Tayob, 'An analytical survey of al-Ṭabarī's exegesis of the cultural symbolic construct of *fitna*', in G. R. Hawting and A.-K. A. Shareef (eds), *Approaches to the Qurān* (New York, 1993), p. 158.
18 Ibn Manẓūr, *Lisān al-'Arab*, 15 vols (Beirut, 1955–56), vol. 5, p. 3334.
19 R. Saad, 'War in the social memory of Egyptian peasants', in S. Heydemann (ed.), *War, Institutions, and Social Change in the Middle East* (Berkeley, 2000), pp. 240–57.
20 I. R. Netton, 'Riḥla', in B. Lewis *et al.* (eds), *Encyclopedia of Islam*, 2nd edn (Leiden, 1995), vol. 8, p. 328; H. Touati, *Islam and Travel in the Middle Ages*, trans. L. G. Cochrane (Chicago, 2010); C. F. Beckingham, 'The Riḥla: Fact or fiction?', in I. R. Netton (ed.), *Golden Roads: Migration, Pilgrimage and Travel in Medieval and Modern Islam* (Richmond, 1993), pp. 86–94.
21 Y. Dejugnat, 'À L'Ombre de la *fitna*, l'Émergence d'un Discourse du Voyage: À propos du *Tartîb al-riḥla* d'Abû Bakr ibn al-'Arabî', *Médiévales* 60 (2011), 85–101.
22 Netton, 'Basic structures and signs of alienation', pp. 29–30.
23 Ibn Jubayr, *Riḥlat Ibn Jubayr* (Beirut, 1964), p. 54.
24 Ibn Jubayr, *Riḥlat*, pp. 55–6.
25 Ibn Jubayr, *Riḥlat*, p. 55.
26 Ibn Jubayr, *Riḥlat*, p. 56.
27 Ibn Jubayr, *Riḥlat*, p. 29.
28 M. Brett, *The Fatimid Empire* (Edinburgh, 2017), p. 291; R. C. Smail, *Crusading Warfare 1097–1193*, 2nd edn (New York, 1995), p. 34.
29 H. Möhring, *Saladin: The Sultan and his Times, 1138–1193*, trans. D. Bachrach (Baltimore, 2008), pp. 27–9.
30 Ibn Jubayr, *Riḥlat*, p. 210.
31 For a detailed view of Ibn Jubayr's depictions of Saladin, see Phillips, 'The travels of Ibn Jubayr', pp. 75–87.
32 Ibn Jubayr, *Riḥlat*, p. 43.
33 Ibn Jubayr, *Riḥlat*, p. 229.
34 Though they refrain from sharing this information with the masses around the well for fear they would be attacked: Ibn Jubayr, *Riḥlat*, p. 119.
35 Ibn Jubayr, *Riḥlat*, p. 260.
36 Ibn Jubayr, *Riḥlat*, p. 261.
37 Ibn Jubayr, *Riḥlat*, p. 261.
38 J. France, *Western Warfare in the Age of the Crusades 1000–1300* (Ithaca, 1999) pp. 218–21; Smail, *Crusading Warfare*, pp. 34–37, 148–56.

39 Ibn Jubayr, *Riḥlat*, pp. 271–3.
40 Ibn Jubayr, *Riḥlat*, pp. 299–300.
41 Ibn Jubayr, *Riḥlat*, pp. 316–17. For more on the condition of Muslims living under Frankish rule, see B. Catlos, *Muslims of Medieval Latin Christendom, c.1050–1614* (New York, 2014), pp. 144–53, and B. Z. Kedar, 'The subjected Muslims of the Frankish Levant', in J. M. Powell (ed.), *Muslims under Latin Rules 1100–1300* (Princeton, 1990), pp. 135–74.
42 Ibn Jubayr, *Riḥlat*, p. 275.
43 Qur'ān, VII:155.
44 Rouzati, *Trial and Tribulation in the Qur'an*, p. 30.
45 On alienation, see Netton, 'Basic structures and signs of alienation', p. 31.
46 Davis-Secord, 'Bearers of Islam', demonstrates that Ibn Jubayr presents this woman not as a sign of sexual temptation but of Christian cultural domination. Also illustrating the allure of Christian culture, Ibn Jubayr describes a Sicilian church as provoking a similar *fitna*: Ibn Jubayr, *Riḥlat*, p. 306.
47 Qur'ān, XII:21.
48 Ibn Jubayr, *Riḥlat*, pp. 279–80.
49 S. Davis-Secord, 'Muslims in Norman Sicily: The evidence of Imām al-Māzarī's fatwās', *Mediterranean Studies* 16 (2007), 46–66; S. Getz, 'Permission to stay in "enemy" territory? Ḥanbalī juristic thinking on whether Muslims must emigrate from non-Muslim lands', *The Muslim World* 103 (2013), 94–106; M. Brett, 'Muslim justice under infidel rule: The Normans in Ifrīqiya, 517–555H/1123–1160 AD', *Cahiers de Tunisie* 43 (1995), 325–68; M. K. Masud, 'The obligation to migrate: The doctrine of hijra in Islamic law', in D. F. Eickelman and J. Piscatori (eds), *Muslim Travellers: Pilgrimage, Migration, and the Religious Imagination* (Berkeley, 1990), pp. 29–49.
50 For other readings of Ibn Jubayr's account of Sicily, see A. Metcalfe, *The Muslims of Medieval Italy* (Edinburgh, 2009), pp. 214–24; J. Johns, *Arabic Administration in Norman Sicily: The Royal Dīwān* (Cambridge, 2002), pp. 248–9; Granara, *Narrating Muslim Sicily*; J. C. Birk, *Norman Kings of Sicily and the Rise of the Anti-Islamic Critique: Baptized Sultans* (Cham, 2016), pp. 243–50; Davis-Secord, 'Bearers of Islam'.
51 Ibn Jubayr, *Riḥlat*, p. 298.
52 For more on the Sicilian eunuchs see Birk, *Norman Kings*, pp. 173–205.
53 For other evidence that Sicilian Muslims retained their Islamic faith, see J. Johns and N. Jamil, 'Signs of the times: Arabic signatures as a measure of acculturation in Norman Sicily', *Muqarnas* 21 (2004), 189–90.

54 Metcalfe, *Muslims of Medieval Italy*, pp. 195–6; Johns, *Arabic Administration*, pp. 250–4.
55 Ibn Jubayr, *Riḥlat*, p. 300.
56 Birk, *Norman Kings*, p. 247.
57 Ibn Jubayr, *Riḥlat*, p. 309.
58 Ibn Jubayr, *Riḥlat*, p. 301.
59 On conversion, see J. Johns, 'The Greek church and the conversion of Muslims in Norman Sicily?', *Byzantinische Forschungen* 21 (1995), 133–57.
60 Ibn Jubayr imagines children and especially women as seminal markers of Muslim cultural identity in Sicily. He expresses anxiety that young Muslims can use conversion to Christianity to escape parental authority. See Davis-Secord, 'Bearers of Islam'.
61 For more see Metcalfe, *Muslims of Medieval Italy*, pp. 222–33; Ibn Jubayr, *Riḥlat*, p. 313.
62 Qur'ān, XVI:106.

7

Bellum civile: urban strife and conflict management in early twelfth-century Benevento

Markus Krumm

Since the beginning of papal rule in Benevento in the mid-eleventh century, local conflicts within the urban community posed a challenge to the pope's authority.[1] A good example of this nexus between urban rule and papal authority is the *bellum civile* on 14 March 1114, which, despite being unusually well documented, has been little studied. This conflict seems at first glance to have been the result of a strange turn of events. In 1112, Archbishop Landulf II of Benevento and an urban judge hurried to Rome to warn Pope Paschal II of two conspiracies brewing in his unruly enclave. The plots, aimed at installing a rector without papal consent, were thwarted and ended with the pope's sentencing of a number of his Beneventan subjects to prison or exile in 1113.[2] Having salvaged his authority, Pope Paschal II sought to secure it further by appointing a local nobleman, Landulf of Greca, as his constable to defend the city from external threats. This move, however, occasioned new trouble for the pope. Only one year later (March 1114) he received word that the very same archbishop who had earlier warned him of Beneventan conspiracies now stood accused of undermining papal authority. The charges against Archbishop Landulf II were grave. He was said to have acted against the pope by encouraging citizens to establish a sworn association (*conspiratio*) against the pope's constable, by participating in a 'civil war' (*bellum civile*) that led to the invasion of Benevento's papal palace, by forcing Landulf of Greca to give up the *comestabilia* and driving him from the city and, finally, by acting in accord with the same Normans against whom the constable had been warring for almost a year. Paschal II responded without hesitation and demanded the archbishop's removal from office. Consequently, in October 1114 the Council of Ceprano deposed Landulf II for having 'acted against St Peter and our lord the pope'.[3] The archbishop's eclipse was, however, brief. He regained his former position in 1116 with the help of the monks of Montecassino.[4]

This chapter investigates the circumstances leading to the *bellum civile* in Benevento and the archbishop's temporary downfall as a case study in the complex dynamics of conflict management in southern Italy. The material basis for this study would appear to be excellent, since, thanks to Falco of Benevento, the Beneventan *bellum civile* is one of the best documented urban conflicts for early twelfth-century southern Italy. Falco witnessed the events and wrote around 3,500 words on the conflict and the pope's response to it.[5] However, Falco's account has never been comprehensively examined, only simply retold and more often than not misunderstood.[6] As I will show, this is partly due to the fact that Falco, who usually relates events in chronological order, chose to recount the *bellum civile* in a nonlinear, unchronological narrative. Moreover, it is usually overlooked that Falco's depiction of the archbishop's dealings is not neutral but instead paints a black-and-white picture intended to inculpate the archbishop in the escalation of violence. Writing judgementally, Falco sees the papal constable as having acted correctly and the archbishop wrongly, the former a *fidelis Beati Petri*, the latter an *adversarius Beati Petri*.[7] Accepting this verdict uncritically, some scholars have even labelled Archbishop Landulf as the Pope's local antagonist.[8] This interpretation does not withstand close examination.

Thus, Falco's account obscures many aspects of the history it purports to narrate. At the same time, it contains many details of the events and, although partisan, offers clear insights into the conflict's development. A critical reading of his eyewitness report will show how the conflict arose following the logics of honour and developed a momentum that the participants could only partially control. I draw from recent research on medieval conflicts and conflict management which underline the importance of the concept of honour for the medieval nobility and the role of mediators in communicative interaction between warring parties.[9] I am also heavily indebted to Graham Loud's research on Benevento and in particular to his seminal work on Beneventan charters and

Falco's chronicle.[10] This study follows in his footsteps by offering a rereading of Falco's text and drawing on the evidence of a hitherto unknown deathbed donation by Landulf of Greca which appears in the appendix.

Some scholars have seen the origins of the Beneventan *bellum civile* in latent tensions between the pope and the archbishop of Benevento.[11] There are, however, indications that Archbishop Landulf II acted as the pope's *locum tenens* in Benevento before the events in question. Besides his trip to Rome in 1112, we know of other encounters between the archbishop and Pope Paschal II in Benevento and elsewhere in the two years preceding March 1114.[12] This would speak for a good understanding between the two men. A remark in Falco's chronicle even suggests that the noteworthy absence of papal rectors in Benevento for several years after 1108 might be explained by the fact that the archbishop, ordained that year, performed that function himself.[13] This hypothesis appears all the more credible considering that, prior to becoming archbishop of Benevento, Landulf II probably was the cardinal priest of St Lawrence in Lucina and belonged to the closest circle of papal advisors.[14]

Paschal II's appointment of a constable for Benevento early in 1113 has been interpreted as a strategic move to weaken the archbishop's position and would as such seem to fit in the scenario of growing tensions between the pope and Landulf II.[15] Falco's chronicle, however, does not support this theory. The chronicler explains that Paschal II hoped to free the city from the Norman yoke by appointing Landulf of Greca.[16] Having suppressed the internal challenge to his authority, he intended to protect Benevento from external threat through the military service of the *comestabulus*. One may even assume that Archbishop Landulf II played a part in this decision. As Falco relates, the pope took counsel regarding the matter beforehand.[17] In appointing Landulf of Greca, the pope was probably following the advice of trusted local authorities such as the civic judges John and Persicus, later counted among Landulf's supporters.[18] It is also more than likely that the decision was made on the advice of the influential archbishop of Benevento, known to have been near the pope at this time.[19] There is, indeed, no reason for projecting the later conflict between Archbishop Landulf II, the pope and the new constable Landulf of Greca backwards in time to the constable's appointment in March 1113. On the contrary, everything suggests that the relationship between the pope and his men in Benevento was initially harmonious. The archbishop and the constable seem to have worked together in the first year without notable conflict. They even resided near one another with Landulf of Greca's residence, the *palatium Dacomarii*, only a stone's throw from the cathedral and archbishop's palace.[20]

Thus, it seems that the conflict did not arise from latent tensions between the pope and the archbishop. To understand the origins of the *bellum civile*, one must consider the relationship between Landulf of Greca and the Norman nobility surrounding Benevento. Five months after Landulf was appointed *comestabulus*, Prince Robert I of Capua and Counts Robert of Caiazzo and Jordan of Ariano joined 'with all the Normans of the neighbouring areas' in a sworn association (*coniuratio*) against him by making an oath 'to levy war and rapine against the Beneventans as long as Landulf remained as their constable'.[21] The local nobility's adamant opposition to Landulf of Greca is usually seen as a reaction against the constable's aggressive behaviour towards Normans in the urban hinterlands.[22] Falco, however, connects the Norman animosity with their hatred towards the *gens Longobardorum* and their envy of Landulf of Greca. He claims that they were struck by an *invidiae telum* as they watched Landulf 'daily increasing in fame and wealth'.[23] Taken seriously, these explanations become plausible motives when we consider Landulf's origin and his position relative to the regional nobility.

Falco's use of the term *gens Longobardorum* in this context is conspicuous, since it only appears this once in his chronicle. Historians, consequently, have generally rejected the theory that a Norman–Lombard antipathy is important in understanding Falco's text.[24] It remains, however, unclear why he speaks of the *gens Longobardorum* at this very point. A possible explanation is that Falco in this case evokes the long-standing *odium* of the Normans towards the Lombards in general with particular reference to the role of Landulf's family in this conflict. We learn something of Landulf's genealogy through his deathbed donation to the monastery of St Sophia in Benevento. There, he writes of himself as the son of a Lombard count named Madelfrid.[25] This information allows probable identification of Landulf's mother in the Beneventan charters as Sikelgarda, daughter of a certain Count Landulf.[26] Another of Landulf's ancestors was most likely an earlier *comes* Madelfrid who buried his nephew, fallen in battle against the Normans, in the same monastery endowed by Landulf of Greca.[27] Thus, it was perhaps a long-standing animosity between the Normans and Landulf's family to which Falco refers in speaking of the hatred of the *gens Longobardorum* that provoked the Norman opposition to Landulf the constable.

The second motive named by Falco, *invidia*, reflects his awareness of the prestige Landulf gained through his appointment as constable. Landulf himself underlined the importance of the *comestabilia* to his self-image. In his deathbed endowment, he styles himself *olim comestabulus* despite having been deposed more than five years earlier.[28] Years later, in September 1137, his son Daddaeus still referred to the title.[29] However, it was not only Landulf's newly won prestige that provoked the hostility of the local nobility, but rather more his gain in military capabilities. We know Landulf was wealthy. He owned estates between Benevento and Montefusco in the south, all located near those of nobles opposing him.[30] As constable of the Beneventan forces, Landulf was considerably more powerful than before.[31] Many of his local rivals would have viewed this as an unfair advantage and threat.

Although there are no concrete reports that Landulf was engaged in feuds with future members of the *coniuratio* before becoming constable, such conflicts are more than probable. Indeed, given the political landscape, smaller and larger feuds were seemingly the order of the day in the *Terra Beneventana*. Landulf's earlier engagement in this local warfare is indicated by his re-engagement in it after losing the *comestabilia* in 1118. He even fought side by side with Normans who had opposed him in 1114.[32] As Falco relates, it was Landulf's 'warlike spirit' which prompted the pope to appoint him as constable in the first place, as he apparently 'would not put up with injuries and menaces, and was every day a threat to his enemies'.[33]

The decisive factor in the conflict's escalation was that the sworn association against Landulf of Greca did not target only Landulf's territories but declared war on Benevento.[34] Shortly before the outbreak of the *civile bellum*, Landulf suffered a defeat at the hands of his enemies. The loss must have been considerable: Falco found it worth noting that 'twelve noble knights of the city were captured with all their war gear'.[35] It was in this situation, faced with the hostility of the local nobility sworn to depose constable Landulf and the complaints of the Beneventan citizens suffering under this feud, that Archbishop Landulf II and Abbot Rachisius of St Modestus informed the pope of their difficulties and asked for help.[36] According to Falco, Paschal II commissioned them 'to secure peace for the city and to help the poor, lest the Apostle Peter lose the city which he had by chance acquired; the terms however of the peace treaty they should leave to him'.[37] This is the point in Falco's narrative where the sequence of events becomes a list of charges against Archbishop Landulf. According to him, the archbishop's conflict with the *comestabulus* of Benevento arose as the former deviated from the orders given to him by the pope:

> But when the archbishop returned from Rome he acted differently from what he had been told and sent to Landulf the Constable saying that, constrained by the plight of the poor, he should resign as Constable until the time when the lord pope should come to Benevento. Afterwards, indeed, either for money and services or by the prayers of the citizens they would request the pope to restore him to his original honour; he did this only because the Normans were unwilling to make peace, for they were prevented, as has been said, by their oath. However, on hearing this, Landulf the Constable, in the Sacred Beneventan Palace in front of the *fideles* of St Peter, replied saying that he would never relinquish the constable's position unless he was captured and kept prisoner by main force. He also wanted to see what peace the Normans wanted to make with the Beneventans, and he wanted to send this peace to the pope in writing.[38]

Falco's report suggests that, on his return from Rome, Archbishop Landulf II immediately disobeyed the pope's instructions quite deliberately. However, closer examination of the archbishop's activities reveals that the chronicler is here not relating them in chronological order. This discrepancy between 'discours' and 'histoire', between the sequence of events as related in the text and the order in which they occurred, is quite unusual for Falco's chronicle. He effectively places the result of the archbishop's dealings, the request that the constable renounce the *comestabilia*, at the beginning of his narrative and then goes back in time to relate what had happened previously.[39] The occurrences between the archbishop's return and the scene with Landulf of Greca, a period of four days, are thus narrated in flashback, which fosters the incorrect impression that Archbishop Landulf II immediately began acting *aliter quam acceperat*.

Besides this, Falco's confusingly unchronological narrative has caused an important fact to be overlooked: Archbishop Landulf did not return from Rome alone but was accompanied by two cardinal legates, Cardinal Bishop Peter of Porto and a cardinal deacon named Romuald – probably Romuald of St Mary in Via Lata.[40] As Falco relates in flashback, all three had been sent by the pope to Benevento *pro pace invenienda*.[41] The chronicler even reports that Cardinal Bishop Peter delivered a lengthy speech in the *sacrum palatium* one day after arriving in Benevento in which he clearly said that Pope Paschal II had 'sent us, along with your archbishop, so that, with God's aid, you may have peace'.[42] Thus, the archbishop of Benevento was acting not alone but together with two cardinal legates as a papal delegate on a peace mission. This is important for understanding how he came to demand that Landulf of Greca lay down his office. I now will reconstruct the archbishop's dealings during the four days between his arrival and his act of disobedience against the pope by rereading Falco's chronologically murky narrative.

Landulf II's first task would have been to restore broken channels of communication between the hostile parties.[43] The archbishop was certainly well qualified for this, since he apparently had good connections to Landulf of Greca's enemies.[44] As we can gather from Falco's flashback narrative, the papal peace delegation was under considerable pressure from the outset. As they arrived and 'even before they had found their lodgings', a furious mob followed the mediators to the constable's residence, the *palatium Dacomarii*, and loudly threatened them: 'If you do not make peace at once as we want, we shall draw our swords and there will be death in the streets.'[45] Apparently, they also attacked the constable verbally by saying that 'they ought not to suffer a war and so lose their lives wretchedly just to keep one man in the constable's office'.[46] The next day, Falco reports, weapons were gathered in the cathedral tower to launch an attack on Landulf of Greca in his neighbouring palace and 'to expel him'.[47] One day later, the house of the civic judge Persicus was assaulted – presumably because he was close to the constable.[48] The situation was so threatening that Cardinal Bishop Peter of Porto left town the next day.[49] He seems to have taken his colleague, Cardinal Deacon Romuald, with him.[50] Thus, Archbishop Landulf II found himself henceforth responsible for negotiating peace alone.

Despite this, the archbishop apparently achieved some measure of success, since the Normans were prepared to accept a peace agreement.[51] Falco does not recount how this agreement was negotiated or what it entailed but instead focuses on the Normans' central precondition: Landulf of Greca's surrender of his *comestabilia*. This demand, which led to the ensuing *bellum civile*, was not the wish of the archbishop, who was only a mediator, but a condition set by the Normans. One may, however, suppose that the archbishop did indeed attempt to make the demand palatable to Landulf of Greca by invoking his pity for the suffering of the poor, as Falco relates, and assuring him that the thankful citizens would offer the pope money, services or prayers to restore him to his 'original honour'. Besides suggesting that loss of the *comestabilia* would not be permanent, Falco even hints that money was offered to Landulf to entice him to resign.[52] Falco's account also reveals something about the circumstances of the archbishop's negotiations with Landulf.[53] Apparently they took place in the *sacrum palatium*, where the constable had withdrawn on orders from the Cardinal Bishop of Porto.[54] The archbishop did not negotiate with Landulf personally but through delegated mediators.[55] Besides these participants, the constable's remaining supporters were also present at the negotiations.[56]

In sum, it seems that Archbishop Landulf II became involved in this conflict not by deliberately disobeying the pope but by following his orders to resolve the conflict with the Normans peacefully. According to Falco, Landulf of Greca initially even welcomed the papal peace initiative and accompanied Cardinal legate Peter of Porto to the *sacrum palatium*, where the cardinal publicly proclaimed the pope's orders in *conspectu omnium*.[57] Regardless of what Landulf thought of the peace efforts, by participating in this public ceremony he tacitly consented to the *negotium pacis*.[58] Why, then, did the mediators fail? Since peace negotiations usually aim at finding an acceptable solution for both parties to a conflict, the negotiators probably began by offering Landulf favourable conditions.⁵⁹ An example of what such an agreement could have entailed is offered in Falco's account of negotiations between Count Jordan of Ariano and Count Rainulf of Caiazzo in May 1120. Unable to break Rainulf's siege of his castle Tufo, Count Jordan engaged mediators who negotiated peace agreements. The process included a meeting of the two counts in the presence of a 'great assembly of nobles' on the Ponte San Valentino east of Benevento. In a gesture symbolising their equality in status, each rival promised the other fidelity before confirming the peace.⁶⁰ This made it easier for them to accept its conditions, since both parties kept face. Landulf of Greca by comparison was confronted with accepting a one-sided loss of face, the surrender of the *comestabilia* as a precondition of peace. Following the 'logic of honour', such a humiliation would have been unacceptable for the proud constable. As already noted, Falco characterises Landulf as a 'warlike spirit' who 'would not put up with injuries and menaces'. He apparently would have preferred to die rather than suffer an enemy who had harmed him to retire unpunished.⁶¹ And Landulf had already sustained a painful blow to his honour from his enemies: after receiving the *comestabilia* a year earlier, he demonstrated his military potency in a series of successful raids,⁶² but had recently suffered a defeat by the Normans who now demanded his abdication.⁶³ He had even been publicly humiliated by insults and threats from the Beneventan *populus* and obliged to retreat from the *palatium Dacomarii* to the *sacrum palatium* to 'escape the howling of the furious people'.⁶⁴ This repeated loss of face severely limited his readiness to compromise. When the archbishop's mediators now confronted him with his enemies' demand, he answered in the presence of his supporters, Falco's '*Beati Petri fideles*', 'that he would never relinquish the constable's position unless he was captured and kept prisoner by main force'.⁶⁵

As we have seen, the contending parties found themselves in quite entrenched positions shortly before violence erupted on Saturday, 14 March 1114. On one hand, the Normans had sworn an oath to continue their attacks on Benevento as long as Landulf of Greca remained *comestabulus*. On the other, Landulf, unable to stop the attacks by military means, had agreed to peace negotiations but was now faced with having to agree to an unacceptable humiliation. As mediator, Archbishop Landulf found himself caught between two uncompromising positions. At the same time, both he and the constable had seen public discontent explode into violence and were under considerable pressure from the Beneventan *cives* to end the Norman attacks. Under the weight of these events, they each sought ways to end the impasse. These were unfortunately quite different.

In his account, Falco is quite definite that Landulf of Greca followed the pope's orders while Archbishop Landulf II did not. As he relates, Landulf the constable was thrice asked to renounce the *comestabilia* to facilitate a peaceful solution and thrice answered that the peace agreement should first be laid before the pope to decide. He would then, he repeated, be willing to obey the pope's will, even if it meant resigning his office.[66] According to Falco, Landulf in insisting on this was loyally following Pope Paschal II's instructions to Archbishop Landulf.[67] But it is unclear if the pope had formulated his mandate in this way or if this was merely a ploy by Landulf of Greca to gain time. Falco reports that there was indeed uncertainty in Benevento over whether the pope need ratify the terms negotiated by the archbishop. The archbishop claimed to have received the order from the pope to make a treaty, so it was unnecessary to send the pontiff the agreement's details.[68] The question may well have been raised because Archbishop Landulf seemed to have no written mandate from the pope.[69] But, if Paschal II had dispatched his envoys for negotiations with only verbal instructions, then Archbishop Landulf alone could have known what they were, since the other legates were no longer in Benevento.

Seeing the constable obdurate in his refusal to resign, the archbishop and his men started working on a solution that would enable peace with the Normans without Landulf of Greca's consent. According to Falco, Archbishop Landulf and a man named Fulco held regular public meetings in the cathedral. These seem to have served to form consent on how best to proceed in the deadlocked negotiations. On 13 March, one day before the *civile bellum* began, Benevento's *cives* gathered at such a meeting and swore (*coniuraverunt*) 'that they would not consent to Landulf of Greca being their constable from that point on until the pope with the advice of the Normans had restored him to that honour'.[70] Thus, the citizens formed a sworn association to depose Landulf, since he would not step down voluntarily. The Normans seem to have accepted this solution, since Archbishop Landulf II advised his followers the next day to prepare for possible conflict with the constable 'so that they might together with the Normans confirm the peace which they had resolved on'.[71]

Landulf of Greca's reaction to this followed the 'logics of honour'. Armed and accompanied by a host of faithful followers, he made his stand in 'the midst of the square' in front of the *sacrum palatium* and proclaimed his wish to see those people who dared threaten him.[72] The situation escalated rapidly and led to battles in Benevento's streets, the *'bellum civile'* in which Landulf was roundly defeated. Wounded, he was forced to retreat to the *sacrum palatium* and obliged to promise the archbishop under oath 'that he would not accept the constableship, the rectorate or any other public office without the agreement of the archbishop, the archpriest, the archdeacon and other Beneventans and that he would not do harm to the archbishop nor to any Beneventan and that, if anyone wanted to harm them, he would hinder him without trickery or malice'.[73] The *milites* who had supported him swore the same oath. The day after, the Normans met on the *pons maior*, a bridge over the Sabato, to confirm the peace agreement.[74] A week later, Landulf and his few remaining *milites* fled Benevento.[75]

In conclusion, the conflict leading to the 'civil war' in Benevento did not originate from poor relations between Pope Paschal II and Archbishop Landulf II, nor from antipathy between the archbishop and the papal constable Landulf of Greca, but rather in the context of local rivalry between Landulf of Greca and the Norman nobility. As the Normans formed a common front against Landulf and attacked Benevento to force his dismissal from the *comestabilia*, the pope sent the archbishop with two other papal legates to negotiate a peace. It was, paradoxically, this peace mission which led to the outbreak of civil war in Benevento. The negotiations became gridlocked on the Normans' precondition that Landulf resign as constable, a demand Landulf could not accept without compromising his honour. Caught between the uncompromising positions of the antagonists and under pressure from the civil population to end the conflict, the archbishop sought to end the impasse by building public support to undercut Landulf of Greca's position. Conflict with the constable was the inevitable consequence. In any case, this was the lesser evil for the Beneventans, who were able to defeat Landulf and attain peace with the Normans. But the solution had consequences for Archbishop Landulf II: under the charge of having disobeyed papal orders, he was declared *adversarius Beati Petri* and removed from office, if only briefly. This punishment for an action which, in its results, not only honoured the pope's intention but was also successful seems strange. Perhaps the pope's judgement may be explained by the fact that Landulf's version of events portraying the archbishop's dealings as disobedience was first to reach his ears. However that may be, feeling his authority put in question by how Archbishop Landulf II had carried out his orders, Paschal II was obliged to demand satisfaction for his own honour, even if he was probably well pleased with the results.[76]

Appendix

1123 November, Montefusco
Scriptum dispositionis
Landulf of Greca lying on his deathbed donates a piece of land near Leocubante to St Sophia, Benevento. Beneventan script, poorly legible. Conjectures in []; standard abbreviations without brackets; emendations in (). Benevento, Museo del Sannio, Fondo S. Sofia, XII, 40.[77]

In nomine Domini. Anno millesimo centesimo v[icesimo tert]io ab incarnatione domni nostri Ihesu Christi et quinto anno pontificatus domini nostri summi pontificis et universalis pape secundi Ca[l]ix[ti] | mense novembris secunda indictione. Ego Landulfus olim com[estabulus] filius quondam M[a]delfridi comitis qui de Greca fuit cognominatus, declaro me a gravissima infirmitate cor|[pori]s mei omne detentu(m)[78] et nisi divina pietas mihi subvene[rit ci]tius me hanc vitam finiri credo. Sed data mihi protectione[79] a Domino sanam et rectam in me | agnosco habere memoriam et dum in lecto iaceo tamen dum recte [l]oqui valeo adeo de rebus [m]eis disponere et iudicare previdi qualiter post meum obitum disposite | et iudicate pro anima mea secundum legem permanea(n)t.[80] Iterum [...] legibus pertinentem habeo rem que est silva que dicitur Sancte Rufine foras in finibus Locubanti | prope [pon]tem pianum et munimen inde habeo. Nunc autem i[n]tegram ipsam silvam meam ob remedio et salvatione anime mee et animarum parentum me[orum o]ffero Deo in monast[erio] | Sancte Sophie [ubi nunc, Deo tuent]e, domnus Iohannes [religiosus a]bb[as preesse] vide[tur]. Qua propter quoniam congruum mihi est bona mea voluntate ante Iohannem iudicem et alios ydoneos homines, per hoc scriptum | dispono et iudico in prephato monasterio totam et integram ipsam silvam quam ut supra me declaravi pertinentem habere foris in predicto loco. Que videtur esse per hos | fines: de una parte fine via puplica que vadit ad predictum pontem pianum usque in termino posito inter hoc et terram Sancti Felicis. De alia parte revolvit ab eodem termino et qualiter | vadit inter hoc et ipsam terram Sancti Felicis usque in alio termino et ab inde qualiter vadit cum proprio limite inter hanc meam oblationem et terram predicte ecclesie Sancti Felicis us[que] in | alio [termino]; de alia parte revolvit ab ipso termino et qualiter vadit ascendendam inter hoc et terram pertinentem de aliis hominibus meis de silva Canosa et sicut termini positi | [... u]sque [in] alio termino; de alia capite qualiter revolvit ab eodem termino et vadit revolvendam inter hanc meam oblationem et ipsam paludem quam mihi reser[v]avi et | [coniungit se] in ipsa via puplica priori fini. Infra hos autem fines nec mihi nec cuiquam alteri reservavi. Sed integram ipsam silvam per cunctos predictos fines una cum in[fe]rio|ribus et superiori[bus] et cum viis et anditis suis et cum omnibus aliis inde pertinentiis, transactionem illam Deo in prephato monasterio optuli, habendam et possidendam. Ea quidem ratione | ut a modo [et] semper pars predicti monasterii eiusque custodes et rectores integram eandem meam oblationem sicut dictum est habere et possidere valeant securiter | inde [faciendo omnia] quecumque voluerint sine mea meorumque heredum contradictione et sine cuiuscumque requisitione. Unde obligo me et meos heredes antistare et de|fendere ipsam meam oblationem ad partem predicti monasterii et quibus ab eius datum paruere et illorum heredum amodo et semper ab omnibus hominibus ab omnibusque partibus. | Quod si aliquo tempore ego vel mei heredes cum parte predicti monasterii vel cum quibus ab eius datum paruere vel cum illorum heredum ex predicta mea oblatione per | quamcumque inventam rationem causare aut contendere presumpserimus querendam inde eis aliquid tollere aut contrare vel minuere aut de illorum | subtrahere proprietate et dominatione et si qualiter dictum est illam eis non defensaverimus aut si hoc removere quesierimus ducentos solidos constantinatos penam eis componere | obligavimus; et inantea omni tempore exinde adversus eos inviti, taciti et contempti maneamus [a] tque inviti illut eis antistemus et defendamus sicut supra legitur | per eandem obligatam penam; et quando voluerint potestatem habeant hoc scriptum et quanta alia munimina inde habuerint pertinentes et continentes ad legem hostendere et cum suis | causatoribus inde causare et contendere omnemque diffinitionem cum eius inde facere sicut nos facere debuissemus et predictam meam oblationem per se ipsos illam sibi defendant | et securiter possideant. Hoc scriptum dispositionis tibi Servato clerico et notario taliter scribere iussi eo quo interfuisti. | Actum in castello Montisfusculi. Feliciter.

+ Ego qui supra Iohannes iudex (S).
+ Ego presbiter Milo.
+ Ego Paganus me subscripsi.

Notes

1 On the structural conditions of papal rule over Benevento, see G. A. Loud, 'Politics, piety and ecclesiastical patronage in twelfth-century Benevento', in E. Cuozzo and J.-M. Martin (eds), *Cavalieri alla conquista del Sud. Studi sull'Italia normanna in memoria di Léon-Robert Ménager* (Rome, 1997), pp. 283–312; reprinted in G. A. Loud, *Montecassino and Benevento in the Middle Ages: Essays in South Italian Church History* (Aldershot, 2000). On the beginnings of papal rule over Benevento, see P. Oldfield, *City and Community in Norman Italy* (Cambridge, 2009), pp. 21–2, 24–5, 41–3.
2 *ChBen*, 1112.3.1–3.5.
3 *ChBen*, 1114.1.1–5.45.
4 *ChBen*, 1116.3.1; *Chronica monasterii Casinensis*, ed. H. Hoffmann, MGH SS 34 (Hanover, 1980), pp. 523–4 (hereafter *CMC*).
5 *ChBen*, 1113.1.1–5.45.
6 O. Vehse, 'Benevent als Territorium des Kirchenstaates bis zum Beginn der avignonesischen Epoche. I', *QF* 22 (1930–31), 87–160, at pp. 121–4; D'Angelo in *ChBen*, pp. xvii–xix; C. Lavarra, 'Coscienza civica e tensioni sociali nel Mezzogiorno normanno: Benevento nella prima metà del XII secolo', in C. Lavarra, *Mezzogiorno Normanno: Potere, spazio urbano, ritualità* (Galatina, 2005), pp. 97–140, at pp. 104–6; D. Siegmund, *Die Stadt Benevent im Hochmittelalter* (Aachen, 2011), pp. 153–5. An exception is Loud, 'Politics', pp. 294–5, who points to the 'extensive land holdings' of both Archbishop Landulf II and the abbot of St Modestus 'in the Valle Caudine … and hence far enough away to be very vulnerable to outside interference' to explain their engagement during the conflict.

7 In *ChBen*, 1114.1.7, 1114.2.6 and 1114.3.22, Falco mentions Landulf of Greca together with other *Beati Petri fideles*; at 1114.3.22, he stresses that Landulf of Greca endured his sufferings *pro Beati Petri fidelitate*; at 1114.4.1, Falco describes Archbishop Landulf II's followers as *adversarii Beati Petri*. On Falco and his chronicle, see M. Krumm, *Herrschaftsumbruch und Historiographie. Zeitgeschichtsschreibung als Krisenbewältigung bei Alexander von Telese und Falco von Benevent* (Berlin/Boston, 2021).

8 See D'Angelo in *ChBen*, pp. xvii–xviii; Lavarra, 'Coscienza', pp. 104–6.

9 G. Althoff, 'The rules of conflict among the warrior aristocracy of the High Middle Ages', in K. Esmark *et al*. (eds), *Disputing Strategies in Medieval Scandinavia* (Leiden, 2013), pp. 313–32; G. Althoff, 'Satisfaction: Peculiarities of the amicable settlement of conflicts in the Middle Ages', in B. Jussen (ed.), *Ordering Medieval Society: Perspectives on Intellectual and Practical Modes of Shaping Social Relations* (Philadelphia, 2001), pp. 270–84.

10 Loud's essays on Benevento and Falco are collected in his *Montecassino and Benevento*; see also the translation of Falco's chronicle in his *Roger II*, pp. 130–249; all translated quotes come from this translation if not explicitly stated otherwise.

11 D'Angelo in *ChBen*, pp. xvii–xviii. Lavarra, 'Coscienza', pp. 104–6.

12 *Italia Pontificia*, ed. W. Holtzmann, vol. 9 (Berlin, 1963), pp. 62–3, nos 37–45. The archbishop is found in every papal charter issued during the pope's stay in Benevento in early 1113 and signed by witnesses; cf. *Regesta Pontificum Romanorum*, ed. P. Jaffé *et al*., 2 vols, 2nd edn (Leipzig, 1885–88) (henceforth JL), vol. 2 nos 6336 and 6340; *Italia Pontificia*, vol. 8, pp. 161–2, no. 174; JL, vol. 2, no. 6341.

13 When Paschal II accuses the Archbishop in Ceprano of having taken *regalia Beati Petri* the latter answers: 'Vere regalia Beati Petri non alia de causa accepi, sed vestra pro fidelitate; nam, cum Beneventi aderas, civitatem mihi commendasti.' *ChBen*, 1114.5.30. Trans. in *Roger II*, p. 144.

14 On this possibility, see R. Hüls, *Kardinäle, Klerus und Kirchen Roms 1049–1130* (Tübingen, 1977), p. 181, n. 8.

15 See *ChBen*, pp. xvii–xviii.

16 *ChBen*, 1113.1.1–1.4.

17 *ChBen*, 1113.1.1.

18 *ChBen*, 1114.2.13 and 1114.3.27, refers to both judges as Landulf of Greca's partisans. Moreover, Persicus *iudex* in 1104/05 confirms a donation issued by Landulf's mother: *Le più antiche carte del capitolo della cattedrale di Benevento (668–1200)*, ed. A Ciarelli, V. de Donato and V. Matera (Rome, 2002) (henceforth, *Cattedrale di Benevento*),

p. 164, no. 53. John *iudex* was present in November 1123 at Landulf's deathbed in Montefusco; Benevento, Museo del Sannio, Fondo S. Sofia (henceforth FSS), XII, 40.
19 See n. 12 above.
20 *ChBen*, 1114.2.2; on the vicinity of the *palatium Dacomarii* and the archbishop's palace, see 1102.1.7.
21 *ChBen*, 1113.2.1; similarly in 1113.6.1, 1114.1.6 and 1113.2.2; 1113.5.2 and 1114.3.18. Falco mentions Robert Sclavus, Gerard della Marca, Hugh Infans, Rao of Ceppaloni and Landulf Burrellus as members of the *coniuratio*; Robert Sclavus and the count of Ariano had only made *pacta* with Landulf of Greca shortly before joining the sworn association; cf. 1113.1.5–1.10. On sworn associations in general, see O. G. Oexle, 'Peace through conspiracy', in Jussen (ed.), *Ordering Medieval Society*, pp. 285–322.
22 D'Angelo in *ChBen*, p. xviii; Lavarra, 'Coscienza', p. 105.
23 *ChBen*, 1113.2.1.
24 G. A. Loud, 'History writing in the twelfth-century kingdom of Sicily', in S. Dale, A. W. Lewin and D. J. Osheim (eds), *Chronicling History: Chroniclers and Historians in Medieval and Renaissance Italy* (University Park, 2007), pp. 29–54, at p. 42; G. A. Loud, 'Norman traditions in southern Italy', in S. Burkhardt and T. Foerster (eds), *Norman Tradition and Transcultural Heritage: Exchange of Cultures in the 'Norman' Peripheries of Medieval Europe* (Farnham, 2013), pp. 35–56, at p. 38.
25 See the edition in the appendix.
26 A Beneventan charter of 1104/05 is issued by 'Sikelgarda filia Landolfi comitis et que fui uxor Madelfridi comitis Adelferii comitis'; her son *Landolfus* is named as Sikelgarda's *mundoald*: *Cattedrale di Benevento*, p. 164, no. 53.
27 FSS, XII, 16 (1045 July). The nephew was also called Madelfrid. He cannot be one of Landulf's direct ancestors since he had *nec filium nec filiam de sua uxore quia non habuit uxorem in coniugio sociata*. He and his uncle Madelfrid are also mentioned in a charter from July 1045 issued by an uncle called Dauferius and the latter's wife Altruda, Frascati, Archivio Aldobrandini, Pergamene, I, 36 (1145 June); on both charters see D. Girgensohn, 'Documenti beneventani inediti del secolo xii', *Samnium* 40 (1967), 262–317, at p. 269, n. 37; G. A. Loud, 'A Lombard abbey in a Norman world: St Sophia, Benevento, 1050–1200', *ANS* 19 (1997), 273–305, at p. 276, n. 6.
28 FSS, XII, 40.
29 *Codice diplomatico verginiano*, ed. P. M. Tropeano, 13 vols (Montevergine, 1977–2000), vol. 3, p. 177, no. 242, and p. 183, no. 244.

30 ChBen, 1114.3.21 and 1118.2.1. Falco mentions *domos suas* (i.e. Landulf's) *et possessiones* in Benevento. In 1104/05 Landulf's mother Sikelgarda donated 'rem quam pertinentem habui foris hac Beneventana civitate in loco ubi Rosetum nominatur' (located about three kilometres north of Benevento, near the Torrente Fasanella), *Cattedrale di Benevento*, p. 164, no. 53. A charter from November 1110 mentions an 'ortus Landulfi comitis filii quondam Madelfridi comitis' near Benevento's Port'Aurea, FSS, XXXIV, 4. A charter from August 1121 mentions 'rem Landulfi de Greca' as well as 'terra predicti Landulfi de Greca' near the 'casale Leocubante' (south-east of Benevento), FSS, XXXIV, 3. On his deathbed Landulf donated 'rem que est silva que dicitur sancte Rufine foras in finibus Locubanti prope [pon]tem pianum', FSS, XII, 40 (1123 Nov.). Finally, Landulf held land near the *castrum* Montefusco (some thirteen kilometres south of Benevento), ChBen, 1114.3.26, 1119.2.11, 1120.8.1 and 1122.1.14. In 1137 Landulf's son Daddaeus donated land near Montefusco to the monastery of Montevergine, *Codice diplomatico verginiano*, vol. 3, pp. 175–8, no. 242. The dowry of Daddaeus's wife was located in the same area (vol. 3, pp. 183–4, no. 244). In October 1175 a *terra de Grecisis* near Montefusco is mentioned in FSS, XXXIV, 1; an edition of this charter is provided by E. M. Jamison, *Admiral Eugenius of Sicily: His Life and Work and the Authorship of the* Epistola ad Petrum *and the* Historia Hugonis Falcandi Siculi (London, 1957), p. 318, no. 1.
31 On Landulf's military resources see *ChBen*, 1113.4.1: 'Guerra Normandorum ... durius incepta est; in qua innumeram auri et argenti copiam, et equorum, distribuit.' At 1113.3.1, Falco mentions 180 *milites* and 4,000 *cives*, with whom Landulf attacked the *castellum* Terra Rubea.
32 ChBen, 1119.2.11–2.12.
33 ChBen, 1113.1.2–1.3.
34 See e.g. ChBen, 1113.2.1, 1113.6.1.
35 ChBen, 1113.5.3.
36 ChBen, 1114.1.2–1.3.
37 ChBen, 1114.1.4.
38 ChBen, 1114.1.5–1.7: 'Archiepiscopus vero Roma reversus, aliter quam acceperat, faciens, misit Landulpho comestabulo dicens ut, condolens necessitatis pauperum, comestabiliam poneret, quoadusque dominus papa Beneventum veniret. Postea vero aut pretio, servitiisve seu civium precibus papam ipsum precarentur, eumque honori pristino rederent, dummodo Normandi pacem facere nolint, sacramento, ut dictum est, eorum interveniente. Landulphus autem hoc audiens

comestabulus in Sacro Beneventano palatio coram Beati Petri fidelibus respondens ait, se nunquam comestabiliam dimissurum, nisi manu ad manum captus esset, et virtute retentus; insuper videre vellet, quam Normandi pacem Beneventanis facere voluissent, et domino papae pacem ipsam descriptam delegaret.' My translation differs in some parts from Loud's (*Roger II*, pp. 137–8).

39 *ChBen*, 1114.2.1, makes this explicit: 'Qualiter autem in Sacro Beneventano palatio comestabulus ipse affuerit, retexam.'
40 *ChBen*, 1114.2.2. Peter of Porto was the former rector of Benevento; see G. A. Loud, 'A provisional list of the papal rectors of Benevento, 1101–1227', in Loud, *Montecassino and Benevento*, pp. 1–11, at pp. 1–2. If Cardinal Romuald is to be identified with Cardinal Deacon Romuald of St Mary in Via lata, he also knew Benevento from personal experience; see Hüls, *Kardinäle*, p. 238.
41 *ChBen*, 1114.2.2.
42 *ChBen*, 1114.2.6–2.10.
43 On mediators, cf. H. Kamp, *Friedensstifter und Vermittler im Mittelalter* (Darmstadt, 2001).
44 On 17 July 1109 Count Robert of Caiazzo donated an estate (*tenimentum*) called *Pulveca* to the church St Peter in Tocco. Archbishop Landulf II was present and confirmed the charter, Naples, Biblioteca Nazionale, XII.A.A. 1, 1. This charter was wrongly considered to be destroyed during the Second World War, G. Tescione, 'Roberto conte normanno di Alife, Caiazzo e S. Agata dei Goti', *Archivio storico di Terra di Lavoro* 4 (1975), 9–52, at pp. 18–19 and 40 (wrongly dated to 16 August 1109 instead of *XVI kalendas Augusti*). Tescione's knowledge of the charter's content was based on its 'certamente imperfetta' edition in G. Marcarelli, *L'oriente del Taburno. Storia dell'antica città di Tocco e dei suoi casali* (Benevento, 1915), pp. 22–3. This edition was not available to me. On 30 August 1109 Count Robert confirmed the donation of several churches to the archbishop, *Cattedrale di Benevento*, p. 166, no. 54. In May 1112 Hugh Infans transferred, with the archbishop's consent, some churches to the abbey of Montecassino; cf. *Cattedrale di Benevento*, pp. 25–7, no. 4; CMC, IV, 47, p. 514.
45 *ChBen*, 1114.2.2–2.3.
46 *ChBen*, 1114.2.4.
47 *ChBen*, 1114.2.5.
48 *ChBen*, 1114.2.13.
49 *ChBen*, 1114.2.14.
50 Falco just stops mentioning the cardinal.
51 On the following see n. 38 above.

52 *ChBen*, 1114.3.10.
53 On this information, see again n. 38 above.
54 On the importance of privacy for peace talks, see Kamp, *Friedensstifter*, pp. 192–3.
55 Among these may already have been the bishop of Avellino and some of his priests, whom Falco mentions at a later stage of the negotiations (*ChBen*, 1114.3.7).
56 *ChBen*, 1114.1.7.
57 *ChBen*, 1114.2.6–2.12.
58 *ChBen*, 1114.2.6. On the binding character of public gestures, see G. Althoff, 'Symbolic communication and medieval order: Strengths and weaknesses of ambiguous signs', in W. Jezierski *et al.* (eds), *Rituals, Performatives, and Political Order in Northern Europe, c.650–1350* (Turnhout, 2015), pp. 63–75.
59 Kamp, *Friedensstifter*, pp. 186–215.
60 *ChBen*, 1120.2.3–2.6. On comparable peace agreements, see Althoff, 'Satisfaction'.
61 *ChBen*, 1113.1.3.
62 *ChBen*, 1113.3.1–4.3.
63 *ChBen*, 1113.5.3.
64 *ChBen*, 1114.2.14.
65 *ChBen*, 1114.1.7.
66 *ChBen*, 1114.3.3.
67 *ChBen*, 1114.1.4.
68 During a public meeting in the cathedral Archbishop Landulf II told his followers: 'We have notified the lord pope of your need and he has ordered us to make a treaty with the Normans; thus it seems superfluous to send him the full details.' *ChBen*, 1114.3.5. Trans., *Roger II*, p. 139.
69 Papal legates were usually given one or more letters of recommendation. They received their instructions, however, verbally. See C. Zey, 'Die Augen des Papstes: zu Eigenschaften und Vollmachten päpstlicher Legaten', in J. Johrendt and H. Müller (eds), *Römisches Zentrum und kirchliche Peripherie. Das universale Papsttum als Bezugspunkt der Kirchen von den Reformpäpsten bis zu Innozenz III* (Berlin, 2008), pp. 77–108, at p. 80.
70 *ChBen*, 1114.3.6: 'quod Landulphum illum de Greca comestabulum esse non consensissent, exin et dum dominus papa consilio Normandorum illum honori non rediddisset'. My translation differs slightly from Loud's (*Roger II*, p. 139). In *ChBen*, 1114.3.7, Falco explicitly states that he renders the text of a promissory oath.

71 *ChBen*, 1114.3.11: 'ut cum Normandis, quam posuerant, pacem firmarent'. My translation differs slightly from Loud's (*Roger II*, p. 139).
72 *ChBen*, 1114.3.8–3.10.
73 *ChBen*, 1114.3.12–3.16: My translation of the last paragraph ('et, si aliquis redere vellet, disturbaret sine fraude et malo ingenio') differs slightly from Loud's (*Roger II*, p. 140).
74 *ChBen*, 1114.3.18.
75 *ChBen*, 1114.3.26.
76 On the trial against Archbishop Landulf II, see M. Krumm, 'Streiten vor (und mit) dem Papst. Beobachtungen zur kurialen Gerichtspraxis anhand der Klosterchronik von Montecassino und des *Chronicon Falcos von Benevent*', in J. Nowak and G. Strack (eds), *Stilus – modus – usus. Regeln der Konflikt- und Verhandlungsführung am Papsthof des Mittelalters* [Rules of Negotiation and Conflict Resolution at the Papal Court in the Middle Ages] (Turnhout, 2019), pp. 67–95, at pp. 88–94.
77 I would like to thank Paola Massa and Duane Henderson for their support in editing this charter.
78 Ms: datam mihi protectionem.
79 Ms: detentus.
80 Ms: permaneat.

8

Norman rulers and Greek-speaking subjects: the *Vitae* of Italo-Greek saints (twelfth and thirteenth centuries) and the negotiation of local identities

Eleni Tounta

The question of how the Italo-Greek communities of southern Italy and Sicily perceived and responded to the cultural changes introduced by the Norman conquests is important for a deeper understanding of the society of Norman Italy. The *Vitae* of the Italo-Greek saints of the twelfth and thirteenth centuries can contribute to this avenue of research, since, for the Italo-Greeks, hagiography, alongside secular poetry, was the literary genre *par excellence* for communicating the hopes, fears and expectations engendered by their encounter with the Normans. In narrating the lives of their saints they sought to redefine their self-perception, strengthen the bonds of their communities and converse with the new rulers – in other words, to negotiate their identities. The saints became their literary *personae*; they were invested with specific social traits and were given a life scenario that in narrative terms represented the social experiences of Italo-Greek communities.[1] It is no exaggeration to argue that, from the early twelfth until the early thirteenth century, the *Vitae* of the Italo-Greek saints narrate the evolution of the Italo-Greek communities, from the refashioning of their identity under Latin rule, through their subsequent heyday, until their decline. This social function of hagiography was no innovation of the Norman period. It is evident in the *Vitae* of the Italo-Greek saints in the Byzantine era of the Mezzogiorno (ninth–eleventh centuries),[2] whose main traits are worth outlining so that readers will understand the changes that hagiographical narrative underwent in the new cultural context. Those saints, natives of Sicily and southern Calabria, were ascetics who wandered in the mountains of Calabria and Lucania before establishing their own monasteries, which after their deaths became the focus of their cults. In their *Vitae* no other power, either ecclesiastical or secular, is cast as having supreme authority. Yet the saints did not hesitate either to judge the secular authorities and inflict on them severe punishments when necessary or to defend the interests of their local communities against the imperial centre.[3]

Luke, bishop of Isola Capo Rizzuto (1035/40–1114): the role of his *Vita* in creating the space of the county of Sicily

In the southern Calabrian territory of the county of Sicily – whose first governmental seat had been established in Mileto – the Normans encountered a majority Greek-speaking population to which they entrusted important administrative offices because of its relevant skills and Byzantine *paideia* (cultural education).[4] This is how Greek language and Byzantine culture came to play such an important role in the new political entity. The first count, Roger I of Hauteville (1071–1101) took pains to revive the county's ecclesiastical structure by establishing Latin bishoprics in Sicily, where the Church had been dissolved under Muslim rule. Southern Calabria's network of Italo-Greek bishoprics survived, and its bishops remained in their seats and were replaced by Latins only after their deaths. The lower clergy was unaffected by this and continued to offer spiritual services following the Eastern Church's rite and doctrine. The Hauteville rulers recognised the bishops, regardless of their ethno-cultural origins, as important supporters of their policy and fostered their authority.[5]

It is against this backdrop that we should place the emergence of an Italo-Greek bishop-saint, Luke of Isola Capo Rizzuto. His *Vita* [*Bibliotheca hagiographica graeca* (*BHG*) 2237], written c. 1116–20 by a priest or monk,[6] reveals the enhancement of episcopal power, something absent in the Italo-Greek *Vitae* of the Byzantine era. The saint, a native of southern Calabria, is presented as undertaking all the functions of the ascetic saints: a spiritual guide for monks and laymen (pp. 86–8), a mediator in conflicts (pp. 92–4) and a miracle-worker (pp. 90–2, 94–8). Ascetic saints typically expelled wild beasts, an act symbolic, *inter alia*, of the civilising of the wild, untamed countryside and the protection of monastic property.[7] In Luke's *Vita*, this act is moved into an urban context as a means to shape the people's piety and facilitate the bishop's control over his flock. A wild wolf terrorising Squillace was exterminated after the people had fasted, confessed and prayed in the cathedral (pp. 98–100).

By redefining the sanctity of a bishop in this inaugural phase of Norman rule in southern Calabria and Sicily, the Italo-Greeks contributed to the organisation of the county of Sicily and the shaping of its political unity, thus fashioning their own identity in order to integrate themselves into the new political situation. Luke is the only Italo-Greek saint from the ninth century onwards who travels from southern Calabria to Sicily, a route opposite to that followed by his peers of the Byzantine era, who left Sicily for Christian southern Italy. In Sicily, Luke preached and consecrated priests, since the island had become a 'voiceless land' (γῆ ἄλαλος) because of the 'infidel enemies' (ἀθέων ἐχθρῶν), the Muslims (p. 90).[8] Luke's travels helped to produce the space of the county of Sicily by influencing how the Italo-Greeks experienced and gave meaning to the county's political and ecclesiastical unity, in accordance with their own mental horizons, spatial practices and expectations.[9] This production of space favoured both the establishment of Norman rule – which by the time of the *Vita*'s composition had transferred its seat to Palermo (1112) – and the redefinition of the identity of the southern Calabrian Italo-Greeks, who settled on the island in order to acquire positions in the new system of power. These settlements, which continued throughout the twelfth century, had been promoted by Roger I, who offered the Italo-Greeks lands and administrative offices in Sicily in an effort to increase the island's Christian population.[10] Thus, an Italo-Greek elite was gradually forged thanks to its office-holding at the comital court and, from 1130 onward, when the kingdom of Sicily was established under Roger II (1105–54), at the royal court. Its members were steadfast supporters of the dynasty's policy and maintained their socio-political status through intermarriage and creation of kinship networks at court, as well as by preserving their cultural traits, Greek language and Byzantine *paideia*, to which they owed their importance.[11]

In light of these narrative strategies and the harmonious symbiosis of the Italo-Greek and Latin communities, Luke's brutal doctrinal conflict with the Latins, which could have cost him his life, seems out of place. In a *disputatio* concerning the Latin use of unleavened bread, the saint gravely insulted his interlocutors by accusing them of Pharisaism, the adoption of Jewish religious rites and heresy. They, enraged by his accusations, had a hut built and ordered the saint to enter it for execution by burning. Luke asked their permission to celebrate Holy Communion a last time and, with their consent, entered the hut together with a little boy to assist with the liturgy. When he had finished the ceremony, the Latins set the hut afire but saint and child survived unscathed (pp. 106–8). This strange episode raises questions about its narrative function.[12] I argue that it constitutes a strategy of constructing otherness with the aim of maintaining community discipline. The conflict presents the bishop as a guardian of the correct religious rites. The shaping of identity is inconceivable without the simultaneous construction of the other, in this case the otherness of the Latins, which must be presented as an existential threat to the values the bishop fosters.[13] The more inimical and violent the portrayal of otherness, the more the flock will gather round the bishop, the defender of its spiritual life, recognise his authority to control its spiritual and, therefore, social behaviour, and thereby establish him as regulator of the community's life. After Luke's death and probable replacement by a Latin bishop, the priests assumed his role. They displayed his sanctity and were eager to produce and disseminate his *Vita* in an effort to persuade the community, as well as Latin authorities, to accept their socio-religious role. A posthumous miracle by the saint can be interpreted in the same way, since it might refer to tensions provoked by local Latin magnates who demanded abusive taxes from the Italo-Greek clergy.[14] A certain 'Frank' (Φράγκος) from Briatico named Revetos behaved badly towards the priests and subjected them to a 'yoke of slavery' (ζυγὸ δουλείας), the bishop's admonitions notwithstanding. Revetos then fell ill, visited the late saint's tomb, promised to reform his behaviour and was cured. However, he did not keep his promise and eventually died (pp. 120–2).

Bartholomew of Simeri (d. 1130): shaping the identity of the Italo-Greek elite

Throughout the twelfth century the Norman rulers protected Italo-Greek monasticism by offering privileges to existing monasteries and by founding new ones.[15] One of the most important new foundations was Holy Saviour in Messina, created by Roger II in 1130 and associated with the southern Calabrian saint, Bartholomew of Simeri. The monastery was established to become the mother house of a congregation of southern Calabrian and Sicilian monasteries that had lost their independence, although the richest among them retained the right to elect their own abbots. The abbot of Holy Saviour, who bore the title of archimandrite, was elected by all the congregation's monks, although the choice required the king's sanction, to whom the abbot was directly subordinate.[16] I argue that the monastery's close bonds with the Hauteville dynasty, as well as the transfer of the centre of power to Sicily – which turned the island into a meaningful space for the fulfilment of the Italo-Greek elite's expectations – led Holy Saviour to become associated with a saint. The narrative representation of Bartholomew draws on the social traits of the Italo-Greek elite; therefore, his *Vita* becomes an essential tool for that elite's self-perception and the fashioning of its identity.

The *Vita* of Bartholomew of Simeri (*BHG* 236), who died on 19 August 1130, was written in the middle of the twelfth century.[17] The narration of his entry into monastic life is typical of the Italo-Greek hagiography of the Byzantine period. In his early youth he renounced earthly pleasures and abandoned his family to live ascetically in the mountains of Rossano, where he attracted many disciples through his grace-filled life (chs 2–16, pp. 206–16). The new cultural context is, nevertheless, revealed in the account of the establishment of his first monastery (*c.* 1101–5), the *Nea Hodegetria* (the new *Hodegetria* = 'she who shows the way'), today St Mary of Patire in Rossano. Unlike the saints of the previous era who relied on their own powers and those of their disciples for founding their monasteries, Bartholomew had the support of an important court official, the Sicilian Italo-Greek 'admiral' (ἀμιρᾶς) Christodoulos, who is presented as a spiritual son of the saint who 'depended on his counsel' (τῆς νουθεσίας ἐξηρτημένος) (ch. 17, p. 216).[18]

Christodoulos persuaded 'King' (ῥήξ) Roger II to finance the foundation of the monastery. The royal family, moreover, entrusted the saint not only with money but also with their souls, as the author underlines (ch. 17, pp. 216–17). Bartholomew is cast as a member of the Italo-Greek elite who, thanks to kinship networks at court, here spiritual in form, enters the new hierarchy of power and gains an important position at the court, thus shaping his socio-political status. The saint is no longer a mediator between rulers and local communities, like his Byzantine-era peers, but he fosters relations with the holder of power on whom he is dependent.[19] Given the date of the monastery's foundation, the titles attributed to Roger II and Christodoulos, named admiral in 1107, are anachronisms and reveal the author's aim to associate Bartholomew with both the Italo-Greek elite and the ruling royal dynasty.

The author pursues the same narrative strategy when he has Bartholomew visit the Byzantine emperor in Constantinople, unlike the saints of the Byzantine era, who were portrayed as consciously avoiding the emperor in an effort to shape their own and consequently their communities' autonomy from the imperial policy.[20] In Bartholomew's case, the journey to Constantinople, his recognition by Alexius I, and imperial donations of holy vessels, books and icons (ch. 25, pp. 221–2) construct the saint's identity as a bearer of Byzantine *paideia*. This increases his own and his community's symbolic capital, since Byzantine culture and the Greek language were the distinct cultural traits of the Italo-Greek elite and its main qualifications for a courtly career. With the same aim, the author associates Bartholomew with the main centre of Byzantine monasticism, Mount Athos, by recording that a Byzantine magnate called Basil Kalimeris donated to the saint the monastery he had founded there, which subsequently became known as 'the monastery of the Calabrian' (μοναστήριον τοῦ Καλαβροῦ) (ch. 26, p. 222). However, this monastery had borne this name since at least 1080 because of its founder's origin, not the saint's.[21]

The symbolic capital that Bartholomew had acquired paved the way for his close association with Holy Saviour. The saint was accused by two Italo-Greek monks of giving the gold offered to him by the king to his relatives and spending it with his kinsmen on a life of debauchery and heresy.[22] Roger summoned Bartholomew and his slanderers to Messina to appear before the

'Senate' (σύγκλητος), the royal judicial court. Since the saint did not defend himself, he was sentenced to be burnt to death by the king. Bartholomew asked for Roger's permission to celebrate Holy Communion a last time and he was guided outside the city to the church of St Nicholas of Punta, accompanied by the king and the Senate. When he raised the chalice, a great miracle happened: a column of fire rose from his feet up to the sky and angels came to assist him. The king, seeking to show repentance, granted Bartholomew any wish he desired and the latter requested that a monastery dedicated to the Holy Saviour be erected on the site of the miracle. Roger II founded the monastery and donated to it lands, money and holy vessels. Bartholomew appointed Luke, a monk of *Nea Hodegetria*, as abbot and sent him to Messina (chs 28–30, pp. 224–6). Before his death, the saint appointed the same monk as abbot of *Nea Hodegetria*. Bartholomew was buried in this monastery (ch. 31, pp. 226–8).

The founding myth of Holy Saviour relates to the Italo-Greek elite's strategy of shaping its socio-political status by offering its loyalty to the new rulers.[23] The outcome of the trial shows Bartholomew's sanctity but the process affirms Roger II's power in a way which prompts me to suggest that the *Vita* was written by someone who understood and sought to legitimise the royal policy. In sharp contrast to the Italo-Greek *Vitae* of the Byzantine period, Bartholomew does not judge or punish the holder of secular power but openly submits to his authority.[24] Roger II is thus presented as the only person responsible for rendering justice. One can grasp the function of these narrative representations by considering the importance that Roger II assigned to his own role in the administration of justice, an essential underpinning of the royal dynasty vis-à-vis its magnates. In 1140 the king issued a legal code for his kingdom, the so-called 'Assizes of Ariano', a novelty by medieval standards, since Roger II assumed complete legislative authority without asking his magnates' leave. He, furthermore, introduced new laws largely influenced by the Justinian codification and he abolished the existing laws in case they contradicted the old ones.[25] The founding myth of Holy Saviour, therefore, reflects and legitimises Roger II's perception of justice and in no way undermines his authority. The king, righteous judge he was, realised his mistake and restored justice.

The importance of this founding myth for the saint's association with Holy Saviour is considerable, since Bartholomew's relationship with the monastery is obscure. The monastery was established after his death, since Roger II's founding charter dates from May 1131. A royal charter of 1133 clearly states that the founder was Luke, Bartholomew's successor.[26] There is no mention of the founding myth in the funerary sermon composed on the first anniversary of the saint's death by Philagathos of Cerami, a famous Italo-Greek preacher and Bartholomew's disciple at the *Nea Hodegetria*.[27] In the *Typicon* of Holy Saviour, written by Abbot Luke in his final years,[28] Luke says that he had followed Bartholomew's counsels and insists that Roger II made great efforts to persuade him to assume the abbacy.[29] However, like the *Vita*'s author and the Italo-Greek elite, Luke supports the prerogatives of the royal power and declares that he accepted the king's offer since 'it is known how dangerous it is to offend God and the king'.[30]

John Theristis (tenth–eleventh centuries): questioning identities in the thirteenth century

John Theristis probably lived in the tenth century. His thirteenth-century *Vita* (*BHG* 894 and 894a) draws on a previous – now lost – account of his life, also the source for extant hymns written in the saint's honour in the eleventh century.[31] Temporal distance and striking differences between the two *Vitae* permit us to examine the construction of collective memory and thus the negotiation of identities in the cultural context of the thirteenth century, an era when the assimilation into the Latin culture of the Italo-Greeks, especially those of the upper social strata, was ongoing.

According to the thirteenth-century *Vita*, John was a native of Stilo in southern Calabria and was descended from a rich Christian family. His father was the lord of the village of Cursano and was killed during a Muslim raid. His mother, while pregnant with the saint, was captured and transported to Palermo. There she was married to a Muslim magnate who raised John – in the *Vita* the saint is unnamed before his baptism – as his own son. The mother secretly taught the saint Christian doctrine and, when he was fourteen, she revealed the truth of his origins and sent him to

Calabria to find the family palace and treasure in Cursano and to be baptised as a Christian (chs 1–2, pp. 137–9). The hymns that drew on John's first *Vita* give a different version of the saint's descent. According to them, John was a native of Sicily, the legitimate son of a Christian woman and a Muslim man, and was forced to go to Calabria to become a Christian because his father did not permit it.[32] While the eleventh-century *Vita* presents John's journey to southern Calabria as a flight from an environment hostile to his faith, in the thirteenth-century *Vita* the saint's *xeniteia* (migration and wandering) emerges as an action necessary for him to discover his family and *patria* and thus re-establish his identity. A treasure was waiting for him in his ancestral home to boot.

It is difficult to gauge to what extent such tales dealing with fluid identities fascinated the Italo-Greek audience, whether John's story reflected its own anxieties or even its lived experiences concerning the quest for an identity that had sunk into oblivion. From the second half of the twelfth century onward, the Greek-speaking communities of the kingdom started to decline, since their elite, facing fierce competition from a Latin elite to occupy positions of authority, abandoned its specific cultural traits, language and Eastern doctrine in order to assimilate into the Latin system of power. Within this framework, the use of Greek in public documents significantly receded. Italo-Greeks, moreover, adopted Latin names or Latinised their family names.[33] In many cases, traces of Italo-Greek descent were confined to a cognomen, such as William Ipatus or Angerramus de Maniachi. Thus, the distance was accentuated between the symbolic and the experienced cultural identity of the bearers of these names, who might have not been conscious of their Italo-Greek origins.[34] Self-identification became more complicated because many southern Calabrian Italo-Greeks had moved to Sicily since the end of the eleventh century. In the same period, Sicilian Muslims who converted to Christianity adopted Eastern, not Latin, doctrine.[35] After three generations, the way individuals identified themselves would have therefore undergone many changes and some persons might have sought their cultural origins. Such fluidity in identity may explain why John Theristis was given a different life in his thirteenth-century *Vita*.[36]

It should also be taken into consideration that, from the reign of William I (1154–66) onward, the kingdom's Muslim population had been defined as a threatening otherness and faced persecution and ultimately an extreme population decline.[37] Against this backdrop, the transformation of John's identity, so that it was 'purged' of any fearful Muslim trait, appears totally reasonable. The thirteenth-century account of the saint's arrival in southern Calabria constitutes a typical narrative of fashioning otherness and of the anxiety caused by religious conversion.[38] When John arrived at Stilo, the people who saw him 'wearing clothes of a barbarian' (ἐνδεδυμένον ἔνδυμα βαρβάρου) regarded him as a 'barbarian' (βάρβαρο) and took him to the bishop, who asked him where he had come from. John replied that he had come from 'barbaria' (βαρβαρία) in order to become a Christian. The bishop wanted to test him and told him that he was too old for such a thing and, in order to be judged as capable, he first should be baptised in hot oil. Obviously, this trial was deemed necessary to ascertain the truth of a 'barbarian's' words and avoid a case of incomplete conversion. John agreed to the trial and, when he was about to enter the cauldron of hot oil, the bishop stopped him, baptised him and taught him Christian doctrine (ch. 3, pp. 139–40). After this, the saint began his ascetic life, found the family treasure and distributed it to the poor.

Cyprian of Calamizzi (first half of the twelfth century – c. 1210–15): the experience of decline

The *Vita* (*BHG* 2089) of Cyprian, a native of Reggio and abbot of St Nicholas of Calamizzi, was written in the mid-thirteenth century, an era of decline for the kingdom's Italo-Greek element.[39] It has, therefore, important historical value since the perception of Cyprian's sanctity, which differs substantially from that of the Byzantine- and Norman-era saints, reveals how the Italo-Greek communities experienced this decline and to what extent they had integrated themselves into the kingdom's society. The first difference concerns the medical knowledge imparted to the saint by his physician father (p. 88). In fact, his *patria*, Reggio, was an important centre of medical science throughout the Middle Ages.[40] So, Cyprian cured people 'through art and science, albeit mainly through the grace of the Holy Spirit' (τέχνῃ καὶ ἐπιστήμῃ, μᾶλλον δὲ τοῦ Παναγίου Πνεύματος χάριτι) (pp. 92-4). The second difference concerns the transformation of a function of the ascetic saints central to the development of Italo-Greek monasticism, the founding of monasteries. Cyprian does not fulfil this role, since he is presented as renovating a pre-existing one. The saint was leading an ascetic life in family lands where he had gathered disciples around him when he was elected abbot of St Nicholas of Calamizzi by its monks and the archbishop of Reggio (pp. 88-90). The *Vita* later focuses on his efforts to renovate the monastery and its dependencies through restoration and the construction of new buildings. Moreover, he increased the monastic property – cultivated lands, buildings and animals – through either purchases or donations (p. 92). Yet, according to the author, Cyprian 'suffered a lot' (κακοπάθησε), since 'disorders and irregularities of that era' (τὸ ἀκατάστατον καὶ ἀνώμαλον τοῦ τότε καιροῦ) forced people – magnates and the populace alike – to harm the monastery and its interests. Nevertheless, Cyprian managed to convince some of them to repent and offer annual donations to it (p. 92).

The reason for these two innovations in the perception of sanctity should be sought in the cultural context of the thirteenth century. Cyprian's activity as a physician, which rejects the clash between divine grace and secular medicine typical of most *Vitae*, hinges on the scientific progress of the twelfth century, which led to the foundation of universities and the appreciation of science as a tool for improving the quality of life. The kingdom of Sicily played a pioneering role in shaping the new mentalities, especially regarding medical knowledge and the development of the concept of public health. The kingdom's second legal code, the *Constitutiones* of Melfi issued by Frederick II (1198-1250) in 1231, as well as many of his *Novels* issued from 1240 onward, provided for the profession of physician (necessary studies, final examinations, obtaining a licence to practise), as well as for the profession of pharmacist and the process of drug production. In fact, the provisions for preventing air and water pollution in residential areas were groundbreaking for medieval Europe.[41] Frederick II's health laws reveal a different perception of political power. The protection of public health was considered to require state regulation and was, therefore, included among the sovereign's duties.[42] I suppose that Cyprian's *Vita* is an example of how this policy had influenced the kingdom's subjects, to the extent that they cultivated a different perception of sanctity. They added to the saint's functions the medical treatment of people, thus bridging the gap between tradition and innovation.

The second transformation relates to difficulties faced by the Italo-Greek monasteries due to the decline of the Italo-Greek communities and the consequent loss of their importance for the ruling dynasty. Although Frederick II ratified privileges given to Italo-Greek monasteries by his predecessors, he offered new ones only to Latin monasteries. In fact, in the same era, Italo-Greek monasteries were subject to Latin ones and were obliged to convert to Latin doctrine and rite under the pretext of their financial incapacity and loose morals.[43] This situation is mirrored in the *Vita* in multiple ways. Cyprian is presented as abandoning the monastery in which he had taken the monastic tonsure and leading an ascetic life in family lands 'in order to avoid occasions for scandals in the coenobium' (τὰς τῶν σκανδάλων ἀφορμὰς ἐν τῷ κοινοβίῳ ἐκκλίνων) (p. 88). The monastery of St Nicholas of Calamizzi, founded in the tenth century and prosperous in the eleventh,[44] seems to have been in decline. The author, therefore, attaches more importance to the abbot's role in preserving an existing monastery than in founding a new one. In the same vein, the 'disorders and irregularities of that era' would have concerned financial problems and property disputes, which contributed to the moral degeneration of the monastic communities. Against this backdrop of decline, it is easy to see why the monks chose to bury Cyprian in the monastery's church – after having sought and obtained the archbishop's consent – despite the saint's wish to the contrary (p. 96): They aimed to construct an important *lieu de mémoire* for his cult, capable of sustaining the monastery.

The Norman conquests changed the cultural context of the Mezzogiorno and transformed the social lives of the Italo-Greek communities, which used the *Vitae* of their saints to shape, legitimise and convey new definitions of self. The changes in the hagiographical narratives, when compared with those of the Byzantine period, testify to the emergence of new perceptions of sanctity and enable us to study the strategies adopted by the Italo-Greeks to negotiate their identities in their efforts to integrate themselves into the new political system. The southern Calabrian Italo-Greeks offered allegiance to the Hauteville family and, consequently, cultivated new self-perceptions. The *Vita* of Luke, Bishop of Isola Capo Rizzuto, provides evidence of the way in which they perceived their settlement in Sicily and their involvement in the formation of the county of Sicily thanks to their Greek language and Byzantine *paideia*. The saint's travels from southern Calabria to Sicily and his preaching on the island helped to produce the county's space and organise the Italo-Greeks' lived experiences, which enhanced their new self-perception. The assumption of offices at the Palermitan court created an Italo-Greek elite which tried to strengthen its community by presenting the southern Calabrian saint Bartholomew of Simeri as a quasi-patron of the royal family. Bartholomew is thus presented as having all the identity traits of this elite: the Greek language and Byzantine *paideia*, court networks and close relations with the rulers for whose policy he offered ideological support and legitimacy.

From the second half of the twelfth century onwards, the assimilation of the Italo-Greek elite into the Latin culture, alongside the cultural interaction between Christian and Muslims, would have generated experiences of fluid identities, since memories of origins had faded into oblivion. The change in John Theristis's identity over time mirrors this fluidity. The saint, offspring of a mixed Christian–Muslim marriage in tenth-century Sicily, became in his thirteenth-century *Vita* the legitimate son of a southern Calabrian Christian family who had been raised by a Muslim stepfather in Sicily. His journey to southern Calabria is thus cast as a quest for origins, *patria* and culture. In the thirteenth century the ongoing Latinisation of the Italo-Greek elite led to the decline of the Italo-Greek communities, which became unable to sustain their traditional cultural point of reference, the monasteries. The new context is personified by Cyprian of Calamizzi, no longer the glorious founder of prestigious monasteries but a man struggling to combat the material and moral degeneration of an existing one. Cyprian is also the first Italo-Greek saint openly appreciated for his medical knowledge. Considering the development of the concept of public health in the kingdom of Sicily during this era, this new perception of sanctity possibly indicates the dynamics of social and cultural integration in the kingdom's society.

Notes

1 For the social function of hagiography, there is an abundance of relevant studies. See, among others, J. Kreiner, *The Social Life of Hagiography in the Merovingian Kingdom* (Cambridge, 2014); M. Kuefler, *The Making and Unmaking of a Saint: Hagiography and Memory in the Cult of Gerald of Aurillac* (Philadelphia, 2014); M. Goullet, *Écriture et réécriture hagiographiques. Essai sur les réécritures de Vies de saints dans l'Occident latin médieval (VIIIe–XIIIe s.)* (Turnhout, 2005); and T. Head, *Hagiography and the Cult of Saints: The Diocese of Orléans, 800–1200* (Cambridge, 1990).
2 For southern Calabrian saints, see E. Tounta, 'Conflicting sanctities and the construction of collective memories in Byzantine and Norman Italo-Greek Southern Calabria: Elias the Younger and Elias Speleotes', *Analecta Bollandiana* 135 (2017), 101–44.
3 See, among others, E. Follieri, 'I santi dell'Italia greca', in A. Jacob, J.-M. Martin and G. Noyé (eds), *Histoire et culture dans l'Italie byzantine. Acquis et nouvelles recherches* (Rome, 2006), pp. 103–26; S. Efthymiades, 'Les saints d'Italie méridionale (IXe–XIIe s.) et leur rôle dans la société locale', in D. Sullivan, E. Fisher and S. Papaioannou (eds), *Byzantine Religious Culture: Studies in Honor of Alice-Mary Talbot* (Leiden, 2012), pp. 347–72.
4 For the Norman conquests and the formation of the county of Sicily, see G. A. Loud, *The Age of Robert Guiscard: Southern Italy and the Norman Conquest* (Harlow, 2000), pp. 92–145. For the Greek-speaking communities in the Byzantine era, see A. Peters-Custot, *Les Grecs de l'Italie méridionale post-byzantine (IXe–XIVe siècle). Une acculturation en douceur* (Rome, 2009), pp. 85–221.
5 Peters-Custot, *Les Grecs de l'Italie méridionale*, pp. 234–63; G. A. Loud, *The Latin Church in Norman Italy* (Cambridge, 2007), pp. 259–78, 364–5, 494–500.
6 *Vita di S. Luca vescovo di Isola Capo Rizzuto*, ed. and trans. G. Schirò (Palermo, 1954).
7 D. Alexander, *Saints and Animals in the Middle Ages* (Woodbridge, 2008), pp. 1–19, 39–40, 48–51.
8 The 'enemies' were definitely the Muslims, not the Normans, as had been argued. For a bibliographical survey of this subject, see G. Strano, 'Echi storici nei testi agiografici italo-greci di età normanna. Le Vitae di San Luca, vescovo di Isola Capo Rizzuto, di San Bartolomeo da Simeri e di San Cipriano di Calamizzi', *Aiônos* 17 (2011–12), 104–6.
9 For the production of space which results from the interaction between the objectives of agents of power and the spatial practices and lived

experiences of the people, see H. Lefebvre, *The Production of Space*, trans. D. Nicholson-Smith (Oxford, 1991), pp. 38–46.

10 V. von Falkenhausen, 'The Greek presence in Norman Sicily: The contribution of archival material in Greek', in G. A. Loud and A. Metcalfe (eds), *The Society of Norman Italy* (Leiden, 2002), pp. 260–1.

11 Von Falkenhausen, 'The Greek presence', pp. 258–9; V. von Falkenhausen, 'I logoteti greci nel regno normanno. Uno studio prosopografico', in P. Corrao and I. E. Mineo (eds), *Dentro e fuori la Sicilia: studi di storia per Vincenzo D'Alessandro* (Rome, 2009), p. 107; A. Peters-Custot, '"Byzantine" versus "Imperial" kingdom: How "Byzantine" was the Hauteville kingdom of Sicily?', in F. Daim *et al.* (eds), *Menschen, Bilder, Sprache, Dinge. Wege der Kommunikation zwischen Byzanz und dem Westen*, 2. *Menschen und Worte* (Mainz, 2018), pp. 239–40.

12 Schirò (ed.), *Vita di S. Luca vescovo*, pp. 56–60, suggests that after a doctrinal conflict with Latins the bishop did enter a hut that accidentally caught fire, and afterwards the people's imagination associated the two events. Peters-Custot, *Les Grecs de l'Italie méridionale*, p. 368, argues for probable tensions between Italo-Greek bishops and Latin rulers. P. Oldfield, *Sanctity and Pilgrimage in Medieval Southern Italy, 1000–1200* (Cambridge, 2014), pp. 135–6, regards the episode as indicating possible inter-religious conflicts that could occur because of inflexible doctrinal positions. Loud, *The Latin Church*, pp. 501–2, underlines the privileges that Luke had accepted from the Latin rulers for his own monastery and argues for tensions caused by the arrival of Latins in an exclusively Italo-Greek area. In Strano, 'Echi storici', p. 107, the episode reflects the reaction of an Italo-Greek bishop who was facing the gradual Latinisation of the southern Calabrian bishoprics.

13 For construction of identity and the role of boundaries relating to 'us' and 'them', see S. Hall, 'Who needs "identity"?', in S. Hall and P. du Gay (eds), *Questions of Cultural Identity* (London, 1996), pp. 1–17.

14 For the interpretation of this episode, see Strano, 'Echi storici', pp. 108–9, who presents the relevant literature.

15 Peters-Custot, *Les Grecs de l'Italie méridionale*, pp. 266–302; Loud, *The Latin Church*, pp. 501–11.

16 M. Scaduto, *Il monachesimo basiliano nella Sicilia medievale. Rinascità e Decadenza sec. XI–XIV* (Rome, 1982), pp. 165–213, supposes that the monastery was established in order to provide financial support for the other monasteries of Sicily and southern Calabria, which were in decline. A similar view is shared by Loud, *The Latin Church*, pp. 507–9. Peters-Custot, *Les Grecs de l'Italie méridionale*, pp. 289–302, underlines the political reasons behind its

foundation, namely the king's wish to impose himself as patron of Italo-Greek monasticism, and thus enhance his autonomy from the Roman Church.

17 Follieri, 'I santi dell'Italia greca', pp. 122–4. The *Vita* has been edited by G. Zaccagni (ed.), 'Il Bios di san Bartolomeo da Simeri (*BHG* 235)', *Rivista di studi bizantini e neoellenici* 33 (1996), 193–274 (pp. 205–28 text). The exact date of the text's composition is unknown. Contrary to Zaccagni, who places it nearly fifty years after the saint's death (p. 201), I suggest that the *Vita* was written in the middle of the twelfth century, before 1149, when Luke, first abbot of Holy Saviour, died, since in the text he is given the title 'ἁγιώτατος' (the most holy) used to address living religious authorities. Besides, nothing in the text indicates that Roger II was then dead. On the contrary, when the author mentions the Byzantine Emperor Alexius I (1081–1118), he points out that he was no longer on the throne by the time of the *Vita*'s composition.

18 For Christodoulos, see V. von Falkenhausen, 'Cristodulo', in *Dizionario Biografico degli Italiani* 31 (1985), pp. 49–51.

19 To explain Bartholomew's policy, A. Peters-Custot argues for a new type of monasticism influenced by the Benedictines, which favoured the relations of the abbots with secular authorities without downgrading the spiritual life. See A. Peters-Custot, 'Le monachisme italo-grec, entre Byzance et l'Occident (VIIIe–XIIIe siècles): autorité de l'higoumène, autorité du charisme, autorité de la règle', in J.-F. Cottier, D.-O. Hurel and B.-M. Tock (eds), *Les personnes d'autorité en milieu régulier. Des origines de la vie régulière au XVIIIe siècle* (Saint-Étienne, 2013), pp. 256–7.

20 E. Tounta, 'Saints, rulers and communities: The Vitae of the Italo-Greek saints (tenth to eleventh centuries) and their audiences', *JMH* 42 (2016), pp. 434–7, 446–7.

21 A. Pertusi, 'Monasteri e monaci italiani all'Athos nell'alto medioevo', in *Le Millénaire du Mont Athos 963–1963. Études et Mélanges*, 2 vols (Chevetogne/Venice, 1963–64), vol. 1, pp. 238–41.

22 S. Caruso, 'Il santo, il re, la curia, l'impero. Sul processo per eresia contro Bartolomeo da Simeri (XI–XII sec.)', *Bizantinistica* 1 (1999), pp. 59–68, has proved that the slanderers were Italo-Greeks, not Latins, as previous research had maintained.

23 Oldfield, *Sanctity and Pilgrimage*, pp. 134–5, rightly treats the episode as the hagiographical motif of the falsely accused saint. F. Burgarella, 'Aspetti storici del *Bios* di san Bartolomeo da Simeri', in V. Ruggeri and L. Pieralli (eds), *EUKOSMIA. Studi miscellanei per il 75° di Vincenzo Poggi S.J.* (Soveria Mannelli, 2003), pp. 127–9, argues that the accusations should be associated with scandals occurring at that time

on Mount Athos, which Bartholomew had visited. He also believes that the miracle alludes to the superiority of the Eastern Church. His view is shared by Strano, 'Echi storici', pp. 117–18. Caruso, 'Il santo, il re', pp. 70–2, argues that the accusations could be explained by Bartholomew's journey to Constantinople. The saint should have gone there as a legate of the Roman Church to negotiate an alliance between the Byzantine Empire and the Holy See against Roger II. Furthermore, he suggests that the miracle testifies to the intervention of the Roman churches to the saint's benefit. Nevertheless, no source supports such a view, since the Italo-Greeks's loyalty to Norman rule was beyond question.

24 Peters-Custot, *Les Grecs de l'Italie méridionale*, pp. 369–70, underlining Roger II's support for the founding of Bartholomew's monasteries, argues that the *Vita* is a politico-theological manifesto that aims to familiarise the Italo-Greeks with Latin power. Strano, 'Echi storici', p. 119, supports the view that the author attributes to Roger II traits of the Byzantine emperor Alexius I, who had chaired trials against heretics.

25 K. Pennington, 'The Normans in Palermo: King Roger II's legislation', *Haskins Society Journal* 18 (2006), 140–67; H. Houben, *Roger II of Sicily: A Ruler between East and West*, trans. G. A. Loud and D. Milburn (Cambridge, 2002), pp. 135–47.

26 *Le Typicon du monastère du Saint-Sauveur à Messine, Codex Messinensis Gr 115 A.D. 1131*, ed. M. Arranz (Rome, 1969), pp. xx–xxi.

27 Filagato da Cerami, *Omelie per i vangeli domenicali e le feste di tutto l' anno*, vol. I: *Omelie per le feste fisse*, ed. G. R. Taibbi (Palermo, 1969), sermon no. 34, pp. 232–8.

28 M. Re, 'Il copista, la datazione e la genesi del *Messan. gr. 115* (*Typicon de Messina*)', *Bollettino della Badia Greca di Grottaferrata* 44 (1990), 145–56.

29 *Novae Patrum Bibliothecae*, ed. G. Cozza-Luzi, Tom. 10:2 (Rome, 1905), p. 121. It should be noted that the first folio of the manuscript has been lost and the beginning of the text is, therefore, obscure, *Le Typicon du monastère du Saint-Sauveur*, ed. Arranz, p. xiv.

30 *Novae Patrum Bibliothecae*, ed. Cozza-Luzi, p. 121: '[...] τὸ δὲ θεῷ προσκρούειν καὶ βασιλεῖ οὐκ ἠγνόηται ὅσος ὁ κίνδυνος.'

31 It is difficult to establish the exact dates of the saint's life. Acconcia Longo dates his death at the end of the tenth or the beginning of the eleventh century, since one of the hymns in his honour had probably been written by Abbot Bartholomew of Grottaferrata, who died in 1050. See A. Acconcia Longo, 'S. Giovanni Terista nell'agiografia

e nell'innografia', in A. Acconcia Longo, *Ricerche di Agiografia Italogreca* (Rome, 2003), pp. 139–41. His *Vita* has been edited by S. Borsari (ed.), 'Vita di San Giovanni Terista', *Archivio Storico per la Calabria et la Lucania* 22 (1953), 13–21 (introduction), 136–51 (text). It was written to legitimise, through John's performance of miracles, the property of the same named monastery against persons who claimed its lands. John was not the founder of the monastery, which was a family one founded in the second half of the eleventh century and was associated with the saint in an effort to protect its property. See *Saint-Jean-Théristès (1054–1265)*, ed. A. Guillou (Vatican City, 1980), pp. 23–4.

32 The hymns have been edited by A. Peters (ed.), 'Joannes Messor, seine Lebensbeschreibung und ihre Entstehung' (PhD dissertation, University of Bonn, 1955), pp. 7–27. For an analysis, see Acconcia Longo, 'S. Giovanni Terista', pp. 130–2. Mixed marriages were not unknown in Muslim Sicily: see A. Metcalfe, *Muslims and Christians in Norman Sicily: Arabic Speakers and the End of Islam* (London, 2003), pp. 15–17.

33 Peters-Custot, *Les Grecs de l'Italie méridionale*, pp. 418–19, 435–58, 476–503.

34 Peters-Custot, *Les Grecs de l'Italie méridionale*, p. 452.

35 V. von Falkenhausen, 'Friedrich II. und die Griechen im Königreich Sizilien', in A. Esch and N. Kamp (eds), *Friedrich II. Tagung des Deutschen Historischen Instituts in Rom im Gedenkjahr 1994* (Tübingen, 1996), p. 238.

36 Acconcia Longo, 'S. Giovanni Terista', p. 137, argues that the monastery changed the saint's origins, since his Calabrian descent served its interests better.

37 A. Metcalfe, *The Muslims of Medieval Italy* (Edinburgh, 2009), pp. 181–92, 275–98.

38 For this anxiety, see, among others, H.-R. Benveniste, 'Crossing the frontier: Jewish converts to Catholicism in European history', in E. R. Dursteler *et al.* (eds), *From Florence to the Mediterranean and Beyond: Essays in Honour of Anthony Molho* (Florence, 2009), pp. 447–74.

39 G. Schirò (ed.), 'Vita inedita di S. Cipriano di Calamizzi dal cod. Sinaitico n. 522', *Bulletino della Badia greca di Grottaferrata* n.s. 4 (1950), 88–97. For the dates of the saint's life, see D. Stiernon, 'Saint Cyprien de Calamizzi (+ vers 1210–1215). Notule chronologique', *Revue des Études Byzantines* 32 (1974), 247–52.

40 F. Russo, *Medici e veterinari calabresi (sec. VI–XV). Ricerche storico-bibliografiche* (Naples, 1962), pp. 71–101.

41 W. Stürner, *Friedrich II.* Part 2: *Der Kaiser 1220–1250* (Darmstadt, 2003), pp. 375–85; D. Porter, *Health, Civilization and the State: A History of Public Health from Ancient to Modern Times* (London, 1999), pp. 23–36. See also G. Geltner, *Roads to Health: Infrastructure and Urban Wellbeing in Later Medieval Italy* (Philadelphia, 2019) which demonstrates the myriad of factors that were responsible for developing precocious strategies and regulations on public health in medieval Italy.
42 Stürner, *Friedrich II.*, pp. 384–5.
43 Peters-Custot, *Les Grecs de l'Italie méridionale*, pp. 480–83, 511–15, 518–23.
44 A. Cilento, *Potere e monachesimo. Ceti dirigenti e mondo monastico nella Calabria Bizantina, sec. IX–XI* (Florence, 2000), pp. 142–3.

9

Griffones and the city of Messina: urban encounters with crusading

Paul Oldfield

The complex entanglement of Norman Italy and crusading has long underpinned research on the region for the twelfth and thirteenth centuries, and this includes several important works of Graham Loud, whose enduring guidance and groundbreaking scholarship fundamentally inspire my own work and this chapter in particular.[1] Here, this current chapter re-examines one notable case of such entanglement: the antagonistic encounter between the citizens of Messina in Sicily and the Anglo-Norman contingent stationed nearby during the winter of 1190–91 on its journey on the Third Crusade. This encounter is a particularly revealing case of different realms colliding, of developments in Norman Italy intersecting with those on an international scale. Several Anglo-Norman narratives relate the violent tensions that emerged between Messina's inhabitants and, in particular, King Richard I (the Lionheart) and his crusading force. Some accounts label a segment of Messina's community as *Griffones*, a term sometimes directed pejoratively at citizens of Greek or Greco-Arabic origin. These events, consequently, can be viewed as part of a wider emergent Latin Christian animus towards the 'other', another sign of the cultural misunderstandings between northern and southern Europe and, more evidently, between Latins and Greeks, which would eventually lead to the sack of Constantinople in 1204.[2] Alternatively, scholarship has fitted the events within wider discussions of the Third Crusade, international diplomacy, Richard's temperament and growing friction between the Anglo-Norman and Capetian monarchs.[3]

All these approaches have been fruitful; however, the scholarship has primarily explored this encounter at Messina from the external perspective presented by the (mostly) Anglo-Norman narratives associated with the crusading parties. This chapter instead will examine the encounter through a different optic: the urban perspective. While the sources offer insight into religious, cultural and Anglo-French tension, viewed from a different angle and situated alongside South Italian and other sources, they also allow us to see how these tensions could equally be shaped by the dynamics of an encounter between, on the one hand, an increasingly assertive and diverse urban community, and, on the other, powerful external forces, in this case crusading contingents which brought logistical and leadership challenges.

There are several useful Anglo-Norman narratives of the encounter at Messina.[4] These include, among others, the works of Ambroise, the anonymous author of the *Itinerarium Peregrinorum et Gesta Regis Ricardi* (henceforth: *IP*), Richard of Devizes and Roger of Howden, as well as the briefer accounts by Ralph de Diceto and William of Newburgh.[5] All were composed within approximately a decade of the Third Crusade and at latest by *c.* 1220. It seems very probable that Ambroise, Roger of Howden and perhaps the author of the *IP* were present at Messina in Richard I's contingent.[6] The story they tell collectively is well known and need not be recounted in detail here. In outline it reads thus: King Philip II Augustus of France and his army arrived at Messina in September 1190 and the king was quartered in the city. King Richard I of England and his force arrived soon after but Richard ultimately stationed himself and his contingent outside the city walls, occupied a local Greek monastery and built a fortification nearby which he named Mategrifon (Griffon-killer). Tensions erupted during the winter between the citizens and Richard I's army and caused casualties on both sides and the storming of Messina by Anglo-Norman forces. Frictions, moreover, arose between Richard I and the recently crowned, but vulnerable, King Tancred of Sicily, and between Richard I and Philip II. Fragile truces were eventually reached between all parties. Philip sailed for the Holy Land in late March 1191; Richard followed in April.

The aforementioned authors will be drawn upon in conjunction with other contemporary, 'internal' and contextual evidence on Messina. The intention here is not to reconstruct a narrative of events nor revisit analyses of the cultural perspectives, reliability, content or agendas of the Anglo-Norman accounts. For this, the reader should consult the work of Lindsay Diggelmann, who notes that during the Third Crusade 'their [the Anglo-Norman commentators] willingness to impose unitary and uncomplicated definitions on those other peoples whom they encounter reinforces their own "national" or cultural worth: "we" are part of a complex, sophisticated society; "they" are a simple, headstrong people who lack our obviously superior values'.[7] Thus, the 'truth' of these accounts is problematic, but they can be read in ways that improve our understanding of the urban context underpinning the encounter. Indeed, the aim here is to highlight the wider potential for resituating some of the tensions exposed in those Anglo-Norman sources within an urban framework by exploring three themes: (1) the multicultural meeting-point; (2) markets; and (3) autonomy and ritual.

The multicultural meeting-point

The twelfth century saw rapid urban transformation. Demographic, topographic and economic growth turned cities into increasingly significant actors commercially, politically and culturally. The crusaders who arrived at Messina in 1190 encountered a city at the forefront of these changes, but one particularly distinctive through its role as key transit point for east–west Mediterranean movement, a role enhanced in the twelfth century by crusading and pilgrimage. This generated an especially diverse and transient urban population. The city's affluence, diversity and vibrant activity inspired scholarly comment. Muḥammad al-Idrīsī in his geographical treatise of c. 1154 noted that 'travellers and merchants from every sort of country, Christian and Muslim' were encountered in Messina. Visitors such as Benjamin of Tudela, who passed through southern in Italy in c. 1170, noted that 'most of the pilgrims assemble [at Messina] to cross over to Jerusalem', and Ibn Jubayr, in the city in the 1180s, mentioned its abundance of commodities, ships and foreigners.[8] Indeed, Amalfitan, Pisan and Genoese trading colonies had been established in Messina from at least the early twelfth century.[9] Overlaying this diversity of visitors to the city was the conspicuous mixed heritage of Messina's permanent urban populace. In c. 1190 it was home to both Latin and Greek communities. It must be remembered that, prior to the Norman conquest of Sicily in the eleventh century and subsequent Latin Christian immigration, Messina's Christian population was effectively Greek. The Latin Christians in Messina in the twelfth century were relative newcomers with an immigrant background.[10] But the influx of Latin settlers of diverse origins and the gradual Latinisation of Messina had not by the second half of the twelfth century entirely displaced the city's Greek community.[11] The Sicilian chronicle of the so-called Hugo Falcandus, covering the years 1154 to 1169, demonstrates that the city had a powerful and distinct Greek community which participated in (sometimes violent) civic faction and retained political agency.[12] Moreover, the vibrancy of the Greek community was aided by a nearby cultural focal point, the influential Greek archimandrite monastery of Holy Saviour in *Lingua Phari*. The house enjoyed significant royal patronage and headed a confederation of more than thirty Greek Orthodox monasteries.[13] Indeed, the *De Viis Maris* – a late-twelfth century portolan possibly composed by Roger of Howden – records that the monastery (*abbatia Griffonum*) housed 'one hundred griffon monks, that is Greeks' (*centum monachos griffones, id est Grecos*).[14] Civic administration still reflected Messina's diversity too. The city's chief urban official bore a Greek title, *stratigotus*. The office's first Latin holder appears in the 1150s, but at the end of the twelfth century the city sometimes simultaneously employed two *stratigoti*, one Greek, the other Latin. The city, moreover, had a sizeable Jewish community and quarter.[15] An (at least partially authentic) privilege of Henry VI in 1194 exemplifies Messina's multicultural reality by addressing the city's Latin, Greek and Jewish inhabitants and establishing that the city would have three judges, two Latin, one Greek.[16]

At the same time, this diversity could no doubt be confusing and unsettling. Hugo Falcandus's account notes the malleable affinities within the multicultural port city: he characterises the citizens' loyalty as 'typical both of Greek perfidy [*greca perfidia*] and of the reliability to be expected from pirates'.[17] He elsewhere records a particularly noteworthy episode of entangled relationships in which Messina's Greek community allied with local Latins against recent, politically powerful French immigrants. A riot was sparked when some drunken Frenchmen broke up the gaming of some Greeks.

Falcandus presents both Messina's Greeks and its Latins as victims of French abuse and financial extortion, particularly demands for money from ships bound for the Holy Land.[18] The city's *stratigotus* lost control over events, the leader of the French 'party' was gruesomely executed by the Messinesi, and it was said that 'during this time the Greeks [*Greci*] were busy slaughtering anyone from north of the Alps [*transalpinos*] they could find'.[19]

All the contextual factors above – a commercial hub with a transient, multicultural community and a history of tension between Messinesi and 'outsiders' who transgressed local customs – must have contributed to how the crusaders and their Anglo-Norman commentators made sense of their encounters with Messina. The Anglo-Norman sources are permeated by an evident anxiety and uncertainty regarding Messina, its potential power and its fluid community. This may too have been framed by universal tropes on the 'evil city' that associated wealth and profit with sin, corruption and malevolence and often implicitly transposed these attributes onto a city's inhabitants.[20] Indeed, among his many scathing critiques of the key actors in his work, Falcandus describes Messina as a city 'composed of immigrants, pirates and brigands [*hec enim civitas ex convenis, piratis, predonibus adunata*]. It held within its walls almost every type of human being, free from no kind of wickedness, rejecting no crime, thinking that nothing that it had the power to do was forbidden'.[21] This connecting of urban environment with human behaviour appears early in Anglo-Norman narratives of the encounter at Messina. Ambroise notes that 'Messina was full of comforts, but we found them an evil people'.[22] Likewise, the *IP*'s author, apparently drawing on Ambroise, comments that Messina 'abounds in every good and essential thing, but its people are cruel and the very worst sort [*pessimos et crudeles*]'.[23]

More generally, the Anglo-Norman narratives certainly reflect, as Diggelmann has shown, 'strategies of cultural distancing' between the Anglo-Norman and Mediterranean worlds.[24] The fluidity of identity in Messina seems to have intensified that distancing and created both interest and confusion. Some Anglo-Norman commentators spoke generically of the *cives* of Messina.[25] In places they attempted more precision. Richard of Devizes, Ralph de Diceto, Roger of Howden, Ambroise and the *IP* opted for the term *Griffones/Grifones* for Greeks, and both Ambroise and the

IP employed the term *Li Longebardi/Longobardi* (Lombards) for the city's Latins.[26] But the shifting allegiances at Messina must have bewildered the Anglo-Norman observers. This is reflected particularly in Ambroise and the *IP*, for at times they signal the *Griffones* as troublemakers, sometimes the Lombards, at other times both, and at yet others the Lombards in alliance with Philip II's French contingent. Roger of Howden adds to this list the Pisans and Genoese, who had trading colonies in Messina and for some unknown reason attacked the English fleet on Christmas Day, 1190.[27] This picture could only have been complicated further by Messina's complex historical demography. When the *IP*'s author (again perhaps following Ambroise) called the citizens a 'wicked bunch, commonly known as Griffons [*Cives namque nequam, vulgo dicti Griffones*]. Many of them were the offspring of Saracen fathers [*patribus progeniti plures eorum Saracenis*], and they were absolutely opposed and hostile towards our people', he not only denigrated the Messinesi but also seemed to allude (although not entirely accurately) to the long-term immigration and acculturation that had shaped the city's urban communities.[28]

While the alleged hostility and threat of the *Griffones* partially served a useful literary function for some Anglo-Norman commentators, it may quite possibly have been influenced by the current status of the Greek community in Messina and also may have resonated with civic remembrance of earlier conflict. Both Roger of Howden and Richard of Devizes note that the *Griffones* were, before Richard I's arrival, the region's most powerful group. If the Greek community's influence had been steadily declining elsewhere in Sicily in the second half of the twelfth century, it endured at least in Messina. Both authors also mention the *Griffones*' hatred of all *Ultramontanos* (those from beyond the Alps).[29] Richard of Devizes adds that 'While they [the *Griffones*] had always hated the *Ultramontanos*, now, irritated by fresh injuries, they burned more fiercely than ever'. He tells us that the English were attacked and 'slain both by day and night by forties and fifties' by the enraged *Griffones*. Apparently the 'slaughter increased every day and it was planned to continue with this madness till every one of them was killed or put to flight'.[30] This account of a desire for vengeance that fomented a seemingly wide, indiscriminate attack on individuals from north of the Alps mirrors Falcandus's earlier account of the

Greeks' role in disorder in Messina in the 1160s. There was thus a precedent for such violent cross-cultural tension in Messina between Greeks and *Ultramontanos*, albeit in the 1160s the outsiders were French and labelled with a synonym, the *Transalpinos*. Ambroise and, with slight amendment, the *IP* imply that both sides were influenced by memory. Ambroise charges that 'The Lombards and the townsfolk always had bitterness against us, for their fathers said to them that our ancestors conquered them'.[31] Of course, Messina was conquered by the Normans as early as 1061, when no Lombards were in the city, but a distant past could clearly be mobilised and reinscribed with new cultural meaning.

One of those 'fresh injuries' inflicted on Messina's urban community seems to have been connected to the important nearby archimandrite Greek monastery of Holy Saviour in *Lingua Phari*. As noted above, in c. 1190 it was Sicily's leading Greek monastery, a large community. Vera von Falkenhausen has shown how, with its active scriptorium and patronage from the kingdom's Greek elites, the monastery was a spiritual and cultural safeguard for Messina's Greek community. Its distance from Palermo conversely meant that it had less chance of stemming the Greek community's gradual decline in the island's 'capital'.[32] Given the demographic change in Messina from the second half of the twelfth century and the pressure placed on the city's Greek community, Holy Saviour's cultural significance undoubtedly increased in Messina. The sense of threat and insult thus posed by Richard I's decision to occupy the monastery was palpable. According to Roger of Howden, Richard expelled the monks and their servants, installed his knights and guards, and even used it as a storehouse for victuals. Messina's citizens, cognisant also of Richard's takeover of a site across the strait at Bagnara and fearing that he was preparing to conquer the whole island, henceforth 'considered him to be suspect'. Roger of Howden thus presents the occupation of Holy Saviour as a significant event in 'the origin of the discord' (*principium discordiae*) between the Messinesi and Richard.[33] Richard of Devizes' account notes that after the occupation of Holy Saviour the king of England made the '*Griffones* a laughing-stock to his men'.[34] If this was part of Richard's strategy to pressure the Sicilian king Tancred in negotiations over the return of his sister's dowry, it was simultaneously an inflammatory manoeuvre for the Messinesi, especially the city's Greeks. Soon afterward, open hostility erupted and the citizens closed the city gates, armed themselves and took to the walls.[35]

Markets

Understanding the importance of precedent and the sociodemographic transitions within Messina during the twelfth century is clearly central to accomplishing a more complete reading of events in 1190/91. In this context, it is also significant that some of the flashpoints for tension with the Messinesi in 1190/91 related to long-standing issues associated with markets, logistics and resources. Messina historically faced one overriding challenge in the twelfth century as the city boomed from commercial and crusading traffic. Proximity of the Peloritani mountain range rendered Messina's hinterland too restricted to produce sufficient grain for the city, so its civic administration had to ensure supplies from elsewhere in eastern Sicily and from Calabria.[36] The city, consequently, was especially vulnerable to embargo. In 1168, for example, the Sicilian monarchy punished Messina for its role in an uprising by cutting off grain from Catania, an 'action [that] imposed starvation on the people of Messina'.[37] The city's precarious grain supply and susceptibility to embargo was aggravated by the unpredictable flows of pilgrims or crusaders into Messina. Scarcity and higher prices could ensue. Moreover, because of this hinterland-city interrelationship and the imperative to be competitive with the Genoese and Pisan trading communities, the Messinesi had always fought to secure more lenient taxation and to retain control of their domestic economy and the trade moving through their city.[38] Indeed, in the 1160s the Messinesi beseeched King William II of Sicily for the restoration of a privilege granted by Roger II (d. 1154) 'regarding the city's freedoms from taxation', and the issue of taxes levied on boats heading for Syria was at the heart of the aforementioned violent uprising against a French contingent in the city.[39] Commerce and the functioning of markets in the city had long been sources of tension.

By 1190, therefore, with Messina a thriving commercial and transit port, its citizens were long accustomed to logistical supply-and-demand challenges. Uneven surges of commerce, pilgrimage and crusading would have been routine. But it appears that those logistical challenges were significantly intensified in 1190 by the arrival of such a large Anglo-French contingent. This clearly strained the city's supplies and capacity and exacerbated the cultural preconceptions harboured by both the Messinesi and the northern European visitors. Access to resources and the provision of supplies appear to underpin the fluctuating, interconnected phases of hostility, but so too does mistrust of strangers. William of Newburgh claims that at the outset the Messinesi rejected Richard I's request to reside in the city because the burden of hosting two monarchs would be too great. In the fallout, some of Richard's men were allegedly killed.[40] The *IP* presents a slightly different picture of slowly escalating tension between the Messinesi and the English. The Messinesi, angered by some of the English 'chatting to their wives', harassed the English and pre-emptively enhanced the city's fortification.[41] The tipping point was apparently reached with a dispute about the price of bread between a local woman and an Englishman, an incident simultaneously pragmatic and symbolic. The former claimed the latter offered too little for the loaf and in the ensuing commotion a crowd of citizens attacked the Englishman.[42] The following day another fight erupted and from there the path of the dispute ultimately led to the violent capture of Messina by Richard and his army.[43] Soon afterward, to pressure Richard following his construction of the Mategrifon, the *Griffones* reportedly prohibited the sale of food to the English contingent.[44] When peace was finally restored among Richard I, Philip II and Messina's citizens, the terms mandated the return of looted precious metal and money to the citizens and enactment of legislation to ensure security and peace; consequently, according to the *IP*, 'Now necessary foodstuffs for humans and horses were laid out for sale at a reasonable price'.[45] The provision of supplies and a just price were reinstated. Access to markets and the provisioning of crusader forces had always been a logistical challenge and a flashpoint for conflict on earlier expeditions, particularly in the Byzantine Empire. Those tensions seem to have been ever-present at Messina and exacerbated by the city's own historic supply-and-demand challenges. It is no surprise that those frictions should re-emerge after the arrival of the large crusading contingents in 1190.

Autonomy and ritual

Messina was not only a vibrant commercial port city, but also a politically and military powerful entity able to act autonomously when the circumstances dictated. As Julia Becker notes, Messina with good reason was described in hyperbolic terms in contemporary sources – as *clavis Siciliae* in Geoffrey Malaterra's chronicle and as *megalopolis* or *magna civitas* in charters – and its strategic location and distinctive openness to the wider Mediterranean world endowed it with an 'internazionalità' that distinguished it from other cities in the kingdom of Sicily.[46] Moreover, the limited hinterland meant there were few landed estates to grant out in support of a local nobility; political power was thus more firmly controlled by the city's urban elite.[47] Consequently, the monarchy since the kingdom's founding in 1130 had established an often uneasy but pragmatic interrelationship with Messina. Falcandus's account shows clearly that the Messinesi were politically active, acutely aware of their privileges, willing to protect them and open to conspiracy and rebellion with influential elites and other cities if necessary. Yet, at the same time, the Sicilian monarchy's authority was recognised, even welcomed, as a mediator in local urban disputes. The city hosted a royal palace, the one which Ibn Jubayr had probably marvelled at and where Philip Augustus was lodged on his arrival.[48] The Sicilian monarchs, moreover, were fairly regular visitors, given that they mostly remained in Palermo. During his reign, William II (1166–89) was in the city on at least ten occasions.[49] Falcandus records this intricate dynamic between monarchy and city: despite their perceived loyalty to the king, the Messinesi in *c*. 1168 registered a charge of abuse of their rights through a choreographed protest in which they placed 'their accusations in writing, and stuck them up on poles and raised an enormous clamour in front of the palace'. On another occasion a letter composed by William in response to rumours of plotting at Palermo was to be read out to the assembled citizenry at the city's cathedral.[50] As Messina's *stratigotus* prepared to read the letter, more rumours circulated among the assembled citizenry and sparked a further cycle of violence in the city. The monarchy thus had to tread carefully and be cognisant of the nuances of public political discourse, ritual and violence within a city whose assorted communities could rapidly assert autonomy of action. Unsurprisingly, the monarchs of France and England were less attuned to these local discourses. Richard's royal entry into the city seems to have simultaneously inspired not only awe but also suspicion and concern within Messina, because it apparently transgressed established norms. As Caterina Lavarra states:

> the solemn rituals of welcome were extraordinary instruments of interaction between people, or groups of people, but above all of communication, as they conveyed non-verbal messages, whose content was mediated by symbolic elements intelligible to all the participants, protagonists or recipients (the public), and they lent themselves to being used for the representation of relationships of power, manifesting thus an extremely political character.[51]

The *IP* contrasts Philip's understated, almost secretive entrance into Messina with the power and spectacle of Richard's.[52] The author undoubtedly was aiming to establish an opposition between a cowardly and a courageous monarch. We thus must be cautious with embellishment, but such a display of royal magnificence is not out of the question and is echoed across a number of the accounts. According to the *IP*, the Messinesi were apparently underwhelmed by Philip's arrival and 'accused him of being timid and jeered him, saying that this king could not easily accomplish great deeds of valour since he was so wary of human gaze'. Conversely, Richard's magnificent entrance astounded the crowds. The sea seemed to 'boil [*mare fervescere*]' from the approaching fleet's oars, its trumpets 'thundering [*tubarum intonationibus*]', and Richard standing on the prow for all to see. Such 'great magnificence [*tanta gloria*]' 'stunned [*attonitum*]' the Messinesi, who proclaimed, 'This man is certainly worthy of authority! [*Hic quidem dignus imperio!*] He deserves to be set over peoples and kingdoms [*super gentes et super regna*]. We had heard of his great reputation [*fama*], but the reality that we see is far greater'. If the agenda of the Anglo-Norman author is clear, equally so is the perceived impact on the Messinesi. The *IP* claims that the *Griffones*' 'arrogance was somewhat checked [*in parte repressa est arrogantia*]' by the manner of the arrival and

'They realised that the kings were stronger and more glorious than they'. More explicitly, Ambroise acknowledges that 'the Grifons were angry and the Lombards grumbled because he came into their city with such a fleet and such pomp and circumstance'.[53] Roger of Howden states that 'fear [*tremor*] overtook those who were in the city' and Richard of Devizes also notes that 'so great was the noise of trumpets and clarions that the city trembled and grew afraid'.[54] These authors display the power of the English monarch to astonish, but they also reveal how a stark message of hierarchy, subordination and threat was conveyed to the Messinesi. John Gillingham rightly questions if the arrival was 'tactful'.[55] Indeed, in framing his entry around the dominion of the sea, Richard was encroaching on the very lifeblood of many Messinesi. William of Newburgh in contrast says that Philip's arrival 'was welcomed with joy by the citizens', and both Roger of Howden and a rare and brief French perspective (Rigord's *Gesta Philippi*) claim that Philip was received 'honorifice'.[56] The contrasting ritualised advents of the respective monarchs seem to have created a cornerstone for future relationships with Messina. Unsurprisingly, Philip was hosted within the city at the royal palace, and Richard eventually was compelled to station himself outside Messina's walls, with the consequent distancing (real and metaphorical) that this generated. Perhaps Richard had only intended to stay in the city for a short time and made a powerful statement sustainable only briefly in the context of the city's politics. But, according to Roger of Howden, adverse winds apparently prevented the fleets from moving on and forced a prolonged winter stopover.[57] In any event, it seems that Richard made a miscalculation that set a path towards dispute between royal and urban conceptions of power.

Conclusion

The encounter between Messina and the Anglo-French contingents during the Third Crusade has long been considered primarily within the framework of the latter group. This can only provide half the picture; the urban perspective is essential to understanding the events which unfolded during the winter of 1190–91. At points across that winter, Messina was without doubt often a pawn in the high diplomatic struggles among the three kings, Richard, Tancred and Philip. But, in addition, a multicultural urban community, cross-cultural tensions, the functioning of markets and their city–hinterland interrelationship, civic autonomy and public ritual within Messina all coalesced to present a framework within which the Third Crusaders, and more markedly the royal conceptions of power and the logistical challenges that travelled with them, had to be accommodated somehow. Such accommodation was difficult and sometimes impossible, while at other times uneasy truces were accomplished. Within the fluctuating relationship between city and crusaders, precedent and memory (past events in Messina and the city's long-standing norms) played a central formative role. But, it is also important to note how the Messinesi experienced what must have seemed to be the 'underbelly' of crusading. The Third Crusaders who encountered Messina appear to have first and foremost made pragmatic and logistical demands on the city, and, particularly in the case of the Anglo-Normans, framed them in an ideology of royal prerogative and superiority. The Anglo-Norman sources may have on occasion termed the Anglo-French contingents at Messina as *peregrini* (pilgrims) who were *in via perigrinatione*.[58] Indeed, according to Richard of Devizes, the English monarch openly linked the struggle at Messina to the recovery of Jerusalem and the struggle with Saladin and implied that violence could be legitimately applied against sinful *Griffones* at Messina.[59] But to the Messinesi, crusading piety must have seemed tangential, and there is evidence that other medieval cities had comparable encounters with large crusading forces, particularly when 'otherness' was an important dynamic between local community and visiting crusader.[60] To the Messinesi, who oversaw their city's infrastructure of travel and trade (hospitals, *fondachi*, markets), the visitors were *prima facie* the sort of consumers, transient visitors and potential transgressors whom they had encountered in their port city for decades. In 1190–91, however, the combination of the magnitude, pre-eminence and difference of those visitors also brought to the city a cultural threat, a socio-economic and political challenge and a source of spectacle which proved particularly volatile, and it just so happened that the eyes of the wider Latin Christian world were now watching.

Notes

1 For example: G. A. Loud, 'Norman Italy and the Holy Land', in B. Z. Kedar (ed.), *The Horns of Hattin* (Jerusalem, 1992), pp. 49–62; G. A. Loud, 'A new document concerning the bishopric of Sebastea', *Crusades* 16 (2017), 21–31. I would like to thank Professor Jonathan P. Phillips for kindly commenting on an early draft.

2 See especially L. Diggelmann, 'Of Grifons and tyrants: Anglo-Norman views of the Mediterranean world during the Third Crusade', in L. Bailey, L. Diggelmann and K. M. Phillips (eds), *Old Worlds, New Worlds: European Cultural Encounters, c.1000–c.1750* (Turnhout, 2009), pp. 11–30, and also A. P. Kazhdan and A. Wharton Epstein, *Change in Byzantine Culture in the Eleventh and Twelfth Centuries* (Berkeley, 1985).

3 J. Gillingham, *Richard I* (New Haven, 1999); S. Spencer, '"Like a raging lion"': Richard the Lionheart's anger during the Third Crusade in medieval and modern historiography', *EHR* 132 (2017), 495–532.

4 In applying the label 'Anglo-Norman' in this chapter I of course acknowledge the problem in using it as term for a collective identity in *c.* 1200. On English historical writing of this period see M. Staunton, *The Historians of Angevin England* (Oxford, 2017).

5 *The History of the Holy War: Ambroise's Estoire de la guerre sainte*, ed. and trans. M. Ailes and M. Barber, 2 vols: vol. 1 (Old French Text); vol. 2 (Translation) (Woodbridge, 2011) (henceforth: Ambroise, *History*); *Itinerarium Peregrinorum et gesta regis Ricardi*, ed. W. Stubbs, in *Chronicles and Memorials of the Reign of Richard I*, Rolls Series 38, vol. 1 (London, 1864) (henceforth: *IP*, Stubbs); *Chronicle of the Third Crusade: A Translation of the Itinerarium Peregrinorum et gesta regis Ricardi*, trans. H. J. Nicholson (Aldershot, 1997) (henceforth: *IP*, Nicholson); *The Chronicle of Richard of Devizes at the Time of King Richard the First*, ed. and trans. J. T. Appleby (London, 1963); the two works by Roger of Howden: *Gesta regis Henrici secundi et gesta regis Ricardi*, ed. W. Stubbs, Rolls Series 49, 2 vols (London, 1867) and *Chronica magistri Rogeri de Houedene*, ed. W. Stubbs, Rolls Series 51, 3 vols (London, 1868); *Ymagines Historiarum of Ralph de Diceto* in *Opera Historica*, ed. W. Stubbs, Rolls Series 68, vol. 2 (1876); *Historia Rerum Anglicarum of William of Newburgh* in *Chronicles of the Reigns of Stephen, Henry II, and Richard I*, ed. R. Howlett, Rolls Series 82, vol. 1 (1884).

6 Diggelmann, 'Grifons', pp. 13–15.

7 Diggelmann, 'Grifons', p. 30.

8 English translation in *Roger II*, p. 361; French translation in Idrîsî, *La Première Géographie de l'Occident*, rev. trans. H. Bresc et al. (Paris, 1999), p. 312; *The Itinerary of Benjamin of Tudela*, trans. M. N. Adler (London, 1907), p. 137; *The Travels of Ibn Jubayr*, trans. R. J. C. Broadhurst (London, 1952), pp. 338–9.
9 E. Pispisa, *Messina medievale* (Galatina, 1996), p. 17; D. Abulafia, 'Pisan commercial colonies and consulates in twelfth-century Sicily', *EHR* 93 (1978), 68–81.
10 V. von Falkenhausen, 'Die griechischen Gemeinden in Messina und Palermo (11. bis 13. Jahrhundert)', in T. Jäckh and M. Kirsch (eds), *Urban Dynamics and Transcultural Communication in Medieval Sicily* (Paderborn, 2017), p. 42; see also evidence from local charters: *Les Actes grecs de S. Maria di Messina*, ed. A. Guillou (Palermo, 1963), and *Les Actes latins de S. Maria di Messina (1103–1250)*, ed. L.-R. Ménager (Palermo, 1963); Pispisa, *Messina*, pp. 13–22.
11 On the Italo-Greek community in southern Italy generally, see A. Peters-Custot, *Les Grecs de l'Italie méridionale post-byzantine: une acculturation en douceur* (Rome, 2009).
12 *Falcandus*, pp. 183–5, 199–208; Latin edition: *La Historia o Liber de Regno Sicilie e la Epistola ad Petrum Panormitane Ecclesie Thesaurium di Ugo Falcando*, ed. G. B. Siragusa, FSI 22 (Rome, 1897), pp. 131–3, 147–55 (henceforth: *Historia*).
13 V. von Falkenhausen, 'L'Archimandritato del S. Salvatore in lingua phari di Messina e il monachesimo italo-greco nel regno normanno-svevo (secoli XI–XIII)', in G. Fallico, A. Sparti and U. Balistreri (eds), *Messina: il Ritorno della memoria* (Palermo, 1994), pp. 41–52.
14 P. Gautier Dalché (ed.), *Du Yorkshire a l'Inde. Une'geographie urbaine et maritime de la fin du XII siècle (Roger de Howden)* (Geneva, 2005), pp. 206, 210–11.
15 Benjamin of Tudela (*Itinerary*, p. 137) noted around 200 Jews (or this figure may represent heads of families) living at Messina in c. 1170; E. Pispisa, 'Organizzazione urbana di Messina e i suoi rapporti con il territorio nel medioevo', in G. Fallico, A. Sparti and U. Balistreri (eds), *Messina: il Ritorno della memoria* (Palermo, 1994), p. 339.
16 J. Becker, '... ut omnes habitatores Messane tam latini quam greci et hebrei habeant predictam libertatem ... Vita cittadina e cittadinanza a Messina tra Normanni, Angioni er Aragonesi', in T. Jäckh and M. Kirsch (eds), *Urban Dynamics and Transcultural Communication in Medieval Sicily* (Paderborn, 2017), p. 170; F. Martino, 'Una ignota pagina del Vespro: la compilazione dei falsi privilegi Messinesi', *Archivio Storico Messinese* 57 (1991), pp. 22–7.

17 *Falcandus*, p. 184; *Historia*, p. 132; here Falcandus follows conventional twelfth-century Latin Christian tropes on Greeks; for discussion see Diggelmann, 'Grifons', especially pp. 16–22.
18 *Falcandus*, pp. 199–208; *Historia*, pp. 147–55.
19 *Falcandus*, p. 206; *Historia*, p. 153.
20 P. Oldfield, *Urban Panegyric and the Transformation of the Medieval City, 1100–1300* (Oxford, 2019), pp. 95–110.
21 *Falcandus*, p. 156; *Historia*, p. 108.
22 Ambroise, *History*, vol. 2, p. 37.
23 *IP*, Nicholson, pp. 154–5; *IP*, Stubbs, p. 154.
24 Diggelmann, 'Grifons', p. 12.
25 For example, Roger of Howden: *Chronica*, pp. 56–8; William of Newburgh: *Historia*, bk IV, XII, pp. 324–5.
26 Diggelmann, 'Grifons', pp. 16, 22; for the Lombards, see, for example, Ambroise, *History*, vol. 1, p. 10, line 615; *IP*, Stubbs, pp. 154–5, 157.
27 *Chronica*, p. 93. The author of the *IP* claimed the Italians had 'got drunk on neat wine' (*IP*, Nicholson, p. 172; *IP*, Stubbs, p. 174). It is also worth noting the presence of yet another community with its own interests: the military monastic orders. The Templars and Hospitallers had a presence in Messina in the twelfth century, and the city was temporarily placed under their (apparently neutral) custody after Richard I had captured it. See also Roger of Howden's *Chronica*, p. 58, and also A. Luttrell, 'Gli ospedalieri nel mezzogiorno', in G. Musca (ed.), *Il mezzogiorno normanno-svevo e le crociate* (Bari, 2002), pp. 290, 298–9.
28 *IP*, Nicholson, pp. 155–6; *IP*, Stubbs, pp. 154–5; Ambroise, *History*, vol. 2, p. 38; see generally A. Metcalfe, *Muslims and Christians in Norman Italy: Arabic Speakers and the End of Islam* (London, 2003).
29 *Chronica*, p. 67; *Chronicle of Richard of Devizes*, p. 19.
30 *Chronicle of Richard of Devizes*, p. 19.
31 Ambroise, *History*, vol. 2, p. 39; *IP*, Stubbs, pp. 157–8.
32 Von Falkenhausen, 'Die griechischen Gemeinden', pp. 39–40; and von Falkenhausen, 'L'Archimandritato', pp. 41–52.
33 *Chronica*, p. 56; see the slightly different version in Roger of Howden's *Gesta*, vol. 2, p. 127; In *Ymagines Historiarum*, p. 85, Ralph de Diceto speaks of Richard capturing a *castellum* called 'monasterium Griffonum'.
34 *Chronicle of Richard of Devizes*, p. 17.
35 As noted by Roger of Howden in both *Chronica*, p. 56 and *Gesta*, vol. 2, p. 127.
36 Pispisa, *Messina*, pp. 11, 22.
37 Falcandus, p. 207; *Historia*, pp. 154–5.

38 The authenticity of a set of twelfth-century royal charters conferring privileges on Messina, including commercial rights, is still much debated. Most of the charters appear problematic and probably were forged in the thirteenth century, but it remains possible that some of the contents of the false charters were based on contemporary concessions. See *Rogerii II Regis Diplomata Latina*, ed. C.-R. Bruhl, Codex Diplomaticus Regni Siciliae, Ser. I.ii(1) (Cologne, 1987), no. 11, pp. 29–35; *Guillelmi I Regis Diplomata*, ed. H. Enzensberger, Codex Diplomaticus Regni Siciliae, Ser. I.iii (Cologne, 1996), no. 28, pp. 74–7; no. 30, pp. 80–2; Martino, 'Una ignota pagina del Vespro', pp. 19–76.
39 *Falcandus*, pp. 183, 200; *Historia*, pp. 131, 147.
40 *Historia*, bk IV, XII, p. 324.
41 *IP*, Nicholson, pp. 158–9; *IP*, Stubbs, pp. 157–8.
42 *IP*, Nicholson, p. 159; *IP*, Stubbs, pp. 158–9. Roger of Howden in his *Chronica*, pp. 59–60, includes what purports to be a full copy of the agreement reached between King Richard and King Philip after the former had stormed and captured Messina and a dispute had arisen between the two monarchs over the placing of Richard's standards on the city's walls. The charter reveals some of the overriding concerns of the Crusade leadership. It established terms of conduct for the crusading armies. Sizeable sections of it are given over to rules on gaming and its punishments, debts, making and selling bread, and procurement of associated foodstuffs such as flour and corn. A Capetian source also notes issues associated with market-supply: 'in that time, whatever goods were found there were extremely expensive. A sextarius of grain was worth 24 Angevin solidi; barley, 28 solidi; wine, 15 solidi; poultry, 12 denarii'. See also the record of Rigord in *Gesta Philippi Augusti Rigordi Liber/Histoire de Philippe Auguste*, ed. and trans. E. Carpentier, G. Pons and Y. Chauvin (Paris, 2006), ch. 79, pp. 286–8.
43 *IP*, Nicholson, pp. 159–63; *IP*, Stubbs, pp. 159–64. Ambroise, *History*, vol. 2, pp. 39–43, offers broadly the same narrative.
44 *IP*, Nicholson, p. 167; *IP*, Stubbs, p. 168; Ambroise, *History*, vol. 2, p. 44. *Chronicle of Richard of Devizes*, p. 19, also notes, in a slightly different order of the narrative, that an edict was issued to prevent trade with the English.
45 *IP*, Nicholson, p. 169; *IP*, Stubbs, p. 170.
46 Becker, 'Vita cittadina', pp. 159 (and footnotes 1–4 across pp. 159–60 for full references to the aforementioned contemporary sources), 171. Estimates of Messina's population in *c.* 1190 can only be speculative. The *IP*, Stubbs, p. 162, reckons that those defending the city from Richard's assault numbered more than 50,000. Of course we must be

cautious in using such calculations. Pispisa, *Messina*, p. 10, estimates the figure to be around 20–25,000.
47 Pispisa, *Messina*, pp. 10–13.
48 *Travels*, p. 340.
49 H. Enzensberger, 'Messina e i re', in G. Fallico, A. Sparti and U. Balistreri (eds), *Messina: il Ritorno della memoria* (Palermo, 1994), pp. 332–4.
50 *Falcandus*, pp. 184, 202; *Historia*, pp. 132, 150.
51 C. Lavarra, 'Rituali di accoglienza e spazio urbano nel Mezzogiorno normanno', in C. Lavarra, *Mezzogiorno normanno: potere, spazio urbano, ritualità* (Galatina, 2005), p. 47.
52 For the translated quotes from the *IP* in the following paragraph: *IP*, Nicholson, pp. 156–8; and for the Latin: *IP*, Stubbs, pp. 155–7.
53 Ambroise, *History*, vol. 2, p. 39.
54 Roger of Howden: *Chronica*, p. 55 and *Gesta*, vol. 2, pp. 125–6; *Chronicle of Richard of Devizes*, p. 16.
55 Gillingham, *Richard I*, p. 131.
56 William of Newburgh: *Historia*, bk IV, XII, p. 324; Roger of Howden: *Chronica*, p. 54 and *Gesta*, vol. 2, p. 124; Rigord, *Gesta Philippi*, ch. 79, p. 286.
57 *Chronica*, p. 55.
58 For example, Roger of Howden: *Chronica*, p. 58; *IP*, pp. 158–9, 169; Ambroise, *History*, vol. 2, pp. 38, 46.
59 The *Chronicle of Richard of Devizes*, p. 20, claims that Richard entreated his army in preparation for the assault on Messina as follows: 'Will we overcome Turks and Arabs, will we be the terror of the most invincible nations, will our right arms make a way for us to the ends of the earth after the Cross of Christ, will we restore the kingdom of Israel, if we show our back to these vile and effeminate Griffons?' See also *Chronicle of Richard of Devizes*, p. 23 for the idea of legitimate violence against the 'damned Griffons [*maledictos Grifones*]'. On this application of violence, see Diggelmann, 'Grifons', pp. 17–18.
60 Most starkly in the case of the anti-Jewish pogroms of the First Crusade.

Part III

Religion and the Church

10

The foundation of St Euphemia in Calabria: a 'Norman' church in southern Italy?

Benjamin Pohl

It is impossible to overestimate the importance of Graham Loud's work on the medieval Mediterranean and its churches. Anyone wishing to study Norman Italy will struggle to do so without consulting his seminal scholarship and primary source translations.[1] In writing this chapter, I aim to pay fitting tribute not just to a great scholar, but also to a generous mentor and friend.[2] This chapter focuses on one specific church in Norman Italy and asks questions which, largely due to lack of original manuscripts and archival documents, have eluded scholarly attention: What kind of institution was the Benedictine monastery founded in honour of the Virgin Mary in the Calabrian town of St Euphemia, and how does it compare to other churches in Norman Italy? What drove its foundation, who were its patrons and intellectual architects, and whose vision and ambitions did it reflect? To what extent was St Euphemia a ducal foundation, and was it, ultimately, a 'Norman' church?

In *The Latin Church in Norman Italy*, Loud identifies three 'notable features' characterising the 'Hauteville foundations', that is, the churches established in Apulia, Calabria and Sicily by the descendants of Tancred de Hauteville, a minor Norman lord from the Cotentin.[3] First, the monastic communities founded in southern Italy (unlike those in Sicily) were subject directly and exclusively to the Roman See – a privilege traditionally considered, optimistically, to mirror the so-called 'Cluniac exemption'.[4] Second, the individual foundations were connected closely to one another through a dense institutional and interpersonal network. Third, the founders of these churches were, at least on the mainland, exclusively Normans and thus foreigners in the regions in which they planted 'their' monastic communities.[5] Tancred de Hauteville had no fewer than twelve sons, several of whom abandoned Normandy to seek their fortune in southern Italy. Two brothers became successful rulers in their own right and founded and patronised churches in their conquered territories: Roger, count of Sicily (1071–1101), and the elder Robert Guiscard, duke of Apulia, Calabria and Sicily (1059–85).[6] Many of the churches established and endowed by Roger and Robert during the second half of the eleventh century have been studied in detail, primary evidence permitting, though one of the first and arguably most important of them remains elusive. Compared with other Hauteville foundations, particularly Venosa and Mileto,[7] modern scholarship on St Euphemia in Calabria is scarce, though the *état present* is not quite as bleak as sometimes suggested.[8]

Most information about St Euphemia's foundation in narrative sources comes from non-contemporary writers, primarily Orderic Vitalis, a Benedictine monk-historian writing a generation after the event. Orderic's interest in St Euphemia was no coincidence, given that his home monastery of St Évroult in Lower Normandy was heavily invested, in every sense of the word, in Norman Italy's monastic revival.[9] Orderic's version of events is supplemented, and sometimes relativised, by the accounts of Geoffrey Malaterra – possibly another St Évroult monk who had emigrated to Sicily – and Amatus of Montecassino, though neither provides as much detail as Orderic.[10] Between them, these three (pro-)Norman historians offer considerable information in stark contrast to the almost complete lack of original archival and manuscript sources. St Euphemia's medieval library and archives were destroyed in an earthquake in 1638.[11] The sole surviving document, albeit only through later copies, none earlier than the first half of the sixteenth century, is the abbey's foundation charter (1062).[12] Due to its significance, the charter's text is given here in translation:

> In the name of the holy and indivisible Trinity. I, Robert Guiscard, by God's grace duke of Apulia, Calabria and Sicily, for the redemption of my own soul and those of my father and mother, as well as of my brothers William, Drogo, Serlo, Humphrey and Mauger, and of my other brothers, sisters and relatives, both living and dead, restore a certain [church], amongst those other churches located under our rule (*inter alias ecclesias que site sunt sub monarchia nostra*), [which

was] founded in honour of our Lord, Jesus Christ, and his mother, the eternally blessed Virgin Mary, but ruined by its evil inhabitants, which is situated in the valley of Nicastro by the seashore known today as Santa Euphemia, formerly called *Lametinum* by the Greeks, in the one thousandth and sixty-second year after the incarnation of the Lord, in the twelfth indiction, with Emperor Constantine reigning in the East, Philip in France, Henry in Saxony and our lord, Pope Alexander, in Rome. I declare [this said church] free (*facio liberam*), and I concede (*concedo*) everything that I have given and will give, and whatever the faithful will give for their souls, to be free and without anyone's lordship (*absque dominatione nullius hominis*) but within the power (*in potestate*) of Abbot Robert of that same place, to whom I gave all these things. I promise, as do my heirs, that after this abbot's death, the election of a new abbot shall occur according to the monks' choice (*arbitrio*), in recognition of their will (*voluntatis*) and with our assent (*assensu nostro*), in accordance with the *Rule* of St Benedict. We also confirm the grounds of this monastery and the buildings of the lay people who dwell therein to be protected and free, so that if any fugitive, captive, enemy or adversary of ours, or anyone who is compelled by whatever reason should take refuge there, he shall have the power to come and go as he pleases, or to stay in perpetuity. Further, these are the [things] that I grant [as being] in the possession (*sub potestate*) of that church at the present point in time: the territory of the old city [Lamezia] near the two rivers all the way to the sea; the port of the river Amato that divides the territories of Nicastro and Maida; the wood/forest or land that lies between the two rivers and runs just like a road from that same port to the ford of the other river; the ports of St Senator and Fico; the entire seashore with all its rents and profits, and all the nearby woods from the mouth (*portu*) of the river Amato to St Maria of Cipusa; the twenty tenants/villeins (*villanos*) in the territory of Nicastro along with their hereditary possessions. In addition, Eremburga, our niece, gave her share of the said woodlands with four tenants to the same monastery, with our affirmation. I also gave the imperial monastery of St Elia, along with its tenants and all its dependencies and appurtenances (*omnibus pertinentiis et appenditiis*) as they are contained in the records of that monastery. I further [give] five monasteries with all their dependencies in the district (*pago*) of Orientano, whose names are: St Mary of Gallano, St Peter of Episcopio, St Gregory, St Vesanatus and St Nicolas. In addition, we have also conceded Gizzeria with all its tenants/villeins, dependencies and appurtenances, both on land and sea, to the same place in perpetuity, in the way that this same land of Gizzeria is divided from the territory of Nicastro, with their border running along the river from the port of Fico all the way to the source of that river, and from there to the right up to the great rock, and then further to another great rock, and from there onwards to the territory of Marturana, and then to the west across the mountain plateau up to the twin-peaked mountain, and thence via its [*lacuna*] all the way to the sea along the brook that runs near St Maria of Apeza. After this, I also conceded [*lacuna*] with all its dependencies and appurtenances and [its] church to the same monastery, to be held in a similar fashion. Meanwhile, Ansketil of Maida gave the monastery of St Peter of the same city with its appurtenances, with our consent and permission, to be held in that place in perpetuity. Thorald donated, likewise with my permission, to the same monastery the church of St Mary of Nicastro with all its dependencies. I concede to the aforementioned monastery of St Mary [= St Euphemia] everything listed above to be had and held freely and in perpetuity, just as I myself hold these entire lands lawfully. We therefore ratify to God and Our Lady, St Mary, all these things with our own hands, and with those of our archbishops, Arnulf and Alo, and with those of my brother, Count Roger, and all our other faithful men; by ratifying we strengthen them, and by strengthening we corroborate them, and by corroborating we enact (*sancimus*) them, so that they may endure perpetually. If, however, anyone amongst my successors or heirs, or any other person however great or small, should be tempted by rash temerity knowingly to break, destroy or in any way disturb these alms and this decree (*preceptum*) of ours, let him be subject to the shackles of anathema, erased from the book of the living and not listed amongst the righteous (*deleaturque de libro viventium et cum iustis non scribatur*), and let him be *anathema maranatha!* until, having been admonished once or twice, he renders fully appropriate satisfaction. Whoever may assist us in ensuring that this our confirmation remains intact and authentic shall earn himself the reward of eternal blessing. Amen. I, Robert, by God's grace duke, made this sign + and ordered for this privilege to by sealed with my seal; I, Arnulf, archbishop of Cosenza, signed [it] and made this sign +; I, Alo, archbishop of Siponto, signed and made this cross +; I, Count Roger, made this cross +; I, Hugh; I, Romald; I, William Capriolus.[13]

Issued, 'signed' and sealed by Duke Robert Guiscard, the charter *prima facie* presents St Euphemia as a ducal foundation whose revival and renovation on the site of a derelict (presumably Greek) church were motivated, in the first instance, by princely piety and a concern for the salvation of souls. As has been established, 'the foundation and endowment of monasteries was something expected of a ruler, not just that he would wish to make provision for his soul – and there is nothing to indicate that Robert [Guiscard] was other than conventionally pious – but also as a necessary part of his *bella figura*'.[14] Orderic in his *Historia ecclesiastica* relativises the duke's agency in the foundation of St Euphemia and instead emphasises the role of one of St Évroult's own monks – its second abbot, no less – Robert (II) de Grandmesnil (1059–61), who, after having been deposed by Duke William II, fled Normandy for Italy with a group of loyal disciples.[15] Most modern scholarship, whilst mindful of the chronicler's vested interest, his unapologetic bias in favour of his community's former abbot and, not least, his obvious benefit of hindsight, has embraced this version of events. Orderic's account thus goes some way towards recalibrating the relationship between ducal and abbatial initiative and participation in the foundation of St Euphemia, though arguably not far enough. A fresh study of the foundation charter and related documents reveals Abbot Robert as the project's primary (if not sole) intellectual architect. Before analysing these documents, it is worth recalling briefly the milestones of Robert II's career as portrayed by St Évroult's twelfth-century monk-chronicler.[16]

Robert was the second child of Robert I de Grandmesnil and Hawisa, a daughter of Giroie, and he had at least two brothers, Hugh and Arnold, and a sister, Adeliza. His lineage combined two of the most powerful, well-connected aristocratic families of eleventh-century Normandy, the Grandmesnils and the Giroies.[17] The family demesne comprised considerable estates around Grandmesnil and further westward, towards the Giroie lands.[18] Connected by marriage, members from both families decided to co-found a Benedictine monastery which, after the initial location had been ruled out by Robert's maternal uncle, William FitzGiroie, was established at St Évroult in the Pays d'Ouche *c.* 1050.[19] Apart from William FitzGiroie, the founders included his brother, Robert FitzGiroie, and his nephews, Hugh and Robert II de Grandmesnil, all of whom feature, alongside other secular and ecclesiastical lords, as witnesses in a redaction of the abbey's foundation charter (see below).[20] By that point, Robert II de Grandmesnil was in his early twenties and had built a prosperous career in the service of Duke William II, but he abandoned the knightly lifestyle soon after – or probably upon the occasion of – the abbey's foundation to become one of its monks and make his profession to Abbot Thierry (1050–57).[21] Robert quickly, perhaps instantly, rose to the rank of prior and, after a formative sojourn at Cluny, was elected abbot following Thierry's death. Orderic places this decision squarely with the monks themselves, though it seems likely that Duke William II, then still an avid supporter of his former squire, might have influenced the process beyond the ritual of ducal assent and investiture with the pastoral staff (*baculum*) customary in eleventh-century Normandy.[22]

If we can trust Orderic's testimony, Robert's abbacy (1059–61) was an instantaneous success and a blessing for St Évroult's monks that continued – and eclipsed – Thierry's legacy by leading the community to unprecedented wealth and prosperity. It ended prematurely when Robert became 'collateral damage' in the conflict between his brother and co-founder Hugh and Duke William II, a conflict which put the entire Grandmesnil-Giroie family into the duke's crosshairs. We are told that the abbot's adversaries in this episode were his own prior, Rainer, and the duke himself. The latter deposed his former protégé and forced him to leave Normandy. In Robert's place, William II appointed Osbern, who in Orderic's narrative serves as a foil to the unjustly banished abbot: whilst Robert had been elected by the monks' free choice in 1059, Osbern was imposed against their will in 1061. According to Orderic, the monks 'found themselves on the horns of a dilemma', having had their decision overthrown and their abbot expelled 'through the tyranny of the raging prince (*per tirannidem furentis marchisi*)', though they had little choice but to 'endure the violence and obey the master who had been gratuitously thrust upon them'.[23] Despite having papal support, Robert finally relented and left Normandy together with eleven loyal monks whose names are listed, not without admiration, in Orderic's work.[24] Their destination was southern Italy, where some of Robert's relatives and members of St Évroult's extended *familia* had established themselves recently. Indeed, Robert's half-sister Judith married Robert Guiscard's younger brother Roger that same year.[25] Following a fruitless appeal to Richard of Capua, Robert then turned to Robert Guiscard, who supported his exiled kinsman by granting him and his monks land in his recently conquered powerbase of Calabria, where they could (re-)build a monastery.[26] The result was the foundation of St Euphemia with Robert as its first abbot (c. 1062–82), an appointment cemented and confirmed in the foundation charter. The charter's opening sentence combines formal elements of the *invocatio, intitulatio, arenga* and *narratio*, and it shows the duke as the primary agent of St Euphemia's restoration as a religious site ('Ego Robertus [...] restauro'), singled out from amongst all churches under his rule ('inter alias ecclesias que site sunt sub monarchia nostra'). This is a peculiar phrase, and its use of 'monarchia' when referring to Robert Guiscard's rule in Apulia and Calabria in the early 1060s has caused debate amongst scholars, some of whom have ascribed it to the pen of the charter's sixteenth-century copyist, Alessandro Barbaro, though the act's authenticity in general remains intact.[27] This usage of 'monarchia' is unique in the surviving corpus of Robert Guiscard's charters, but it finds a parallel in a limited number of early- to mid-eleventh-century *diplomata* from north-western Europe. There it is applied to the rule of bishops or secular princes like Count Baldwin V of Flanders (1037–67) and three dukes of Normandy, Richard II (996–1026), Robert I (1027–35) and William II (1035–87).[28] Is it possible that St Euphemia's foundation charter was based not on local or regional diplomatic custom but on precedents from north of the Alps? And if so, whose design did it reflect, and whose vision did it seek to implement?

Careful analysis of the charter's wording points away from Lombard or Byzantine exemplars and towards the north, specifically Normandy. Take, for example, the *sanctio*, whose use of Psalm 68:29 ('Deleantur de libro viventium, et cum iustis non scribantur') combined with the curse *anathema maranatha!* has no parallel in Robert Guiscard's other known charters, but is found repeatedly in eleventh-century Norman and (northern) French documents, especially under Duke William II.[29] Even more striking is the charter's *intitulatio*, which identifies Robert Guiscard as 'by God's grace duke of Apulia, Calabria and Sicily' ('gratia Dei dux Apulie, Calabrie Sicilieque'). Robert carried the title 'dux' – as well as 'comes', and sometimes 'dux et comes' – ever since Pope Nicholas II had invested him at the Synod of Melfi in August 1059, but there is no evidence that he used the specific titulature 'gratia Dei dux' between 1059 and 1062.[30] Of the seven extant ducal diplomata from this period, only St Euphemia's foundation charter uses 'gratia Dei dux'.[31] The earliest other examples of 'gratia Dei dux' date from 1082–85,[32] and they form no more than 10 per cent of the thirty-nine ducal charters issued during the period 1063–85, most of which use either 'Divina favente clementia dux' (36 per cent) or simply 'dux' or 'comes' (23 per cent).[33] After 1080 Robert Guiscard's charters almost exclusively use 'Divina favente clementia dux' in the *intitulatio*, as is attested in no fewer than fourteen extant documents, and this chimes well with Horst Enzensberger's reconstruction of the development of a ducal chancery in Apulia and Calabria from *c.* 1079/80 onwards.[34] Early in his reign, Robert Guiscard had neither a chancery nor a dedicated notary (let alone a *cancellarius*), and most of the charters he issued were prepared by their beneficiaries (*Empfängerausfertigungen*).[35] It is thus entirely plausible, indeed likely, that St Euphemia's foundation charter was drawn up not by a ducal official, but by a beneficiary, almost certainly a Norman immigrant accustomed to foreign diplomatic traditions.

The most likely explanation, therefore, is that the charter was the work of Abbot Robert de Grandmesnil, who either composed it *manu propria* or dictated it to a monk who had followed him from St Évroult.[36] The *intitulatio*, whilst standing in stark contrast with Robert Guiscard's spare use of the formula 'gratia Dei dux' – sporadic during the years 1063–85 and virtually non-existent before 1062 – finds a close parallel in the titulatures of Duke William II of Normandy. By 1062, William II had issued no fewer than nine charters using the formula 'gratia Dei (Normannorum) dux' (or minor variants thereof), most of them to monastic communities enjoying ducal patronage and receiving privileges not dissimilar from St Euphemia's.[37] For a beneficiary like Robert de Grandmesnil, a recent émigré for whom Normandy's diplomatic custom remained an intuitive frame of reference, adopting formulaic elements such as titulatures, sanctions, etc. from records in St Évroult's monastic archives and transplanting them onto the foundation charter of his new community made perfect sense.

We can go further still. Evidence suggests that St Euphemia's foundation charter was modelled not just on any Norman charter but specifically on St Évroult's foundation charter (*c.* 1050). As with

St Euphemia, St Évroult's original charter does not survive, though there are two copies (resembling two redactions; see below) in the abbey's thirteenth-century cartulary (Paris, Bibliothèque nationale de France, MS Lat. 11055–11056), copies whose content is deemed essentially authentic, with the possible exception of a single exemption clause.[38] Comparison reveals that St Euphemia's charter both mimics and adopts verbatim some wording of St Évroult's foundation charter. This is true not only of the idiosyncratic formulae in the *intitulatio* and *sanctio* discussed above, but also of the *corroboratio* and the exemption clause.

These similarities leave little doubt that St Euphemia's charter was inspired by, and sought to imitate, St Évroult's. Several phrases were transplanted carefully into the foundation charter for St Euphemia, which resembles St Évroult's much more closely than those of the other churches founded by Robert Guiscard and Roger, including Venosa and Mileto.[39] As we will remember, Robert de Grandmesnil had been one of St Évroult's four founders, together with his brother Hugh and his uncles, Robert and William FitzGiroie. His name figures prominently in St Évroult's foundation charter, though there are crucial differences between the two redactions contained in the cartulary. In the first redaction (B), Robert assumes the role of interlocutor, from whose intervention ('intercedente Roberto fideli meo') the monks receive the right of free abbatial election.[40] Even though Robert is mentioned by name together with his Grandmesnil/Giroie relatives ('Robertus et Hugo frater eius, Willelmus et fratres eius et filii'), neither he nor William FitzGiroie appears in the witness list, which includes only Hugh and Robert FitzGiroie alongside other magnates. This changes drastically in the second redaction (C), dated 25 September 1050, where Robert takes centre stage and, by placing his name and signature cross before (!) those of his brother Hugh, confidently refers to himself as the charter's 'author' and 'maker' ('Signum Robertis huius cartule auctoris et factoris').[41]

As the self-proclaimed redactor of St Évroult's foundation charter, Robert – possibly a monk at that point – demonstrates crucial administrative insight. If a single aspect of Robert's abbacy was remembered at St Évroult, it was his business acumen. Normandy's twelfth-century monks often looked to their abbots for economic leadership, but Orderic's unbridled praise for Robert goes beyond that. He reports how '[h]e [Robert] laboured ceaselessly to mitigate

Table 10.1 Foundation charters of St Euphemia and St Évroult

	St Euphemia	St Évroult	MS BnF Lat. 11055
Intitulatio (incl. *arenga*, *promulgatio*)	'Ego Robertus, **gratia Dei dux** Apulie, Calabrie Sicilieque, **inter alias ecclesias que site sunt sub monarchia nostra restauro unam quondam fundatam** [...] ad honorem Domini nostri Iesu Christi ac beate semper virginis Marie, matris eius, [...] **que sita est in valle Neocastri** [...].'	'Ego Guillelmus, Normannorum dux gratia Dei, [...] Proinde notum esse volo [...] quod **inter ceteras ecclesias que infra regnum nostrum site sunt specialiter ecclesiam** sancti Petri et sancti Ebrulfi **que infra Lisiocacensium comitatum sita** [...].'	Fol. 15r, lines 2–9 (Figure 10.1).
Exemption clause	'[F]acio liberam et omnia [...] concedo tam **libera ut absque dominatione nullius hominis sint** sed sint in potestate Roberti abbatis [...]; post mortem vero illius electionem abbatis **in monachorum arbitrio** eiusdem loci et in requisitione eiusdem voluntatis **secundum regulam sancti Benedicti** assensu nostro, ego simul et heredes mei promitto fieri.'	'[...] **ut libera et ab omni subiectione maneat immunis.** De electione autem abbatis loci eiusdem, intercedente Roberto fideli meo, hoc totum concede, consilio fratrum, tam ego quam successores mei,* **salva tamen regularis,** id est ut non [...] vota eligentium corrumpat.' [*alternative version in C: '...ego quam successores mei, absque potestate mei sive cuiuslibet, **in arbitrio monachorum** solummodo pendeat.']	Fols 15r, lines 12–15 (B; Figure 10.2), 16v, lines 17–19 (C; Figure 10.3).

Corroboratio	'Et ego [...] hec omnia manibus nostris nostrorumque archiepiscoporum Arnulfi et Alonis et fratris mei [...] firmamus [...].'	'Hanc donationis cartulam ego [...] scribi feci et manibus archiepiscopi Rothomagensis et Episcoporum abbatumque ac principum quorum nomina et signa subter scripta habentur [...] tradidi.'	Fol. 16r, lines 20–3 (Figure 10.4).
Sanctio	'Si quis autem [...] tentaverit, anathematis vinculo innodatus subiaceat deleaturque de libro viventium et cum iustis non scribatur sitque illi anathema maranata nisi semel aut bis admonitus condigne satisfecerit.'	'Ut si quis eam infringere presumpserit [...], ex auctoritate Dei [...] ab omni christianitate, **si non emendaverit**, excommunicatum et in eternum maledictum se noverit, [...] deleatur de libro viventium et cum iustis non scribatur.'	Fol. 16r, lines 23–7 (Figure 10.4).

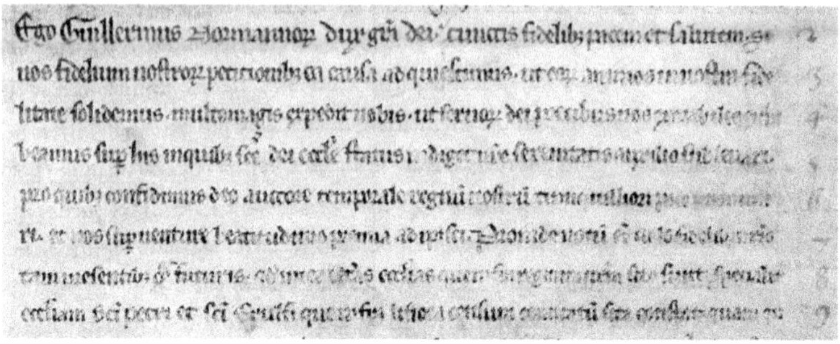

Figure 10.1 Paris, Bibliothèque nationale de France, MS Lat. 11055, fol. 15r, lines 2–9 (detail).

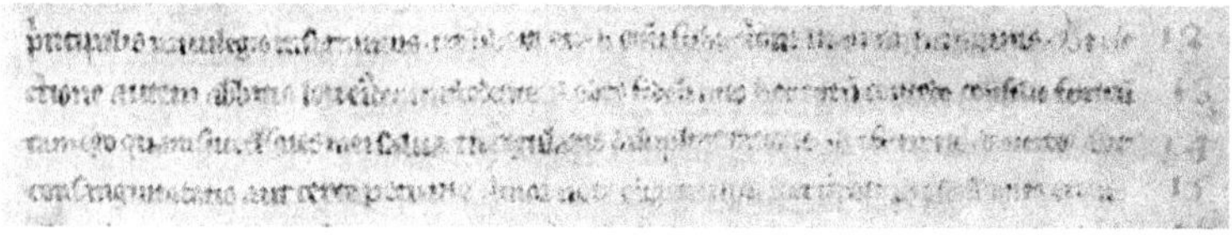

Figure 10.2 Paris, Bibliothèque nationale de France, MS Lat. 11055, fol. 15r, lines 12–15 (detail).

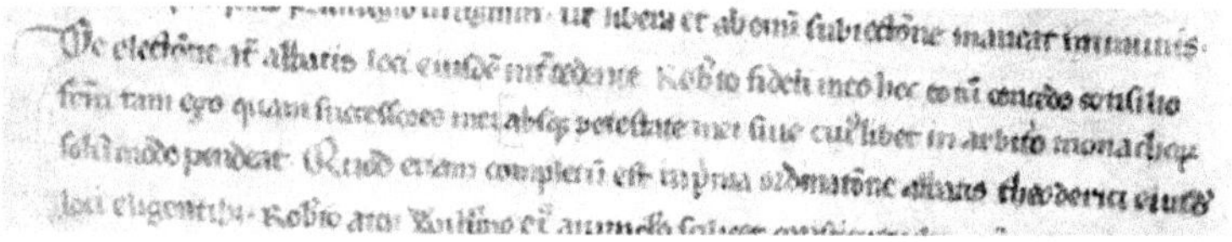

Figure 10.3 Paris, Bibliothèque nationale de France, MS Lat. 11055, fol. 16v, lines 17–19 (detail).

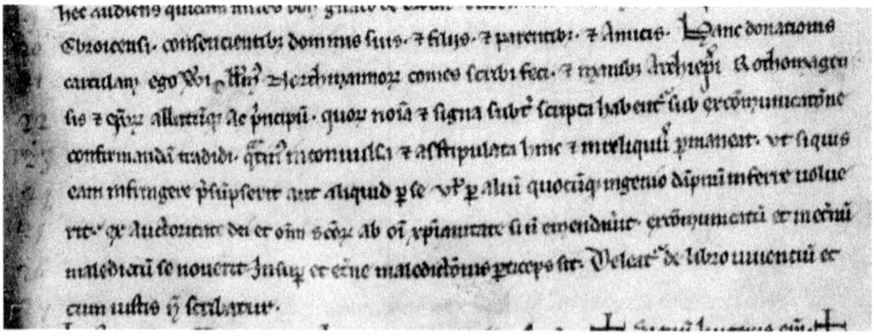

Figure 10.4 Paris, Bibliothèque nationale de France, MS Lat. 11055, fol. 16r, lines 20–7 (detail).

the poverty of the church', and even 'appropriated the riches of his [own] over-wealthy relatives' and 'procured many other gifts for his church, both ecclesiastical ornaments and useful revenues'.[42] Orderic even copied Robert's redaction of the foundation charter into his *Historia ecclesiastica*.[43] Aware of his own abilities, Robert had become a vocal critic of Abbot Thierry's lack of managerial leadership and business sense, because he considered it the abbot's duty to grow his community's wealth by procuring lands and revenues to expand the monastic demesne, as well as to increase its architectural footprint.[44] Acting as an abbot-architect and *magister operis*, Robert had initiated and overseen several building campaigns during his short abbacy at St Évroult, including the new abbey church, and after his banishment he continued, and perfected, his architectural vision in southern Italy.[45]

As Giuseppe Occhiato has shown, the ambitious Romanesque structures that Robert ordered built not only at St Euphemia, but also at Venosa and Mileto, all showed unmistakable Norman influence. They in fact carried the familiar imprint of St Évroult and some of the great abbeys connected to it, Bernay and Cluny (II). Robert had visited the latter as prior of St Évroult.[46] If, to paraphrase Occhiato, Robert's church of St Euphemia provided southern Italy's closest link with Normandy's monastic architecture,[47] its foundation charter claims a similarly unrivalled status with regard to diplomatic influences. When Robert was given abbatial 'overlordship' for Venosa and Mileto in the 1060s/80s, he assumed a role not unlike that of William of Volpiano in early eleventh-century Normandy, though, unlike William, Robert did not rule over these abbeys himself (*Personalunion*) but appointed deputies whom he had confirmed as abbots. Like St Évroult, St Euphemia never turned into a so-called 'Cluniac monastery', and its liberties and influence never equalled those of the great Burgundian reform centre.[48]

Robert de Grandmesnil's creation of St Euphemia – as it was essentially *his* creation, not Robert Guiscard's – remained the favourite monastery of Italy's Norman rulers until the mid-1080s, when it was superseded by Venosa.[49] Still, for the best part of twenty years it was, to quote Hubert Houben, 'the centre of Norman monasticism in Southern Italy' ('[der] Mittelpunkt des normannischen Mönchtums in Süditalien').[50] Returning to the notable features of the Hauteville foundations mentioned above, St Euphemia emerges as a case apart. Whilst many churches established by Robert Guiscard and Count Roger 'undoubtedly reflected the wishes of the founders',[51] St Euphemia fundamentally followed the specific vision and aspirations of its first abbot, Robert de Grandmesnil. It was less a ducal church, therefore, than it was an abbatial one. More specifically, it was the brainchild of an exiled Norman abbot who, according to St Évroult's institutional memory, had always been personally invested in the architectural, economic and spiritual renovation of his former community. With Robert's banishment before his work could bear fruit, many of these efforts were undone by his ducally appointed successor, Osbern. Robert learned from these experiences, and he applied them in carefully crafting the foundation charter for his new home, St Euphemia. What he (re)created for both himself and those who had followed him into exile was meant to be more than simply another 'Norman' church in the south, but a new St Évroult in the valley of Nicastro on the shores of the Tyrrhenian Sea.

Notes

1 Particularly his monographs G. A. Loud, *Church and Society in the Norman Principality of Capua, 1058–1197* (Oxford, 1985); G. A. Loud, *The Age of Robert Guiscard: Southern Italy and the Norman Conquest* (Harlow, 2000); G. A. Loud, *The Latin Church in Norman Italy* (Cambridge, 2007).

2 I first met Graham during the final year of my Master's degree at the University of Bamberg, when he agreed, in the absence of any formalised institutional arrangement, for me to come to Leeds and be mentored by him whilst writing up my thesis on Orderic Vitalis and the Norman Diaspora – a commitment which he extended by supervising my subsequent PhD project (2009–13) on cultural memory in the manuscript tradition of Dudo of Saint-Quentin's *Historia Normannorum* together with Christoph Houswitschka (University of Bamberg). Since then, Graham has always been a source of great support and encouragement, and of sage advice – a true patron. Unfortunately, the editors' instruction to keep notes brief must prevent me from offering Graham the ultimate gift of the 'Germanic footnote', a trademark upon which he never failed to remark when reading my work.

3 A. P. Via, 'Tancred of Hauteville, Sons of', in C. Kleinhenz (ed.), *Medieval Italy: An Encyclopedia*, 2 vols, 2nd edn (New York, 2004), vol. 2, pp. 1068–9; see also the genealogical tables of the Hauteville family in Loud, *Age of Robert Guiscard*, p. 299, and G. A. Loud (ed.), *Roger II and the Creation of the Kingdom of Sicily* (Manchester, 2012), p. xii.
4 See the discussion on pp. 199–201. For a conceptual discussion of monastic exemption, see B. Pohl, 'The problem of Cluniac exemption', in S. G. Bruce and S. Vanderputten (eds), *A Companion to the Abbey of Cluny in the Middle Ages* (Leiden, forthcoming).
5 Loud, *Latin Church*, pp. 89–91.
6 On Robert's biography, see E. Albu, 'Robert Guiscard', in Kleinhenz (ed.), *Medieval Italy*, vol. 2, pp. 969–70; R. Bünemann, *Robert Guiskard 1015–1085: Ein Normanne erobert Süditalien* (Cologne, 1997); V. D'Alessandro, 'Roberto il Guiscardo nella storiografia medievale', in C. D. Fonseca (ed.), *Roberto il Guiscardo tra Europa, Oriente e Mezzogiorno* (Galatina, 1990), pp. 181–96. On Roger (I), see J. Becker, *Graf Roger I. von Sizilien: Wegbereiter des normannischen Königreichs* (Tübingen, 2008).
7 Especially L.-R. Ménager, 'Les fondations monastiques de Robert Guiscard, duc de Pouille et de Calabre', *QF* 39 (1959), 1–116; L.-R. Ménager, 'L'abbaye bénédictine de la Trinité de Mileto, en Calabre, à l'époque normande', *Bulletino dell'archivio paleografico italiano* 4–5 (1958–59), 9–94; H. Houben, *Die Abtei Venosa und das Mönchtum im normannisch-staufischen Süditalien* (Tübingen, 1995); H. Houben, 'Una grande abbazia nel Mezzogiorno medioevale: la SS. Trinità di Venosa', in H. Houben, *Medioevo monastico meridionale* (Naples, 1987), pp. 85–108; H. Houben, 'Roberto il Guiscardo e il monachesimo', in Houben (ed.), *Medioevo monastico meridionale*, pp. 109–27; H.-W. Klewitz, 'Studien über die Wiederherstellung der römischen Kirche in Süditalien durch das Reformpapsttum', *QF* 25 (1933), 105–57; V. Ramseyer, *The Transformation of a Religious Landscape: Medieval Southern Italy, 850–1150* (Ithaca, 2006); Loud, *Latin Church*, pp. 430–93.
8 Daniel Roach's assessment, according to which '[t]he existing scholarship on St Euphemia is of limited value', seems unduly pessimistic given the important work published during the twentieth century by Italian and German scholars; D. Roach, 'Saint-Évroul and southern Italy in Orderic's *Historia ecclesiastica*', in C. C. Rozier et al. (eds), *Orderic Vitalis: Life, Works and Interpretations* (Woodbridge, 2016), pp. 79–99 (p. 86, n. 42). Giuseppe Occhiato's studies in particular have generated transformative information, much of which, however, sadly seems to have gone unnoticed in anglophone scholarship (see below, n. 10).

9 An excellent overview of St Évroult's close relationship with Norman Italy as portrayed in Orderic's *Historia ecclesiastica*, as well as in his interpolations to William of Jumièges' *Gesta Normannorum ducum*, is provided by Roach, 'Saint-Évroul and southern Italy'. See also M. Chibnall, 'Les moines et les patrons de Saint-Évroult dans l'Italie du Sud au XIe siècle', in P. Bouet and F. Neveux (eds), *Les Normands en Méditerranée dans le sillage des Tancrède* (Caen, 1994), pp. 161–70; J. Decaëns, 'Le patrimoine des Grentemesnil en Normandie, en Italie et en Angleterre aux XIe et XIIe siècles', in Bouet and Neveux (eds), *Les Normands en Méditerranée*, pp. 123–40.

10 The most recent edition and French translation of Geoffrey Malaterra's *De rebus gestis Rogerii et Roberti* is that by M.-A. Lucas-Avenel, *Histoire du Grand Comte Roger et de son frère Robert Guiscard, Vol. 1: Livres I & II* (Caen, 2016), available online: www.unicaen.fr/puc/sources/malaterra/ (accessed 8 October 2018). An English translation is provided by K. B. Wolf, *The Deeds of Count Roger of Calabria and Sicily and of his Brother Robert Guiscard by Geoffrey Malaterra* (Ann Arbor, 2005). For Amatus, see *The History of the Normans by Amatus of Montecassino*, trans. P. N. Dunbar and rev. G. A. Loud (Woodbridge, 2004). Also cf. Roach, 'Saint-Évroul and southern Italy', p. 78; G. Occhiato, 'Robert de Grandmesnil: un abate "architetto" operante in Calabria nell'XI secolo', *Studi medievali* 28 (1987), 609–66 (p. 617).

11 E. Pontieri, 'L'Abbazia benedettina di Sant'Eufemia in Calabria e l'abate Roberto di Grantmesnil', *Archivio storico per la Sicilia* 22 (1926), 92–115. See also Loud, *Latin Church*, p. 91; Loud, *Age of Robert Guiscard*, p. 272.

12 For a discussion of this date, see Ménager, 'Les fondations', pp. 12–19.

13 My translation. I would like to thank Richard Barton and Richard Allen, who checked the text and assisted me in phrasing some challenging passages. The charter's Latin text has been edited on the basis of all the known extant copies by L.-R. Ménager in *Recueil des actes des ducs normands d'Italie, 1046–1127, Vol 1: Les premiers ducs (1046–1087)* (Bari, 1980), pp. 38–47 (no. 11). It was previously printed, albeit with an erroneous attribution, by P. Giuliani, *Memorie istoriche della città di Nicastro da' tempi più remoti fino al 1820* (Nicastro, 1867), pp. 2–5 (Appendix).

14 Loud, *Age of Robert Guiscard*, p. 270. Also cf. the discussion in Loud, *Latin Church*, pp. 84–7.

15 *The Ecclesiastical History of Orderic Vitalis*, ed. and trans. M. Chibnall, 6 vols (Oxford, 1969–80), II, pp. 40–3, 58–75, 88–105; *The Gesta Normannorum Ducum of William of Jumièges, Orderic Vitalis, and*

Robert of Torigni, ed. and trans. E. M. C. van Houts, 2 vols (Oxford, 1992–95), vol. 2, pp. 152–9. For context, see Roach, 'Saint-Évroul and southern Italy', pp. 84–8. On Robert's biography, see Occhiato, 'Robert de Grandmesnil'; V. Gazeau, *Normannia monastica (Xe–XIIe siècle): Princes normands et abbés bénédictins*, 2 vols (Caen, 2007), vol. 1, pp. 275–6.

16 For what follows, see *Ecclesiastical History*, ed. Chibnall, vol. 2, pp. 64–7, 74–5, 88–103; *Gesta Normannorum ducum*, ed. van Houts, vol. 2, pp. 152–5, 158–9.

17 On the Giroies, see J.-M. Maillefer, 'Une famille aristocratique aux confins de la Normandie: les Géré au XIe siècle', *Cahier des Annales de Normandie* 17 (1985), 175–206; P. Bauduin, 'Une famille châtelaine sur les confins normanno-manceaux: les Géré (Xe–XIIIe s.)', *Archéologie médiévale* 22 (1992), 309–56. On the Grandmesnils, see M. Hagger, 'Kinship and identity in eleventh-century Normandy: The case of Hugh de Grandmesnil, *c.*1040–1098', *JMH* 32 (2006), 212–30. A combined Grandmesnil/Giroie family tree is provided in H. Wolter, *Ordericus Vitalis: ein Beitrag zur kluniazensischen Geschichtsschreibung* (Wiesbaden, 1955), pp. 253–4.

18 Hagger, 'Kinship and identity', p. 215; Decaëns, 'Le patrimoine des Grentemesnil'.

19 On the foundation of St Évroult, see Wolter, *Ordericus Vitalis*, pp. 18–23, 29–32; C. Potts, *Monastic Revival and Regional Identity in Early Normandy* (Woodbridge, 1997), pp. 113–15; H. E. J. Cowdrey, *Lanfranc: Scholar, Monk, Archbishop* (Oxford, 2003), pp. 16–18; Bauduin, 'Une famille châtelaine', pp. 318–19; Maillefer, 'Une famille aristocratique', pp. 176–86.

20 St Évroult's foundation charter has been edited, in its two redactions (B and C), in *Orderici Vitalis Historiae ecclesiasticae, libri tredecim*, ed. A. Le Prévost, 5 vols (Paris, 1838–55), vol. 5, pp. 173–80 (nos II–III), as well as, in the shape of a single text with variants, in *Recueil des actes des ducs de Normandie de 911 à 1066*, ed. M. Fauroux (Caen, 1961), pp. 287–92 (no. 122). We no longer possess the original(s), and the two earliest and, presumably, most authoritative copies survive in the first volume of the abbey's thirteenth-century cartulary, Paris, Bibliothèque nationale de France, MS Lat. 11055, fos 15r–16v (no. 14) and 16v–18r (no. 15). On Orderic's use of these and other charters, see T. Roche, 'Reading Orderic with charters in mind', in Rozier *et al.* (eds), *Orderic Vitalis*, pp. 145–71.

21 Wolter, *Ordericus Vitalis*, pp. 33–4; Occhiato, 'Robert de Grandmesnil', pp. 632–35. According to Hagger, 'Kinship and identity', pp. 216–17, Hugh de Grandmesnil was born around 1023–5, which probably

places the birth of the second-born Robert in the latter half of the 1020s.
22 *Ecclesiastical History*, ed. Chibnall, vol. 2, pp. 74–5. As Cassandra Potts has observed, even the founders of St Évroult 'sought the approval of Duke William [II] at every stage ... seeking his permission to appoint an abbot, which in itself underlines that this was his ducal right'; Potts, *Monastic Revival*, p. 113. In some regards, the Norman dukes of the early- to mid-eleventh century (and sometimes later) continued to treat their monastic foundations as if they were proprietary churches (*Eigenkirchen*), as was the case with, for example, Fécamp; see B. Pohl and S. Vanderputten, 'Fécamp, Cluny, and the invention of traditions in the later eleventh century', *Journal of Medieval Monastic Studies* 5 (2016), 1–41. On the Norman dukes' customary participation in abbatial elections and investitures, see J.-F. Lemarignier, *Étude sur les privilèges d'exemption et de jurisdiction ecclésiastique des abbayes normandes depuis les origines jusqu'en 1140* (Paris, 1937).
23 *Ecclesiastical History*, ed. Chibnall, vol. 2, pp. 92–3: 'Illi autem ancipiti discrimine anxiati sunt. Nam vivente abbate suo, qui præfatam ecclesiam fundaverat, eosque ad monachatum susceperat, et sine probabilibus non per iudicium synodi, sed per tirannidem furentis marchisi expulsus fuerat.' On the significance of this statement, see G. Melville, 'Aspekte zum Vergleich von Krisen und Reformen in mittelalterlichen Klöstern und Orden', in G. Melville and A. Müller (eds), *Mittelalterliche Orden und Klöster im Vergleich: methodische Ansätze und Perspektiven* (Berlin, 2007), pp. 139–60 (pp. 148–9).
24 *Ecclesiastical History*, ed. Chibnall, vol. 2, p. 96. Cf. Roach, 'Saint-Évroul and southern Italy', p. 85.
25 Loud, *Latin Church*, pp. 85–6.
26 *Ecclesiastical History*, ed. Chibnall, vol. 2, pp. 98–103.
27 Ménager, 'Les fondations', p. 7; H. Houben, 'I benedettini e la latinizzazione della terra d'Otranto', in B. Vetere (ed.), *Ad Ovest di Bisanzio, il Salento medioevale* (Galatina, 1990), pp. 71–89 (pp. 82–3).
28 See J. F. Niermeyer and C. van de Kieft (eds), *Mediae Latinitatis Lexicon minus*, rev. edn, 2 vols (Leiden, 2002), vol. 1, p. 914. The charter mentioning Baldwin V is found in the monastic cartulary of St Peter in Ghent, dated 1047; see C. Du Cange (ed.), *Glossarium mediae et infimae Latinitatis*, 10 vols (Niort, 1883–87), vol. 5, p. 477. Duke Richard II's charter was issued to the Norman abbey of Fécamp in 1017 × 25, now Fécamp, Palais Bénédictine Museum and Archive, no. 2bis, edited in C. H. Haskins, *Norman Institutions* (Cambridge, MA, 1918), pp. 255–6. Robert I's charter was issued on behalf of Jumièges in 1027 × 35, edited in Fauroux, *Recueil*, pp. 214–16 (no. 74). The

charter issued under William II (*regnante [...] Willelmo illustri comite tenente Normanniae monarchiam*) was included in the cartulary of the abbey of St Peter of Chartres, where it is dated to 'before 1061' (*Ante a. 1061*); *Collection des cartulaires de France: Cartulaire de l'abbaye de Saint-Père de Chartres*, ed. M. Guérard, 2 vols (Paris, 1840), vol. 1, pp. 178–9 (no. 52); also cf. *Annales ordinis S. Benedicti occidentalium monachorum patriarchae*, ed. J. Mabillon, 6 vols (Paris, 1703–39), vol. 4, p. 536.

29 Ménager, *Recueil*, p. 41; H. Enzensberger, 'Roberto il Guiscardo: documenti e cancellaria', in Fonseca (ed.), *Roberto il Guiscardo*, pp. 61–81 (pp. 63, 75–6). The curse *anathema maranatha!* features in charters issued by Dukes Richard I, Robert I and, in particular, William II of Normandy; Fauroux, *Recueil*, pp. 72–4 (no. 4; dated 962 × 96), 214–16 (no. 74; 1027 × 35), 287–92 (no. 122; 1050) and 402–8 (no. 214; 1056 × 66). The website 'Chartes originales antérieures à 1121 conservées en France' (TELMA) lists a further eight examples from France for the period *c.* 1000–62; www.cn-telma.fr//originaux/index/ (accessed 8 October 2018). An early example is the foundation charter of Solignac (632), edited in M. Aubrun, *L'ancien diocese de Limoges des origines au milieu du XI siècle* (Clermont-Ferrand, 1981), pp. 417–18.

30 On Robert's investiture and acclamation by his army, see the sources in J. Déer, *Das Papsttum und die süditalienischen Normannenstaaten, 1053–1212* (Göttingen, 1969), pp. 15–18 (investiture), 18–20 (acclamation). On the Synod of Melfi, see G. Gresser, *Die Synoden und Konzilien in der Zeit des Reformpapsttums in Deutschland und Italien von Leo IX. bis Calixt II., 1049–1123* (Paderborn, 2006), pp. 48–51. Also cf. Loud, *Age of Robert Guiscard*, pp. 128–31; B. Pohl, 'Schnittpunkt Süditalien: Päpste, Patriarchen und Normannen im späteren 11. Jahrhundert, 1054 und 1098', in M. Altripp (ed.), *Byzanz in Europa: Europas östliches Erbe* (Turnhout, 2012), pp. 97–113.

31 The foundation charter apart, the titulatures used in Robert Guiscard's pre-1062 diplomata are: 'Dei gratia et sancti Petri dux' (33 per cent), 'Divina favente clementia dux' (17 per cent), 'Divina misericordia inclitus comes et dux' (17 per cent), 'dono Domini dux' (17 per cent) and simply 'dux' or 'comes' (17 per cent); see Ménager, *Recueil*, pp. 27–38 (nos 4–10). Also cf. the discussion in Enzensberger, 'Roberto il Guiscardo', pp. 67–70.

32 Ménager, *Recueil*, pp. 130 (no. 41; issued in 1082), 143 (no. 44; 1084), 147 (no. 45; 1085).

33 Ménager, *Recueil*, pp. 47–150 (nos 12–45). The titulatures used by Robert Guiscard in 1063–85 are: 'Divina favente clementia dux' (36

per cent), 'dux' or 'comes' (23 per cent), 'Dei gratia dux' (10 per cent), 'Dei gratia et sancti Petri dux' (10 per cent), 'universorum dispositoris permissione dux' (8 per cent), 'Divina misericordia inclitus comes et dux' (3 per cent), 'Divina opitulante misericordia dux' (3 per cent), 'Divina optinente potentia dux' (3 per cent), 'dono Domini dux' (3 per cent) and 'gratia Domini comes et dux' (3 per cent). Also cf. Déer, *Papsttum*, p. 20. A similar distribution emerges from Robert's post-1062 charters for the abbey of Venosa, edited in Houben, *Die Abtei Venosa*, pp. 241–77 (nos 9–45).

34 Enzensberger, 'Roberto il Guiscardo'; H. Enzensberger, 'Bemerkungen zu Kanzlei und Diplomen Robert Guiskards', in *Roberto il Guiscardo e il suo tempo: Relazioni e comunicazioni nelle prime Giornate normanno-sveve* (Rome, 1975), pp. 107–13 (pp. 112–13); H. Enzensberger, 'Chanceries, charters and administration in Norman Italy', in G. A. Loud and A. Metcalfe (eds), *The Society of Norman Italy* (Leiden, 2002), pp. 117–50. See also G. A. Loud, 'The chancery and charters of the kings of Sicily (1130–1212)', *EHR* 124 (2009), 779–810.

35 See F. Beck and E. Henning (eds), *Die archivalischen Quellen: Mit einer Einführung in die Historischen Hilfswissenschaften*, 5th edn (Cologne, 2012), p. 39.

36 A similar conclusion is reached by Enzensberger, 'Roberto il Guiscardo', p. 63.

37 The charters exhibiting this titulature are Fouroux, *Recueil*, pp. 246 (no. 94; issued in 1035 × 40), 259 (no. 102; 1037 × 45), 269 (no. 109; 1047–8), 278 (no. 115; 1048), 289 (no. 122; 1050), 301 (no. 128; 1040/7 × 53), 312 (no. 136; 1055) and 331 (no. 148; 1061). Cf. the discussion on pp. 49–50.

38 On the cartulary manuscript(s), see the references provided above, n. 20. Marjorie Chibnall believed that the exemption clause allowing the monks to choose any bishop they liked for the blessing of their abbots (rather than having to rely on the diocesan bishop of Lisieux) was a subsequent interpolation, which she dated to c. 1114 × 37; M. Chibnall, 'Le privilège de libre élection dans les chartes de Saint-Evroult', *Annales de Normandie* 28 (1978), 341–2. Also cf. Lemarignier, *Étude*.

39 The (forged) charter for Venosa (1053) has been edited in Houben, *Die Abtei Venosa*, pp. 232–5 (no. 4); for Mileto's charters (1080/81), see Ménager, 'L'abbaye de Mileto', pp. 14–16 (no. 2), 20–4 (no. 4).

40 MS BnF Lat. 11055, fol. 15r; Fauroux, *Recueil*, p. 289.

41 MS BnF Lat. 11055, fol. 16r; Fauroux, *Recueil*, p. 292.

42 *Ecclesiastical History*, ed. Chibnall, vol. 2, pp. 40–3.

43 *Ecclesiastical History*, ed. Chibnall, vol. 2, pp. 32–41; B. Pohl, 'What sort of man should the abbot be? Three voices from the Norman Abbey of Mont-Saint-Michel', in S. Vanderputten (ed.), *Abbots and Abbesses as a Human Resource in the Ninth- to Twelfth-Century West* (Zurich, 2019), pp. 101–24.
44 M. Chibnall, *The World of Orderic Vitalis* (Woodbridge, 1984), p. 75.
45 Occhiato, 'Robert de Grandmesnil', pp. 624–8, 642–8.
46 G. Occhiato, 'Rapporti culturali e rispondenze architettoniche tra Calabria e Francia in età romantica: l'abbazia normanna di Sant'Eufemia', *Mélanges de l'Ecole française de Rome. Moyen Âge, temps moderne* 93 (1981), 565–603 (pp. 585–7). Like Cluny (II) and Bernay, St Euphemia's abbey church had a stepped choir with multiple apses. On Bernay's foundation (1025), see Potts, *Monastic Revival*, p. 69. On the buildings of St Évroult, see the recent archaeological reports by A.-S. Vigot, 'Archaeological investigations at the abbey of Saint-Évroult-Notre-Dame-du-Bois', in Rozier *et al.* (eds), *Orderic Vitalis*, pp. 375–84; A.-S. Vigot, 'La salle capitulaire de l'abbaye de Saint-Évroult-Notre-Dame-du-Bois: Rapport final d'opération archéologique' (2014), http://openarchive.eveha.fr/uploads/documents/280-rapport.pdf (accessed 8 October 2018).
47 Occhiato, 'Rapporti', p. 568. Also cf. Occhiato, 'Robert de Grandmesnil', p. 629.
48 Chibnall, 'Le privilège'; *Ecclesiastical History*, ed. Chibnall, vol. 2, pp. 74–5, n. 1; Houben, *Die Abtei Venosa*, pp. 141–2.
49 Loud, *Latin Church*, p. 87.
50 Houben, *Die Abtei Venosa*, p. 39.
51 Loud, *Latin Church*, p. 89.

11

King Roger II's legislation on the celebration of marriage

Elisabeth van Houts

Amongst the laws issued by King Roger II (c.1095–1154), clause xxvii is entitled 'On the legitimate celebration of marriage'.[1] It is part of his wide-ranging assizes promulgated, perhaps in stages, not later than the early 1140s.[2] Exceptionally for a European ruler, the king reserved the right to decide on the legitimacy of a marriage by making the exchange of property associated with the marriage bond dependent on a priest's blessing in a church. He thereby fused what elsewhere in Europe were distinct prerogatives of the secular ruler and of the Church. This chapter will investigate Roger II's motivations for his innovative marriage legislation.

In a period when notions of what constituted a legitimate marriage were fluid and much debated, Roger II combined customary and ecclesiastical elements in an unprecedented way. Until then, in his kingdom, as elsewhere in Western Europe, a distinction had been made between the property arrangements between the couple's families (the betrothal) and the wedding celebration, a festivity that for most people was a domestic affair.[3] The union's legitimacy, for purposes of property and inheritance, was rooted in customary law without any interference by the Church. In the eleventh and twelfth centuries this began to change. As a result of the Church's reform movement, canon lawyers and theologians formulated ideas of marriage alongside those of customary law. Moreover, deeper engagement of lay society with the ideas of consent by the couple (rather than parents or kin), the indissolubility of marriage and the symbolic equating of marital union with the bond between Christ and his Church brought a change in practice. From c. 1180, when Pope Alexander III issued his edict *Veniens ad nos*, Christian society accepted that a marriage's legitimacy was rooted in the exchange of words of consent by the couple, not by the assent of parents

King Roger II's legislation on marriage   213

or kin at the property exchange. The Church urged but did not require couples to express their consent at the church door with a priest ready to bless the union.[4] It is crucial to understand that from c. 1180 in most of Europe the legitimacy of marriage depended on the couple's expression of consent, not on the property exchange between families or a priest's blessing in a church. It is noteworthy that Roger II's legislation regarding marriage followed Pope Anacletus II's approval of his kingship of southern Italy and Sicily in 1130 and Innocent II's confirmation in 1139. This enactment made Roger II the first king in Western Europe to insist on a church celebration, consisting of a priest's blessing after the betrothal, in order to legitimate any property transaction made at that time. In this way Roger II combined the authority of a secular and an ecclesiastical ruler and spelled out the repercussions on property-holding for those who broke that law, especially women.

The contents of clause xxvii

Let me begin with the contents of clause xxvii.[5] In his code's prolegomenon, quoting Proverbs 8:15, Roger II argues that through God kings rule and legislators exercise justice.[6] He furthermore points to his responsibility as king 'to draft laws, govern the people, instruct them in morals and extirpate evil customs' ('leges condere, populum gubernare, mores instruere, pravas consuetudines extirpare').[7] An evil custom in particular need of stamping out, 'as though some calamity or pestilence' ('que quasi clades et lues') was the long-standing habit neither to celebrate marriage in church nor have it blessed by a priest. Roger in fact does not explicitly describe the evil custom but we can infer it from what follows. The comparison of the evil custom to a 'calamity or pestilence' resonates with reform literature condemning clerical marriages as (moral) contagion.[8] Roger explains that 'it goes against custom to contract matrimony, to procreate legitimate progeny and bind oneself indissolubly to a consort, unless seeking the favour and grace of God in these matters of marriage and "concerning Christ and the Church" as the Apostle says, by confirming the sacrament through the priestly ministry'.[9] Roger and his advisers draw upon thinking about marriage in canon law and theology. They knew of

St Augustine's doctrine of marriage as an indissoluble monogamous union, an idea based upon Paul's letter to the Ephesians, which compares marriage to Christ's union with his Church.[10] The Church's propagation of this symbolism has been extensively studied by David d'Avray.[11] Roger II's edict particularly reflects the notion of marriage as a sacrament, a conception developed in the late eleventh and early twelfth century by Anselm of Laon and Hugh of St Victor.[12] For Hugh the sacrament of marriage was given by the couple to one another through the symbolism of Christ's bond with the Church and also as an act of love freely given. The act of love and the sacrament were only valid if given each to the other by the couple's free consent, not by leave of parents or kin or lords, let alone through coercion.[13] For our purpose, it is crucial to understand that marriage was not therefore like other sacraments such as baptism or the eucharist, which were bestowed by a priest. Furthermore, the concept of free consent in clause xxvii is implicit, not explicit.[14]

Given the theology (and canon law) of marriage as a sacrament, it is most surprising that Roger II's clause refers to 'the confirming of the sacrament through the priestly ministry' ('sacramentum confirmandum per sacerdotum ministerium').[15] The wording suggests that in Roger's eyes marriage needed validation by a priest. Unlike the Byzantine Church, the Latin Church had always recommended a priestly blessing but never required it to make a marriage sacramentally valid. Either Roger or his advisers clearly pushed the boundaries of contemporary thinking in Western Europe by stipulating 'that it is necessary for all those wishing to contract a legitimate marriage to have the marriage solemnly celebrated after the betrothal and each for his own measure and comfort to take the path to a church and priestly blessing'.[16] Furthermore, exceptional in a Western European context, Roger II explained in the second half of the clause what exactly he wanted to see happening. The priestly blessing was a requirement for a marriage's validity if the couple 'wished to bequeath succession [to their property] to their future heirs' ('si volunt futuris heredibus successionem relinquere'). There would be repercussions for the couple who failed to have a church celebration: 'They should know that they are acting against our royal precept and would have no legitimate heirs either by will or by intestacy from those born to an illicit marriage contrary to our law.'[17] The legitimacy of the marriage concerned the legitimacy of the property transaction. Under Lombard and Roman arrangements for marital property, this was usually negotiated before the betrothal. The men of the two families would agree on land and movables, a compact with force of law. This arrangement's validity was not dependent on a priest's blessing, except in areas under Byzantine authority, such as southern Italy and Sicily in the tenth and eleventh centuries.[18] Finally, the clause stipulates that in case of a non-church wedding and, thus, an illegitimate marriage, 'women would have no right to the dowers proper [i.e. the husband's property set aside for their upkeep during the marriage and their widowhood] for those legitimately married'.[19] It is significant that Roger II reminded his *barones* to whom he addressed his assizes that it would be their *mulieres* (mothers, sisters and wives) who would lose out. By spelling out the consequences, especially for married women and widows, Roger ensured that his men (and presumably women) would think twice before skipping a church celebration. Roger, however, foresaw problems in enforcing his edict and thus ended it with a reassurance that the new law would not apply to those already married nor to widows wishing to remarry.

Motivations of Roger II

Why did Roger II include this far-reaching law in his legislation of the early 1140s? Scholars have debated this. According to Marongiu, Roger was compensating for an inferiority complex regarding the papacy by establishing himself as *adiutor Christianorum*, a role for which the Byzantine emperors formed a template. This did not mean for Marongiu that Roger imposed a Byzantine legal system on southern Italy but more that he favoured a pick and mix of Byzantine ingredients.[20] According to Joanna Drell, we should see clause xxvii as 'merely [reflecting] the prevailing mood of the day' given the uncertainty of what constituted a legitimate marriage and the priesthood's role in it.[21] In my view three reasons may be distinguished: first, legitimation of Roger's position as king and legislator in a context of conquest; second, sacral kingship of an imperial kind; and, third, the potential for royal control over aristocratic inheritance and property.

The king as lawgiver

The legislation, including clause xxvii, should first be seen as part of Roger II's campaign to legitimise his position. Roger II was a new king, acclaimed first by Pope Anacletus II and then reluctantly confirmed by Innocent II.[22] It was customary for kings after their accession and coronation to set out their legislative programme, as we know from elsewhere in Europe, especially in a context of conquest. For example, in eleventh-century England King Cnut embarked on an extensive legislative campaign after his conquest of the kingdom and coronation, not least to legitimise himself as a Christian king.[23] After the Norman Conquest of England in 1066, the Norman kings issued coronation charters containing mini-blueprints of their legislative agendas.[24] Roger's royal acclamation in 1130 and its confirmation in 1139 were accompanied by a political campaign that included a reorganisation of the counties of southern Italy, to which I will return.[25] A fresh legislative programme such as this one would validate his kingship, but evidence for a specific date remains elusive.[26] Roger II had inherited Sicily but had conquered southern Italy and, by combining the two regions, he consolidated his rule over them by being made king of both. His kingship was controversial not only in Italy but across Western Europe, where many saw him as a tyrant or upstart.[27] The act of legislating was a God-given prerogative reserved for kings; being seen to issue laws therefore underlined his newly-acquired position.[28]

The ruler as king-priest

Being a new king enabled Roger to legislate over his newly unified kingdom. He did so innovatively by imbuing his rulership with far greater symbolism of authority than any earlier ruler. By conditioning a marriage's legitimacy on a church celebration and priest's blessing, he was encouraging his subjects to display greater awareness of their responsibility as Christians. In this sense he not only took on a pastoral role to entice his subjects to frequent churches for important moments in their lives, but he also enabled priests to stipulate to their parishioners that marriage in church was important for the property transactions agreed at betrothal. As others have argued, Roger II modelled himself as much on

Byzantine imperial rulership as on western Christian models of kingship. His legislative campaign must be seen in the context of the visual expressions of his rulership in architecture and art such as the mosaics at the Martorana in Palermo, which depict Christ himself bestowing the crown on him in a Byzantine style of leadership.[29] If this visual representation of kingship echoed the Byzantine imperial pattern, does this mean that his legislative programme was inspired by Byzantine imperial law? Although Houben's biography is silent on this, others have suggested Greek influence. Addressing the innovative nature of clause xxvii, Pennington finds possible Byzantine inspiration in the requirement for a priestly blessing to validate a marriage, a law that originated with Emperor Leo VI *c.* 907.[30] Furthermore, Graham Loud points out that there was considerable Byzantine influence in legal and liturgical matters and finds it plausible that Roger II and his advisers picked up this Byzantine tradition in southern Italy.[31] The Byzantine emperor combined secular authority with greater ecclesiastical authority than any king, or indeed emperor, in Western Europe. Roger II's law set him not only above priests and bishops but also above the papacy.

Gratian's *Decretum*, its latest revision in circulation by the 1140s, includes in its section on marriage a papal decree by Pope Urban II (1088–99) pertaining to a marriage case involving a Norman count, Jordan I of Capua, whose daughter refused to marry a Norman ruler of Gaeta, Rainald Ridel.[32] Jordan's unnamed daughter (d. 1090) was given in marriage by her 'coerced and grieving' ('coactus et dolens') father to Rainald Ridel of Gaeta as part of peace negotiations between warring second-generation Norman settlers in southern Italy. According to Urban, she had been 'unwilling, weeping and resisting with all her might' ('nolentem, flentem, et pro viribus renitentem'). Although Urban felt that the marriage should stand if the girl, her mother and her relatives were willing, we do not know the outcome.[33] Urban's argument was that 'those whose body is one ought to be of one spirit' ('Quorum enim unum corpus est, unus debet esse et animus'), but when a couple disliked each other that did not bode well for a marriage's success.

We do not know if Roger II was aware of this particular papal ruling about a potential marital alliance several decades earlier in southern Italy. However, there seems to be no doubt that with clause xxvii Roger II wanted to prevent any reason for ecclesiastical interference in marriage-making and inheritance in his kingdom. In his mind, if a marriage's validity was questioned, he as king or his royal judges, not a Church official, would decide the matter. As arbiter of the validity of marriages, dependent on a church ceremony, Roger II, as pointed out, makes no allusion to consent. The lack of explicitness regarding consent is significant. As king-priest, Roger II could be expected to know that the Church demanded the couple's consent. In an era of arranged marriages, however, such consent was often trumped by that of parents or indeed their lord. By not addressing consent, Roger II and his lawyers created room to manoeuvre whenever needed by couples, parents or lords in marriage-making.[34] This tells us something, I suggest, about Roger II's ambition to gain greater control over marital property transactions.

The king and prerogatives of lordship

Transfers of marital property were traditionally regulated by secular custom. As Drell has argued for southern Italy, property arrangements surrounding marriage combined Lombard and Roman law.[35] The Lombard *Morgengabe* or morning gift – the husband's gift to the wife – was standard throughout the twelfth century and represented the greatest financial outlay for families. The morning gift evolved gradually into the dower arrangement, the approximately quarter or third of the husband's property set aside for the wife's or widow's maintenance. These practices represent customary law upheld by local rulers, including the Normans.[36] The reorganisation of counties in Apulia and Calabria after 1140 resulted in the counts becoming the king's vassals.[37] The document most often cited in scholarly debate on potential feudalisation of southern Italy is the famous 'Catalogue of Barons' (*Catalogus Baronum*).[38] Hubert Houben described it as 'an inventory of military obligations in the duchy of Apulia and the principality of Capua', datable to 1150–52 and revised in 1167.[39] It seems, therefore, that within just over a decade of Roger II's acceptance as king not only did he issue a programme of laws but he also held lordship over a considerable number of nobles who were thought to hold lands of him in return for military obligations. The question arises whether Roger's lordship over his tenants-in-chief extended to authority over the marriages of their women, like that exercised by the kings of England. Due to the expansion of lordship in medieval Europe, kings as lords tried to extract from the aristocracy prerogatives previously controlled by custom; consent for marriage by aristocrats was a target.[40] In particular, royal or lordly financial demands in return for consent to marry became financial assets. Every level of the feudal hierarchy from the king downward each increasingly tried to control the exercise of feudal prerogatives as sources of income. Thus a king could demand that a tenant-in-chief acquire royal permission for a daughter to marry and similar leave was necessary for a tenant-in-chief's widow to remarry or for a male or female minor in royal wardship to wed. The rationale for this was the ruler's need to know who could perform the military service owed for the land held of him. Having such control over marriages enabled the king to provide loyal followers with land by marrying them to heiresses and widows and thus to assure himself a reliable military force. The practice was abused in Angevin England. King John was ultimately confronted by an irate aristocracy with Magna Carta (1215), which decried the king's abuse of his prerogatives.[41] Whether King Roger II aspired to implement such control is a tricky question because his power over his aristocracy was not as strong as that of his English counterparts.[42]

In this context it is interesting, however, that clause xxvii has been discussed by historians as potential evidence for the aristocracy's need to ask King Roger II's permission to marry off their women. Charter evidence from Conversano and Bari discussed by Marongiu (1171 and 1180) refers to marriages celebrated in Roger II's time 'according to the legitimate and sacred solemnities of the lord king's constitutions'. This, in my view, alludes to marriages celebrated in accordance with royal law: in a church with a priest's blessing.[43] There is no reference to royal permission. We know that assent to marry became an important issue under Roger II's successors William I and William II because contemporary chroniclers report the nobility's concern with seeking leave to arrange the marriages of their womenfolk.[44] But we find the requirement to seek royal consent for the transfer of property on marriage (for men and women) incorporated only in the *Liber Augustalis* of Frederick II, issued at Melfi in 1231, where clause xxiii explicitly mandates that:

no count, baron or knight, or anyone else who holds in chief from us baronies or fiefs in the records of our diwan, should dare to marry without licence. They should not dare to marry off their daughters, sisters or granddaughters or any other girls whom they can and should arrange marriages for, or to marry their sons with movable or immovable property, notwithstanding the contrary custom which is said to have been observed in some parts of the kingdom.[45]

As far as I have been able to establish, there was no such requirement in Roger II's time.

Despite scholarly hesitancy to assess whether clause xxvii says anything explicit about a requirement for royal consent for marriage, there is no ambiguity.[46] Clause xxvii contains nothing about royal permission to marry.

However, Roger II reserved for himself the right to sanction any breach of clause xxvii. Couples who had been betrothed and had made agreements on property but had not subsequently sought a priest's blessing in a church were breaking the king's law and could be punished. Royal sanction would, we might imagine, vary from imposition of fines to confiscation of lands. Both would have been a lucrative source of royal income and would fit with Roger II's keen interest in administration and finances, as we know from his biographer Alexander of Telese.[47] A comparison with English kings Henry I (1100–35) and Henry II (1154–89) springs to mind.[48] The Pipe Rolls (for 1129–30 and then from 1154 onwards) leave no doubt about the sums levied.[49] The *Rotuli de dominabus et pueris et puellis* for 1184–85 lists the widows and wards from twelve counties with the value of their lands and sometimes the fines payable for not having asked the king's permission to marry.[50] The main difference between the English and the southern Italian cases is that the English kings never legislated on the legitimacy of marriages and instead left this matter to the Church. Once a decision on legitimacy had been reached in a bishop's court, it would come to the secular courts where the common law on property applied.[51] We have no evidence for the levying of fines resulting from Roger II's clause xxvii, but the clause seems to have paved the way for his successors – William I and William II – to pressure their tenants-in-chief to seek permission to marry off their women and for Frederick II's *Constitution of Melfi* explicitly to require barons to seek royal permission for marriages and property transfers for both men and women.

Finally, there is the issue of Roger II's concern for aristocratic women. As we have seen, he ended clause xxvii with a warning to his barons that breaching his law would rebound particularly on women. Without a marriage in church and a priestly blessing, a 'woman' or 'wife' (*mulier*) would be unable to control income from the *Morgengabe* assigned to her in church during her life as spouse or widow. This royal warning can be viewed as paternal or pastoral concern of an anxious ruler expected to take care of the vulnerable and weak. It can also be viewed more cynically as Roger making his barons responsible as fathers, brothers and husbands for their womenfolk's destitution if they failed to have their daughters, sisters and wives wed in church. But then Roger II, perhaps mindful of his mother Adelaide del Vasto's failed second marriage, may have been genuinely concerned about the fate of betrothed women. We do not know. What seems incontrovertible is that his legislation making a properly solemnised wedding a prerequisite for legitimate transfer of property increased his control over both aristocratic marriages and the lives of aristocratic men and women in his kingdom.

Conclusion

In this chapter I have taken a fresh look at King Roger II's innovative clause xxvii in which he makes the legitimacy of marital property arrangements dependent on couples being blessed by a priest in a church. His innovation has been explained as part of his campaign to seek legitimation as king (and thus lawgiver), as king-priest insisting on control over a combined secular and ecclesiastical legislative clause, and as lord financially exploiting breaches of his law on marriage by confiscation of land or levying fines. He, however, did not insist that his barons seek his permission to arrange marriages. Yet retrospectively, it is evident how his law helped pave the way for his successors to insist on this. Roger II's moral concern for betrothed aristocratic women in an exclusively domestic wedding ceremony would be touching were it not simultaneously in his financial interest to get them into church on their wedding day.

Notes

1 'Le Assise del Cod. Vaticano con il testo del Cod. Cassinese e quello delle costituzioni relative di Federico II', edited in G. M. Monti, *Lo Stato Normanno Svevo. Lineamenti e ricerche* (Trani, 1945), pp. 114–84 at pp. 137–9 (henceforth: Monti); *Roger II and the Making of the Kingdom of Sicily*, trans. G. A. Loud (Manchester, 2012), pp. 314–28 at pp. 322–3 (henceforth: *Roger II*). The clause has been discussed extensively by canon lawyers and historians; amongst the most important are P. Vaccari, 'La celebrazione del matrimonio in una assisa di Ruggero II', in *VIII centenario della monte di Ruggero II. Atti del convegno internazionale di studi Ruggeriani (21–25 aprile 1954)*, 2 vols (Palermo, 1955), vol. 1, pp. 205–11; A. Marongiu, 'La forma religiosa del matrimonio nel diritto bizantino, normanno e svevo', *Archivio storico per la Calabria e la Lucania* 30 (1961), 1–30, reprinted in A. Marongiu, *Byzantine, Norman, Swabian and Later Institutions in Southern Italy* (London, 1972), no. xiv; and A. Marongiu, *Matrimonio e famiglia nell'Italia meridionale (sec. viii–xiii)* (Bari, 1976), pp. 74–7; J. Drell, *Kinship and Conquest: Family Strategies in the Principality of Salerno during the Norman Period 1077–1194* (Ithaca, 2002), pp. 60–2.

2 For the dating of the whole collection between 1130 and 1140 and the caveat that any clause not taken from Roman law was issued probably early in that period, see K. Pennington, 'The birth of the *ius commune*: King Roger II's legislation', *Rivista internazionale di diritto comune* 17 (2006), 23–60 at p. 52. Loud suggests a date in the 1140s as he wonders how likely it would have been that before 1139 – Roger's reconciliation with Innocent II – the king could have had access to lawyers from Bologna (*Roger II*, p. 43, n. 125).

3 For what follows in this paragraph see E. van Houts, *Married Life in the Middle Ages, 900–1300* (Oxford, 2019), pp. 1–15 and 29–86.

4 The most accessible edition is Gregory IX's *Liber Extra*, 4.1.15 (*Corpus iuris canonici*, ed. A. Friedberg, 2 vols (Leipzig, 1879–81), vol. 2, pp. 666–7).

5 I follow the numbering by Gennaro Monti and Graham Loud, not Kenneth Pennington's, which refers to the clause as number xxvi (Pennington, 'The birth', pp. 52–9).

6 'per me reges regnant et conditores legum decernunt iustitiam', Monti, p. 115, and *Roger II*, p. 314.

7 See Monti, p. 137, and *Roger II*, p. 322 (slightly revised).

8 See, for example, Peter Damian's Letter 61, in *Die Briefe des Petrus Damiani*, ed. K. Reindel, 4 vols, MGH Die Briefe der deutschen

Kaiserzeit (Munich, 1983–93), vol. 2, p. 208 (*scelus … pestis*); *The Ecclesiastical History of Orderic Vitalis*, ed. and trans. M. Chibnall, 6 vols (Oxford, 1968–81), vol. 3, pp. 120–3 (*letalis consuedo*).

9 Monti, p. 137: 'repugnans sacrorum canonum institutis, christianis auribus inauditum est matrimonium velle contrahere, legitimam sobolem procreare indivisibile vitae consortium alligare nec Dei favorem et gratiam in ipsi nuptiarum instabulis querere et tantum "in Christo et Ecclesia", ut dicit Apostolus, sacramentum, confirmandum per sacerdotum ministerium creare.'

10 Ephesians 5:32; Augustine, *De bono coniugali; de sancta virginitate*, ed. and trans. P. G. Walsh (Oxford, 2001); P. L. Reynolds, *Marriage in the Western Church: The Christianisation of Marriage during the Patristic and Early Medieval Period* (Boston, 2001), pp. 241–314.

11 For the symbolism, see D. d'Avray, *Medieval Marriage: Symbolism and Society* (Oxford, 2005), pp. 74–130.

12 H. J. F. Reinhardt, *Die Ehelehre der Schule des Anselm von Laon. Eine theologie-und kirchenrechtsgeschichtliche Untersuchung zu den Ehetexten der frühen Pariser Schule des 12. Jahrhunderts*, Beiträge zur Geschichte der Philosophie und Theologie des Mittelalters, n.s. 14 (Münster, 1974), and M. Müller, *Die Lehre des hl. Augustinus von der Paradiesesehe und ihre Auswirkung in der Sexualethik des 12. und 13. Jahrhunderts bis Thomas von Aquin* (Regensburg, 1954), pp. 44–7 (Anselm) and pp. 75–84 (Hugh).

13 On coercion, see below.

14 Others disagree; see in particular Vaccari, 'La celebrazione', pp. 205–7; Drell, *Kinship*, p. 61.

15 Monti, p. 138; trans., *Roger II*, p. 323.

16 Monti, p. 138; trans., *Roger II*, p. 323: 'Deo propitio perpetuo valitura, volentibus omnibus legitimum contrahere matrimonium necessitatem imponi, quatinus post sponsalia nuptias celebraturi sollempniter quisquis pro suo modulo seu commodo limen petant ecclesie [et] sacerdotum bennedictionem.'

17 Monti, p. 138; trans., *Roger II*, p. 323: 'Alioquin noverint ammodo molientes contra nostrum regale preceptum neque ex testamento, neque ab intestato se habituros heredes legitimos, ex illicito per nostram sanctionem matrimonio procreatos.'

18 Marongiu, 'La forma religiosa', pp. 1–30 at pp. 3–10. For a recent discussion of the Italian areas under Byzantine control and what happened after the Norman conquest, see G. A. Loud, 'Communities, cultures and conflict in southern Italy from the Byzantines to the Angevins', *Al-Masāq: Islam and the Medieval Mediterranean* 28 (2016), 132–52 at pp. 135–44; for a discussion of the survival of

Greek liturgy, see pp. 137–40, though it lacks a discussion of marriage practices. For this, see, briefly, *Roger II*, pp. 43–4.
19 Monti, p. 138; trans., *Roger II*, p. 323: 'mulieres etiam dotes et aliis nubentibus legitime debitas non habere.'
20 A. Marongiu, 'A model state in the middle ages: The Norman and Swabian kingdom of Sicily', *Comparative Studies in Society and History* 6 (1963–64), p. 318, and Marongiu, 'La forma religiosa', pp. 11–12, 17–20, on the psychological explanation for Roger and his 'complesso di inferiorita' vis-à-vis the pope.
21 Drell, *Kinship*, p. 61 and n. 19.
22 *Roger II*, pp. 20–6.
23 *The Laws of the Kings of England from Edmund to Henry I*, ed. and trans. A. J. Robertson (Cambridge, 1925), pp. 140–5 (Cnut's proclamation 1020); P. Stafford, 'The laws of Cnut and the history of Anglo-Saxon royal promises', *Anglo-Saxon England* 10 (1981), 172–90.
24 *The Laws of the Kings of England*, pp. 239–43 (the Ten Articles of William I), 276–83 (coronation charter of Henry I); *Regesta regum Anglo-Normannorum 1066–1154. Vol. III: Regesta regis Stephani ac Mathildis imperaticis et Gaufridi et Henrici ducum Normannorum, 1135–1154*, ed. H. A. Cronne, R. H. C. Davis and H. W. C. Davis (Oxford, 1968), nos 270–1, pp. 95–7 (King Stephen).
25 G. A. Loud, 'William the Bad or William the Unlucky? Kingship in Sicily 1154–1166', *Haskins Society Journal* 8 (1999), 99–113 at pp. 105–7, and H. Fernández Aceves, 'The re-arrangement of the nobility under the Hauteville monarchy: The creation of the south-Italian counties', *Ex Historia* 8 (2016), 58–90 at pp. 68–81.
26 Ortensio Zecchino's suggestion that the legislation was promulgated at Ariano in September 1140 has been rejected by H. Houben, *Roger II of Sicily: A Ruler between East and West*, trans. G. A. Loud and D. Milburn (Cambridge, 2002), pp. 73–4, and, also, as we have seen above in note 2, by Pennington and Loud.
27 Houben, *Roger II of Sicily*, pp. 4–5.
28 On kings as law givers, see, for example, J. L. Nelson, 'Legislation and consensus in the time of Charles the Bald', in P. Wormald, D. Bullough and R. Collins (eds), *Ideal and Reality in Frankish and Anglo-Saxon Society: Studies Presented to J. M. Wallace-Hadrill* (Oxford, 1983), pp. 202–27, and J. L. Nelson, 'Kingship and empire', in J. H. Burns (ed.), *The Cambridge History of Medieval Political Thought c.350–c.1450* (Cambridge, 1988), pp. 211–51 at pp. 213–29; D. Pratt, *The Political Thought of King Alfred the Great* (Cambridge, 2007), pp. 214–41; and J. B. Freed, *Frederick Barbarossa: The Prince and the Myth* (New Haven, 2016), pp. 115–16.

29 Houben, *Roger II of Sicily*, pp. 113–34, especially Figure 2 at p. 114.
30 Pennington, 'The birth', p. 54, without reference to Marongiu, 'La forma religiosa', pp. 5–10, who made the same point.
31 *Roger II*, pp. 43–4.
32 Gratian, Decretum, Pars secunda, Causa 31, questio 2, c. 1 and 4, *Corpus Iuris Canonici*, ed. Friedberg, vol. 1, pp. 113–14 (for Urban's quotes); for what follows, see J. T. Noonan, 'Marriage in the Middle Ages I: Power to choose', *Viator* 4 (1973), 419–34 at pp. 419–20 (on the canon law), and P. Skinner, *Family Power in Southern Italy: The Duchy of Gaeta and its Neighbours 850–1139* (Cambridge, 1995), pp. 156–8 (on the two families but without reference to this marriage case).
33 The other case concerned an unnamed niece of Sancho-Ramirez, king of Aragon-Navarre (1076–94), who refused her royal uncle's arrangement for a marriage (admittedly forced upon him) and found papal support; see Noonan, 'Marriage in the Middle Ages', p. 421.
34 For the role of parents and the couple's customary practice of seeking parental approval (*per licentiam*) for marriage, see Drell, *Kinship and Conquest*, pp. 62–4.
35 Drell, *Kinship and Conquest*, pp. 73–4.
36 Drell, *Kinship and Conquest*, pp. 61–2.
37 Houben, *Roger II of Sicily*, pp. 154–5, based on E. Cuozzo, '*Quei maleditti Normanni'. Cavalieri e organizzazione militare nel Mezzogiorno normanno* (Naples, 1989).
38 *Catalogus Baronum*, ed. E. Jamison, FSI 101 (Rome, 1972).
39 Houben, *Roger II of Sicily*, pp. 154–5.
40 Van Houts, *Married Life*, pp. 52–7 and 143–53, for European geographical variation as well as English royal abuse of the practice.
41 *Magna Carta*, ed. and trans. D. Carpenter (London, 2015), pp. 105 and 450–1.
42 E. Cuozzo, 'Le feudalità del "Regnum" nell'età di Ruggero II', in O. Zecchino (ed.), *Le Assise di Ariano 1140–1990*, Centro Europeo di studi Normanni. Fonti e Studi 1 (Ariano Irpino, 1994), pp. 165–78.
43 Marongiu, 'La forma religiosa', pp. 29–30.
44 Drell, *Kinship and Conquest*, p. 61.
45 *The Liber Augustalis or Constitutions of Melfi Promulgated by the Emperor Frederick II for the Kingdom of Sicily in 1231*, trans. J. M. Powell (New York, 1971), pp. 117–18.
46 Drell, *Kinship and Conquest*, p. 61.
47 *Alexandri Telesini abbatis Ystoria Rogerii regis Sicilie Calbrie atque Apulie*, ed. L. de Nava, commentary by D. R. Clementi, FSI 112 (Rome 1991), IV, c.3, p. 82; Houben, *Roger II of Sicily*, pp. 156–7.

48 This is not the place to investigate whether Roger II might have been inspired by English royal practices with regard to the exploitation of feudal incidents concerning marriages of his tenants-in-chief. For the close contacts between England and Sicily, see G. A. Loud, 'The kingdom of Sicily and the kingdom of England, 1066–1266', *History* 88 (2003), 540–67.

49 *The Great Roll of the Pipe for the Thirty First Year of the Reign of King Henry I Michaelmas 1130 (Pipe Roll 1)*, ed. and trans. J. A. Green, Publications of the Pipe Roll Society, vol. 95, n.s. vol. 57 (London, 2012); for the king and his financial arrangements surrounding aristocratic marriages, see pp. xii, xxvii, xix and xx.

50 *Widows, Heirs and Heiresses in the Late Twelfth Century: Rotuli de dominabus et pueris et puellis*, ed. and trans. J. Walmesley (Tempe, 2006).

51 J. Hudson, *The Oxford History of the Laws of England: Volume II 871–1216* (Oxford, 2012), pp. 778–83.

12

The battle against simony in Norman Italy: perceptions, interpretations, measures and consequences

Lioba Geis

Beginning with Pope Leo IX (1049–54), papal interest in the lands south of Rome gained a new intensity. This shift of focus reflected on one hand the evolving self-conception of Roman pontiffs aspiring to extend their scope of influence beyond Rome, an ambition befitting their universal pretentions.[1] On the other hand, developments in southern Italy stimulated papal interest. In the wake of the consolidation of Norman rule, the southern Italian Church underwent profound change leading by the end of the twelfth century to the extensive Latinisation of previously Greek and Muslim areas, the almost complete reorganisation of the ecclesiastical landscape and the territorial expansion and cultural flowering of Benedictine monasticism.[2] Watching and guiding these transformations, Pope Leo IX and his successors were concerned with ensuring that they conformed to canon law, especially in their ecclesiastical structures. In so doing, they sought to strengthen the bonds between the southern Italian Church and the See of Rome. A particular concern in this context was the promotion of reform ideals and the battle against clerical abuses.[3]

According to the contemporary chronicler Amatus of Montecassino, the major issue confronting Leo IX on his first visit to southern Italy in 1050 was simony, the purchase and sale of Church offices: 'Pope Leo fought against simony and went through the cities making holy sermons whereby he filled the Church with the faithful of Christ. He convoked the synod (that is the congregation) of Salerno and found that all the orders of the Church were involved in the crime of simony.'[4] Amatus depicts simony as a grave and widespread problem not only practised by individuals but also infesting the entire southern Italian Church.[5] Was this merely a commonplace of reform polemics, railing against the illegal practice of selling Church offices and other such abuses and condemning them as the apex of ecclesiastical misconduct?[6] Or was simony for Amatus and his contemporaries such a grave problem that it threatened the southern Italian Church's very existence? Seeking to contextualise the chronicler's pointed assertions, I will investigate how simony was perceived and interpreted and what concrete measures were taken against it in southern Italy from the middle of the eleventh to the end of the twelfth century. By so doing, it will be possible to judge what role simony played in the transformation of the southern Italian Church and whether the response to it was typical of contemporary approaches elsewhere or merely a regional peculiarity.

An important means of disseminating knowledge on simony and how to combat it were Church synods that, from the mid-eleventh century, popes convened in southern Italy with increasing frequency. Particularly before 1130, when the popes repeatedly visited parts of the region, they used synods not just to cement political relations with the Norman rulers but also to propagate their vision of Church reform.[7] Simony was by no means always an issue at these assemblies. The few extant synodal records reveal that simony was dealt with only at Melfi (1089), not at Benevento (1091) or Troia (1093).[8] This impression is confirmed by the narrative sources that, for lack of official records, are one of the main sources for synodal history in southern Italy. Although these materials report on topics addressed at Church assemblies, they rarely mention simony.[9] Furthermore, the authors who do expressly refer to simony speak so generally that it is difficult to determine what measures, if any, were adopted.[10]

Nevertheless, the evidence suggests that simony was indeed an issue in particular for the earlier reform popes from Leo IX to Urban II (1088–99) and that the convocation of the first synod in southern Italy was used to promulgate the programmatic battle against simony. Confirming indirect reports regarding earlier synods, the canons of the synod of Melfi begin with a clearly worded definition and prohibition of simoniacal practices: No one 'should strive to gain the episcopal dignity either by payment given or promised, or by service rendered with that intention, or by prayers, nor should anyone grant it on the aforesaid terms'.[11] The synodal canons then extend this ban to cover all other Church titles and offices. Within his see, the bishop alone was to confer Church offices and benefices, without regard for personal gain; contravention was to be punished with the loss of office for both parties involved.[12] The prohibition on simony formulated at Melfi is thoroughly representative of contemporary thought: in its emphasis on tradition, its acceptance of Gregory the Great's (590–604) understanding of simony in both its material and immaterial form and in sanctions against it. However, the emphasis placed on the papal authority underpinning the canon indicates that Pope Urban II was here not just thinking within the framework of existing prohibitions but also pointedly of the southern Italian context where it was to be implemented.[13]

Unfortunately, the lack of adequate sources for other synods makes further reconstruction of the normative discourse on simony at these assemblies impossible.[14] However, Church synods are not just interesting for their legislative activity against simony but also as a judicial forum in which this problem was dealt with at a practical level. Simony processes conducted against archbishops and bishops under Popes Leo IX, Nicholas II (1059–61) and Alexander II (1061–73) in all cases ended with conviction and removal from office.[15] This rigorous prosecution deviated clearly from the line of papal decrees since Clement II (1046–47) which allowed simoniacal offenders to do penance and remain in office, though this milder regulation seems to have been well known in southern Italy.[16] The case of Bishop Landolf of Tertiveri, whom Alexander II permanently removed from office 'without hope of restoration', is exemplary of the peculiar severity of this practice.[17]

The resolute prosecution of simony by the popes in these cases may perhaps be explained by the fact that the offending prelates held office in Basilicata and Apulia, areas where papal influence was struggling to assert itself.[18] Thus, it would have been particularly important for the popes to know that the Church there was in the hands of morally upright bishops who adhered to their reform ideals. These processes therefore illustrate how synodal practice could adopt quite diverse positions on dealing with simony offences and flexibly apply prevalent Church law to the concrete situation in question.

Beyond Church synods, the popes generally took the leading role in prosecuting simony in southern Italy, either by personally holding court during visits there[19] or by appointing a *locum tenens* empowered to investigate accusations and report his findings to Rome or, alternatively, authorised to make rulings on site as the delegated judge.[20] In contrast, there are few known cases in which the secular rulers of southern Italy took an active role in battling simony. In 1137, a court inquiry into the election of Abbot Rainald I of Montecassino, who was charged – among other things – with having bought votes, was held before Emperor Lothar III of Supplinburg.[21] In the 1140s, Robert of Selby, the chancellor of King Roger II of Sicily and temporary administrator of the kingdom's mainland territories, investigated the election of the bishop of Avellino and found all candidates guilty of simony.[22] And finally, King William II of Sicily commissioned Archbishop Rainald of Bari to investigate simony charges against Maraldus, the bishop-elect of Minervino, between 1171 and 1177.[23]

This legal prosecution of simony by the rulers reflects their general conception of the king's duty to care for the state of the Church and thus assume partial responsibility for ecclesiastical legal affairs.[24] Correspondingly, in the so-called Assizes of Ariano, King Roger II expressly prohibited and sanctioned the simoniacal acquisition of Church office, making simony a secular offence.[25] Nevertheless, the secular authorities seem to have preferred to leave the prosecution of simony in southern Italy to the pope. When the clearly pro-imperial chronicler Peter the Deacon reports on the trial of Abbot Rainald in 1137 for simony and other offences, he mentions Pope Innocent II's (1130–43) resentment of secular investigation of an abbatial election and gives Lothar III's response: He was merely helping to enforce papal law and he invited the Pope to send his own representatives to examine the matter.[26]

Often, however, it was neither pope nor secular ruler who initiated legal investigation of simony in southern Italy but a private plaintiff. This practice casts light on the local context for implementing the prohibition of simony. In all cases in which the plaintiffs were named, they had had personal contact with the accused bishop or abbot and frequently they had apparently been directly affected by the alleged simoniacal practice. While the records sometimes suggest that the plaintiffs were primarily interested in seeing the offence righted and the offender punished, in other cases the charge of simony could well have served other ends. An example of this is Bishop Constantine of Caiazzo's charge of simony against the monks of San Lorenzo in Aversa over their acquisition of the monastery of the Holy Spirit in Caiazzo. Although Pope Urban II ultimately judged in favour of the monks and his successor, Paschal II (1099–1118), confirmed their rightful possession of the monastery in 1100, it was not until six years later that Bishop Constantine's successor Paul, having received in compensation a parcel of land and a yearly rent from the monks, finally accepted this judgement. Obviously, the bishops were not primarily interested in ferreting out simony in their bishoprics but instead used the allegations to assert their own claims to the monastery.[27]

In another case, personal motives apparently played a major role. Responding to the accusations raised by Archdeacon Hugo of Mottola against the bishop of Mottola, Pope Innocent III (1198–1216) instructed Bishop William of Conversano and the archdeacon of Oria in June 1198 to investigate. Most seriously, Hugo accused the bishop of Mottola of nepotism for having provided his nephew with the bishopric's most lucrative benefices: the archdeaconate of Massafra and the archpriesthood in Mottola.[28] Among lesser offences Hugo alleged against his bishop were an uncanonical ordination, squandering his office's goods, simony and association with unworthy persons such as adulterers. It appears, however, that Hugo had a strong personal motive for raising these charges. The bishop of Mottola had recently removed him from his archdeaconate on unknown grounds, which deprived him not just of status but also of income. While nepotism was obviously the central allegation, simony seems to have been a standard smear to discredit the bishop's character.[29] Unfortunately, the sources do not inform us if Hugo's strategy was successful.

Not only clergymen but also laymen appeared before the papal court as plaintiffs in simony cases, as in the allegations raised by some citizens of Benevento in 1123, who charged their archbishop, Roffrid II, with having bought his office. The accusations ultimately failed to convince Pope Calixtus II (1119–24), who freed the archbishop on the basis of a purgatory oath.[30] Although the chronicler Falco of Benevento, who recorded this case, does not elucidate its background, the raising of charges four years after Roffrid's election and three years after his ordination by Pope Calixtus II suggests that the citizens were not primarily moved by the circumstances of the election.[31] Falco's chronicle does not reveal the plaintiffs' motives. The citizens' contestation of the election may have arisen from differences the archbishop had with one civic group but did not affect his relations with the broader community of Benevento. In his narrative of the finding of the relics of St Barbatus, which directly follows this account, Falco emphasises that the archbishop successfully sought the participation of Benevento's citizens as a means to generate common identity in the community.[32]

Finally, not just local conflicts in southern Italy but also the situation in Rome played a role in bringing simony charges to court, as in the case of Abbot Rainald of Montecassino, a process clearly bearing the stamp of the papal schism. Although principally accused of simony, in the course of the hearings held before Emperor Lothar III, as related by Peter the Deacon, Rainald was less and less confronted with this crime than with the circumstances of his ordination. In the end, he was apparently convicted and deposed for having been ordained sub-deacon by excommunicates.[33] He had, in effect, been ordained by (anti)pope Anacletus II (1130–38), he had been elected abbot of Montecassino during the schism and he had repeatedly promised fealty to Anacletus II and King Roger II of Sicily, both excommunicated by Pope Innocent II at the synod of Pisa in 1135.[34] His deposition followed the findings of the papal representatives investigating the case. Thus, it is obvious that not simony but allegiance to the opposite side in the papal schism was Rainald's prime offence in the eyes of Innocent II, who was primarily interested in removing him from office and thereby finally bringing Montecassino back into the fold of obedience.

Although, as Pope Gregory VII (1073–85) had already pointed out in the autumn synod of 1078,[35] simony and the papal schism presented equally grave problems for the validity of ordinations to Church office, schismatic ordinations presented the additional complication of being directly relevant to papal power. This was certainly concerning for Pope Innocent II, who was seeking to re-establish authority in southern Italy, and probably coloured the judgement of contemporary commentators, who generally saw schismatic ordination as a more serious problem than simony.[36] As the 1130s passed, Innocent II conducted more processes against schismatic bishops. He deposed them or declared their ordination by Anacletus II and his followers invalid, without, however, charging them with simony.[37] By contrast, there are no known simony processes at this time unrelated to the schism.

Contemporary interpretations of simony in southern Italy are particularly well documented in the case of the abbey of Montecassino. In the monastic authors' treatment of simony, it is viewed not as an isolated problem leading to misconduct in selective situations, but as a general malaise with grave consequences for the simoniac person as a whole. An eloquent critic of simony is Desiderius, the abbot of Montecassino and later Pope Victor III (1086–87). In the third book of his *Dialogi*, a collection of pedagogic dialogues between the author and a monk named Theophilus (probably a pseudonym for the monk Alberic of Montecassino), which Desiderius wrote as abbot between 1076 and 1079,[38] he discusses simony explicitly. After remarks on the prevalence of simony and the disastrous condition of the Church prior to Leo IX's pontificate, he relates miracle-stories to illustrate this, the most impressive being that of the priest Gibbertus. Gibbertus accepted payment from a suspended bishop for his help in having the bishop's sentence lifted. At Rome, Gibbertus is said first to have pursued legal means and then, as these failed, to have tried to bribe the papal chancellor to issue a false charter. Hearing of this, the pope summoned Gibbertus, demanded that the money be surrendered and cursed the malfeasant in words reminiscent of those spoken by St Peter against Simon Magus (Acts 8:20). Thereupon, Desiderius relates, Gibbertus lost his mind and lived his remaining days in restless wandering.[39] Desiderius was not the only writer to depict how simoniacal dealings could afflict their perpetrators with mental or physical disability. In other accounts, simoniacs suffered sudden loss of speech or a fatal stroke.[40] Such drastic stories were certainly intended to scare and deter contemporary readers from making the same mistake. Their authors conceived simony not only as a problem to be regulated by the provisions of canon law but also as a sin and a crime with potentially grave human consequences.[41]

A different but no less broad interpretation of simony appears in a poem on St Peter written by Amatus of Montecassino, probably in 1078. Amatus adapts the diverse traditions regarding Simon Magus to make them speak to the complex contemporary situation. Simon

Magus becomes more than just the prototypical simoniac. He is St Peter's eternal adversary responsible for the apostle's martyrdom through his intervention before the Emperor Nero. Bridging the centuries, Amatus considers Pope Gregory VII as St Peter's vicar and successor in the war against Simon Magus's brood, the simoniacs of the eleventh century. Thus, he depicts the contemporary battle against simony as a fight for survival, its fatal consequences flowing from Simon Magus's role in the first apostle's death. The parable gains additional relevance in the figure of the Emperor Nero, who not only persecuted the Church but through his association with Simon Magus also personified the simoniacal ruler, an implicit parallel to Emperor Henry IV. At the same time, Amatus positions himself regarding another contemporary problem, the schismatic rivalry between Gregory VII and Guibert of Ravenna (antipope Clement III, 1080–1100) by expressly declaring Gregory VII to be St Peter's successor and rightful pope.[42]

In all these respects, Amatus's poem reflects the sustained contemporary interest in the legends of St Peter and Simon Magus, and he interprets them and applies them to events during Gregory VII's pontificate.[43] In this context, the battle against simony became decidedly political. While in later discussion of this subject during the 1130s simony was clearly overshadowed by the schism, the two issues were here seen as closely connected. In so doing, Amatus and his contemporaries positioned themselves in the acute political situation as 'strong supporter[s] of the moral reform of the Church' and upholders of the 'political aims of the Gregorian papacy'.[44] Their views on simony are thus closely associated with the contemporary situation and are unique to that time.[45]

Our conspectus of legal rulings, judicial practice and literary texts unfortunately offers a body of incongruous information yielding something less than a cohesive vision of how simony was perceived and interpreted in Norman Italy. This is partially the product of gaps in evidence. Not only are synodal records scarce but other sources for the history of the southern Italian Church, particularly regarding the secular clergy, are largely lacking due to the enormous losses in cathedral archives and the absence of collective episcopal biographies comparable to the northern European *Gesta episcoporum*.[46] Moreover, a writer's intention and a work's character will predetermine a source's interest in simony, sometimes extensive, sometimes wholly absent. Simony's negative connotations since the Church reforms of the eleventh and twelfth centuries led in some cases to hiding discussion of it from public view and even banning of written discourse.[47] Beyond this, present-day researchers face the problem, just as contemporary observers must have, of clearly defining simoniacal practices and distinguishing them from the widespread and accepted practice of exchanging gifts.[48] This line was all the more difficult to draw, since the poorer clergy relied on material and pecuniary gratuities to secure life's necessities and found themselves thus permanently in a grey zone between legitimate behaviour and simoniacal acquisitiveness. For example, Lando of St Vincent in Capua on being charged with simony declared himself willing to renounce his claims to the Church on condition that he be provided other means of subsistence. In the end, Pope Stephen IX (1057–58) granted him the monastery of Holy Cross on Monte Marsico as compensation.[49] Finally, the perception and interpretations of simoniacal behaviour was largely dependent on the perspectives and intentions of the persons involved. Not only did the plaintiffs levelling charges of simony formulate their accusations differently according to their individual interests but the literary treatment of the subject also varied considerably, as, for example, with simony's politically charged connotations during Gregory VII's pontificate.

With all of these variables, enforcing the prohibition of simony was fraught with difficulty for the popes. The early reform popes, motivated by reforming zeal, in particular sought not only to imprint their concept of simony onto the normative ecclesiastical structures of southern Italy but also to apply it in concrete legal instances, which anchored it in public consciousness. Beyond this, a few sources indicate that the popes attempted to publicise and apply normative rulings made outside southern Italy in southern Italy.[50] Once again, the available sources do not reveal if or how these impulses were received south of Rome. There are a few records of provincial and diocesan synods, but these contain no legislative acts indicating how the rulings made at the papal synods were applied locally in the lower echelons of the diocesan clergy.[51] As counter-evidence, however, it appears that several abbots and bishops condemned for simony were able to remain in office despite the papal sanction,[52] which suggests that the papacy was viewed in some places, such as Calabria or Sicily, as a distant authority with little power in local affairs.[53] This led in the course of the twelfth century to the increasing importance of regional authorities, such as bishops or abbots, to whom the popes entrusted the examination of cases and sometimes even delegated their judicial authority.

The intensity and diversity of discourse regarding simony in southern Italy does not seem to match that in Rome, northern Italy or transalpine Europe, where the validity of ordinations, the need for re-ordination, simoniacal entry into monastic life and the impact of simony on the administration of sacraments entered the conversation. This may again reflect the poor survival of sources, especially synodal records.[54] There is some evidence that individual bishops and abbots from southern Italy participated in synods beyond their own cultural borders and may have been exposed to the hotly discussed questions of the day. However, the few participants in such assemblies were scattered across the region, so the matter was certainly not common knowledge across southern Italy.[55]

In conclusion, it appears that the parameters for discussion of simony in southern Italy were set by the reformed papacy rather than by local clergy or secular Norman rulers. The papacy's leading role is documented not only, as we have seen, in their activities but also in a remarkable letter addressed to an anonymous Byzantine official in Calabria. Expounding volubly on simony in southern Italy, the author calls on the official to proceed vigilantly against this most contagious disease and poisonous venom.[56] If indeed, as has been supposed, this letter was written by Humbert of Silva Candida, whom Pope Leo IX had nominally appointed archbishop of Sicily, it offers a unique insight into the papal perception of simony as a problem afflicting southern Italy and it documents the intent to battle simony even in more remote regions.[57] In contrast, we have only very thin evidence that the southern Italian clergy themselves took the initiative in dealing with simony. Even at the abbey of Montecassino, there seems to have been little interest in a deeper engagement with the topic. Although Peter Damian's *Liber gratissimus*, in which the author comprehensively presents his views on the validity of simoniacal ordinations, was certainly known in Montecassino, no allusion to this appears in his other correspondence with the abbey.[58]

Furthermore, the battle against simony appears to have had no notable influence on the transformation of the southern Italian Church, although, as mentioned above, this process unfolded under papal guidance. A symptomatic example of how the topic of simony fell by the wayside is the founding of the bishopric of Sarno undertaken by Archbishop Alfanus I of Salerno in 1066 with papal assistance. Writing to the new bishopric's clergy and populace, Alfanus laid down rules for the ordination of new members of the clergy without explicitly mentioning the prohibition of simony, though an indirect allusion may have been intended in requiring candidates for ordination not to commit offences which would preclude them from holding office.[59] The restructuring of southern Italy's ecclesiastical landscape created more than 140 bishoprics, the majority extremely small and often very poor, which made them, compared with transalpine bishoprics, quite unattractive for ambitious, wealthy candidates.[60] This did not, however, effectively forestall simony, since the – albeit sporadic – perseverance of legal cases indicates that simoniacal practices continued into the thirteenth century. On the contrary, it could well be that the cathedral chapter tacitly tolerated simony as compensation for the poor endowment of the bishop's office. Also in contradistinction to the north, simony allegations were not raised extensively in southern Italy purposefully to curb the influence of laymen and their holding of so-called 'proprietary churches'. Contemporaries in southern Italy sought other ways to transfer control of Church institutions from laymen to the clergy.[61] Correspondingly, there is no evidence in southern Italy that simony aroused the moral panic it did elsewhere in Europe, where contemporaries interpreted simony as an omnipresent problem which entirely subverted sacramental practice.[62]

Notes

1 See R. Schieffer, 'Motu proprio. Über die papstgeschichtliche Wende im 11. Jahrhundert', *Historisches Jahrbuch* 122 (2002), 27–41.
2 See G. A. Loud, *The Latin Church in Norman Italy* (Cambridge, 2007).
3 See K. G. Cushing, *Reform and Papacy in the Eleventh Century: Spirituality and Social Change* (Manchester, 2005).

4 *Storia de' Normanni di Amato di Montecassino*, ed. V. De Bartholomeis, FSI 76 (Rome, 1935), III, 15, pp. 129ff.; *The History of the Normans by Amatus of Montecassino*, trans. P. N. Dunbar, rev. G. A. Loud (Woodbridge, 2004), III, 15, p. 91.

5 J. Drehmann, *Papst Leo IX. und die Simonie. Ein Beitrag zur Vorgeschichte des Investiturstreits* (Leipzig, 1908), p. 19. Drehmann views Amatus's remarks as restricted to conditions in Salerno.

6 See for example, *Brunonis episcopi Signini Libellus de symoniacis*, ed. E. Sackur, MGH Libelli de lite 2 (Hanover, 1892), pp. 543–62, here pp. 546ff.: 'Mundus totus in maligno positus erat, defecerat sanctitas, iusticia perierat, et veritas sepulta erat. Regnabat iniquitas, avaritia dominabatur, Symon magus aeclesiam possidebat, episcopi et sacerdotes voluptati et fornicationibus dediti erant. Non erubescebant sacerdotes uxores ducere, palam nuptias faciebant ... Sed quod his omnibus deterius est, vix aliquis inveniebatur qui vel symoniacus non esset vel a symoniacis ordinates non fuisset' ['The whole world had been placed in wickedness, sanctity had disappeared, justice had perished and truth had been buried. Iniquity reigned, avarice ruled, Simon Magus possessed the Church, bishops and priests had given themselves to pleasure and fornications. The priests did not redden with shame to draw wives to themselves, they openly celebrated nuptuals ... But, what is worse than all these things, scarcely anyone was found who either was not a simoniac or had been ordained by simoniacs']. Trans. D. Routt.

7 On papal travel see J. Johrendt, 'Die Reisen der frühen Reformpäpste. Ihre Ursachen und Funktionen', *Römische Quartalschrift für christliche Altertumskunde und Kirchengeschichte* 96 (2001), 57–94. It is, however, to be considered that synods were not always convened in connection with a papal visit. This is, for example, the case under Popes Gregory VII and Calixtus II; see Loud, *Latin Church*, p. 182; B. Schilling, *Guido von Vienne – Papst Calixt II* (Hanover, 1998), pp. 706–16. On the synodal practice of the popes, see G. Gresser, *Die Synoden Konzilien in der Zeit des Reformpapsttums in Deutschland und Italien von Leo IX. bis Calixt II.*, 1049–1123 (Paderborn, 2006).

8 Cf. 'The canons of Melfi', in *Pope Urban II, The Collectio Britannica, and the Council of Melfi (1089)*, ed. R. Somerville and S. Kuttner (Oxford, 1996), c. 1, p. 252 and c. 5–7, p. 254. On the following synods, 'Appendix II. The canons of the Councils of Benevento (1091) and Troia (1093)', in *Pope Urban II*, ed. Somerville and Kuttner, pp. 302–5.

9 Cf. for example, *Guillaume de Pouille, La geste de Robert Guiscard*, ed. M. Mathieu (Palermo, 1961), II, 392–9, pp. 152, 154 (on the synod of

Melfi, 1059); *Chronica monasterii Casinensis*, ed. H. Hoffmann, MGH SS 34 (Hanover, 1980), IV, 33, p. 499 (on the synod of Benevento, 1108) (hereafter *CMC*).

10 See particularly n. 4 above; *Die Touler Vita Leos IX.*, ed. H.-G. Krause, MGH SS rerum Germanicarum in usum Scholarum 70 (Hanover, 2007), II, 14 (6), p. 206.

11 'The canons of Melfi', c. 1a, pp. 252 and 259 (English translation): 'Sanctorum patrum sententiis consona sentientes, ex Dei et apostolorum eius parte precipimus ne quis ulterius vel dato vel promisso pretio vel servitio ea intentione impenso vel precibus episcopalem nitatur assequi dignitatem, nec ullus eam pretaxato tenore indulgeat. Hoc idem et de omni ecclesiastica dignitate vel officio apostolice potestatis auctoritate prefigimus. Alias et dator et acceptor proprii ordinis dignitate priventur.'

12 'The canons of Melfi', c. 1b, p. 252.

13 On Urban II's position between tradition and innovation in Church law, see A. Becker, *Urban II*, vol. 3 (Hanover, 2012), pp. 184–9.

14 For the consequences of the lack of records for contemporary synods in general, see R. Somerville, 'The councils of Gregory VII', *Studi Gregoriani per la storia della 'libertas ecclesiae'* 13 (1989), 33–53, here p. 35: 'these texts, simply stated, often do not reveal what historians would like to know about synods'.

15 *Touler Vita Leos IX*, II, c. 14 (6), p. 206; A. Zavarrone, *Note sopra la bolla di Godano arcivescovo dell'Acerenza* (Naples, 1755), pp. 1–5, here p. 2 (for a discussion of the authenticity of the charter printed by Zavarrone, which refers to the deposition of the bishop of Montepeloso, see H.-W. Klewitz, 'Studien über die Wiederherstellung der römischen Kirche in Süditalien durch das Reformpapsttum', *QF* 25 (1934–35), 105–57, here pp. 147–9); *Epistolae pontificum Romanorum ineditae*, ed. S. Loewenfeld (Leipzig, 1885), no. 118, p. 58.

16 Amatus of Montecassino remarks that Leo IX did not punish all simoniacs at the synod of Salerno in 1050 but absolved them after they had done fitting penance (*Storia*, III, 15, p. 130). This indicates that the more clement approach to dealing with simony discussed at the synod of Rome in 1049 and thereafter (cf. Peter Damian's *Liber Gratissimus*: *Die Briefe des Petrus Damiani*, ed. K. Reindel, MGH Briefe der deutschen Kaiserzeit vol. 1 (Munich, 1983), no. 40, pp. 390ff., 489ff.) was also adopted in southern Italy.

17 See *Epistolae*, no. 118, p. 58: 'absque spe restitutionis eiectus'.

18 Known to have been deposed on grounds of simony are the bishop of Montepeloso in 1059 and in 1067 Bishop Landolf of Tertiveri and Bishop Lantinus of Lucera. Cf. n. 15 above.

19 See for example the cases of Archbishop Roffrid II of Benevento in 1123 (*ChBen*, 1123.3.4, and Bishops Maraldus of Vieste and William of Caiazzo (*Le Liber Pontificalis*. *Texte, introduction et commentaire*, ed. L. Duchesne, vol. 2 (Paris, 1892), p. 419).

20 See for example the case of Archbishop William of Palermo in 1111 (P. Hinschius, 'Über Pseudo-Isodor-Handschriften und Kanonessammlungen in spanischen Bibliotheken', *Zeitschrift für Kirchenrecht* 3 (1863), 122–46, here pp. 142–4), or the trial of the Bishop of Mottola in 1198 (*Die Register Innocenz' III. 1. Pontifikatsjahr, 1198/99. Texte*, ed. O. Hageneder and A. Haidacher (Graz, 1964), no. 255, pp. 357ff.).

21 Cf. *CMC*, IV, 120: 'quod pro sua electione munus a lingua, munus a manu, munus ab obsequio promisisset' ['that for his election he had promised a gift by tongue, a gift by hand, a gift by complaisance'] (trans. D. Routt). This phrase was often used to circumscribe simoniac practices. See, for the first time, Gregory the Great, *Homiliae in evangelia*, ed. R. Etaix, Corpus Christianorum Series Latina 141 (Turnhout, 1999), IV, c. 4, p. 31.

22 See John of Salisbury: *Ioannis Saresberiensis Episcopi Carnotensis Policratici De nugis curialium et vestigiis philosophorum libri 8*, ed. C. C. I. Webb, vol. 2 (Oxford, 1909), c. 19, pp. 173ff. See also n. 47 below.

23 See *Codice diplomatico Barese*, vol. 1, ed. G. B. Nitto de Rossi and F. Nitti di Vito (Bari, 1897), no. 54, pp. 103–7; H. Enzensberger, *Beiträge zum Kanzlei- und Urkundenwesen der normannischen Herrscher Unteritaliens und Siziliens* (Kallmünz, 1971), p. 131, no. *130.

24 Cf. A. Schlichte, *Der 'gute' König. Wilhelm II. von Sizilien (1166–1189)* (Tübingen, 2005), pp. 134–9; Loud, *Latin Church*, p. 285.

25 G. M. Monti, 'Il testo e la storia esterna delle assise normanne', *Storia del diritto* 1 (1940), 295–348, here c. 16, pp. 319ff. Significantly, this was one of the few Assizes not to be adopted in Frederick II's Constitutions.

26 *CMC*, IV, 121, pp. 595ff. On Montecassino's role in the schism and the position of Peter the Deacon, see W. Treseler, 'Lothar III. und die Privilegien des Klosters Montecassino: symbolische Kommunikation während des Konfliktes zwischen Kaiser und Papst im Jahr 1137', *Frühmittelalterliche Studien* 35 (2001), 313–28.

27 See *Regii Neapolitani Archivi Monumenta. Edita ac illustrata*, vol. 5 (Naples, 1857), no. 501, p. 261; no. 523, pp. 306ff.; cf. G. A. Loud, *Church and Society in the Norman Principality of Capua, 1058–1197* (Oxford, 1985), p. 116. Significantly, the second charter makes no

more mention of the simony charges but deals exclusively with the question of ownership.
28 See *Register Innocenz' III*, no. 255, pp. 357ff.
29 See also N. Kamp, *Kirche und Monarchie im staufischen Königreich Sizilien*, vol. 2 (Munich, 1975), p. 710, speaking in this connection of the 'usual accusations'.
30 Calixtus II, who himself ordained Roffrid and must therefore have known him to be qualified, obviously had no fundamental mistrust of the archbishop, since he sent him shortly thereafter on a diplomatic mission to Constantinople; see M. Stroll, *Calixtus II (1119–1124): A Pope Born to Rule* (Leiden, 2004), p. 445. For a similar instance where the charges of simony were dropped on the basis of a purgatory oath, see the case of Archbishop Walter of Palermo in 1111: Hinschius, 'Handschriften', pp. 142ff.
31 On his election and ordination, see *ChBen*, 1119.41, 1120.10.1–10.2.
32 See P. Oldfield, 'Urban government in southern Italy, c.1085–c.1127', *EHR* 122 (2007), 579–608, here pp. 605–7; P. Oldfield, *Sanctity and Pilgrimage in Medieval Southern Italy, 1000–1200* (Cambridge, 2014), pp. 73, 103.
33 See *CMC*, IV, 122, p. 596.
34 *Innocentii II Concilium Pisanum*, ed. L. Weiland, MGH Constitutiones 1 (Hanover, 1903), no. 402, pp. 577–9, here c. 6f., p. 579. For context, see G. A. Loud, 'Innocent II and the kingdom of Sicily', in J. Doran and D. J. Smith (eds), *Pope Innocent II (1130–43): The World vs the City* (Abingdon, 2016), pp. 172–80.
35 *Das Register Gregors VII.*, ed. E. Caspar, MGH Epistolae selectae 2,2 (Berlin, 1923), no. 6,5b, pp. 400–7, here c. 5 (11), pp. 403ff.
36 For another, but special example, the case of Archbishop Peter of Capua, who was deposed in 1134–35, see Loud, *Latin Church*, pp. 534ff.
37 See for example Pope Innocent II's case against the Bishop of Acerra on the grounds of being a schismatic (*Innocentii II Concilium Pisanum*, c. 5, p. 578) or the same pope's annulment of all ordinations undertaken by Anacletus II and the Beneventan rector Rossemanus (*ChBen*, 1139.11.1).
38 On the dating of this work, see R. Grégoire, 'I dialoghi di Desiderio abate di Montecassino († 1087)', in F. Avagliano and O. Pecere (eds), *L'età dell'abate Desiderio III,1: Storia arte e cultura. Atti del IV convegno di studi sul medioevo meridionale (Montecassino – Cassino, 4–8 ottobre 1987)* (Montecassino, 1992), pp. 215–34; alternatively, dating the work in the 1060s: W. McCready, 'Dating the dialogues of Abbot Desiderius of Montecassino', *Revue Bénédictine* 108 (1998), 145–68.

39 *Dialogi de miraculis sancti Benedicti auctore Desiderio abbate Casinensi*, ed. G. Schwartz and A. Hofmeister, MGH SS 30, 2 (Leipzig, 1934), III, c. 2, p. 1144.

40 See for example, *Dialogi* III, c. 5, p. 1148; *Bonizonis episcopi Sutrini Liber ad amicum*, ed. E. Dümmler, MGH Libelli de lite 1 (Hanover, 1941), p. 592; *Briefe des Petrus Damiani*, vol. 2, no. 72, pp. 344ff.; *Touler Vita Leos IX*, c. 10 (4), p. 194.

41 In this, Desiderius was following Gregory the Great, whose dialogues were the model for Desiderius's own work. Gregory characterises simony as the first step on the road to ruin corrupting humans both in their way of life and in their character: Gregory the Great, *Registrum epistolarum*, 2 vols, ed. D. Norberg, Corpus Christianorum Series Latina 140 and 140a (Turnhout, 1982), bk V, 24, p. 291; bk V, 58, pp. 355–7; bk V, 62, pp. 365ff.; bk IX, 216, pp. 777–9. On the copy of his dialogues made under Abbot Desiderius, see F. Newton, *The Scriptorium and Library at Monte Cassino, 1058–1105* (Cambridge, 1999), pp. 57, 59ff.

42 Amatus of Montecassino, *Liber Amati monachi Casinensis in honore b. Petri apostoli*, in *Il Poema di Amato su S. Pietro Apostolo*, ed. A. Lentini, vol. 1 (Montecassino, 1958), pp. 57–143.

43 See in general J. Szövérffy, 'Der Investiturstreit und die Petrus-Hymnen des Mittelalters', *Deutsches Archiv für Erforschung des Mittelalters* 13 (1957), 228–40; for the southern Italian context in particular, H. E. J. Cowdrey, 'Simon Magus in South Italy', *ANS* 15 (1993), 77–90, particularly pp. 83–8. By contrast, Geoffrey Malaterra makes no allusion to the Simon Magus motif in his poem on Rome and the simoniac practices there during the exile of Pope Gregory VII: *De rebus gestis Rogerii Calabriae et Siciliae Comitis et Roberti Guiscardi Ducis fratris eius*, ed. E. Pontieri, RIS 2nd ser. 5:1 (Bologna, 1925–28), III, 38, pp. 80ff. The motif does appear, however, in the works of William of Apulia (*La geste*, IV, 34–7, p. 206).

44 G. A. Loud, in *History of the Normans*, pp. 15ff. On the not always harmonious relations between Montecassino and Gregory VII, see pp. 17ff., and more expansively G. A. Loud, 'Abbot Desiderius of Montecassino and the Gregorian papacy', *Journal of Ecclesiastical History* 30 (1979), 305–26.

45 It is notable that the history of the pontificate of Pope Victor III in the chronicle of Montecassino written in the 1140s, returned to identifying the antipope with Simon Magus; see *CMC*, particularly, III, 70, pp. 452ff. This illustrates how closely this image was connected with the political situation in these years, even from a retrospective position. For context, see T. Haye, *Päpste und Poeten. Die mittelalterliche*

The battle against simony in Norman Italy 243

Kurie als Objekt und Förderer panegyrischer Dichtung (Berlin, 2009), p. 105. As the author points out, the transmission of panegyric poetry on the papacy declines dramatically after Gregory VII.

46 See Loud, *Latin Church*, pp. 250, 266. In comparison to the hagiographical literature north of the Alps, the *vitae* of southern Italian bishops hardly reflect on simony. An exception to this is the *vita* of Berard of Marsica. For a critical examination of this text, J. Howe, 'St Berardus of Marsica (d.1130): "Model Gregorian bishop"', *Journal of Ecclesiastical History* 58 (2007), 400–16; Oldfield, *Sanctity*, pp. 79ff.

47 On the aspect of publicity, see the depiction of Robert of Selby's electoral examination in 1150 in John of Salisbury's *Policraticus* (cf. n. 22 above). As John relates, Robert secretly accepted the candidates's bribes in order to expose them publicly as simoniacs, whereupon he gave the bishopric of Avellino to a monk of untarnished reputation. On John of Salisbury's view of simony, see F. Lachaud, 'La simonie et les clercs simoniaques dans le Policraticus de Jean de Salisbury. Un aspect de la réforme morale et religieuse au milieu du XIIe siècle en Angleterre', in J. Barrow, F. Delivré and V. Gazeau (eds), *Autour de Lanfranc (1010–2010). Réforme et réformateurs dans l'Europe du Nord-Ouest (XIe – XIIe siècles)* (Caen, 2015), pp. 313–28.

48 On the principle of exchanging gifts, see the classical but not unchallenged study of M. Mauss, 'Essai sur le don. Forme et raison de l'échange dans les societies archaïque', *L'Année Sociologique*, 1 (1923–24), 30–186.

49 See *Chronicon Vulturnense del monaco Giovanni*, ed. V. Federici, vol. 3, FSI 60 (Rome, 1938), pp. 88ff. (hereafter *CV*); *Monumenta Corbeiensia*, ed. P. Jaffé, Bibliotheca Rerum Germanicarum 1 (Berlin, 1864), no. 236, p. 355 (on the deposed Archbishop Peter of Capua, see n. 36 above). Significantly, the Bishop-Elect, Maraldus of Minervino, was deposed as a simoniac on the grounds that he had promised the cathedral chapter to raise their share of the tithes and oblations if they elected him. See *Codice diplomatico Barese* 1, no. 54, pp. 103ff.

50 See for example Pope Nicholas II's letter of 1059 to the bishops of the church province of Amalfi in *Die Konzilien Deutschlands und Reichsitaliens 1023–1059*, ed. D. Jasper, MGH Concilia 8 (Hanover, 2010), no. 43 G, pp. 402–4.

51 On provincial and diocesan synods in general, see Loud, *Latin Church*, pp. 378ff.

52 See for example the cases of Lando of St Vincent (*CV*, p. 88) and Lantinus of Lucera (F.-J. Schmale, 'Synoden Papst Alexanders II. (1061–1073). Anzahl, Termine, Entscheidungen', *Annuarium*

Historiae Conciliorum 11 (1979), 307–38, here p. 325, n. 89) or, in contrast, that of the bishops of Caiazzo (n. 27 above).

53 In Sicily, the only known simony process prosecuted by the papacy is that of Walter of Palermo; see n. 30 above.

54 The synod of Melfi (1089) is the only southern Italian assembly known to have ruled on the issue. It prohibited abbots from taking money from those wishing to enter their monasteries, without, however, explicitly speaking of simony; see 'Canons of Melfi', c. 7, pp. 254ff.; on the background to this ruling, see J. H. Lynch, *Simoniacal Entry into Religious Life from 1000 to 1260: A Social, Economic and Legal Study* (Columbus, 1976), pp. 68–70.

55 Cf., for example, the participation in the Lateran Council of 1059 (*Konzilien Deutschlands und Reichsitaliens*, no. 43, B, pp. 388–93, and C, p. 394), in the synod of Piacenza in 1095 (Gresser, *Synoden*, p. 295) or in the Lateran Council of 1179 (G. Tangl, *Die Teilnehmer an den allgemeinen Konzilien des Mittelalters*, 2nd edn (Cologne, 1969), p. 213).

56 J. J. Ryan, 'Letter of an anonymous French reformer to a Byzantine official in south Italy: De simoniaca heresi (Ms Vat. Lat. 3830)', *Mediaeval Studies* 15 (1953), 233–42, here pp. 239–42.

57 On the attribution of the letter to Humbert, see also C. West, 'Competing for the Holy Spirit: Humbert of Moyenmoutier and the question of simony', in F. Depreux, F. Bougard and R. Le Jan (eds), *Compétition et sacré au haut Moyen âge. Entre mediation et exclusion* (Turnhout, 2015), pp. 327–40, here p. 331.

58 On Peter Damian's connections to Montecassino, see J. Howe, 'Peter Damian and Montecassino', *Revue bénédictine* 107 (1997), 330–51; on the reception of his works in Montecassino, see S. Freund, *Studien zur literarischen Wirksamkeit des Petrus Damiani* (Hanover, 1995), pp. 16–37; on his letters in particular, Newton, *Scriptorium*, pp. 76ff., and on the *Liber gratissimus*, see also n. 16.

59 See *Italia sacra*, ed. F. Ughelli, vol. 7 (Venice, 1721), p. 571; for the context, see V. Ramseyer, *The Transformation of a Religious Landscape: Medieval Southern Italy, 850–1150* (Ithaca, 2006), p. 138.

60 Loud, *Latin Church*, p. 367.

61 For a European comparison, see T. Reuter, 'Gifts and simony', in E. Cohen and M. B. De Jong (eds), *Medieval Transformations: Texts, Power, and Gifts in Context* (Leiden, 2001), pp. 157–68. For the situation in southern Italy, Loud, *Latin Church*, pp. 383, 411ff.

62 For the European context, see again Reuter, 'Gifts', pp. 160, 163.

13

Some reflections on the women's monasteries of southern Italy in the eighth to twelfth centuries

Jean-Marie Martin

These few reflections are based particularly on documents copied into the most important monastic cartularies composed in Lombard central Italy during the first half of the twelfth century (*Chronicon Sanctae Sophiae*, *Chronicon Vulturnense*, *Registrum Petri Diaconi*)[1] and bear especially on the establishments well studied by Graham Loud for the Norman period.[2] They seek to clarify these monastic houses' earlier history.

Women's monasticism, it is known, has a particular history: its unique characteristics in comparison with men's monasticism are important. Female monasteries had in fact to accommodate clerics, who were men. They were of course particularly vulnerable and developed above all in an urban setting. Finally, personal law sometimes assigned women inferior status. This was particularly true for Lombard law, which predominated in the region and did not recognise the personhood of women. They were always subject to male authority.[3]

Under these conditions it is easily enough understood that Lombard central Italy, which lost a good part of its cities during the crisis of the sixth and seventh centuries,[4] was not a choice environment for women's monasticism. In southern Italy, it was truly developed only in Naples, which stayed beyond reach of the Lombard invasion and where, moreover, traditions of paleochristian origin remained alive in the Middle Ages. The original private Neapolitan documents inventoried by Bartolomeo Capasso[5] for the first half of the tenth century mention several female monasteries: Sts Nicander and Marcian,[6] Sts Festus and Desiderius,[7] St Martin,[8] St Euphemia[9] and Sts Gregory and Sebastian.[10] The monastery of Sts

Marcellinus and Peter, which was directed in 763 by the *diacona et abbatissa Eufrosina*, became Greek in the eleventh century.[11] In the interim, it would be refounded in the ninth century by Duke Anthime's widow, who would place her niece there as abbess. Despite the absence of documents from the seventh century, a continuity from the tradition of women's monasteries (if not of their individual existence) since late antiquity can be presupposed. These houses seem to have been no less important than their male counterparts.

Foundations

In Beneventan territory, on the contrary, female abbeys were rare. The first were founded only in the eighth century: St Mary *in Cingla* probably in the 740s, St Mary of Piumarola about 750, St Sophia of Benevento around 760, and Holy Saviour of Alife a bit later. The founding of each of these establishments is documented. The impetus always came from aristocrats or, above all, members of ruling families, who asked for the collaboration of men's abbeys; moreover, these foundations were inspired by models foreign to southern Italy.

Let us consider in detail these various cases. The founding of St Mary *in Cingla* is known to us thanks to three charters of Duke Gisulf II of Benevento drawn up respectively in 743, 745 and 747 and copied into the *Registrum Petri Diaconi*.[12] In the oldest, the duke gave Montecassino and Abbot Petronax a church, St Cassian, founded by the *sculdahis* Sarracenus, with all its property except for his slaves, who were emancipated according to the duke's wish. In the charter of 745, it is learned that Abbot Petronax decided to found a women's monastery, St Mary *in Cingla*, in the place of the church of St Cassian. The duke permitted Deusdedit, abbot of St John (*de Porta Aurea*) of Benevento, to sell to this new foundation the *cella* of Holy Cross with all the territories it possessed. The ducal intervention was particularly owed to the fact that Abbot Deusdedit himself had bought this *cella* from a certain priest Anastasius, who was foreign and whose fortune normally would have had to revert to the palace. With the charter of 747, the same Duke Gisulf II at last presented the monastery of St Mary *in Cingla* to Abbess

Gausani and to the nuns Pancrituda and Gariperga. He did it jointly with Abbot Petronax, since the women's monastery 'pertinet de iure Sancti Benedicti' ['belongs by right of St Benedict']. One learns finally that the abbess and the two religious were strangers to the duchy: they had, in effect, given up their families and their wealth to come as pilgrims into the *Terra Beneventana* ('quoniam postposuistis parentes et substantias vestras et venistis peregrinare in terra nostra Beneventana' ['since you left your parents and your fortunes and came to sojourn in our Beneventan land']). The three women were probably Lombard aristocrats (the two nuns' names make one think it) and very certainly came from the Lombard kingdom. Of St Mary *in Cingla*, only ruins remain, found today on a 'large farm' (*masseria*) situated a kilometre and a half south-southwest of Ailano (province of Caserta), close to the confluence of the rivers Ete and Volturno.

The second case, St Mary *in Plumbariola*, is much less well documented. It was situated very near Montecassino – Piumarola is a 'hamlet' (*frazione*) of the commune of Villa Santa Lucia, to the northwest of Montecassino – and apparently nothing remains of it. According to the *Chronica monasterii Casinensis*,[13] this female monastery was founded by Tasia and Rottruda, respectively wife and daughter of the ancient Lombard king Ratchis, 'concedente et adiuvante prefato abbate' ['with the aforesaid abbot conceding and supporting'] (this is to say the same Petronax, he himself a native of Brescia in the Lombard kingdom). The founders were once again Lombards from northern Italy and belonged to a royal family; they richly endowed their foundation ('multisque ditatum opibus' ['and endowed with many resources']) and ended their lives there.

The last two monasteries of the series were foundations of Arichis II, duke of Benevento, who took the title of prince and refused to recognise Charlemagne as king of the Lombards in 774. A native of Friuli (like nearly all dukes of Benevento), he was, moreover, the son-in-law of Desiderius, the last Lombard king, whose daughter Adelperga he had married.

The founding of St Sophia of Benevento occurs well before the overthrow of the Lombard kingdom: the translation to St Sofia of the relics of the Twelve Martyr-Brothers was effected on 15 May 760[14] (Arichis had become duke of Benevento in 758). If, by its name and also by its domed architecture, St Sophia of Benevento is of clear Byzantine inspiration, the founding of this women's monastery linked to the palace seems to me in the first place to repeat the model of Holy Saviour (today St Julia) of Brescia. Indeed, Holy Saviour of Brescia was founded by the parents-in-law of Arichis II – Desiderius and his wife Ansa – without doubt in 753, and its church was consecrated in 763 (it is thus practically contemporary to St Sophia). It received as abbess one of the royal couple's daughters, Anselperga (Arichis's sister-in-law); in the same way, St Sophia had for its first abbess Arichis's sister. St Sophia's endowment was considerable. It is known by the precepts copied at the beginning of the cartulary of the *Chronicon Sanctae Sophiae*, systematically dated (or probably redated) from November 774. It was, moreover, from the outset, placed under Montecassino's control. The *Chronicon Sanctae Sophiae*, composed at the beginning of the twelfth century to demonstrate the Beneventan abbey's independence, does not of course speak of this dependence, but the *Registrum Petri Diaconi* has transmitted the copy of the princely precept 'conceding' St Sophia to Montecassino (dated as well from November 774);[15] there are many other proofs of this dependence.

Finally, Arichis II founded another women's monastery, Holy Saviour of Alife, to which he gave as abbess his daughter and which he entrusted to the men's monastery of St Vincent on Volturno. This foundation, subsequent to that of St Sophia, was considered by Erchempert at the end of the ninth century as being parallel to it.[16]

In the eighth century, women's monasticism on the whole in the duchy (afterwards principality) of Benevento was practised only in very rare monasteries.[17] All were tied to the high aristocracy and repeated models imported from northern Italy. These female monasteries were, upon their founding, richly endowed. They finally were placed under the control of an important male monastery, Montecassino in three cases, St Vincent on Volturno in the fourth.

Each house was governed by an abbess. But at St Sophia there was found as well a *prepositus* who represented Montecassino.[18] Several of them are known: Bassacius (without doubt the future abbot of Montecassino) in 833–35, Antony in 840, Pergolfus in 856, Criscius *medicus* from 868 to 894, Gisepertus towards 920, Autpertus in 923, Ragempertus in 937 and Ursus before December 941. In the same way, St Mary *in Cingla* has a Cassinese *prepositus*: the deacon Laurence, then John to the end of the ninth century,[19] Faroaldus in 944[20] and John in 969.

But what did this subjection mean? On the spiritual level, the nuns of course needed offices from clergy; on a material level, the Cassinese provosts were in charge of the management of the wealth of women's abbeys. At the end of the ninth century, the two *prepositi* of St Mary *in Cingla* carried out exchanges of property with the consent of the abbot of Montecassino and Abbess Gaitruda; Criscius, *prepositus* of St Sophia, was, with the abbot of Montecassino Ragemprandus, the addressee of an *entalma* from Symbatikios, *strategos* of Macedonia, Thrace, Cephalonia and Longobardia,[21] who took under his protection the property of Montecassino and the three women's abbeys that depended on it, St Sophia, St Mary of Piumarola and St Mary *in Cingla*. But each of these monasteries had its own temporal property, over whose management Montecassino indeed had a right of inspection, but that remained its own. One even sees this temporal property increase: this is evident for St Sophia according to documents transcribed in its cartulary. At the very beginning of the tenth century, Prince Atenulf I offered to St Mary *in Cingla* the *mons Sancti Eleutherii* (near the abbey) 'pro pascuis videlicet animalium ipsius loci nec non et pro lignis faciendis ad diversas utilitates' ['the mountain of St Eleutherius for the pasture namely of animals of the place itself and indeed for the making of wood for various uses'] and permitted it to use water from the river Ete;[22] one recalls a legal proceeding concerning this area in 944.[23]

Thus, the female monasteries of the principality of Benevento around the ninth century were not very numerous but immensely rich and relatively autonomous. They indeed received protection from Montecassino (or from St Vincent), but this did not damage their temporal autonomy. The protection, moreover, tended in the tenth and eleventh centuries to lose some of its effectiveness, because it was less and less understood how women's monasteries could depend on a men's abbey. But once again in the ninth century, papal privileges (there are from the eighth century only fraudulent ones, like Zachary's for Montecassino[24]) placed female abbeys under Montecassino's control: in this way, those of Nicholas I (858–67),[25] John VIII (882)[26] and John IX (899).[27] These documents indeed first cite as dependencies of Montecassino two nearby monasteries ('sub prephato monte constructum' ['built under the aforesaid mountain']): St Scholastica, situated four kilometres from Cassino to the west of Montecassino, which disappeared after 985;[28] Holy Saviour, founded by the abbot of Montecassino Gisulf (796–817) and reconstituted around 885, which was already no longer a monastery at the time of Abbot Richerius (1038–55) and became the principal church of the town of San Germano (today Cassino).[29] But, in the papal privileges, after these two Cassinese foundations, there are only 'quattuor monasteria puellaria' ['four women's monasteries'] cited in the list of dependencies: St Mary of Piumarola, St Mary *in Cingla*, St Sophia of Benevento and finally St Mary 'in civitate Cosentia constructum' ['built in the city of Cosenza' (in Calabria)].

But it is remarkable that the copy of John VIII's privilege in the *Registrum Petri Diaconi* does not repeat the enumeration of these four monasteries (or Holy Saviour) and makes do with adding, after St Scholastica, 'et ecclesie per singula loca constructa' ['and churches built in separate places']. On the contrary, the full list draws on another copy of the same privilege made in the eleventh century.[30] Since the *Registrum Petri Diaconi* is not in the habit of passing in silence over Montecassino's property and rights, one wonders if the scribe who copied this document in the 1130s omitted this passage by absentmindedness, or if he judged it incongruous to place under Cassinese authority on one hand a church which was no longer monastic, on the other hand women's abbeys, something no longer done in his time. As for John IX's privilege, it assigns to Montecassino the monastery of Holy Saviour 'ad pedem ipsius prephati montis' ['at the foot of the aforesaid mountain itself'] and the four female monasteries but not St Scholastica. It, moreover, gives up the generic appellation of *monasteria puellaria*.

The next privilege, which does not seem modified in the copy in the *Registrum Petri Diaconi* and is owed to Pope Marinus II (944), cites in general Montecassino's dependencies 'tam in monasteriis virorum quam et ancillarum Dei necnon et cellis et prediis' ['so in the monasteries of men and of maidens of God as in both the cells and estates']. The list includes Holy Saviour *ad pedem ipsius prephati montis*, St Mary of Piumarola, St Mary *in Cingla*, St Sophia, the *monasterium* (apparently male) of St Mary *de Canneto in finibus*

Beneventanis on the river Trigno[31] and finally St Mary of Cosenza. A certain normalcy seems re-established, since the dependencies were no longer exclusively women's houses.

The oldest papal privileges preserved in the *Chronicon Vulturnense* go back only to the tenth century.[32] That of Stephen VII (930)[33] assigns to St Vincent several dependencies, without specifying whether they were men's or women's: St Peter on the Sabato, Holy Saviour of Alife and seven *celle*. The list of Marinus II (944)[34] includes a score of monasteries regarded as *celle* of St Vincent.

Evolution

It was in the tenth century that the first independent female abbeys appeared. The most famous example, despite the relative obscurity of its beginnings, was St Mary of Capua,[35] built in 969 outside the city close to the *porta S. Angeli* and subject to the archbishop of Capua. Let us remember that the metropolis of Capua was created in 966.[36] It was at this time that a true episcopal network was put in place, which until then had been absent in the principalities where the majority of churches were private, many held by the prince. It is known that the duke in 764 could decide that a baptismal church, claimed as such by the bishop, depended in fact on a monastery, the duke judging the 'usus nostre provincie' ['the practice of our province'] to be superior to the *canones*.[37] The rarity and weakness of bishoprics explain, at least partially, the importance of monasteries in the ecclesiastical organisation of *Longobardia minor* during the early Middle Ages and especially the role assigned to the most important among them – which, moreover, enjoyed exemption[38] – as guardians of women's monasticism.

And yet, St Mary of Capua would have been founded by Abbess Carda and the *prepositus* (the priest John) of St Mary *in Cingla*. That is why the official history of Montecassino made it the mere place of refuge of St Mary *in Cingla*, which had been demolished by the Saracens (but in the ninth century). In fact, the monastery near Ailano had afterwards resumed its normal existence.[39] If St Mary of Capua, contrary to the Cassinese assertions, never depended on Montecassino, it consequently without doubt profited from the assistance of St Mary *in Cingla* and especially of its Cassinese *prepositus*, which at the same time dealt a blow to the Cassinese quasi-monopoly on the supervision of female monasteries. This quasi-monopoly was fought all the more willingly because these women's monasteries had from the outset rich endowments of their own, which permitted them to live and could give rise to covetousness not only on the part of the new episcopal organisation but also from lay powers. However, the five abbeys mentioned here knew different destinies.

With Holy Saviour of Alife, a dependency of St Vincent, having been destroyed by the Saracens, its *habitatores* at the beginning of the tenth century fled to Benevento and settled down in a church, Holy Cross, before founding the *cenobiolum* of St Victorinus and there they stayed.[40] The *Chronicon Vulturnense* has preserved two documents of Alexander III concerning St Victorinus: in 1178–79,[41] the Pope wrote 'abbatisse et sororibus Sancti Victorini Beneventani' ['to the abbess and sisters of St Victorinus of Benevento'] that he had received a complaint from the abbot of St Vincent, to whom they should 'obedientiam et reverentiam ... exhibere' ['show ... obedience and reverence']; he reminded them that they could not elect their abbess without the consent of the abbot of St Vincent; moreover, they failed to 'procurationem prestare (without doubt to turn over a revenue) pro multis possessionibus ipsius, quam tenent' ['for the many possessions which they hold of it']. It seems in fact that the abbey of Holy Saviour of Alife recovered after its destruction. It was confirmed to St Vincent by popes and sovereigns until toward the middle of the eleventh century. In 949,[42] Abbot Leo affirmed that Holy Saviour was exempt from the ordinary and subject to St Vincent. In 950,[43] the bishop of Benevento John recognised to the abbot of St Vincent the right to 'ponere et ordinare monachum prepositum suum' ['to place and appoint his own monk provost'] in the monastery of Alife. But once again in 958 and in 964,[44] the female monastery had its own property, distinct from that of St Vincent. It seems still to have been flourishing in the fourteenth century.[45]

It is seen then that, on one hand, the princes attracted the nuns of Alife to Benevento and that, on the other, if the submission of Holy Saviour to St Vincent ultimately continued, it was in adapting itself to the classic canon law put back into force again.

Among the women's monasteries subject to Montecassino, nothing is known of St Mary of Cosenza. It figured in the papal privileges addressed to the abbey up to the time of Innocent II (and in a precept of kings of Italy Hugh and Lothar).[46] It without doubt still existed during the first half of the twelfth century, but one does not know the whole of its actual relations with Montecassino and their evolution.

The history of St Mary of Piumarola seems to have been rather placid. It appears in the same privileges and the same precept. It is known too that it was abandoned at the time of Abbot Bernard who, in 1278, authorised its restoration under the name of St Petronilla. It was still a female monastery, which is mentioned in the fourteenth century in the *Rationes decimarum*.[47] This monastery's survival and its long dependence vis-à-vis Montecassino seem due on one hand to the latter's geographic proximity, but also to the fact it was incorporated into a *castrum* of the abbey (Piumarola), mentioned for the first time in 1057,[48] which underwent the pressure of *Iordanus Pinzzast* at the beginning of the twelfth century,[49] but it belonged to the Cassinese seigneury as it was constituted in the tenth century.

We arrive at the last two of these cases, the most complex and best known. St Sophia's history is well documented,[50] thanks on one hand to the *Chronicon Sanctae Sophiae*, on the other to the *Breviatio de monasterio Sanctae Sophiae*, a memorandum composed around 1101 by Leo of Ostia;[51] moreover, a recently recovered document is more specific about its evolution.[52] Around 940, the abbey experienced two changes: it became male and broke with Montecassino. The first transformation seems to have taken place between 938 (last mention of an abbess, *Rodelgarda*) and 944–45 (first mention of the first abbot, *Ursus*, perhaps the abbey's former Cassinese *prepositus*); the evolution in fact was more complex. Indeed, a fragment of a document (undated, but definitely prior to this period) presents St Sophia as a double monastery, sheltering *monachi* or *fratres* and *monache*. There was then a transitional period during which the abbey was always subject to Montecassino: the charter specifies that the donors' son and daughter, offered to St Sophia, would not be able to be sent to St Benedict, that is to say to Montecassino, or into one of its *cellae*; moreover, the monastery was always directed by an abbess, Teopegisa, and a *prepositus*, the deacon Benedict.

Still, the complete masculinisation of St Sophia is certainly not irrelevant to its emancipation vis-à-vis Montecassino, which we know thanks to Leo of Ostia's account. This last links – without doubt with reason – the emancipation on one hand with the destruction of Montecassino in 883 (the monks only returned there around 950), on the other with the action of the princes of Capua-Benevento, then of Benevento after the division of the principality in 981. According to Leo (who wrote around 1101), the 'Beneventani principes "Sanctae Sophiae monasterium violenter ac nequiter in suum dominium redegerunt, et per annos aliquot a nostre potestatis iure funditus subtraxere"' ['the Beneventan princes "brought back into their own domain violently and badly the monastery of St Sophia and for some years to steal away utterly our power by right"']. They would have restored St Sophia to Montecassino around 940 before 'invading' it again, then returning it in 943. In 944–45, however, Montecassino complained that St Sophia had an abbot, who claimed to be dependent only on the palace. The popes confirmed St Sophia's independence in the first half of the eleventh century and subjected it directly to the Holy See, but the Beneventan abbey continued to figure in privileges addressed to Montecassino until 1023, then again from 1058 to 1112.

The last attempt made to recover St Sophia was that from 1078 to 1097 described by Leo of Ostia. It was without doubt on the occasion of this episode that a fictitious charter of Arichis II summarising dozens of charters concerning the abbey's endowment was fabricated at St Sophia, then inserted at the beginning of the *liber preceptorum* (*Chronicon Sanctae Sophiae*, I, 1), whose compilation was finished in 1119 (and the cartulary, of which only a double leaf remains, was more or less contemporary). In turn, I am persuaded that the compilation of the *Chronicon Sanctae Sophiae* was one of the factors pushing Montecassino to compose the *Registrum Petri Diaconi* between 1131 and 1133. With the town of Benevento having become papal during the third quarter of the eleventh century, the pope no longer had the least wish to restore St Sophia to Montecassino: in 1098, it was the notable Beneventan *Anso*, who then held the town (*Beneventanorum dominus*), whom he charged to judge one such restoration![53]

As in the case of Holy Saviour of Alife, the setting up of a normalised ecclesiastical organisation must have played a role in the change of St Sophia's status; but it was above all the princes' wish to recover (then that of the pope to preserve) a prestigious sanctuary (by the relics it sheltered, as by the personality of its founder) that was the principal driving force. Moreover, St Sophia became a men's monastery.

The vicissitudes of St Mary *in Cingla* have been studied by Graham Loud. Let us recall briefly the facts, more or less precisely known, which should also be placed on two different (but connected) levels: the competition encountered by Montecassino from St Mary of Capua, supported by the local archbishop, for control of the monastery on one hand, the pretensions and usurpations of the region's Norman lords on the other. It is likely that, just after its own birth, St Mary of Capua, founded, it has been seen, by the abbess and *prepositus* of St Mary *in Cingla*, considered St Maria *in Cingla* as its dependency. But, at an unknown date (before 1094), it was the Norman count Robert son of Rainulf who took possession of it.

The individual and his family are well known.[54] Robert's father Rainulf was the cadet brother of the Norman prince of Capua Richard I. Robert, who succeeded Rainulf in 1087–88, was one of the two *magistri* who governed the principality during the minority of Prince Richard II. Until his death in 1116, Robert, who controlled the ancient Lombard counties of Caiazzo, Alife, Telese and Sant'Agata dei Goti, considered himself to be practically independent. His sister married the count of Pontecorvo, whose county fell to him in 1104. His daughter Gaitelgrima married the Norman duke of Apulia William (1111–27), grandson of Robert Guiscard, and his son Rainulf (II) married Mathilda, sister of the future King Roger II (it is known that he would contest with his brother-in-law the title of duke of Apulia). It is understood that, in these conditions, the count of Alife in particular was interested from close by in the rich abbey of St Mary *in Cingla*. However, Robert maintained good relations with Montecassino; also, in December 1094,[55] having learned 'quod idem monasterium antiquitus Sancto Benedicto Montis Casini pertineret' ['that the same monastery from long ago belonged to St Benedict of Montecassino'] (which probably means that he took it from St Mary of Capua), being sorry, moreover, 'quod ex multo tempore per malos ordinatos devastaretur et dissiparetur, et Dei servitium nimis neglegenter ibi fieret' ['that for a long time through bad men it was laid waste and dissipated, and the service of God was done beyond measure negligently'], on the counsel of his *fideles*, he restored St Mary *in Cingla* to Montecassino. Shortly after without doubt, he vowed to Abbot Oderisius I to protect this monastery.[56] Around the same moment, Roger *de Boscione*, one of Count Robert's Norman vassals, swore to the same abbot to respect the lands that St Mary *in Cingla* held from the time of Count Rainulf; he stated, however, that the wanderings of the Volturno could change the boundaries between his own lands and those of St Mary *in Cingla*. In 1098,[57] Pope Urban II could assert that the 'Cinglensis celle causa est definita' ['the case of the Cinglense cell was finished']; he confirmed the return of the monastery to Montecassino, confirmed the abbess of *Cingla* as well and asked Oderisius not to expel the nuns. Abbot Gerard (1111–23) demolished the church of *Cingla* to rebuild it more grandly.[58]

But in 1121–22, a series of documents of Calixtus II addressed to Alferada, abbess of St Mary of Capua,[59] to Count Rainulf [II][60] and to the archbishop of Capua Otto[61] makes a new attack known to us. This time, St Mary of Capua had taken St Mary *in Cingla* away from Montecassino, but with the consent of the archbishop and of the count. The count, as Graham Loud remarks, then had a more hostile attitude than his father vis-à-vis Montecassino, which, for its part, henceforward had interests outside the principality, in the duchy of Apulia (in Apulia and Calabria). One must notice that Rainulf was cited only as the protector of the abbess of Capua. It is without doubt as count of Alife that the pope called on him to restore *Cingla* to Montecassino within twenty days under pain of excommunication and likewise of interdict. The pope too accused some clergy of Capua of having demonstrated publicly against Montecassino by stripping a dead body of the monastic habit given by the monastery. One sees that secular usurpations continued during this politically troubled period, but, in the present case, they strengthened the claims put forth by the ecclesiastical organisation lately set in place.

By the beginning of the twelfth century, however, not only the religious but also the political landscape had changed. It was no longer considered necessary or even appropriate to place women's monasteries under the guardianship of men's abbeys. One sees female houses born again, often from seigneurial origin, in towns: thus in Apulia[62] St Mary *monialium* of Brindisi, St Benedict of Polignano and St John the Evangelist of Lecce. In the twelfth century, all the towns of central Apulia sheltered at least one female monastery. At Bari, St Scholastica, which appeared in 1102, had for abbess in the 1160s the sister of the Emir of Emirs Maio. Constance, wife of Bohemond, even founded a Greek women's monastery, the only known in the region, St Bartholomew of Taranto. The multiplication of female establishments was one of the great novelties of the twelfth century. They were urban and tied themselves to henceforth standardised ecclesiastical institutions.

Conclusion

Apart from the exceptional case of Naples, women's monasticism, which repeated northern Italian models, had only a marginal place in the southern Italy of the early Middle Ages, a region lacking towns and a consistent ecclesiastical hierarchy. These deficiencies pushed the placing of the uncommon female monasteries, of royal, princely, or aristocratic founding, under control of the principal male abbeys. From the tenth century, this situation seems to have passed; the great abbeys were not in a position to protect their rich and vulnerable women's dependencies, which were henceforth claimed by the canonical authorities being set up, as by the lay powers, whose means of action grew with the Norman Conquest. The female monasteries could then multiply themselves in southern Italy in a normalised framework.

Notes

This chapter was translated from French by D. Routt. Translations from Latin appear in square brackets and are also translated by D. Routt.

1 *Chronicon Sanctae Sophiae (cod. Vat. Lat. 4939)*, ed. J.-M. Martin, with a study by G. Orofino, 2 vols, Fonti per la Storia dell'Italia Medievale. RIS 3 (Rome, 2000) (henceforth *CSS*). *Il Chronicon Vulturnense del monaco Giovanni*, ed. V. Federici, 3 vols, FSI 58–60 (Rome, 1925–38) (henceforth *CV*). *Registrum Petri Diaconi (Montecassino, archivio*

dell'abbazia, Reg. 3). Edizione e commento, ed. J.-M. Martin et al., 4 vols, Sources et documents publiés par l'École française de Rome 4; Fonti per la storia dell'Italia medievale. Antiquitates 45 (Rome, 2015) (henceforth *RPD*).

2 G. A. Loud, 'The Norman counts of Caiazzo and the abbey of Montecassino', in *Monastica I. Scritti raccolti in memoria del XV centenario della nascita di S. Benedetto (480–1980)*, Miscellanea Cassinese 44 (Montecassino, 1981), pp. 199–217, reprinted in G. A. Loud, *Montecassino and Benevento in the Middle Ages: Essays in South Italian Church History* (Aldershot, 2000), and see also the whole of this volume. See too G. A. Loud, *Church and Society in the Norman Principality of Capua, 1058–1197* (Oxford, 1985).

3 See E. Cortese, 'Per la storia del mundio in Italia', *Rivista Italiana per le Scienze Giuridiche* 3rd ser. 8 (1955–56), 323–474.

4 See J.-M. Martin, 'L'Italie méridionale', in *Città e campagna nei secoli altomedievali (Spoleto, 27 marzo-1 aprile 2008)*, 2 vols, Centro italiano di studi sull'alto medioevo. Atti delle Settimane 56 (Spoleto, 2009), II, pp. 733–74.

5 *Monumenta ad Neapolitani ducatus historiam pertinentia*, ed. B. Capasso, 2 tomes in 3 vols (Naples, 1881–92), reissued and edited by R. Pilone, 5 vols (Salerno, 2008), II-1.

6 *Monumenta*, no. 2 (914).

7 *Monumenta*, no. 3 (915).

8 *Monumenta*, no. 4 (916).

9 *Monumenta*, no. 6 (920).

10 *Monumenta*, no. 8 (921).

11 *Monumenta*, I, p. 262 (reissued, I, pp. 378–9) and II-1, no. 473 (1041).

12 *RPD*, no. 172 = *Codice diplomatico longobardo, IV-2: I diplomi dei duchi di Benevento*, ed. H. Zielinski, FSI 65 (Rome, 2003) (henceforth *CDL*, IV-2), no. 27 (October 745); *RPD*, no. 173 = *CDL*, IV-2, no. 19 (August 543); *RPD*, no. 174 = *CDL*, IV-2, no. 30 (May 747). Only the second has perhaps been revised.

13 *Chronica monasterii Casinensis*, ed. H. Hoffmann, MGH SS 34 (Hanover, 1980) (henceforth *CMC*), I, 8, p. 34.

14 See *Acta passionis, et translationis sanctorum martyrum Mercurii, ac XII Fratrum*, ed. V. Giovardi (Rome, 1730).

15 *RPD*, no. 175.

16 Erchempert, *Historia Langobardorum Beneventanorum*, ed. G. H. Pertz and G. Waitz, MGH SS rerum Langobardicarum et Italicarum saec. VI-IX 1 (Hanover, 1878), pp. 231–64: here, p. 236: (after the account of the founding of St Sofia) 'pari etiam modo in territorio Alifano ... ecclesiam in honorem Domini Salvatoris construxit, et

monasterium puellarum instituit atque ditioni Sanctissimi Vincentii martiris subdidit' ['also in an equal manner in the Alifanese territory ... he built a church in honour of the Lord Saviour, and he founded a monastery of women and put it under the sway of St Vincent'].

17 It is likely, moreover (but the documentation on the subject is of course nearly nonexistent) that some women practised monasticism individually in their homes: Novel 12 of Arichis II finds fault with widows who 'abitum sanctimonialis in secrete domi suscipiunt', but lead a worldly life that ends 'ut non solum unius, set, quod dici nefas est, plurimorum prostitutionibus clanculo substernantur' ['who assume the habit in the home secretly' but lead a worldly life that ends 'so that not only of one, but, what is execrable to be said, of many, they are made available secretly for dishonourings']: *Le leggi dei Longobardi. Storia, memoria e diritto di un popolo germanico*, ed. C. Azzara and S. Gasparri (Milan, 1992), p. 270.

18 See *CSS*, pp. 45–63. J.-M. Martin, 'À propos d'un feuillet en écriture bénéventaine découvert à Rieti. Quelques considérations historiques', *Mélanges de l'École française de Rome. Moyen Âge* 114 (2002), 219–26.

19 *CMC*, I, 46, p. 123; I, 59, p. 148; II, 3, p. 171.

20 E. Cuozzo and J.-M. Martin, 'Documents inédits ou peu connus des archives du Mont-Cassin (VIIIe–Xe siècles)', *Mélanges de l'École française de Rome. Moyen Âge* 103 (1991), 115–210, doc. no. 83.

21 *RPD*, no. 136 (June 892).

22 *CMC*, I, 51, p. 31.

23 Cuozzo and Martin, *Documents inédits*, doc. no. 83.

24 *RPD*, no. 2.

25 *RPD*, no. 4 (revised).

26 *RPD*, no. 5 (also revised).

27 *RPD*, no. 6.

28 *RPD*, p. 1940.

29 *RPD*, p. 1936.

30 Montecassino, Archive of Montecassino, aula III, ch. VI, 6. On the same parchment is also copied the privilege of Nicholas I.

31 To the southwest of Montefalcone del Sannio (province of Campobasso).

32 With the exception of that of Pope Stephen II (784), which subjects it to Holy Saviour of Alife at a time when it was not yet founded: *CV*, I, no. 17, pp. 166ff.

33 *CV*, II, no. 91, pp. 57ff.

34 *CV*, II, no. 106, pp. 103ff.

35 See *Italia Pontificia*, ed. P. F. Kehr, vol. 8, *Regnum Normannorum-Campania* (Berlin, 1935; reprinted, 1961), p. 231.

36 *Italia Pontificia*, vol. 8, p. 214.
37 *CDL*, IV-2, no. 47.
38 Montecassino was exempt from the ninth century (see the privileges cited of Nicholas I and John VIII, *RPD*, nos 4 and 5), St Vincent at least from 944 (*Italia Pontificia*, vol. 8, no. 11, p. 249).
39 See *CMC*, I, 59, p. 148 (addition). Let us add that St Mary of Capua perhaps succeeded on the spot a homonym monastery founded by the princely family in 901: H. Bloch, *Monte Cassino in the Middle Ages*, 3 vols (Rome, 1986), vol. 1, no. 64A, pp. 243ff.
40 The account of this relocation constitutes the single occasion of speaking about Holy Saviour in the *Chronicon Vulturnense*: 'Tunc quoque monasterium Domini Salvatoris in Aliphis, quod Arichis princeps constituit [ac] rebus multis et possessionibus, servis, et ancillis ditatum Beatissimi Vincencii monasterio subdidit, depredatum et incensum a Sarracenis fuerat, cuius habitatores, qui evadere potuerunt, Beneventum venerunt, et a principibus, ac civibus auxilium postulantes, Sancte Crucis in honore ecclesiam constructam acceperunt, ubi aliquandiu habitantes, Victorini martiris ecclesiam [peci]erunt, ibique cenobiolum edificantes deinceps permanserunt': *CV*, II, p. 40. ['Then too the monastery of Holy Saviour in Alife, which Prince Arichis founded and, with it having been enriched with many things and possessions, servants and maids, placed under the monastery of St Vincent, had been plundered and burned by the Saracens, whose inhabitants, who were able to escape, came to Benevento, asking aid from the prince and the citizens, accepted the church of the martyr Victorinus, and there, establishing a convent, thereafter they remained.']
41 *CV*, I, no. 4, pp. 23–5.
42 *CV*, II, no. 96, p. 74.
43 *CV*, II, no. 97, pp. 75–6.
44 *CV*, II, nos 133 and 140, pp. 190–3 and 216.
45 *Rationes decimarum Italiae nei secoli XIII e XIV. Campania*, ed. M. Inguanez, L. Mattei Cerasoli and P. Sella, Studi e Testi 97 (Vatican City, 1942), no. 2055: it owed the large sum of 2.5 ounces of gold for the *residua secunde decime* in 1308–10.
46 *RPD*, nos 4, 6, 8, 12A, 13, 14, 15, 16, 17, 18, 20, 21, 27, 28, 29, 36, 40, 44, 46, 76 and 115.
47 Inguanez, Mattei-Cerasoli and Sella (eds), *Rationes*, nos 474 (1308–10), 498 (1325), 648 (1358–60); it was in all these cases taxed at twelve tarins.
48 *RPD*, no. 26.
49 *RPD*, nos 633, 634.
50 See *CSS*, pp. 53–63.

51 *RPD*, no. 37.
52 See Martin, 'À propos d'un feuillet en écriture bénéventaine' (the discovery of the manuscript is owed to Virginia Brown).
53 *RPD*, no. 38.
54 See G. Tescione, 'Roberto conte di Alife, Caiazzo e S. Agata dei Goti', *Archivio Storico di Terra di Lavoro* 4 (1975), 9–52; Loud, *The Norman Counts of Caiazzo*.
55 *RPD*, no. 531.
56 *RPD*, no. 624.
57 *RPD*, no. 31.
58 *CMC*, IV, 53, pp. 518–19.
59 *RPD*, nos 49–52.
60 *RPD*, nos 53–55.
61 *RPD*, nos 56–57.
62 J.-M. Martin, *La Pouille du VIe au XIIe siècle* (Rome, 1993), pp. 659–76.

Part IV

Conquering Norman Italy and beyond

14

The Norman siege of Bari, 1068–71

Charles D. Stanton

Significance

Robert Guiscard's blockade of Bari, begun in the summer of 1068 and enduring for two years, eight months, was a watershed in the Norman conquest of southern Italy and Sicily. For compelling reasons, the city was essential to Norman dreams of dominating the central Mediterranean. First, it was the principal and most prosperous port in Apulia and commanded the southern Adriatic and the strategically vital Strait of Otranto. As capital of the Byzantine theme of Longobardia and seat of Constantinople's *catepan* (governor) for the region, Bari was also the last Byzantine bastion in Italy. Capturing it would remove the final Greek threat to Norman pre-eminence in the province. Secondly, its seizure would enable Guiscard to suppress more effectively the stubborn insurgencies among his own Norman nobility by removing their Greek enablers. Thirdly, the city stood directly opposite Dyrrachium (modern Durrës, Durazzo in the Italian sources) on the Balkan peninsula, which made Bari the perfect springboard for future expeditions aimed at expansion into Greek territory. Fourth and perhaps most importantly, the house of Hauteville, represented by Robert and his younger brother Roger, desperately needed Bari's mostly Greek seamen and ships to seize the most coveted jewel in the crown of the conquest: Sicily.[1]

Sources

Fortunately for modern scholars, the three primary Italo-Norman chroniclers cover the confrontation in some detail and generally concur on the basic sequence of events. The first, Amatus of Montecassino, wrote his *Historia Normannorum* to extol the feats of his Benedictine monastery's two main benefactors: Richard of Capua and Robert Guiscard. Therefore, his account of the siege of Bari is mostly from Robert's vantage point.[2] William of Apulia penned his epic poem, the *Gesta Roberti Wiscardi*, at the behest of Guiscard's son Roger Borsa, which ensured a focus on Robert as its main protagonist.[3] On the other hand, Geoffrey Malaterra, a monk of the monastery of St Agatha of Catania, was specifically commissioned to compose his *De rebus gestis Rogerii Calabriae et Siciliae comitis et Roberti Guiscardi ducis fratris eius* as a panegyric to his church's primary patron, Count Roger of Sicily, which meant that the cleric naturally highlighted the younger Hauteville's contributions to the siege.[4]

Providing the Bariot point of view are three intrinsically related Apulian annals: the *Annales Barenses*, the *Anonymi Barensis Chronicon* and the *Annales Lupi Protospatharii*. The first is from the late eleventh century and covers events only up to 1043, while the other two were compiled in the early twelfth century, but all more or less depended upon older indigenous sources, now lost. By dint of their literary format, these accounts are drier and more concise than the Norman chronicles. They nonetheless offer invaluable insights into the attitudes of the city's inhabitants, as well as those of their Byzantine benefactors. Furthermore, the inherent brevity of the medium encouraged a focus on facts at the expense of parochial embellishment.[5]

Situation

Most scholars of the medieval Mediterranean single out the Norman victory at Civitate on 18 June 1053 as pivotal to their subsequent conquest of southern Italy and Sicily. Prior to the battle, the Normans of the Mezzogiorno were nothing more than competing bands of pilgrims-turned-mercenaries engaged in what could most aptly be categorised as organised brigandage. The most prominent among them was the Hauteville clan, led by the disinherited offspring of a minor noble named Tancred of Hauteville from the Cotentin in Normandy. Indeed, two of the three Norman wings at Civitate were commanded by Humphrey and Robert of Hauteville. The latter subsequently assumed the dukedom of Apulia from the former and coalesced many of the victorious Normans into a formidable fighting force with the objective of subjugating all of southern Italy. And Guiscard ('the cunning'), as he came to be known, faced little serious opposition. The Norman triumph at Civitate vanquished the papal coalition of Leo IX: the pope's contingent of Swabian knights had been slaughtered to a man, his Lombard/Italian supporters scattered and his erstwhile Greek allies chased off before they could even join the fray.[6] As a consequence, 'the Normans had an almost free hand to extend their dominations', concludes Graham Loud.[7]

In the aftermath of Civitate, Guiscard's younger brother Roger joined him and the two embarked on the methodical conquest of Calabria. Robert only paused the campaign in August 1059 to solicit papal recognition successfully from Nicholas II at Melfi as 'Duke of Apulia and Calabria, and in the future ... of Sicily'.[8] It was in the process of realising the latter desideratum, the subjugation of Sicily, that Guiscard first came face to face with an inherent limitation in the conventional cavalry-based tactics of the Norman military modus operandi: the lack of naval capability. He sent Roger across the Strait of Messina in early 1060 with a mere sixty knights on what could best be described as a tentative scouting expedition. The young knight was forced to withdraw almost immediately.[9] Early the next year, Roger followed up this reconnaissance with an actual raid by 160 knights and several hundred infantry, but it too was chased back across the strait by Messina's Muslim garrison.[10] The Hautevilles simply did not have the maritime assets necessary to transport enough troops from Reggio to have a measurable impact. Finally, by spring 1061 they had conscripted sufficient merchant vessels to ferry across the strait a force large enough to take Messina by surprise.[11] Progress from that point was slow. Aside from Messina, they could control no other ports and found taking towns in the hinterland all but impossible. The two brothers simply could not muster the manpower to counter the island's Muslim masters, who received reinforcements from their Zirid allies in Mahdiyah through Sicily's open ports. The Hautevilles soon realised conquering Palermo was the key.

Robert first sought to consolidate his hold on Apulia. In hopes of isolating the Salento peninsula from Byzantine Bari, he seized Brindisi and Oria in 1062, while ally Geoffrey Amicus took Taranto.[12] That same summer, however, he suffered a nasty falling out in Calabria with his younger brother over the partition of the region, but the two managed a rapprochement after Roger rescued Robert from unexpected captivity in Gerace.[13] In the autumn, Roger improved his position on Sicily by suppressing a rebellion of the Greek inhabitants of Troina, his stronghold in the Val Demone, prior to winning a lopsided victory in June 1063 over a larger Zirid force at Cerami near Castrogiovanni (modern Enna).[14] His dearth of manpower (a few hundred men at most), however, kept him from capitalising on the triumph to the point that he was even compelled to reject an invitation from the Pisans to join their 6 August raid on Palermo itself.[15] But by early 1064, the two Hautevilles were ready to invest the Muslim metropolis on their own terms. Robert had even stabilised his situation temporarily in Apulia by making a pact with Bari, the city most resistant to his rule. He promised its inhabitants a reprieve from Norman raiding if they would maintain their neutrality in his absence.[16] Guiscard and his brother then gathered around 500 knights (presumably with attendant infantry) at Cosenza for their planned assault on Palermo and crossed the strait to the island's principal port city.[17]

Regrettably, the enterprise was a farcical fiasco from inception. The two brothers began the siege by bivouacking their troops on a tarantula-infested hill. Geoffrey Malaterra describes the grimly comical consequences: 'Anyone who was stung by them [tarantulas] found himself filled with gas and suffered so much that he was unable to keep the same gas from coming out of his anus with a disgusting rattle.' The chronicler adds that they soon transferred to another site, but their prospects of success hardly improved. 'For three months ... the army of the duke and count achieved little against the city.'[18] Amatus explains why:

> When the most wise duke saw the disposition of Palermo and how provisions were being brought there from neighbouring lands, which would be carried there by sea if anyone denied access by land, he prepared himself to seize other cities in order to gather a fleet of ships with which to encircle Palermo and prevent any aid from reaching it by land or sea.[19]

The Hautevilles had encountered a barrier for which they possessed neither the manpower nor the matériel to overcome: the sea. The reduction of Palermo would have to wait until they could acquire the necessary mariners and maritime assets, presumably by conscripting them from port cities in conquered lands. This would have made Bari, the biggest port with the largest mercantile fleet in either Calabria or Apulia, an obvious objective. In the meantime, renewed rebellion by Apulia's fractious Norman nobility, led by Guiscard's nephews Abelard and Geoffrey of Conversano as well as Jocelyn of Molfetta, compelled Robert to return to the mainland, which left Roger with insufficient troops to continue the conquest of the island.[20]

Straws in the wind

Contributing greatly to Guiscard's swift return from Sicily after the Palermo debacle was the arrival in Bari of the new Byzantine *catepan*, Abulchares, who soon conspired with Norman malcontents to foment yet another round of mutinous machinations against Robert's rule in Apulia.[21] Also abetting the simmering resentment of the Norman nobility was Perenos, the Byzantine duke of Durazzo who supplied monetary and material support for the resistance.[22] It was this Byzantine backing that made Robert's campaign to consolidate his authority in the duchy all the more arduous and protracted. Constantinople even contributed considerable manpower at crucial junctures. In 1066, for instance, a Greek naval commander called 'Mabricas' (identified as Michael Maurex) delivered to Bari a sizable contingent of the emperor's feared Varangians (Norsemen who formed the imperial guard).[23] Full-scale rebellion subsequently broke out in fall 1067, led by the usual suspects: Abelard, Geoffrey of Conversano, Roger Toutebouve, Jocelyn of Molfetta and his son-in-law Amicus. Meanwhile on Sicily, Roger's chronic shortage of soldiers meant that he could do little more than maintain his dominance of the Val Demone (the island's north-east corner), while executing the occasional raid into the hinterlands to keep his Saracen protagonists at bay. His most aggressive action was to construct a fortress at Petralia (around twenty-five kilometres south-east of Cefalù), in order to extend his power westward towards Palermo.[24]

Finally, in 1068, after four years of near fruitless campaigning in their respective spheres of influence, the Hauteville brothers became beneficiaries of a fortuitous confluence of occurrences. First, Romanos Diogenes, a prominent Byzantine military commander and husband of imperial regent Eudokia Makrembolitissa, was acclaimed emperor in January with a mandate to halt the incursions by the Seljuk Turks into Cappadocia. To accomplish this, the new *basileus* concentrated his forces on Asia Minor and presumably drew precious manpower from dwindling Byzantine possessions on the Italian mainland.[25] Guiscard capitalised in short order by besieging Geoffrey of Conversano at Montepeloso on 16 February and gaining his capitulation soon afterwards. Jocelyn and Roger Toutebouve fled to Constantinople, while Robert offered clemency to Abelard and Amicus, albeit with forfeiture of lands.[26] Meanwhile, his younger brother Roger was on a *chevauchée* near Misilmeri (twenty kilometres south-east of Palermo), when he encountered a large Zirid force led by the sons of Emir Tamim ibn al Mu'izz of Mahdiyah (Ayub and Ali) and defeated it so decisively that the two brothers were forced to abandon the island.[27] Malaterra claims that Roger announced his triumph in the most intimidating manner possible: 'Among the spoils taken at Misilmeri, the count found baskets with birds [homing pigeons] in them. So he used them to report the unhappy outcome of the battle to the people of Palermo, sending the birds on their way with notes written in blood.'[28] Having cowed all opposition on the island, Roger was then free to respond at will to his brother's inevitable summons for support.

Showdown

Guiscard could no longer tolerate what had become a wellspring of Greek-agitated discontent in the heart of his duchy. As soon as he had dealt with the last of his obstreperous Norman aristocracy, he moved with alacrity to subdue Bari. By early August 1068, he was before the city's walls with a sizable force, mostly from Calabria. He considered the Bariots to be in breach of the bargain that he had made with them prior to his passage to Palermo in 1064. In his view, they had violated their promise of neutrality by subsequently receiving the *Catepan* Abulchares and by hosting a force of the emperor's Varangians in 1066. In restitution, the duke demanded the house of Argyros (a previous *catepan*).[29] 'Robert hoped that by retaining it that he might control the whole city from its elevation', explains William of Apulia.[30] The Bariots, of course, rebuffed his request and Robert responded by besieging the city on 5 August.[31]

Graham Loud labels Guiscard's siege of Bari 'the most ambitious military operation that he had yet undertaken'.[32] The chroniclers brave no reliable estimates of the size of his land contingent or the number of defenders they faced, but Richard Bünemann surmises that the total population of Bari at the time was between 10,000 and 12,000, of which around 3,000 would have been expected to man the walls. Accordingly, he calculated that the Normans would have had to field at least several thousand besiegers.[33] In addition, Robert would have required a massive maritime contingent, composed mostly of Calabrian ships, to establish an effective blockade of the port.[34]

To effectuate the landward side of the siege, the duke had his men dig fosses some distance from the foot of the walls and station wicker mantlets covered with hides near the city gates to guard against inevitable sorties by the inhabitants. William of Apulia testifies that he also had them construct 'a large wooden tower to overtop the city walls, along with every sort of siege engine [battering rams] which might knock down the walls'.[35] In addition, the duke directed his men to build an array of projectile-launching machines, undoubtedly including *pierrières* (stone-throwers) and trebuchets (catapults).[36] Bünemann believes the trebuchets were of the German *Blide* type, but the *Blide* was a counterweight catapult which did not come into common use until the late twelfth century.[37] Robert's trebuchets were more likely of the rudimentary traction variety, such as a mangonel, which could hurl a sixty-kilogram projectile around 110 metres.[38] Since both sides would have had access to widely available tenth-century Byzantine *poliorcetica*, treatises on the art of siege warfare, both would have constructed similar weapons and neither would have accrued any particular advantage.[39] The land siege was soon stalemated. The Bariots were so confident in their defences, Malaterra recounts, that they actually taunted Guiscard by parading many of the city's treasures along the walls in full view of the besiegers.[40] Robert's response would, however, ring menacingly prophetic: 'The things that you are displaying are mine, and I thank you for offering them to me voluntarily. But for now, be careful with them. I plan to be generous in their distribution, while you are crying over their loss.'[41]

Bünemann contends that the Normans did not initially institute a blockade of the port and says it was not until September 1070 that they put one in place, but there is scant corroboration for this assertion in contemporary sources.[42] He is, in fact, alone among modern historians in advancing this hypothesis, because it flies in the face of the lessons that Amatus insists that Guiscard had learned from the failed siege of Palermo – specifically, the need for ships to close off the harbour.[43] Indeed, Geoffrey Malaterra, who describes the blockade in detail, avers the opposite:

> Because the city of Bari was situated on a certain angle of land that extended out into the sea, Robert used his cavalry to close off, from one shore to the other, that part of the city which opened toward the land. *At the same time*, he used his ships, spread out over the sea and firmly joined to one another with iron chains like a fence, to close off the city from the sea, so that there was no opening anywhere through which anyone could leave the city.[44]

While the establishment of the naval blockade concurrent to the initiation of the land siege seems to be borne out by the circumstances, admittedly not all aspects of Malaterra's description are entirely credible. The chronicler goes on to report:

> He [Robert] also constructed two jetties, one on each side of the city, which reached out from the shore on both sides far into the sea and to which the line of ships was attached at each end. He did this so that if by chance the people of Bari tried to attack his ships, there would be a path connecting the knights on shore with the ships, thus expediting their defence.[45]

A seaborne *cordone sanitaire* such as Malaterra describes here would have required a combination of ships and piers as much as a mile and half long, which would have necessitated around 400 vessels, each the size of a Venetian *galea grossa* 'great galley' (i.e. seventeen feet of beam), lashed together gunnel-to-gunnel and anchored to two 500-foot sea bridges. Even if Guiscard had succeeded in building such a colossal waterborne barrier, it would have been nearly impossible to maintain its integrity in the face of inclement weather for a prolonged period.[46] Besides, if he could have gathered that many ships, albeit merchantmen, from Calabrian ports alone, he would not have needed to subdue Bari in order to effect a complete encirclement of his ultimate objective: Palermo.

In all probability, William of Apulia's version of the blockade is closer to the mark. He claims that Guiscard 'filled the sea with ships to prevent the Bariot ships from leaving' and adds that 'He [Robert] built a harbour for his ships, and a bridge on which a tower was placed, so that it was impossible for the inhabitants to make a sortie'. William also tellingly observes, 'The Norman fleet, thus sheltered, guarded the port'.[47] Similarly, a local Apulian source, the annals of Lupus Protospatharius, notes that 'the duke made a bridge in the sea in order to close the port of said city'.[48] Huguette Taviani-Carozzi interprets these last two accounts to mean that the Normans blockaded only the main harbour on the west side of the promontory while leaving the old port to the east open.[49] Given the fact that the blockade was subsequently broken or skirted on several occasions, she is most likely correct. Norman inexperience in naval warfare also adversely affected the blockade's effectiveness. In fact, William of Apulia further relates that no sooner had it been installed than 'the citizens of Bari captured the tower and demolished most of the maritime bridge.'[50] Guiscard must have realised then that the siege was going to be a protracted, difficult undertaking.

Struggle

Given the standoff on both the landward and seaward sides of the city, Robert had little choice but starve the Bariots into submission – a task made all the more challenging by the porousness of the Norman blockade. That said, the duke benefited from a key confederate inside the walls: factionalism. The city was a Mediterranean melting pot with the Lombard majority coexisting with Greek, Armenian, Jewish, Slavic and Arab minorities.[51] Irrespective of these ethnic divisions, there were essentially two factions: a pro-Byzantine party and a pro-Norman party. Most belonged to the pro-Greek group led by a certain *Patrikios* Bizantius who favoured continued allegiance to Constantinople, principally for commercial advantages. He and his followers also remained staunchly resistant to paying Norman

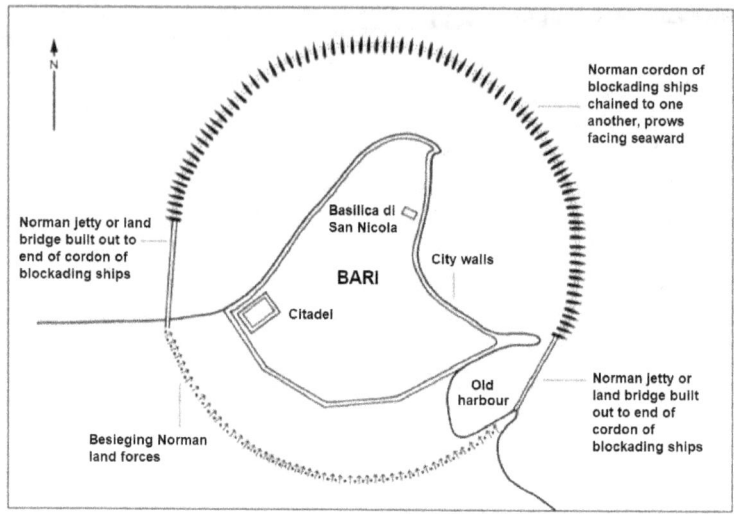

Figure 14.1 Concept of the Norman siege of Bari in 1068, based upon the description of the Italo-Norman chronicler Geoffrey Malaterra.

tribute. The pro-Norman camp was headed by the more pragmatic Argyritzos, who, although Greek, recognised that Robert's power in Apulia was ascendant while that of the distracted *basileus* was waning.[52]

When the Norman stranglehold started to take its toll on Bari's grain supplies, Bizantius broke through the blockade in mid-1069 with a small flotilla to seek help from Constantinople. Argyritzos alerted Robert, who sent four galleys in pursuit, but the quality of Norman seamanship at this stage was still wanting. Only two badly damaged galleys made it back to the duke. The results were no better when the *patrikios* returned that summer: two of the three galleys Guiscard dispatched to intercept him were captured.[53] Worse still, Bizantius's mission was successful. The emperor answered his entreaties for aid by dispatching a relief fleet commanded by the *Praetor* Stephan Pateranos. Aside from fresh troops and supplies, it also carried a newly appointed *catepan* named Avartutele, who brought with him a single *solidus* from the emperor for each citizen.[54] Its passage was not without incident, however. The *Anonymi Barensis Chronicon* reports that the Normans, apparently gaining confidence on the water, ambushed the Byzantine fleet sometime in late summer as it sailed past Monopoli (about forty-five kilometres south-east of Bari) and sank twelve vessels.[55]

This, of course, prolonged the siege, so Guiscard took his frustrations out on Brindisi, which had reverted to Greek control during the rebellion. He apparently hoped that retaking it would help intimidate Bari into submission. In January 1070, he marched a detachment of troops north-west to the target port, while ally Geoffrey of Taranto sailed a fleet up the Apulian coast to besiege it by sea. The operation failed spectacularly. The Greek fleet of Michael Maurex reportedly defeated Geoffrey's flotilla, while Brindisi's Greek garrison dealt a crushing blow to Robert's land contingent. Lupus Protospatharius professes that the heads of forty Norman knights and forty-three attendants were sent back to Constantinople as grisly trophies of war.[56]

By summer 1070, the rivalry between Bizantius and Argyritzos had escalated into open hostility with each hurling public invectives at the other. Inevitably, the truculent exchange resulted in violence. On 18 July, Argyritzos had his nemesis assassinated while en route to the *Catepan* Avartutele's domicile.[57] The malice did not end there. That autumn, in apparent retribution, the *Praetor* Pateranos enlisted the services of 'a knight from foreign parts on whom the duke [Guiscard] had previously inflicted a grave affront', according to William of Apulia.[58] The mercenary, whom Malaterra calls Amerino, stole into the Norman camp at sundown and attempted to murder Robert with a poison-tipped dart (or possibly a javelin) while he dined in his makeshift abode. Amerino missed his quarry when the duke suddenly ducked his head to expectorate.[59] The would-be assassin escaped, but the disheartening disappointment over the failure then prompted Avartutele to send a messenger, Stephan Pateranos according to some reports, to Constantinople in late December or early January 1071 to appeal for desperately needed reinforcements and provisions. In the same timeframe, Robert, impatient with the progress of the siege and the permeability of the blockade, sent for his brother Roger to bring his fleet from Sicily.[60] Events were rapidly coming to a head.

Sea battle

The *catepan*'s call for help did not go unheeded. The Emperor Romanos IV Diogenes could spare no troops of his own at the time, because he was preparing a major campaign against the Seljuks who had reached Iconium (Konya) on the south-western edge of the Anatolian Plateau. As it turned out, he was just months from his fateful encounter with Arp Arslan at Manzikert on 26 August 1071. But in the meantime he tasked Norman renegade Jocelyn of Molfetta and his entourage of disaffected Norman knights to conduct a relief flotilla of twenty 'pirate ships' loaded with 'grain and arms'. It departed from Durazzo in late February.[61] Malaterra divulged that Bari's designated messenger (probably Pateranos) was sent ahead to advise the city's citizens 'to light torches on the ramparts facing toward those who would be approaching by sea so as to make certain that the ships came to the right port'.[62] They did so the very next night.

This, of course, alerted the Normans. Roger, just recently arrived from Sicily, had his men set a seaward watch. Their vigilance was soon rewarded. 'And indeed', writes Malaterra, 'one night the lookout saw lanterns in the distance, shining like stars on the tops of ships' masts'.[63] Roger immediately launched his galleys and had his own flagship head towards an approaching vessel distinguished from the rest by two lanterns affixed to its mainmast: Jocelyn's flagship. When the two vessels engaged, the Normans – still new to the ways of the sea – rushed to one side to engage the enemy, but, instead, capsized their own ship. Malaterra reports 'one hundred fifty were drowned under the weight of their armour'. But Roger's remaining galleys quickly joined the fray and 'the count overcame Jocelyn in battle'.[64] 'Jocelyn and nine ships were taken and the treasure which the ships were carrying became the duke's', adds Amatus. 'The other ships fled.'[65] William of Apulia sums up the significance of the Norman victory at sea, their first:

> The Norman race had, up to this point, known nothing of naval warfare. But by thus returning victorious, they very much enhanced their leader's confidence, for he knew that the Greeks had been unable to carry enough help to the citizens of the town to hinder the siege. At the same time, he greatly rejoiced at the novelty of this naval

victory, hoping in consequence that he and the Normans might in the future engage in battle at sea with more hope of success.[66] The defeat irretrievably demoralised the city's citizens. Bari lingered on until the spring, but its capitulation was inevitable. In the interim, the duke assaulted Brindisi again and this time gained its submission.[67] In April, Argyritzos finally seized a strategic tower inside Bari's walls and sent for Robert. The citizenry had no choice but to surrender.[68] The duke was surprisingly magnanimous in triumph. He permitted no looting, levied no war indemnity and expected only the standard annual tribute due an overlord. In fact, he returned what property had been seized from them and granted them considerable autonomy by entrusting the city's governance to Argyritzos. He even forgave Stephan Pateranos for trying to have him assassinated.[69] As a consequence Robert and Roger marched into Bari as conquerors on 16 April 1071, the Saturday before Palm Sunday.[70]

Sequel

Robert Guiscard's benevolence towards the Bariots in the aftermath of the long, gruelling siege stemmed not from generosity but ruthless pragmatism: he needed their experienced, mostly Greek seamen and Byzantine-built ships.[71] William of Apulia recounts, 'After remaining in the city for some days, the conqueror ordered the Bariots to prepare arms and supplies, and to follow him wherever they saw him go'.[72] Where they saw him go first was Otranto. Robert departed Bari for the strategically located port at the southern end of the Salento Peninsula in mid-May. Malaterra maintains that 'The duke remained in Otranto throughout June and July, making his men level a hill so as to render the descent to the sea easier for getting horses onto ships'.[73] He was apparently gathering vessels from all along the Adriatic coast of Apulia. The chronicler also mentioned that Durazzo's citizens were 'terrified' that they would be the next target of Guiscard's ire and their fears were not unfounded, for in 1081 the great Norman baron would indeed besiege and take the troublesome Greek port.[74] But his premier objective, for the time being, remained what it had been prior to the siege of Bari: the port of Palermo. Lupus Protospatharius records that Robert set sail for Sicily in July with fifty-eight ships.[75] The duke paused briefly at Reggio to collect more recruits and rations.[76] From there, he moved onto Catania, where he joined Roger in gaining that city's submission through subterfuge. They claimed only to be seeking refuge in the harbour on the way to their real objective: Malta. Once the two brothers established control of Catania, Roger headed overland to Palermo, while Guiscard proceeded by sea on his command galley 'accompanied by ten *catti* [large oared warships] and forty other ships'.[77] By mid-August, both brothers were before the walls of Palermo to begin a constricting land–sea siege of the city. The inhabitants sought aid from the Zirids of Ifriqiyah, who soon responded with a fleet of ships. Galleys from Palermo joined those from North Africa to confront Robert's fleet outside the port. The Normans had apparently learned the lessons of naval warfare well from their newly acquired Greek subjects. They prevailed and even broke the harbour chain to pursue their Muslim adversaries into Palermo's ancient port, where they wreaked havoc on the ships moored there.[78] The city fell after a mere five months of stifling investment. Robert and Roger of Hauteville entered Palermo in triumph on 10 January 1072.[79] From that great port city, Roger's progeny would ultimately rule a sea kingdom, which would dominate the central Mediterranean for nearly a century – an eventuality that would not have been possible without the successful siege of Bari.

Notes

1 R. Bünemann, *Robert Guiskard 1015–1085; Ein Normanne erobert Süditalien* (Cologne, 1997), p. 56; C. D. Stanton, *Norman Naval Operations in the Mediterranean* (Woodbridge, 2011), p. 40; H. Taviani-Carozzi, *La terreur du monde: Robert Guiscard et la conquête normande en Italie* (Paris, 1996), pp. 260–1; G. Theotokis, *The Norman Campaigns in the Balkans, 1081–1108* (Woodbridge, 2014), p. 117.

2 *Storia de' Normanni di Amato di Montecassino*, ed. V. de Bartholomaeis, FSI 76 (Rome, 1935); *The History of the Normans by Amatus of Montecassino*, trans. P. N. Dunbar and rev. G. A. Loud

(Woodbridge, 2004). See also G. A. Loud, 'Amatus of Montecassino (Amatus Casinensis)', in G. Dunphy (ed.), *Encyclopedia of the Medieval Chronicle*, 2 vols (Leiden, 2010), vol. 1, p. 34; K. B. Wolf, *Making History: The Normans and their Historians in Eleventh-Century Italy* (Philadelphia, 1995), p. 88.

3 *Guillaume de Pouille, La Geste de Robert Guiscard*, ed. and trans. M. Mathieu (Palermo, 1961). See also J. Becker, 'William of Apulia (Guglielmo di Puglia)', in *Encyclopedia of the Medieval Chronicle*, vol. 2, pp. 1509–10; Wolf, *Making History*, pp. 123–4.

4 *De rebus gestis Rogerii Calabriae et Siciliae comitis et Roberti Guiscardi ducis fratris eius auctore Gaufredo Malaterra*, ed. E. Pontieri, RIS 2nd ser. 5:1 (Bologna, 1925–28); *The Deeds of Count Roger of Calabria and Sicily and of his Brother Robert Guiscard by Geoffrey Malaterra*, trans. K. B. Wolf (Ann Arbor, 2005). See also E. Albu, *The Normans in their Histories: Propaganda, Myth and Subversion* (Woodbridge, 2001), p. 111; M.-A. Lucas-Avenel, 'Le récit de Geoffroi Malaterra ou la légitimation de Roger, Grand Compte de Sicile', *ANS* 34 (2012), 169–92.

5 *Annales Barenses*, ed. G. Pertz, MGH SS 5 (Hanover, 1844), pp. 51–6; *Anonymi Barensis Chronicon*, ed. L. Muratori, RIS 5 (Milan, 1726), pp. 745–80; Lupus Protospatharius, *Annales*, ed. G. Pertz, MGH SS 5 (Hanover, 1844), pp. 51–63. See also W. J. Churchill, 'The Annales Barenses and the Annali Lupi Protospatharii, Critical Edition and Commentary' (PhD dissertation, University of Toronto, 1979); H. Kümper, 'Annales Barenses (Annals of Bari)', in *Encyclopedia of the Medieval Chronicle*, vol. 1, p. 55; J. Kujawiński, 'Anonymi Barensis Chronicon', in *Encyclopedia of the Medieval Chronicle*, vol. 1, p. 100; F. Delle Donne, 'Lupus Apulus Protospatharius (Protospata)', in *Encyclopedia of the Medieval Chronicle*, vol. 2, p. 1051.

6 Bünemann, *Robert Guiskard*, pp. 20–4; F. Chalandon, *Histoire de la Domination Normande en Italie et en Sicile*, 2 vols (Paris, 1907), vol. 1, pp. 134–42; M. Fuiano, 'La Battaglia di Civitate (1053)', *Archivio Storico Pugliese* 2 (1949), 125–33; G. A. Loud, *The Age of Robert Guiscard: Southern Italy and the Norman Conquest* (Harlow, 2000), pp. 118–21; C. D. Stanton, 'The Battle of Civitate: A plausible account', *Journal of Medieval Military History* 11 (2013), 25–55; Taviani-Carozzi, *La terreur du monde*, pp. 205–12.

7 Loud, *Age of Robert Guiscard*, p. 121.

8 *Le Liber Censuum de l'Eglise Romaine*, ed. P. Fabre and L. Duchesne, 3 vols, Bibliothèque des Écoles Françaises d'Athènes et de Rome, 2, série 6 (Paris, 1889–1952), vol. 1, pp. 421–2. See also Loud, *Age of Robert Guiscard*, pp. 123–30.

9 *De rebus gestis Rogerii*, bk II, ch. I, pp. 29–30; *Deeds of Count Roger*, bk 2, ch. 1, p. 86.
10 *Storia de' Normanni*, bk V, chs IX–XI, pp. 231–4; *History of the Normans*, bk V, chs 9–11, pp. 136–7; *De rebus gestis Rogerii*, bk II, chs IV–V, pp. 30–1; *Deeds of Count Roger*, bk 2, chs 4–5, pp. 87–8. See also Stanton, *Norman Naval Operations*, pp. 34–5.
11 *Storia de' Normanni*, bk V, chs XV–XVIII, pp. 235–7; *History of the Normans*, bk V, chs 15–18, pp. 138–9; *De rebus gestis Rogerii*, bk II, ch. X, p. 32; *Deeds of Count Roger*, bk 2, ch. 10, pp. 90–1. See also Stanton, *Norman Naval Operations*, pp. 36–7.
12 Loud, *Age of Robert Guiscard*, p. 132.
13 *De rebus gestis Rogerii*, bk II, chs XXI, XXIII–XXVII, pp. 35–9; *Deeds of Count Roger*, bk 2, chs 21, 23–7, pp. 96–101.
14 *De rebus gestis Rogerii*, bk II, chs XXIX–XXXIII, pp. 39–45; *Deeds of Count Roger*, bk 2, chs 29–33, pp. 102–11.
15 *De rebus gestis Rogerii*, bk II, ch. XXXIV, p. 45; *Deeds of Count Roger*, bk 2, ch. 34, pp. 111–12.
16 *Anonymi Barensis Chronicon*, anno 1064, p. 152. See also Bünemann, *Robert Guiskard*, pp. 57–8; Loud, *Age of Robert Guiscard*, p. 132.
17 *De rebus gestis Rogerii*, bk II, ch. XXXVI, p. 46; *Deeds of Count Roger*, bk 2, ch. 36, p. 114. See also Loud, *Age of Robert Guiscard*, p. 158; Stanton, *Norman Naval Operations*, p. 40.
18 *De rebus gestis Rogerii*, bk II, ch. XXXVI, p. 46; *Deeds of Count Roger*, bk 2, ch. 36, p. 114.
19 *Storia de' Normanni*, bk V, ch. XXVI, pp. 246–8; *History of the Normans*, bk V, ch. 26, p. 143.
20 Loud, *Age of Robert Guiscard*, pp. 133–4.
21 *Anonymi Barensis Chronicon*, anno 1064, p. 152. See also Chalandon, *Histoire*, vol. 1, pp. 177–8; Taviani-Carozzi, *La terreur du monde*, p. 260.
22 *Storia de' Normanni*, bk V, ch. IV, pp. 224–7; *History of the Normans*, bk V, ch. 4, pp. 133–4. See also Chalandon, *Histoire*, vol. 1, pp. 177–9.
23 *Anonymi Barensis Chronicon*, anno 1066, p. 153. See also Chalandon, *Histoire*, vol. 1, p. 183; Loud, *Age of Robert Guiscard*, p. 133.
24 *De rebus gestis Rogerii*, bk II, ch. XXXVIII, pp. 47–8; *Deeds of Count Roger*, bk 2, ch. 38, p. 116.
25 *Guillaume de Pouille, La Geste de Robert Guiscard*, bk III, lines 1–17, pp. 164–5. See also Bünemann, *Robert Guiskard*, p. 56; Chalandon, *Histoire*, vol. 1, pp. 184–5; Loud, *Age of Robert Guiscard*, p. 135.
26 *Storia de' Normanni*, bk V, ch. IV, pp. 224–7; *History of the Normans*, bk V, ch. 4, pp. 133–4; *De rebus gestis Rogerii*, bk II, ch. XXXIX, p. 48; *Deeds of Count Roger*, bk 2, ch. 39, pp. 116–7; *Guillaume*

de Pouille, *La Geste de Robert Guiscard*, bk II, lines 444–78, pp. 156–9. See also Chalandon, *Histoire*, vol. 1, p. 184; Loud, *Age of Robert Guiscard*, pp. 133–4, 239.
27 *De rebus gestis Rogerii*, bk II, ch. XLI, pp. 49–50; *Deeds of Count Roger*, bk. 2, ch. 41, p. 119. See also Loud, *Age of Robert Guiscard*, pp. 158–9.
28 *De rebus gestis Rogerii*, bk II, ch. XLII, p. 50; *Deeds of Count Roger*, bk 2, ch. 42, p. 120.
29 Bünemann, *Robert Guiskard*, p. 58; Taviani-Carozzi, *La terreur du monde*, p. 262.
30 Guillaume de Pouille, *La Geste de Robert Guiscard*, bk II, lines 490–4, pp. 158–9.
31 *Anonymi Barensis Chronicon*, anno 1068, p. 153; Lupus Protospatharius, *Annales*, anno 1069, p. 60. See also Chalandon, *Histoire*, vol. 1, p. 186.
32 Loud, *Age of Robert Guiscard*, p. 134.
33 Bünemann, *Robert Guiskard*, pp. 56–8.
34 Guillaume de Pouille, *La Geste de Robert Guiscard*, bk II, lines 485–6, pp. 158–9. See also Loud, *Age of Robert Guiscard*, p. 135.
35 Guillaume de Pouille, *La Geste de Robert Guiscard*, bk II, lines 496–502, pp. 158–9.
36 Taviani-Carozzi, *La terreur du monde*, pp. 262–3.
37 Bünemann, *Robert Guiskard*, pp. 58–9.
38 P. Contamine, *La Guerre au Moyen Âge* (Paris, 1980), pp. 208–14.
39 Taviani-Carozzi, *La terreur du monde*, p. 264.
40 *De rebus gestis Rogerii*, bk II, ch. XL, p. 49; *Deeds of Count Roger*, bk 2, ch. 40, p. 117. See also Bünemann, *Robert Guiskard*, p. 58.
41 *De rebus gestis Rogerii*, bk II, ch. XL, p. 49; *Deeds of Count Roger*, bk 2, ch. 40, p. 117.
42 Bünemann, *Robert Guiskard*, p. 59.
43 *Storia de' Normanni*, bk V, ch. XXVI, pp. 246–8; *History of the Normans*, bk V, ch. 26, p. 143. See also Bünemann, *Robert Guiskard*, p. 56; Taviani-Carozzi, *La terreur du monde*, p. 261.
44 *De rebus gestis Rogerii*, bk II, ch. XL, p. 48; *Deeds of Count Roger*, bk 2, ch. 40, p. 117.
45 *De rebus gestis Rogerii*, bk II, ch. XL, pp. 48–9; *Deeds of Count Roger*, bk 2, ch. 40, p. 117.
46 Stanton, *Norman Naval Operations*, pp. 41–2.
47 Guillaume de Pouille, *La Geste de Robert Guiscard*, bk II, lines 522–9, pp. 160–1.
48 Lupus Protospatharius, *Annales*, anno 1071, p. 60.
49 Taviani-Carozzi, *La terreur du monde*, p. 261.

50 Guillaume de Pouille, *La Geste de Robert Guiscard*, bk II, line 530, pp. 160–1.
51 Bünemann, *Robert Guiskard*, p. 56.
52 *Storia de' Normanni*, bk V, ch. XXVII, p. 249; *History of the Normans*, bk V, ch. 27, p. 143. See Taviani-Carozzi, *La terreur du monde*, pp. 261–2, 266.
53 *Storia de' Normanni*, bk V, ch. XXVII, pp. 249–50; *History of the Normans*, bk V, ch. 27, pp. 143–4.
54 *Storia de' Normanni*, bk V, ch. XXVII, pp. 249–50; *History of the Normans*, bk V, ch. 27, p. 144. See also Bünemann, *Robert Guiskard*, p. 60; Taviani-Carozzi, *La terreur du monde*, p. 266.
55 *Anonymi Barensis Chronicon*, anno 1069, p. 153.
56 Lupus Protospatharius, *Annales*, anno 1070, p. 60. See also Chalandon, *Histoire*, vol.1, p. 188; Stanton, *Norman Naval Operations*, p. 43.
57 *Storia de' Normanni*, bk V, ch. XXVII, pp. 250–1; *History of the Normans*, bk V, ch. 27, p. 144; *Anonymi Barensis Chronicon*, anno 1069, p. 153.
58 Guillaume de Pouille, *La Geste de Robert Guiscard*, bk II, lines 547–8, pp. 162–3.
59 *De rebus gestis Rogerii*, bk II, ch. XL, p. 49; *Deeds of Count Roger*, bk 2, ch. 40, p. 118; Guillaume de Pouille, *La Geste de Robert Guiscard*, bk II, lines 555–65, pp. 162–3.
60 *Storia de' Normanni*, bk V, ch. XXVII, p. 251; *History of the Normans*, bk V, ch. 27, pp. 144–5; *Anonymi Barensis Chronicon*, anno 1071, p. 153; *De rebus gestis Rogerii*, bk II, ch. XLIII, pp. 50–1; *Deeds of Count Roger*, bk 2, ch. 43, pp. 120–1; Guillaume de Pouille, *La Geste de Robert Guiscard*, bk III, lines 111–2, pp. 170–1. See also Bünemann, *Robert Guiskard*, p. 61; Chalandon, *Histoire*, vol. 1, p. 189.
61 Guillaume de Pouille, *La Geste de Robert Guiscard*, bk III, lines 1–116, pp. 164–71. See also Bünemann, *Robert Guiskard*, pp. 61–2.
62 *De rebus gestis Rogerii*, bk II, ch. XLIII, p. 51; *Deeds of Count Roger*, bk 2, ch. 43, p. 121.
63 *De rebus gestis Rogerii*, bk II, ch. XLIII, p. 51; *Deeds of Count Roger*, bk 2, ch. 43, p. 121. See also Taviani-Carozzi, *La terreur du monde*, pp. 270–1.
64 *De rebus gestis Rogerii*, bk II, ch. XLIII, p. 51; *Deeds of Count Roger*, bk 2, ch. 43, pp. 121–2.
65 *Storia de' Normanni*, bk V, ch. XXVII, p. 253; *History of the Normans*, bk V, ch. 27, p. 145.
66 Guillaume de Pouille, *La Geste de Robert Guiscard*, bk III, lines 132–8, pp. 170–1. For English translation see Loud, *Age of Robert Guiscard*, p. 136.

67 Lupus Protospatharius, *Annales*, anno 1071, p. 60.
68 *Storia de' Normanni*, bk V, ch. XXVII, p. 254; *History of the Normans*, bk V, ch. 27, p. 145.
69 Guillaume de Pouille, *La Geste de Robert Guiscard*, bk III, lines 142–60, pp. 172–3. See also Loud, *Age of Guiscard*, p. 136.
70 *Storia de' Normanni*, bk V, ch. XXVII, pp. 254–5; *History of the Normans*, bk V, ch. 27, p. 146; *Anonymi Barensis Chronicon*, anno 1071, p. 153.
71 Loud, *Age of Robert Guiscard*, pp. 136–7.
72 Guillaume de Pouille, *La Geste de Robert Guiscard*, bk III, lines 163–5, pp. 172–3.
73 *De rebus gestis Rogerii*, bk II, ch. XLIII, p. 51; *Deeds of Count Roger*, bk 2, ch. 43, p. 122.
74 *De rebus gestis Rogerii*, bk II, ch. XLIII, p. 51; *Deeds of Count Roger*, bk 2, ch. 43, p. 122. See also Bünemann, *Robert Guiskard*, pp. 65, 123–8.
75 Lupus Protospatharius, *Annales*, anno 1071, p. 60.
76 Guillaume de Pouille, *La Geste de Robert Guiscard*, bk III, lines 183–92, pp. 174–5.
77 *Storia de' Normanni*, bk VI, ch. XIV, p. 276; *History of the Normans*, bk V, ch. 14, p. 156; *De rebus gestis Rogerii*, bk II, ch. XLV, p. 52; *Deeds of Count Roger*, bk 2, ch. 45, p. 124.
78 Guillaume de Pouille, *La Geste de Robert Guiscard*, bk III, lines 225–54, pp. 176–9.
79 *Anonymi Barensis Chronicon*, anno 1072, p. 153; Lupus Protospatharius, *Annales*, anno 1072, p. 60.

15

The past, present and future of Norman rule in Apulia: Roger II's silver *ducalis*

Sarah Davis-Secord

[Then, after travelling round the whole of the region which his sons had conquered] and making a careful study of everything there, he came to the city of Ariano where he held a court with his nobles and bishops and dealt with a large number of different matters. Among the other dispositions which he made there he promulgated a terrible edict, hated throughout Italy and leading to death and poverty, namely that nobody dwelling in his kingdom should receive *romesinae* or pay them in any transaction, and on the worst possible advice he introduced his own money; the ducat, worth eight *romesinae*, which was reckoned to have been struck far more of copper than of silver. He also introduced copper *follares*, three of which were equivalent to one *romesina*. All the people of Italy suffered and were reduced to poverty and misery by this horrible money, and as a result of these oppressive actions hoped for the king's death or deposition.[1]

Falco of Benevento, *Chronicon Beneventanum*

According to the chronicler Falco of Benevento (d. 1144), King Roger II spent most of 1140 using his and his sons' troops to subdue towns across southern Italy, even closing in on the borders of Roman territory. He then retired to Ariano and issued a series of edicts, among them a coinage reform. No great fan of Roger II, Falco particularly disdained the king's monetary policy.[2] He complained that the king made a twofold error: he both outlawed a good coin (the *romesina*) and introduced a bad one (the silver *ducat* or *ducalis*).[3] This 'terrible edict' brought poverty, death and misery to the entire population of Italy, according to Falco, and caused the locals to wish for Roger's deposition or death. While Falco might be accused of exaggeration or of misplacing local enmity towards

Roger onto coins rather than other aspects of his rule (which was, according to Falco, much hated), it is true that monetary reforms were often perceived by medieval people as attempts at extra taxation or economic oppression. The population of Sicily and southern Italy, long accustomed to using coins of a wide range of values, might have foreseen dire economic consequences from radical and unwelcome changes to their monetary system.[4] And it is true that the *ducalis* was relatively unpopular and short-lived. It did not circulate widely beyond Apulia and was minted only until William II (r. 1166–89) introduced new coinages.[5]

Most discussions about Norman coinages have focused on cultural or economic reasons for adopting Islamic and Byzantine imagery and denominations. As Lucia Travaini wrote: 'Norman Italy created through "borrowing" a complex and mature form of expression.'[6] The *ducalis* has proved confusing, however, due to its apparent novelty. It was 'monete d'argento di tipo del tutto nuovo'.[7] Its unpopularity may have arisen from its newness or perhaps from broader displeasure at Roger's policies. However, the coin was not intended to be novel or to reflect a generalised reliance on Byzantine style, I argue, but rather to invoke a celebrated past and desired future. That past was a moment in the 1080s of expansive Norman power and interconnection with Byzantine imperial authority, a time supremely important for Roger II's conception of his kingdom because of its connection to Robert Guiscard (d. 1085), conqueror in Byzantium and ruler of Apulia. By harkening to this specific history, Roger's *ducalis* called attention to the foundations for his claims to royal power in both Sicily and the mainland, his descent from the celebrated Robert Guiscard and his intentions for the kingdom's future through the succession of his son Roger III, duke of Apulia (1118–48).

The coins of Sicily and southern Italy

The medieval Mezzogiorno's coinages were highly distinctive and diverse, both before and after the arrival of the Normans.[8] While the rest of Latin Christendom used only silver, southern markets were accustomed to tri-metallic coinages because of the Byzantine-Greek and Arab-Muslim political and economic influences in the region. Under Islamic rule from 827 to 1061, Sicily's coinage was a variation of that of the rest of the Islamicate world. Sicily minted a fractional of the gold dinar (*ruba'i*, one-quarter dinar) and a silver fractional (*kharruba*, one-sixteenth dirham; Sicily did not mint a full dirham), but no known copper coinages.[9] The Byzantine coinage system featured a gold *solidus* (or *nomisma*), a silver *miliaresion* and a copper *follis*, but there is no evidence that the *miliaresion* was ever minted or circulated in Byzantine Italy.[10] By the mid-eleventh century, Byzantine gold *nomismata* had been split into two different issues (the *histamenon* and the lighter *tetarteron*), both highly debased, often appearing more silver than gold.[11] The economic role of silver coins in the south was filled by northern *denarii*, especially those from Lucca and Pavia. Various issues, imports or imitations of these coins circulated in different parts of southern Italy. Some regions employed Byzantine standards, other locales used Islamic coins of Sicily (or imitations) and some places relied on Latin *denarii*. Into this diverse monetary world came the Normans, who initially adopted pre-existing coinages and adapted them for their own use. Successive issues featured slightly newer imagery and inscriptions, which suggests a keen awareness of the power of coins to convey messages to their users and the Normans' eagerness to take advantage of this.

Despite Roger II's apparent misstep with the *ducalis*, he clearly had a purpose for introducing this new coin. Contrary to Falco's assertion that the *ducalis* was minted from debased metal, it was of relatively high purity (50 to 60 per cent silver). Reckoned at one-twelfth *solidus*, the *ducalis* weighed between 1.8 to 2.5 grams and was minted in the trachy, or concave, style common to contemporary Byzantine coins, both silver and gold.[12] *Ducales* feature a nimbate bust of Christ holding a Gospel book on the obverse (convex), while the reverse (concave) has two standing figures: King Roger II in Byzantine imperial dress (crown with *pendilia* and the *loros*) holds a *globus cruciger* in his left hand and with the right hand grasps a long patriarchal cross. This cross is also grasped, perhaps either in receipt or offering, by a figure in military dress whom the coin identifies as Roger, duke of Apulia.[13]

One question that often arises about a new coin is that of its prototype. Italy's Norman rulers skilfully adapted pre-existing issues in new contexts, yet the source for the *ducalis* has remained

Figure 15.1 *Ducalis* of Roger II, Palermo, minted from 1140. British Museum, Inv. C.2706. Obverse: +IC XC RG IN ÆTERN around nimbate bust of Christ holding Gospel book. Reverse: R DVX AP and R R SLS ('Rogerius Dux Apulie' and 'Rogerius Rex Sicilie') and AN R X ('Anno regni decimo,' or 1140) with King Roger in imperial dress and Duke Roger in military dress with sword in right hand, both grasping a long patriarchal cross.

unclear for several reasons. There are several possible candidates but none is an exact match in both numismatic and visual detail. It may have made sense to base their new coin on the *denarius*, which would have been the silver coin already familiar to the Normans as northerners, and which was already circulating in the region.[14] Roger may have desired a new silver coinage bearing his name and image to replace northern *denarii*, but the *ducalis* was clearly not meant to be a *denarius* in style or substance. The *ducalis*'s economic value was far greater than the *denarius*'s. Roger's *tertia ducalis* (0.9 grams) was the closer match in value to the *denarius*; the *ducalis*, at about twice that weight, could not have been intended to fill the *denarius*'s monetary role. The *denarius*, moreover, was plainly decorated, while the *ducalis* was visually distinctive and clearly Byzantine in style.

Numismatists often suggest that the *ducalis* was meant to replace the Byzantine *miliaresion*, the common silver coin of the empire, which apparently never circulated in Italy.[15] However, the *ducalis* is an exact match neither in weight nor visual imagery for the *miliaresion*. Their similarity lies in their relationship to the *solidus*: both were figured as one-twelfth *solidus*. There are no known Italian mintings of the *miliaresion*. Produced only in Constantinople, it would have been imported into Italy. However, Grierson asserts, based on the scarcity of hoards containing *miliaresia*, that the coins 'circulated, if they did so at all, only marginally'.[16] And, given that regular minting of *miliaresia* in Constantinople ceased around a century before Roger's 1140 reform, even if it were the prototype for the *ducalis*, Roger would have been using a historical rather than contemporary coin as his model and questions about this choice would remain.

Visually, too, the Byzantine *miliaresion* shares little with Roger's *ducalis*. The early *miliaresion* featured a cross on steps on the obverse, while the reverse had a five-line inscription. This style remained fairly consistent until the tenth and eleventh centuries, when the coin began to feature imperial portraits and a bust of Christ. The final minting of *miliaresia* had a Virgin *orans* standing on the obverse with Emperor Alexius in military attire standing with a long cross on the reverse. This is nearer iconographically to the *ducalis* but still not very close. So, heavier than the *ducalis*, dissimilar in image and style and not in widespread Italian use, the *miliaresion* was not an exact model for Roger's 1140 silver coin, even while it may have been intended to fulfil a similar monetary role.

Iconographically, the model for Roger's *ducalis* is a much rarer and more regionally isolated coin, produced briefly and exclusively in the Byzantine mint at Thessalonica. Alexius I Komnenos (r. 1081–1118) had, early in his reign, issued a very debased version of the *nomisma*, the *histamenon nomisma*, a thin concave coin.[17] Although gold in theory, it was minted with so little pure gold that it in fact appeared to be silver. The *histamenon* was much heavier than the *ducalis* – approximately double its weight (3.29 to 4.4 grams rather than 1.8 to 2.5 grams) – so the *ducalis* was obviously not meant to have the same value, and it seems unlikely that the Normans intended users to mistake this coin for its Byzantine antecedent.[18]

In its imagery, however, the *histamenon nomisma* is a perfect equivalent to Roger's *ducalis*. The obverse shows a nimbate bust of Christ holding a Gospel book in both hands; the reverse has two standing figures: the left-hand one wears military dress, carries a sword to his left and presents the long patriarchal cross to or receives it from Alexius, who wears the *loros* and crown with *pendilia*. The left-hand figure is St Demetrius, an important military figure associated with Thessalonica. A saint, he has a nimbus; Duke Roger does not.[19] Duke Roger also carries his sword in the opposite hand. Apart from these details, the images match precisely.

The *histamenon nomisma* was minted exclusively in Thessalonica, only for the single decade preceding Alexius's 1092 reform and did not circulate beyond the Balkans.[20] A deeply debased, regionally-specific coin minted for less than a decade and separated from Roger's coinage reform by a half century might seem an unlikely model for Roger's *ducalis*. It had neither lasting monetary impact nor wide distribution. Despite the coin's limited, non-Italian circulation, there is good reason to suspect that the Normans had encountered it and that it was available to Roger for imitation. First, the visual match is too close to be coincidental: Roger was

Figure 15.2 *Histamenon* of Alexius I, Thessalonica, minted 1081–92. American Numismatic Society, Inv. 1944.100.81428. Obverse: + KE RO ALES IC XC around nimbate bust of Christ holding Gospel book. Reverse: D/M/I/T/ D/EC/P/ with St Demetrius, with nimbus and in military dress with sword to the left, presenting patriarchal cross to Alexius, in imperial dress.

not simply employing generic imperial dress or Byzantine styling. Travaini notes this iconographic similarity and attributes it to 'una conferma della sua idea del potere e di sovranità: la corona, il globo crucigero, le vesti, sono ripresi dall'immagine imperiale bizantina, indicando come Ruggero II si fosse posto su un piano di parità effetiva rispetto all'imperatore d'Oriente, pur scegliendo di non usare i titoli propri del *basileus*'.[21] Roger II certainly depicted himself regularly in imperial garb (as on the famous Martorana mosaic) and employed the visual imagery of Byzantine power and status. However, Roger's rationale for using this particular coin as a model must have been more than simply an assertion of parity with imperial authority. Why use this coin's image rather than another, especially since it was a rare, regionally-specific, short-lived coin not in local circulation? The answer, I argue, was closely connected to the historical moment at which the Normans in Italy first encountered the *histamenon*, a moment that Roger was intentionally invoking with his new coin and his new kingdom.

The past

Another reason why the *histamenon* was likely to have been the iconographic model for the *ducalis* arises from a historical connection between the Greek coin's first issue and Norman military activity.[22] Roger's uncle Robert Guiscard was present in the Byzantine Balkans as an invader in exactly the years of the coin's first minting; indeed, it was minted at precisely the time that Alexius was marching towards Dyrrachium (modern Durrës) to defend it from Guiscard. It is likely that Norman troops brought plunder back to Italy after their withdrawal and coins may have been part of the loot.[23] Alternatively, they may have circulated in Italy without leaving a trace in hoards discovered to date. Either way, the first issue of the *histamenon* was closely connected to Byzantine–Norman relations. The imperial mint at Thessalonica, closed since 630, was reopened by Alexius in 1081 as he passed through the city to confront Guiscard's troops. The coin was thus minted in direct response to the Norman invasion.

The first half of the 1080s was a period of intense Norman military activity in imperial Balkan territory. Guiscard initially routed Alexius's forces and gained the support of many locals.[24] But the Norman–Byzantine relationship had not always been entirely combative. In the mid-1070s Robert Guiscard, in fact, more resembled an agent of Byzantine power in Italy than a challenger for imperial lands. Emperor Michael VII Doukas (r. 1071–78) chose to ally with Guiscard in 1071 after a decade of successful attacks by the Norman on Greek territories in Italy. Bestowing upon Guiscard imperial honours and titles (significantly, *doux*), the emperor also offered a marriage alliance in 1074.[25] Byzantine–Norman relations were then at a high point, and Guiscard had been accorded Byzantine honours and status.[26] But a series of coups brought to power Alexius, who ended the alliance. This provoked Guiscard's invasion of imperial lands, purportedly to support Michael VII's restoration. In October 1081 Guiscard controlled Dyrrachium, but his triumph was short-lived.[27] By 1084 the tide had turned and Norman forces were forced to withdraw.[28] By his death in July 1085, Guiscard had lost both the lands taken from Alexius and the titles conferred by Michael VII. But in 1081 Guiscard appeared to be on the verge of marching victoriously towards Thessalonica en route to Constantinople. Alexius began minting the *histamenon nomisma* at just this moment.

Timing and circumstance underscore the significance of the images on the *histamenon*: Alexius depicts himself with a local military saint, the protector of the region Alexius is at that moment attempting to defend from a Norman incursion. Alexius, a usurper only a few months on the throne, faced a formidable enemy championing a predecessor.[29] He was clearly using imperial minting and imagery to strengthen his claim to the throne, to arouse local support and to call on the protective power of a significant warrior-saint. Demetrius, alongside George, Mercurius and Theodore, was one of the most important Byzantine military saints and was specifically associated with defence of Thessalonica. Originally cast not as a soldier but as a martyr of the fourth-century persecutions, by the seventh century Demetrius was celebrated for his miraculous defence of Thessalonica. Sometimes alone, sometimes leading an army, Demetrius protected the city against various enemies.[30] Demetrius was regularly depicted in military garb and later moved beyond Thessalonica to become a more universal imperial military patron.[31] This dual saintly role assuredly accounts for his appearance on Alexius's coins.[32] He was both a patron of imperial military projects generally and of the particular city whose mint issued the coin. Alexius's coin conveys a clear message: his legitimate political authority was backed by the saint's spiritual and military power.[33]

Something similar may have been at work in Roger's *ducalis* and his larger effort, if not to replace the Byzantine emperor, at least to join him in stature and prestige. The argument of the *ducalis* is partly that the spiritual power conferred by Demetrius, connected with political power in the Balkans, was, at the specific historical moment in which it was first minted, being transferred from Byzantine emperors to the Normans. And perhaps Roger wanted to suggest that it could be transferred again in the future during the rule of his son Duke Roger III.[34] If St Demetrius was the patron and defender of imperial military authority, Roger III was envisioned as the future protector of Norman territory in Italy and potentially elsewhere. Thus in one image we can see hints of the Norman king receiving the patronage of an important Byzantine military saint connected with the key region of Thessalonica specifically and with imperial war efforts more generally, and, at the same time, the transferral of Demetrius's role as warrior-protector to Roger's son and heir.

The link between Demetrius and Duke Roger III may, however, be less important than the connection this coin sought to make between Roger III and his great-uncle Robert Guiscard. Guiscard and his troops were the ones who were initially successful in imperial territory and were, presumably, the ones first to encounter the *histamenon*. Guiscard was also the duke of Apulia – a title that Roger II later bestowed upon his son and may have considered a precursor to the royal title. Guiscard was powerful throughout southern Italy and into the Balkans, another legacy Roger perhaps hoped his son would revive.

Roger II's adoption of weight standards and iconography from various historical coinages was by no means random. This was an intentional mixing of denomination and iconography to create a specific and unique coin. The linking of his newly recognised royal authority with a historical moment of expansive Norman ascendancy within the imperial hierarchy and territory, and with Guiscard's control of Apulia in particular, was a calculated choice. This choice was related not simply to a general sense of Guiscard's importance as founder of Norman authority in Italy and conqueror of Byzantine territory, however. Rather, it was directly related to both the importance of his memory as justification for the establishment of the kingdom of Sicily and the duchy of Apulia as the key to united power in both Italy and Sicily.[35]

Restitutio Regni Siciliae

Roger's coinage reform of 1140 accompanied a series of legal and administrative reforms undertaken after the conclusion of a lengthy battle for papal recognition of his kingdom. In July 1139, Roger and Pope Innocent II (1130–43) negotiated the Treaty of Mignano, after a decade of conflict between Roger, Innocent and antipope Anacletus II (d. 1138).[36] Innocent agreed to recognise Roger as king, despite the pope's second excommunication of Roger the previous April. On 27 July 1139 the pope issued the bull *Quos dispensatio*, which claimed to establish the kingdom that had been previously declared in 1130 by Roger and Anacletus.[37] The pope disregarded the decade during which Roger styled himself king of Sicily and reached farther back into history for justification of this new kingdom.

Indeed, the pope's endorsement of Roger's right to a new kingdom rested on the argument that there was nothing novel about it. In *Quos dispensatio*, Innocent plumbed both recent and ancient history to support Roger's royal authority. He noted Roger's descent from great warriors who had defended the Church and traced Roger's relationships to his uncle 'Robert Guiscard, Duke of Apulia, that valiant and faithful knight of St. Peter of distinguished memory' and his father Roger, 'of illustrious reputation'.[38] In truth, neither Guiscard nor Roger I had been a 'faithful knight of St. Peter' but had often positioned themselves as foes of Rome.[39] The fact that Guiscard and Roger I had, like Roger II himself, maintained long-standing conflicts with earlier popes was apparently forgotten and forgiven in service of the Norman–papal alliance cementing Innocent's authorisation of Roger's kingdom and Roger's recognition of Innocent's papacy.

Roger's genealogy was important, but so too was the recognition by a previous pope, Honorius II (1124–30), that his 'noble self was descended from the aforesaid distinguished family'. This acknowledgement, combined with Honorius's supposedly positive assessment of Roger's wisdom and justice, merited, according to the bull, Honorius's promotion of Roger to 'higher rank'.[40] This too was a fiction. Honorius had striven to prevent Roger's consolidation of power in southern Italy, especially his accession to the duchy of Apulia.[41] Thus Innocent crafted an invented history that established Roger's descent from (fictive) holy warriors while claiming that he was simply following a previous pope's recognition of the suitability of Roger and his family for kingship.[42]

Innocent then turned to even more ancient history for justification of the kingdom and possibly echoed Roger's own propaganda in claiming that this was in fact a restoration, not a new foundation.[43] Innocent confirms his predecessor's grant to Roger of the right 'by apostolic authority, [to] rule over Sicily, which has undoubtedly been a kingdom, for it is called this in ancient histories, and which was conceded to you by this same predecessor of ours. We grant to you the duchy of Apulia, which he also bestowed upon you' and also the principality of Capua.[44] The pro-Roger chronicler Alexander of Telese had used similar logic when describing how Roger required the urging of his nobles in order to declare himself king in the first place. Their argument was that he had consolidated rule over an ancient kingdom that needed restoration.[45] Such a claim to revival of ancient authority would have been an important part of Norman efforts to establish legitimacy despite their being relative newcomers in Italy.[46]

Alexander claimed that the declaration of the kingdom was not Roger's idea but that of his close supporters. They proposed that, since he ruled 'so many provinces, Sicily, Calabria, Apulia, and other regions stretching almost to Rome', he should hold the title of king rather than duke and place his capital at Palermo, 'which once, in ancient times, was believed to have had kings [who ruled] over this province'.[47] According to Alexander, Roger appointed a group of learned and influential persons to consider the question. The determination, naturally, was that 'it was certain that kingship had once existed in that city [Palermo], governing all Sicily; it seemed to have been in abeyance for a long time, but now it was right and proper that the crown should be placed on Roger's head and that this kingdom should not only be restored but should be spread wide to include those other regions where he was now recognised as ruler'.[48]

At no point in this discussion of the ancient kingdom did the question of its religious identity or language arise, so there is no way of knowing whether they envisaged a Latin or Greek kingdom, a Christian or pagan one. The 'long abeyance' presumably corresponded to the nearly two and a half centuries during which Muslim lords ruled the island, which suggests that it was a formerly Greek kingdom with close ties to Constantinople that Roger was reviving with himself at its head. What is clear is that he used history to justify present political decisions and royal authority. This was not the only instance of Roger looking to the past to promote his royal status. For example, in the famous mosaic at the Martorana, Roger dons crown and dress similar to what he wears on the *ducalis*, a clearly historicising image.[49] But the imagery of the new coin did not simply intend to remind viewers of a onetime kingdom in need of restoration. It was a visual invocation of a specific history in order to establish both the present and future authority of the kingdom.

Future

So, why would Roger choose to mint his own version of a coin depicting himself in the position of the very emperor who forced Roger's ancestor from imperial lands in the Balkans? And why replace a Thessalonican military saint with his son and heir to his kingdom? Coins are essential to promotion of state ideology since they circulate among the population and are seen by everyone in the marketplace, even if their intended messages cannot be fully understood by every user.[50] Roger's message drew upon the history of Norman interconnection with Byzantine power and legitimised Roger's control over Apulia, a key part of his consolidation of power in southern Italy. And there is evidence that the future, as much as the present or the past, was at the front of Roger II's mind when he employed historicising coins and imagery to support his new-old kingdom.

The future that Roger may have envisaged was one that would restore not only an 'ancient kingdom' but also the glory days of

Robert Guiscard and do so in the person of his eldest son and intended heir, Duke Roger III. Given the importance that royal and papal propaganda placed upon history and heritage, especially Roger's descent from 'that valiant and faithful knight of St. Peter of distinguished memory' Guiscard, it makes sense that Roger wanted to associate not only his present rule but his son's future rule with that memory. Even more specifically, the coin's imagery evokes a close linkage with Guiscard's military and political connections to Byzantine power.[51] Whether Roger envisioned the future of his kingdom to include imperial lands or titles is less clear, but in the 1140s he launched a series of campaigns in Greek territories.

The written record hints that Roger was interested in assuring the smooth succession of his son to the throne. The younger Roger had been publicly fulfilling the role of duke of Apulia since at latest 1134, when he first appears in royal charters.[52] Duke Roger III was mentioned in ten of Roger II's extant charters from the 1140s and three were co-issued by the two Rogers.[53] Succession is also mentioned in *Quos dispensatio*, which specified that the kingdom, and the special relationship between papacy and Norman kings, should extend beyond the reigns of the current king and pope. So the *ducalis*'s image of Duke Roger receiving the cross from his father – and with it both leadership of Apulia and future title of king – was intended to herald visually the transfer of power within the Norman realm.

The Normans were skilled imitators, but this was not blind emulation or simply intentional multiculturalism. A closer examination of the *ducalis* in its context also allows us to see the new king's use of it to craft a specific message that at once called to mind a glorious past and future. Roger selected and mixed coinages – in both weight and iconography – in order to suit particular needs. He took a denomination from a century before his own time and iconography from a half century earlier to remind viewers of both Robert Guiscard's past and Duke Roger's future. 1140 was an important moment for Roger's kingdom, one he hoped to see replicated and enhanced under his son's rule. The *ducalis* was intended to smooth that transition by providing a reminder of both his and his son's descent from the hero Guiscard, conqueror in the Balkans and ruler of Apulia.

Roger's plans for succession were thrown into disarray by Duke Roger's early death in 1148 at thirty. His death – the fourth among Roger's five sons with Elvira of Castile (1100–35) – led Roger to seek a new wife in Sibylla of Burgundy (d. 1150) who might produce another heir. That this marriage was likewise unsuccessful in producing a live male heir demonstrates the wisdom behind Roger's concern for matters of succession. No *ducales* were minted showing Roger with his youngest son and eventual successor William I (1154–66, duke of Apulia from 1148). However, William minted *ducales* depicting himself with his eldest son and intended heir (Roger IV, duke of Apulia, 1152–61), who also predeceased his father.[54] This suggests that the patterns set by Roger II – the title duke of Apulia as a precursor to the royal title and minting *ducales* as a visual plan for succession – were maintained, even as the Norman kings struggled to see their eldest sons live to take the throne.

Notes

1 *ChBen*, 1140.4.1–1140.4.4. 'Et eis omnibus studiose perscrutatis, Arianum civitatem advenit, ibique de innumeris suis actibus, curia procerum et episcoporum ordinata, tractavit. Inter cetera enim suarum dispositionum, edictum terribile induxit, totius Italiae partibus aborrendum et morti proximum, et egestati, scilicet ut nemo in toto eius regno viventium romesinas accipiat vel in mercatibus distribuat. Et mortali consilio accepto, monetam suam introduxit unam vero, cui "ducatus" nomen imposuit, octo romesinas valentem, quae magis magisque erea quam argentea probata tenebatur; induxit etiam tres follares ereos romesinam unam appretiatos. De quibus orribilibus monetis totus Italicus populus paupertati et miseriae positus est, et oppressus; et de regis illius actibus mortiferis mortem et depositionem regni optabat.' Trans., *Roger II*, p. 245.

2 For more on Falco and his chronicle, see G. A. Loud, 'The genesis and context of the Chronicle of Falco of Benevento', *ANS* 15 (1993), 177–98. On Falco and other contemporary chroniclers of the Normans, see G. A. Loud, 'History writing in the twelfth-century kingdom of Sicily', in S. Dale, A. W. Lewin and D. J. Osheim (eds), *Chronicling History: Chroniclers and Historians in Medieval and Renaissance Italy* (University Park, 2007), pp. 29–54.

3 P. Grierson and L. Travaini, *Medieval European Coinage Vol. 14: Italy III: South Italy, Sicily, Sardinia* (Cambridge, 1998), no. 212 (henceforth: *MEC*); R. Spahr, *Le monete siciliane dai Bizantini a Carlo d'Angiò (582–1282)* (Zurich, 1976), no. 72. The standard history of

Norman coinage is L. Travaini, *La monetazione nell'Italia normanna* (Rome, 1995); the *ducalis* is no. 241, pp. 210–18; see also *MEC*, pp. 101–25 for Roger's coinages, especially pp. 120–1 for the *ducalis*. See also P. Grierson, 'The coinages of Norman Apulia and Sicily in their international setting', *ANS* 15 (1993), 117–32; L. Travaini, 'La riforma monetaria di Ruggero II e la circolazione minuta in Italia meridionale tra X e XII secolo', *Rivista Italiana di Numismatica* 83 (1981), 133–53; J.-M. Martin, 'Le monete d'argento nell'Italia meridionale del secolo XII secondo i documenti d'archivio', *Bolletino di numismatica* 6–7 (1986), 85–96; and A. Sambon, 'Monetazione di Ruggiero II Re di Sicilia (1130–1154)', *Rivista Italiana di Numismatica* 24 (1911), 437–75. The *romesina* is an unknown coin, usually presumed to be copper or silver billon.

4 Southern Italy and Sicily were much more highly monetised in the pre-Norman and Norman periods than northern Italy or Europe. G. A. Loud, 'Coinage, wealth and plunder in the age of Robert Guiscard', *EHR* 114 (1999), 815–43.

5 The *ducalis* was 'una moneta essenzialmente pugliese' – 'essentially an Apulian coin'; Martin, 'Le monete d'argento', p. 91.

6 L. Travaini, 'The Normans between Byzantium and the Islamic world', *Dumbarton Oaks Papers* 55 (2001), p. 186.

7 'A completely new type of silver coin'; Travaini, *La monetazione*, p. 211.

8 G. A. Loud's many publications on the period before, during and after the Norman conquest are foundational for study of southern Italy. This chapter is particularly reliant upon *The Age of Robert Guiscard: Southern Italy and the Norman Conquest* (Harlow, 2000) and *The Latin Church in Norman Italy* (Cambridge, 2007).

9 Brief overviews of pre-Norman coinages in Sicily and southern Italy are found in *MEC*, ch. 2, pp. 36–75, and P. Balog, 'La monetazione della Sicilia araba e le sue imitazioni nell'Italia meridionale', in F. Gabrieli and U. Scerrato (eds), *Gli Arabi in Italia: cultura, contatti e tradizioni* (Milan, 1979), pp. 611–28.

10 Overviews of Byzantine coinage are available in P. Grierson, *Byzantine Coinage* (Washington, DC, 1999) and D. R. Sear, *Byzantine Coins and their Values*, 2nd edn (London, 1987).

11 M. F. Hendy, *Studies in the Byzantine Monetary Economy c.300–1450* (Cambridge, 1985), p. 513. See also M. F. Hendy, *Coinage and Money in the Byzantine Empire, 1081–1261* (Washington, DC, 1969), pp. 3–9.

12 *MEC*, nos 212 and 213.

13 Travaini, 'The Normans between Byzantium and the Islamic world', 179–96, especially pp. 185–6, where she discusses Norman cooption of imperial dress.

14 *MEC*, p. 3. No *denarii* were minted in the south until 1195 under Henry VI. *MEC*, pp. 2, 40–1, and 154.
15 The *miliaresion* was introduced by Leo III (717–41) with a weight of 2.27 to 3.0 grams. From the mid-ninth century it became standard Byzantine silver, and in the tenth and eleventh centuries the weight fluctuated between 1.8 and 3.0 grams. The final *miliaresia* were minted sparingly and from highly debased metal. Some numismatists think the *miliaresion* was originally minted in imitation of the *dirham* of the Islamic world, or that it was meant to fill a similar market. L. Travaini, 'The monetary reforms of William II (1166–1189): Oriental and western patterns in Norman Sicilian coinage', *Schweizer Münzblätter* 46 (1996), 109–23; P. Grierson, 'The role of silver in the early Byzantine economy', in S. A. Boyd and M. M. Mango (eds), *Ecclesiastical Silver Plate in Sixth-Century Byzantium* (Washington, DC, 1992), pp. 137–46; C. Morrisson, 'Monnaie et prix à Byzance du Ve au VIIe siècle', in C. Morrisson, *Monnaie et finances à Byzance: analyses, techniques* (Aldershot, 1994), pp. 239–60; and C. Morrisson, 'Byzantine money: Its production and circulation', in E. Angeliki (ed.), *The Economic History of Byzantium: From the Seventh Through the Fifteenth Century*, vol. 3 (Washington, DC, 2002), pp. 909–66.
16 *MEC*, p. 40. See also Travaini, *La monetazione*, pp. 187ff., for the uncertainty that any *miliaresia* circulated in eleventh-century Italy.
17 Sear, *Byzantine Coins*, no. 1905. A similar coin from the same mint is Sear, *Byzantine Coins*, no. 1904. The only difference is that the two figures on the reverse hold a *labarum* rather than a patriarchal cross. The *labarum* was a regular part of Byzantine imperial regalia, although not imitated by the Italian Normans, and strongly connoted the emperor's role as military leader.
18 Six of Roger's *ducales* are in the British Museum coinage collection: Inv. 1847,1108.823; Inv. 1906,1103.4002; Inv. C.2706; Inv. C.2707; Inv. 1846,0910.195; and Inv. 1847,1008.822. Four are concave and two are flat. They range in weight from 2.01 grams to 2.78 grams and appear to represent several distinct dies. Several were struck quite roughly and show significant wear. The catalogue does not include find sites and attributes them all to the Palermo mint. The collection contains four *ducales* of William I (1154–66) with his son Roger (1156–61): Inv. 1856,0901.19; Inv. 1860,0703.021; Inv. 1906,1103.3555; and Inv. 1847,1108.833. All trachy, they range between 2.0 grams and 2.58 grams. The collection also contains three silver coins issued by William II (1166–89), but their imagery is entirely distinct from the *ducales* of Roger II and William I.
19 No *miliaresia* ever featured St Demetrius.

20 The Thessalonica mint was active from 330 until 629/30, when it was closed. It was reopened by Alexius in 1081 and operated until the mid-fourteenth century. Hendy, *Studies*, pp. 424ff.

21 'A confirmation of his idea of power and sovreignty: the crown, globus cruciger, and robes emulate the Byzantine imperial image, indicating that Roger II wanted to place himself on an equal plane with the Emperor in the East, even while choosing not to use the title *basileus*.' Travaini, *La monetazione*, p. 213.

22 Much has been written about Byzantine–Italian relations in the pre-Norman and Norman periods. See for example, G. A. Loud, 'Byzantine Italy and the Normans', in J. D. Howard-Johnston (ed.), *Byzantium and the West c.850–c.1200* (Amsterdam, 1988), pp. 215–33; G. A. Loud, 'Southern Italy and the eastern and western empires, c.900–1050', *JMH* 38 (2012), 1–19; and V. von Falkenhausen, 'I rapporti con Bisanzio', in M. D'Onofrio (ed.), *I Normanni. Popolo d'Europa 1030–1200* (Venice, 1994), pp. 350–5.

23 Hendy claims the *ducalis* as a direct copy of the *histamenon* for this reason in *Studies*, p. 314. Travaini dismisses this claim in 'The Normans between Byzantium and the Islamic world', pp. 185–6. For Guiscard as a plunderer, see Loud, 'Coinage, wealth and plunder', pp. 825–7.

24 Paul Stephenson, *Byzantium's Balkan Frontier* (Cambridge, 2009), pp. 165ff.; G. Theotokis, *The Norman Campaigns in the Balkans, 1081–1108* (Woodbridge, 2014), chs 6–7; and Loud, *Age of Robert Guiscard*, pp. 209–23.

25 For the financial benefit to Guiscard from this marriage alliance, see Loud, 'Coinage, wealth and plunder', pp. 827ff.

26 According to Stephenson, *Byzantium's Balkan Frontier*, p. 158, 'He had been brought into the imperial hierarchy, and undertook to rule southern Italy as a vassal of the eastern emperor'. Anna Comnena believed that Guiscard had ambitions to replace the emperor; see Theotokis, *Norman Campaigns*, p. 141; E. Lapina, *Warfare and the Miraculous in the Chronicles of the First Crusade* (University Park, 2015), pp. 59–61; and Loud, *Age of Roger Guiscard*, pp. 216ff.

27 For the battle of Dyrrachium, see Theotokis, *Norman Campaigns*, pp. 154–64.

28 For Guiscard's second expedition, see Theotokis, *Norman Campaigns*, pp. 177–84.

29 Stephenson, *Byzantium's Balkan Frontier*, pp. 165ff.

30 M. White, *Military Saints in Byzantium and Rus, 900–1200* (Cambridge, 2013), especially pp. 15–19; C. Walter, *The Warrior Saints in Byzantine Art and Tradition* (Aldershot, 2003), pp. 67–93; P. Lemerle, 'Note sur les plus anciennes représentations de Saint

Démétrius', Δελτίον ΧΑΕ 10 (1980–81), 1–10; C. Bakirtzis, 'Le culte de saint Démétrius', in E. Dassmann and J. Engemann (eds), *Akten des XII. Internationalen Kongresses für christliche Archäologie*, 3 vols (Munster, 1995–97), vol. 1, pp. 58–68; E. Lapina, 'St. Demetrius of Thessaloniki: Patron saint of crusaders', *Viator* 40 (2009), 93–112; Lapina, *Warfare*, pp. 48ff.

31 Lapina, *Warfare*, pp. 65ff.

32 For Demetrius on coins, see Hendy, *Coinage and Money*, p. 437, and Lapina, *Warfare*, pp. 65–6.

33 Demetrius had been coopted by earlier Latin Christians, including the Carolingians and crusaders, who both sought to transfer Byzantine spiritual and political power to themselves. For example, at the battle for Antioch, as Lapina argues, 'When Demetrius and other saints joined the crusaders, they abandoned the Byzantines'. Lapina, 'Demetrius of Thessaloniki', pp. 93–112. See also R. Forrai, 'Byzantine saints for Frankish warriors: Anastasius Bibliothecarius' Latin version of the Passion of Saint Demetrius of Thessaloniki', in S. Brodbeck *et al.* (eds), *L'Héritage byzantin en Italie (VIIIe–XIIe siècle)* (Rome, 2015), pp. 185–202.

34 There is no evidence that Roger II had a special affinity for Demetrius, although another Byzantine military saint, George, had earlier been spotted aiding the Normans in their efforts to take Sicily from the Muslims at the battle of Cerami (1063), suggesting that the Normans were sometimes keen to claim Byzantine saints as their own. Lapina, 'Demetrius of Thessaloniki', pp. 107–8, and Lapina, *Warfare*, chs 3 and 4.

35 Loud sees Pope Honorius's resistance to Roger II's succession as duke of Apulia in 1127 as an effort to prevent his consolidation of power both across southern Italy and in Sicily. See *Latin Church*, pp. 148–51. Soon after he gained the duchy (1128) and the overlordship of Capua (1129) he declared himself king (1130).

36 For more on the history of Norman–papal relations, see G. A. Loud, 'The papacy and the rulers of southern Italy 1058–1198', in G. A. Loud and A. Metcalfe (eds), *The Society of Norman Italy* (Leiden, 2002), pp. 151–84, and Loud, *Latin Church*, especially ch. 3.

37 Loud, *Latin Church*, pp. 155–7.

38 'Manifestis siquidem probatum est argumentis, quod egregiae memoriae strenuus et fidelis miles B. Petri Robertus Guiscardus, praedecessor tuus, dux Apuliae, magnificos et potentes hostes Ecclesiae viriliter expugnavit, et posteritati suae dignum memoria nomen et imitabile probitatis exemplum reliquit. Pater quoque tuus illustris recordationis Rogerius, per bellicos sudores et militaria certamina,

inimicorum Christiani nominis intrepidus exstirpator, et Christianae religionis diligens propagator, utpote bonus et devotus filius, multimoda obsequia matri suae sanctae Romanae Ecclesiae impertivit.' Innocent II, *Quos dispensatio*, 27 July 1139, *PL*, vol. 179, no. 416, pp. 478–9. Trans., *Roger II*, p. 311.

39 Guiscard had defended the Rome of Pope Gregory VII (1073–85) in 1084 but in a rather incomplete and quite destructive way; see Loud, *Age of Robert Guiscard*, pp. 221–2, and Loud, *Latin Church*, pp. 141–2.

40 'Unde et praedecessor noster religiosus et prudens papa Honorius, nobilitatem tuam de praedicta generositate descendentem intuitus plurimum de te sperans, et prudentia ornatum, justitia munitum, atque ad regimen populi te idoneum esse credens, valde dilexit, et ad altiora provexit.' Innocent II, *Quos dispensatio*, pp. 478–9. Trans., *Roger II*, p. 311.

41 Loud, *Latin Church*, pp. 148–52.

42 Roger's first recorded charter after the 1140 confirmation of his kingdom clearly underscores these genealogical claims as well by pointing to 'predecessores et p(ro)genitores n(ost)ri pie, recordationis et beate memorie Robertus Guiscardus, patruus n(oste)r Rogerius comes, pat(er) noster, et ceteri patrui n(ost)ri atq(ue) consanguinei' ['our predecessors and progentiors of blessed memory and recollection, our uncle Robert Guiscard and our father Count Roger, and our other paternal uncles and relatives']. The focus of praise is his ancestors' efforts to subjugate Muslim territory: 'inimicis fidei Chr(ist)ianae, Sarracenis miserabiliter occupatos universos fines Sicilie, Calabrie, Apulie et Longobardie' ['all of Sicily, Calabria, Apulia, and Lombardy having been unfortunately occupied by the Muslims, enemies of the Christian faith']. In Roger's own words, then, his ancestors' most important deeds appear to have been their efforts against Muslims rather than those directly on behalf of the Roman Church. *Rogerii II Regis Diplomata Latina*, ed. C.-R. Brühl, Codex Diplomaticus Regni Siciliae, Ser. I.ii(1) (Cologne, 1987), doc. 48, 28 April 1140. For more on the Norman royal chancery records, see G. A. Loud, 'The chancery and charters of the kings of Sicily (1130–1212)', *EHR* 124 (2009), 779–810; and J. Becker, 'Charters and chancery under Roger I and Roger II', in S. Burkhardt and T. Foerster (eds), *Norman Tradition and Transcultural Heritage: Exchange of Cultures in the 'Norman' Peripheries of Medieval Europe* (Farnham, 2013), pp. 79–95.

43 Loud, *Latin Church*, pp. 155–6; and H. Wieruszowski, 'Roger II of Sicily, Rex-Tyrannus, in twelfth-century political thought', *Speculum* 38 (1963), 46–78; see pp. 51–3.

44 'regnum Siciliae, quod utique, prout in antiquis refertur historiis, regnum fuisse non dubium est, tibi ab eodem antecessore nostro concessum, cum integritate honoris regii et dignitate regibus pertinente, excellentiae tuae concedimus, et apostolica auctoritate confirmamus. Ducatum quoque Apuliae tibi ab eodem collatum, et insuper principatum Capuanum, integre nihilominus nostri favoris robore communimus, tibique concedimus.' Innocent II, *Quos dispensatio*, pp. 478–9. Trans., *Roger II*, p. 311.

45 For more on Alexander's chronicle, see Loud, 'History writing'.

46 Loud, *Latin Church*, pp. 152ff., places Alexander's passage in the context of Norman–papal relations and Loud, 'History writing', pp. 33ff., compares it to other Norman chroniclers.

47 'sepissima sibi ac familiari quorundam, maximeque Henrici comitis avunculi sui, a quo plus aliis diligebatur, cepit suggeri collocutione; videlicet ut ipse, qui tot provinciis, Sicilie, Calabrie, Apulie, ceterisque regionibus que pene Romam usque habentur, Domino cooperante dominabatur, nequaquam utique ducalis sed Regii illustrari culminis honore deberet. Qui etiam addebant, quod regni ipsius principium et caput, Panhormus Sicilie metropolis fieri deceret; que olim sub priscis temporibus super hanc ipsam provinciam Reges nonnullos habuisse traditur, qui postea, pluribus evolutis annis, occulto Dei disponente iudicio nunc usque sine regibus mansit.' *Alexandri Telesini abbatis Ystoria Rogerii regis Sicilie, Calabrie atque Apulie*, ed. L. de Nava, commentary by D. R. Clementi, FSI 112 (Rome, 1991), 2.1. Trans., *Roger II*, p. 77–8.

48 'Horum itaque amica atque laudanda suggestio, cum infra semet ipsum multipharie tractando versaretur, velletque exinde certum ratumque habere consilium Salernum regreditur; extra quam non longe convocatis ad se aliquibus ecclesiasticis peritissimis, atque competentioribus personis, nec non quibusdam principibus, comitibus, baronibus, simulque aliis qui sibi sunt visi probatioribus viris, patefecit eis examinandum secretum et inopinatum negotium; ac illi, rem ipsam sollicite perscrutantes, unanimiter tandem uno ore laudant, concedunt, decernunt; ymmo, magnopere precibus insistunt ut Rogerius dux in regiam dignitatem apud Panhormum, Sicilie metropolim, promoveri debeat, qui non tantum Sicilie paterna hereditate, verum etiam Calabrie, Apulie, ceterarumque terrarum, que non solum ab eo bellica obtinentur virtute, sed et propinquitate generis antecedentium ducum iure sibi succedere debent. Nam si regni solium in eadem quondam civitate ad regendum tantum Siciliam certum est extitisse, et nunc ad ipsum per longum tempus defecisse videtur, valde dignum et iustum est ut in capite Rogerii diademate posito, regnum ipsum non solum ibi

modo restituatur, sed in ceteras etiam regiones, quibus iam dominari cernitur, dilatari debeat.' *Alexandri Telesini abbatis Ystoria Rogerii*, 2.2. Trans., *Roger II*, pp. 77–8.

49 On the coin he wears the crown with *pendilia* but not the crossed *loros*. D. M. Hayes, 'The political significance of Roger II of Sicily's antiquated loros in the mosaic of Santa Maria dell'Ammiraglio, Palermo', *Allegorica* 29 (2013), 52–69. For scholarship on Byzantine crowns, see n. 11. For the *loros*, see n. 13. Hayes argues that the historicising dress Roger wears in the mosaic is tied to the Norman effort to remind viewers of their long ancestry and history in the region. For the importance of visual images in Roger's self-promotion, see, among others, W. Tronzo, *The Cultures of his Kingdom: Roger II and the Cappella Palatina in Palermo* (Princeton, 1997).

50 The uncertainty of a coin's message being received correctly by people in the marketplace was not isolated to the *ducalis*, but the difficulty of deciphering Roger's claims regarding both the past and future of Norman power may have contributed to the coin's poor reception.

51 Guiscard had issued a (copper) coin featuring himself in imperial garb and used coins to cement the intended succession of his son Roger Borsa (1085–1111). P. Grierson, 'The Salernitan coinage of Gisulf II (1052–77) and Robert Guiscard (1077–85)', *Papers of the British School at Rome* 24 (1956), 37–59.

52 *Rogerii II regis diplomata Latina*, doc. 35.

53 The ones mentioning Roger III are *Rogerii II Regis Diplomata Latina*, docs 57, 58, 59 (co-signed), 65, 66, 67, 71, 72, 73 and 75. The co-issued charters *Rogerii II Regis Diplomata Latina*, D.I, D.II and D.III.

54 *MEC*, no. 290; Spahr, no. 94. British Museum, Inv. 1847,1108.835; Inv. 1867,0514.3; and Inv. 1906,1103.3552.

16

From Alexandria to Tinnīs: the kingdom of Sicily, Egypt and the Holy Land, 1154–87

Alan V. Murray

> He conceived a mortal hatred against the kingdom and its people. Other Christian princes in various parts of the world, either by coming in person or by giving liberal gifts, have amplified and promoted our infant realm. But he and his heirs to the present time have never become reconciled to us to the extent of a single friendly word. Although they could have relieved our necessities by counsel and aid far more easily than any other prince, yet they have always remembered their wrongs and have unjustly avenged upon the whole people the fault of a single individual.

Thus the chronicler William of Tyre, writing in the 1180s, describes the lack of support for the kingdom of Jerusalem by Roger II of Sicily and his heirs up to William's own time. He traces this enmity back to the short-lived marriage of Baldwin I, king of Jerusalem (1100–18), and Roger II's mother Adelaide, widow of Count Roger I of Sicily, which had been contracted in 1113.[1] Baldwin had hoped that this alliance would not only bring a substantial dowry but also secure the naval and military support of the Normans of southern Italy. However, the Sicilians stipulated that, if the marriage produced no issue, the kingdom of Jerusalem would revert to Adelaide's son Roger II on Baldwin's death, and, when Baldwin fell ill during the winter of 1116–17 with no heir yet born, the kingdom's magnates feared that he might die; with the prospect of the throne of Jerusalem passing to an absentee monarch, they persuaded the king to repudiate Adelaide and the marriage agreement.[2]

The Normans of southern Italy had made a significant contribution to the establishment of the principalities of Outremer, and by the second half of the twelfth century the kingdom of

Sicily was one of the leading powers of the Mediterranean. As he worked on his chronicle, William was increasingly conscious of the growing threat to his homeland from the Muslim warlords Nūr al-Dīn and Saladin, and thus did not conceal his disappointment that Roger II and his successors had consistently refused to deploy their might in the defence of the Holy Land, in contrast to other princes of the West. In light of William's damning judgement, it is surprising that within his own lifetime the kingdom of Sicily is known to have launched several naval expeditions against Egypt, the economic hub of the Near East. Historians of Norman Sicily have largely assumed that these expeditions were sent in response to appeals for assistance from King Amalric of Jerusalem and were intended at first to coordinate with Amalric's attempts to seize control of Lower Egypt and later to take pressure off the increasingly beleaguered kingdom of Jerusalem by striking at the main source of Saladin's financial and military power.[3] One of these attacks (launched in 1174) is described in some detail by William himself, so there would appear to be a contradiction between his earlier comments about long-standing Sicilian hostility to the kingdom of Jerusalem and the idea of Frankish-Sicilian co-operation during his own lifetime. Over a century ago, Prutz attempted to resolve this inconsistency with the suggestion that William wrote his account of King Baldwin's repudiation of Adelaide before 1174.[4] Although William probably worked on the chronicle between 1170 and 1184, it is uncertain whether it was written in chronological order or whether he undertook revisions of earlier drafts. So, while Prutz's suggestion cannot be discounted, we should perhaps not take it as a hard and fast indication of the chronology of William's process of research and writing.[5] This chapter broadens the discussion by undertaking a more critical examination of the character of the Sicilian expeditions to Egypt in the geopolitical context of the changing balance of power between the kingdom of Jerusalem and its Muslim enemies.

The Franks who established the kingdom of Jerusalem were well aware of Egypt's wealth and strategic position. Indeed, Baldwin I died from an illness contracted during an expedition directed towards the Nile Delta, which was probably intended to reconnoitre possibilities for a more substantial future invasion. Yet it was not until his successor Baldwin III (1145–63) captured Ascalon, the last

Fatimid base in Palestine, that an offensive policy towards Egypt became feasible. The kingdom's southern frontier was stabilised by the construction of a castle at Gaza, which Baldwin III entrusted to the Templars, while his brother King Amalric (1163–74) built another stronghold at Darum further south. From this time the most southerly point held by the Franks on the Mediterranean coast was the little village of El 'Arish, from where the Nile Delta could be reached in about ten days' march.[6] Baldwin III was clearly planning an invasion at the time of his premature death, so it was left to Amalric to undertake the first serious attempts to profit from military interventions in Egypt.[7]

Until the Frankish capture of Ascalon in 1153, the main thrust of Sicilian expansion had been directed towards North Africa and the western Mediterranean, and, thanks to their powerful navy, under Roger II (1105–54) the Sicilians had secured control over an impressive string of coastal settlements stretching from Sousse in Tunisia as far as Tripoli (modern Tarābulus) in Libya.[8] Roger also directed campaigns against Byzantine territory in 1147–48, and his son and successor William I (1154–66) further developed an interest in the possibilities for aggrandisement in the eastern Mediterranean. The contemporary chronicler Abū Yaʻlā Ḥamza Ibn al-Qalānisī (d. 1160) relates that during the first month of Jumādā in AH 549 (18 March 1154 – 6 March 1155), that is sometime after 14 July, news reached Damascus that a substantial fleet from Sicily had sailed to the city of Tinnīs in Egypt and plundered it for three days before leaving laden with booty and slaves.[9] An expedition of this size directed against a target which had never previously figured in Sicilian war aims could only have been organised with the approval of King William I and his chief minister, Maio of Bari, but, since at this time Baldwin III was still consolidating his new acquisitions in south-western Palestine, it cannot have been intended to coordinate with any initiative from the kingdom of Jerusalem, although the Frankish victory at Ascalon may well have alerted William and his advisors to the increasing military weakness and political instability of the Fatimid state.

Tinnīs was the most remarkable port on the southern Mediterranean seaboard. It was situated on an island in an extensive lagoon (now known as Lake Manzala) separated from the open sea by a narrow spit of land some sixty kilometres long extending from Damietta in the west to al-Farama in the east, which protected it from storms. The port had access to the open sea from the lagoon via two channels which penetrated the spit, while it was also connected with a major branch of the Nile, which fed the lake. The entire island, whose maximum diameter was just over one kilometre from north-west to south-east, was entirely built up with workshops, houses, mosques, warehouses and other storage space; its population, numbering several thousand, was mostly engaged in trade and the manufacture of luxury textiles. The only other economic activity was fishing in the lagoon, the only plentiful local source of food. Since the island had no space for cultivation or pasturage, other foodstuffs had to be brought in by boat. Fresh water came with the annual inundation of the Nile, strong enough to force back the salt water of the lagoon. The island contained large cisterns which were filled with Nile water every year to supply the population for the large part of the year when the water became saline again.[10] In an age when transport by water was faster and provided greater capacity than any equivalent by land, Tinnīs had an enviable, well-connected location as a trading centre. It had a citadel, but it was not strongly fortified and, lacking a substantial garrison, could not resist a strong attack from the sea.

Contextualising the Sicilian attack on Tinnīs is complicated by shorter accounts from later sources. The chronicler 'Izz al-Dīn Ibn al-Athīr (1160–1233) tersely confirms that such an attack took place but assigns it to the previous year in the Islamic calendar, AH 548 (27 March 1153 – 17 March 1154). Ibn al-Athīr is credible since he is especially well informed on Roger II's campaigns in Africa, so it is tempting to assume that both accounts refer to the same event, especially if the preparations for the attack on Tinnīs had actually begun before the Islamic year recorded by Ibn al-Qalānisī.[11] A notice in the *Kitāb al-Mawā'iẓ wa al-'Itibār bi-Dhikr al-Khiṭaṭ wa al-Āthār* by the Mamlūk-era author Taqī al-Dīn Aḥmad b. 'Alī al-Maqrizī (1364–1442) states that in AH 550 (7 March 1155 – 24 February 1156) a fleet of sixty ships sent by the ruler of Sicily appeared at Damietta and then raided Tinnīs, Rosetta and Alexandria.[12] Stanton suggests that al-Maqrizī confused these events with one of the later Sicilian campaigns.[13] We cannot exclude this possibility, although another explanation can be advanced. In keeping with its character as a work of topography, the *Khiṭaṭ* was arranged geographically rather than chronologically, and in this case its information is recorded under a chapter dealing with Damietta, probably because this was where al-Maqrizī's information originated. But neither Damietta nor Tinnīs would be an obvious first target for a fleet with no experience of Egyptian waters. Sicilian ships aiming for Egypt would probably cross to Cape Bon and then use the prevailing currents to sail along the African coast and reach Egyptian territory at Alexandria. They would then need to proceed carefully, especially when passing the difficult currents at the Bughaz mouth of the Nile below Damietta.[14] It is doubtful whether the first Sicilian fleet to enter Egyptian waters would have the navigational knowledge to sail straight into the Tinnīs lagoon; rather, one can envisage the fleet making a gradual exploratory progress along the coast to test the defences of Alexandria, Damietta and Rosetta before deciding to commit its main effort to a strike at the relatively undefended port of Tinnīs. So it is possible that, like Ibn al-Athīr, al-Maqrizī's evidence was simply a year out in its reckoning and actually relates to the first Sicilian naval campaign to Egypt, stressing the route by which the fleet approached Tinnīs.

Whether there were one or more attacks on Tinnīs around 1154, these events seem to mark the beginning of a Sicilian interest in Egypt. However, any such ambitions were set back by a Byzantine invasion of Apulia in conjunction with rebellions by disaffected Norman nobles in 1155–56. The Byzantines were decisively beaten back, but another insurrection followed the murder of Maio of Bari by rivals in 1160. In the meantime revolts in Africa and attacks by the Almohads led to the loss of all the Norman monarchy's African possessions by the time of William I's death in 1166.[15] The regency government for the underage William II, which lasted until the king reached majority in 1171, lacked stability because of internal intrigues and was scarcely in a position to launch long-range campaigns abroad. Stanton has demolished the notion that Sicily contributed to the siege of Damietta carried out by the Franks of Jerusalem and their Byzantine allies in 1169.[16] It was Amalric of Jerusalem, who succeeded his brother in February 1163, who now took the initiative against Egypt and launched no fewer than five separate campaigns against the 'sick man on the Nile', as Yaacov Lev has characterised the increasingly feeble Fatimid regime.[17]

Amalric's campaigns have been described in detail by Schlumberger and Mayer, so it will suffice to outline their salient features as background to the renewed Sicilian interest in Egypt.[18] The first expedition, which set off in September 1163, was intended to secure financial and possibly territorial concessions from the Fatimids.[19] The Fatimid vizier, Dirgham, not only agreed to pay tribute but enlisted Amalric as an ally against a rival, Shāwar, who in turn appealed to Nūr al-Dīn, the Turkish ruler of Aleppo and Damascus. Thus the second campaign (1164) and the third (1167) ended up with Frankish forces and their Egyptian allies fighting troops from Syria commanded by Nūr al-Dīn's Kurdish general Asād al-Dīn Shīrkūh until the Syrians withdrew.[20] The Frankish experience of three years of fighting highlighted both the poor quality of the Fatimid armed forces and the danger that Nūr al-Dīn was becoming increasingly able to win control of the country. The policy Amalric pursued in his fourth (1168) and fifth (1169) campaigns was therefore designed to secure control of as much of Egypt as possible before the Fatimid regime succumbed to pressure from Nūr al-Dīn.

This aim would require substantial forces, especially the naval capacity to take on the Fatimid navy, markedly superior to its army, and to blockade fortified ports such as Damietta and Alexandria. At the siege of Ascalon Baldwin III had deployed a fleet of fifteen galleys commanded by Gerard, lord of Sidon, but the majority of the ships engaged were evidently provided by Western powers, so Amalric would similarly need to seek external support.[21] The kingdom of Sicily also had a powerful navy, but Amalric and his advisors preferred to secure such assistance by cultivating existing ties with Byzantium. Less than a month after he returned from Egypt to his kingdom, on 29 August 1167, Amalric married Maria Komnene, a niece of Emperor Manuel I Komnenos. This was the culmination of two years of negotiations and followed the example of Baldwin III, who had also married a Byzantine princess.[22] Mayer has highlighted the singular circumstance that, against all precedent, Maria was crowned queen before the marriage took place, and at Tyre, her port of arrival. These dispositions were undoubtedly at the insistence of the Byzantines. On his accession, hostility among his barons had forced Amalric to divorce his first wife, Agnes of Courtenay, although his two children by her, Sibylla and Baldwin

(IV), were recognised as legitimate. The Byzantine insistence that Maria be crowned before marrying Amalric derived from anxiety about her future position and indicates that the relationship between the empire and kingdom had not quite reached an optimal state.[23] Once Maria's status was secure, however, diplomatic activities between the two powers intensified. In summer 1168 a Byzantine embassy led by Alexander, count of Gravina, and Michael of Otranto brought a first approach concerning a joint invasion of Egypt. In October William of Tyre, as the kingdom's chancellor, was sent to Constantinople to continue negotiations.[24]

It was not unusual to find two Latin Christians leading a Byzantine legation; numerous Westerners were in imperial service, and it made sense to use French speakers in negotiations with the Franks of Jerusalem. However, it is significant that, as their names suggest, both of them originated in the kingdom of Sicily. Alexander had been count of Conversano, one of only four comital dynasties at the time of the kingdom's creation, which held extensive lands at Conversano, Matera, Gravina and elsewhere in southern Apulia. Alexander and his brother Tancred had belonged to a baronial alliance opposing Roger II during the 1120s and were in rebellion again in 1132. On the latter occasion Roger captured Tancred and Alexander's son Geoffrey, but Alexander fled to Dalmatia and later joined imperial Byzantine service. Since the county of Conversano was given to one of Roger's close supporters, Robert of Bassunvilla, the former count seems to have been known as 'Alexander of Gravina' from this time.[25] In 1156 he went to Apulia with the invading Byzantine army, only to be captured then released. He returned once more to Constantinople. Alexander must have been advanced in age by 1168, but as a long-standing and implacable enemy of the Hauteville monarchy it is unlikely that he would have been employed to lead the embassy if King Amalric had been keen to construct a Christian alliance with both Byzantium and Sicily; indeed, he would be an ideal candidate to persuade Amalric to avoid entering into any agreements with the Sicilians.

The timing and duration of these diplomatic contacts meant that the Byzantines were unable to take part in Amalric's fourth campaign, which began in October 1168.[26] The ambitious nature of this undertaking can be seen in agreements contracted by the Order of the Hospital to provide troops, in which the formulations of the royal chancery clearly envisaged the ultimate conquest of the entire country.[27] The absence of Byzantine naval assistance may have contributed to the failure of the campaign, which Amalric abandoned in January 1169. However, that summer a fleet of 150 ships plus sixty horse transports sailed to Palestine under the commander Alexios Kontostephanos, accompanied by Alexander of Gravina and Theodore Maurozoumes, to join Amalric's fifth campaign, which commenced in August 1169. This huge force was necessary because in January Shīrkūh had seized control of Cairo and appointed himself vizier to the powerless Fatimid caliph al-'Aḍīd, effectively becoming the state's chief executive. When Shīrkūh died two months later he was succeeded by his nephew Saladin, who dismantled the Fatimid regime and made himself the real ruler of Egypt, in defiance of the expectations of his nominal master Nūr al-Dīn. The joint Frankish-Byzantine forces blockaded Damietta on the eastern Delta but abandoned the siege in October, and most of the Byzantine fleet was wrecked by storms during its return voyage. Although Chalandon argues that the Sicilians must have responded to Amalric's appeals for military assistance, the evidence of the participation of Pisan ships and soldiers as described by the *Annales Pisani* indicates that the allies had managed to secure additional naval support without having to come to terms with the king of Sicily.[28] And again, while the presence of Alexander of Gravina with the Byzantine fleet indicates a desire to liaise closely with the Franks of Jerusalem, a man with his history would have been a less obvious choice for an enterprise involving co-operation with Sicilian forces. The lack of success and the losses of men and equipment must have meant that both Manuel and Amalric were unable or unwilling to launch another campaign too soon, especially since Saladin now began to take the offensive against Frankish Palestine with attacks on Darum and Gaza.[29] However, the allies' determination to hold to their grand strategic objectives is evident in the fact that in March 1171 Amalric travelled to Constantinople to negotiate another treaty with Manuel and remained there until May. Amalric's stay had many features of a state visit, with the king being shown the sights and wonders of the Byzantine capital, but it also involved discussions that went on for weeks often involving only the two monarchs and presumably their interpreters.[30]

The projected second Jerusalemite-Byzantine attack on Egypt never materialised. On his return to Palestine, Amalric was obliged to lead the kingdom's host to confront Nūr al-Dīn's army positioned near Banyas, a city north-east of the Sea of Galilee. Banyas had been held by the Franks until October 1168, when Nūr al-Dīn's forces seized it while Amalric was in Egypt. It was an important staging post on the road from Damascus to Galilee and could serve as a springboard for the most obvious invasion route into the kingdom; Banyas would continue to figure in Amalric's strategy, since if he were able to recover the city it would greatly hinder any invasion from Damascus.[31] After seeing off the threat, Amalric led a force north to aid the principality of Antioch against a renegade Armenian prince named Mleh, who had allied himself with Nūr al-Dīn and invaded the Christian kingdom of Cilicia, but the king was then forced to return south on receiving news that Nūr al-Dīn himself had moved against Kerak, one of the main Frankish fortresses in Transjordan. Indeed, throughout 1172 and 1173 the kingdom of Jerusalem was on the defensive against attacks by Nūr al-Dīn from Damascus and Saladin from Egypt. This was no propitious time for another joint Christian invasion of Egypt.

Yet it is a naval expedition launched from the kingdom of Sicily that Chalandon and Stanton have advanced as the most tangible evidence for joint Sicilian-Jerusalemite co-operation against Egypt.[32] There is no doubt that a fleet was sent from Sicily to Alexandria in 1174; the question is whether it was part of an operation coordinated with the leadership of the kingdom of Jerusalem. Ibn al-Athīr claims that former Fatimid officials made approaches to both Amalric and King William II of Sicily, who had meanwhile reached his majority, and invited them to invade Egypt, as Stanton expresses it, 'in order to draw Saladin out of Cairo so that they could foment a popular uprising that would sweep the Ayyubids [...] from power'.[33] In his history of the Ayyūbid and Mamlūk sultans, *al-Sulūk li-Maʿrifat Duwal al-Mulūk*, al-Maqrizī dates the conspiracy to AH 569 (12 August 1173 – 1 August 1174). The named conspirators were evidently mostly administrators, jurists, *qāḍis* (magistrates) and missionaries belonging to the state-supported but minority Ismaʿīlī sect.[34] One might accept that officials who had lost power and status found ways of communicating with both Christian monarchies, but the notion of a popular uprising against Saladin is much less credible. In August 1169 Saladin had bloodily suppressed an uprising by Sudanese and Armenian units of the Fatimid army and then dismantled the structures of the Ismaʿīlī state and religion; on the caliph's death in 1171, he restored mosques and madrasas to Sunnī worship.[35] These acts were highly popular with the majority Sunnī population, which was unlikely to have supported any move to restore the rule of an Ismaʿīlī dynasty. By 1174 Saladin had largely dissolved the Fatimid army, relying instead on his own regiments of Turkish and Kurdish mamlūks. In the event the conspiracy was betrayed and the ringleaders and many potential supporters were arrested and either imprisoned or executed. One can accept that the Fatimid plotters communicated with the governments of Sicily and Jerusalem in the hope of encouraging attacks, but this is a long way from a coordinated campaign. Since the plot was completely defeated by the month of Ramaḍān AH 569 (i.e. spring 1174) it must have been clear to any invading force departing in the summer that it could not count on any uprising in its favour.

By this time Amalric was increasingly hard-pressed by Saladin. In 1172 the sultan besieged the fortress of Montréal in Transjordan without success but returned to ravage the same region the following year and did great destruction to settlements, crops and vines.[36] Saladin had demonstrated his ability to enter the kingdom both along the coast and through the regions south and east of the Dead Sea and do considerable economic damage. In fact, we can identify Amalric's priorities at the point that he received news of Nūr al-Dīn's unexpected death in May 1174. He assembled the 'entire strength of the kingdom and besieged the city of Banyas', but after two weeks' fruitless siege he accepted an indemnity from the Turks and withdrew. On his return journey he fell ill with dysentery and died at Jerusalem on 11 July.[37] Chalandon argues that only the king's death prevented a joint campaign with William II, yet the events of the preceding two years make it unlikely that Amalric would have sent a large proportion of his manpower to march against Egypt while leaving the kingdom open to attack from Damascus.

Let us look at the detail of the campaign. Bahāʾ al-Dīn Ibn Shaddād (1145–1234), who spent considerable time in the service of Saladin and his family, attributes the attack on Alexandria only to 'the Franks', but indicates that it was opportunistic, because of the disruption caused by regime change in Egypt. He places the beginning of the siege at 7 September 1174 and gives hugely inflated figures of 600 ships and 30,000 men. He stresses the importance of siege equipment carried by the fleet, and states that the invaders abandoned the siege after three days of assaults when they learned that Saladin was moving troops against them.[38] Surprisingly, the most detailed description is given by al-Maqrīzī, writing much later, who implies that the attack was carefully prepared on the initiative of William II after he took control of the government. He too offers inflated numbers for troops, but gives more plausible figures for the shipping: 200 galleys, forty troop transports, thirty-six horse transports and six ships carrying siege machinery.[39] By contrast, the Western sources agree that the Sicilian fleet arrived in August; in either case it must have left before Amalric's death and the succession of his underage son Baldwin IV. Yet William of Tyre gives no indication that any Jerusalemite participation had been planned:

> During the first year of this king's reign, about the beginning of August, King William of Sicily sent a fleet of two hundred ships to attack Alexandria. With a splendid force of both cavalry and infantry, it sailed down to Egypt. During the stay of five or six days made before that city, though through the lack of caution displayed by the governors and leaders, both the infantry and cavalry forces sustained great losses by death and capture and were finally obliged to retire in confusion.[40]

Arabic and Western sources alike agree that the Sicilians' objective was Alexandria, which is problematic for the argument that it was intended as a joint operation with the kingdom of Jerusalem.[41] In theory a two-pronged attack could have been directed against separate goals, but this would have been risky for a Jerusalemite army lacking naval support. An attack by the Franks of Jerusalem on any major port would also have been difficult – if not impossible – without ships to fend off the Egyptian navy, to transport heavy siege equipment and supplies and to mount a blockade. So, for a joint operation to have the best chance of success, both forces would have to operate against a common goal, but in this respect the choice of Alexandria raises problems. It was the closest Egyptian city for any fleet sailing from Sicily, and had an excellent harbour. However, an army proceeding by land from Ascalon would face a march of some 450 kilometres to reach Alexandria. Amalric had done this in 1167, but on that occasion he had been able to count on local allies, who were able to boost his numbers and provide logistic support.

The *Annales Pisani* agree with William of Tyre on the total number of ships but makes the important distinction that 150 of these were galleys and fifty were horse transports (*dermonum pro equis portandis*). The horse transport was a new form of naval vessel fully developed only by the second half of the twelfth century. Horses do not take to being transported by sea over long distances. They had to be kept standing and secured by slings to prevent them being thrown around and suffering injuries which would render them useless. Even landing horses could be problematic, so transport ships often had ports which enabled horses to be led ashore rather than being lifted out by winch. Such vessels had to be either constructed or adapted from other ship types and thus were relatively expensive; the number of horses that could be accommodated in any given ship was also much smaller than the number of men that could be carried in the same space.[42] Why would horse transports make up a quarter of the entire Sicilian fleet? Mounted knights could not be employed in any direct assault on Alexandria: their main role in a siege would be to fend off attacks by Saladin's cavalry, although they would become more important if the siege were successful and the Sicilian force could move on to other targets. However, if the attack had been planned as a joint operation, one might assume that the kingdom of Jerusalem would provide sufficient cavalry in the form of knights and lightly armed turcopoles, since horses would be their main means of transport to Egypt. If this were the case, one wonders why the Sicilians devoted so much capacity to transporting horses, rather than carrying as much siege equipment as possible, essential to take Alexandria. The obvious answer is that they did not expect material assistance from the kingdom of Jerusalem. This would explain why the size of the Sicilian fleet was roughly equal to or greater than the Byzantine navy that Manuel Komnenos sent to Damietta in 1169.

The campaign of 1174 was disastrous in terms of Sicilian losses; Alexandria was clearly too tough a nut to crack. Yet the interest of William II and his advisors in Egypt remained undiminished.

According to al-Maqrizī's description of Tinnīs, in AH 571 (22 July 1175 – 9 July 1176), forty vessels from Sicily arrived with a force which occupied the town for two days before withdrawing.[43] It is likely that the Sicilians were able to use captains and pilots who had been involved in the first voyage to Tinnīs in 1154. Then in AH 573 (30 June 1177 – 18 June 1178) another Sicilian force of the same size appeared and seized the town. The admiral Muḥammad b. Isḥāq and some of his troops took refuge in a mosque and during the night emerged and killed 120 of the Sicilians who were off their guard. In the morning the Westerners assaulted the mosque and killed seventy Muslims, which seems to have ended the Egyptian resistance. The Sicilians plundered the city for four days, then sailed towards Alexandria with booty and captives.[44] These attacks were clearly carried out on the initiative of the Sicilians alone. After Nūr al-Dīn's death, Saladin led an army from Egypt to Syria (without opposition from the Franks of Jerusalem) and seized control of Damascus. Nūr al-Dīn's officers accepted Saladin's authority, and he established control over Aleppo and most of Muslim Syria. Thus, from 1174, Saladin was able to carry out attacks against the kingdom of Jerusalem from three directions: along the northern coast of Sinai, from the desert into Transjordan and from Damascus into Galilee. The Franks remained largely in a defensive state until the sultan's great victory at the Horns of Hattin in July 1187. It is no surprise that the kingdom of Jerusalem had neither the capacity nor the enthusiasm for further large-scale invasions by land, but a mobile naval force might have better prospects, as in the case of a flotilla sent against Tinnīs by the Franks of Ascalon in AH 576 (28 May 1180 – 16 May 1181), which was repulsed by the island's governor. The island's fortifications were improved the following year, but in AH 588 (18 January 1192 – 6 January 1193) its population was evacuated, probably because, after Richard the Lionheart refortified Ascalon, there was a prospect that the armies of the Third Crusade might strike out against Egypt.[45]

After 1174 any Sicilian assistance would have been welcome in Outremer, but William II's designs were still set on aggrandisement in Byzantine territory in the hope of exploiting instability following the death of Emperor Manuel I in 1180. In June 1185 a Sicilian army crossed the Adriatic and captured Dyrrachium (modern Durrës) and met the fleet at Thessalonica, which was besieged and sacked; the Sicilian aim was evidently to proceed to Constantinople itself, but in the face of more organised Byzantine resistance the combined forces abandoned their conquests.[46] Tellingly, the Old French continuation of the chronicle of William of Tyre reveals that, while planning his attack on Byzantium, William II 'sent to the land of Outremer and all the lands nearby and recruited knights and sergeants and gave them pay in accordance with each man's status'.[47] Thus the Sicilian invasion of 1185 not only struck at Jerusalem's increasingly debilitated ally but syphoned off existing military resources from the Holy Land.

The foregoing discussion presents a broad-brush overview rather than a comprehensive study, which would require more thorough investigation of the Arabic texts, yet it suggests that, in their designs on Egypt, the kingdoms of Sicily and Jerusalem were rivals, not allies. The initial Sicilian interest in Egypt in 1154 came about on the initiative of William I and his advisors, possibly pursuing an extension of Roger II's policy of acquisition of territory in Tunisia and Libya. As the kingdom of Jerusalem came under increasing pressure from Nūr al-Dīn and his general Saladin, its leadership sent all manner of appeals for aid to the Christian powers of the West, but Byzantium was Amalric's preferred ally in his Egyptian ambitions, whereas Sicilian hostility to the empire had continued unabated since Manuel Komnenos's invasion of Apulia with the support of rebellious Norman barons in 1155–56. After coming of age, William II of Sicily was no doubt keen to make his mark as a ruler with an impressive foreign adventure, but he was unwilling to share the spoils with King Amalric. The Sicilian attack on Alexandria in 1174 can best be understood as an opportunistic attempt to derive economic gain from Egypt before Saladin became too powerful. Similarly, the attacks on Tinnīs in the following years were not coordinated with the Franks of Jerusalem but were probably designed to hit home while Saladin and his forces were occupied in Syria and Palestine. It was not until after Saladin had overrun the kingdom of Jerusalem that William II deigned to send a fleet to aid the few remaining beleaguered Frankish garrisons. William of Tyre's long-term assessment of Sicilian policies towards the Holy Land was both accurate and shrewd.

Notes

1 *Willelmi Tyrensis Archiepiscopi Chronicon*, ed. R. B. C. Huygens, Corpus Christianorum Continuatio Mediaevalis 63–63A (Turnhout, 1986) (henceforth: WT), 11.29, p. 542: 'filius et apud se odium concepit adversus regnum et eius habitatores inmortale. Nam cum reliqui fideles diversi orbis principes aut in propriis personis aut inmensis liberalitatibus regnum nostrum quasi plantam recentem promovere et ampliare sategerint, hic et eius heredes usque in presentem diem nec etiam verbo amico nos sibi conciliaverunt, cum tamen quovis alio principe longe commodius faciliusque nostris necessitatibus consilia possent et auxilia ministrare. Videntur ergo iniurie perpetuo memores et delictum persone iniuste in populum refundunt universum.' Trans. *A History of Deeds Done beyond the Sea by William Archbishop of Tyre*, trans. E. A. Babcock and A. C. Krey, 2 vols (New York, 1943), vol. 1, p. 514. Citations to William's chronicle in this chapter give references to book and chapter as well as to pages in order to facilitate comparison between the Latin edition and the English translation without multiplying references unnecessarily.

2 On Baldwin I's marriage, see H. E. Mayer, *Mélanges sur l'histoire du royaume latin de Jérusalem*, Mémoires de l'Académie des Inscriptions et Belles-Lettres, n.s. 5 (Paris, 1984), pp. 49–72; G. A. Loud, 'Norman Italy and the Holy Land', in B. Z. Kedar (ed.), *The Horns of Hattin* (Jerusalem, 1992), pp. 49–62; A. V. Murray, 'Norman settlement in the Latin kingdom of Jerusalem, 1099–1131', *Archivio Normanno-Svevo* 1 (2009), 61–85.

3 F. Chalandon, *Histoire de la domination normande en Italie et en Sicile*, 2 vols (Paris, 1907), vol. 2, pp. 392–8; H. Wieruszowski, 'The Norman kingdom of Sicily and the crusades', in K. M. Setton et al. (eds), *A History of the Crusades*, 2nd edn, 6 vols (Madison, 1969–89), vol. 2, pp. 3–42; C. D. Stanton, *Norman Naval Operations in the Mediterranean* (Woodbridge, 2011), pp. 146–52.

4 H. Prutz, 'Studien über Wilhelm von Tyrus', *Neues Archiv der Gesellschaft für ältere deutsche Geschichtskunde* 8 (1883), 91–132.

5 P. W. Edbury and J. G. Rowe, *William of Tyre: Historian of the Latin East* (Cambridge, 1988), pp. 23–8.

6 A. V. Murray, 'The place of Egypt in the military strategy of the crusades, 1099–1221', in E. J. Mylod et al. (eds), *The Fifth Crusade in Context: The Crusading Movement in the Early Thirteenth Century* (Abingdon, 2016), pp. 117–34.

7 H. E. Mayer, 'Ein Deperditum Balduins III. von Jerusalem als Zeugnis seiner Pläne zur Eroberung Ägyptens', *Deutsches Archiv für Erforschung des Mittelalters* 36 (1980), 549–66.

8 D. Abulafia, 'The Norman kingdom of Africa and the Norman expeditions to Majorca and the Muslim Mediterranean', *ANS* 7 (1985), 26–49.
9 *The Damascus Chronicle of the Crusades Extracted and Translated from the Chronicle of Ibn al-Qalānisī*, trans. H. A. R. Gibb (London, 1932), pp. 321–2. In the following discussion Islamic dates and their Western equivalents are given according to the tables in J. L. Bacharach, *A Middle East Studies Handbook* (Cambridge, 1984), pp. 8–15, which reflects current practice among historians. Note that Chalandon gives Islamic years according to a different system, e.g. AH 571 (Bachrach) = AH 561 (Chalandon) = AD 1175–76.
10 J. P. Cooper, *The Medieval Nile: Route, Navigation, and Navigation and Landscape in Islamic Egypt* (Cairo, 2014), pp. 214–20.
11 *The Chronicle of Ibn al-Athīr for the Crusading Period from al-Kāmil fī'l-ta'rīkh, Part 2: The Years 541–589/1146–1193: The Age of Nur al-Dīn and Saladin*, trans. D. S. Richards (Aldershot, 2007), p. 65.
12 U. Bouriant, *Description topographique et historique de l'Égypte*, 2 vols [cont. pag.] (Paris, 1895–1900), p. 635; N. Rabbat, 'Who was al-Maqrizī? A biographical sketch', *Mamluk Studies Review* 7 (2003), 1–19.
13 Stanton, *Norman Naval Operations*, pp. 128–9.
14 J. P. Cooper, '"Fear God, Fear the Bogaze": The Nile mouths and the navigational landscape of the Nile delta, Egypt', *Al-Masāq: Islam and the Medieval Mediterranean* 24 (2012), 53–73.
15 G. A. Loud, 'William the Bad or William the Unlucky? Kingship in Sicily, 1154–1166', *Haskins Society Journal* 8 (1999), 99–113.
16 Stanton, *Norman Naval Operations*, pp. 145–6.
17 Y. Lev, *Saladin in Egypt* (Leiden, 1999), p. 153.
18 G. Schlumberger, *Campagnes du roi Amaury Ier en Égypte, en XIIe siècle* (Paris, 1906); Mayer, *Mélanges sur l'histoire*, pp. 140–58.
19 WT, 19.5, pp. 870–2.
20 WT, 19.7, pp. 872–83; 19.13–19, pp. 882–9; 19.25–32, pp. 898–909.
21 WT, 17.23–5, pp. 792–5.
22 WT, 20.1, p. 913.
23 H. E. Mayer, 'The beginnings of King Amalric of Jerusalem', in Kedar (ed.), *The Horns of Hattin*, pp. 121–35; H. E. Mayer, *Geschichte der Kreuzzüge*, 10th edn (Stuttgart, 2005), p. 149–50.
24 WT 20.4, pp. 915–16.
25 H. Fernández Aceves, 'County and nobility in Norman Italy (1130–1189)' (PhD dissertation, University of Leeds, 2017), pp. 20, 45, 111–12, 140–1.
26 WT, 20.5–9, pp. 917–23.

27 A. V. Murray, 'The grand designs of Gilbert of Assailly: The Order of the Hospital in the projected conquest of Egypt by King Amalric of Jerusalem (1168–1169)', *Ordines Militares: Yearbook for the Study of the Military Orders* 20 (2016), 7–24.
28 WT, 20.14–16, pp. 927–33; *Gli Annales Pisani di Bernardo Maragone*, ed. M. L. Gentile, RIS 6, 2 (Bologna, 1930–36), p. 47.
29 WT, 20.19–21, pp. 936–9
30 WT, 20.22–24, pp. 941–6; S. Runciman, 'The visit of King Amalric I to Constantinople in 1171', in B. Z. Kedar, H. E. Mayer and R. C. Smail (eds), *Outremer: Studies in the History of the Crusading Kingdom of Jerusalem* (Jerusalem, 1982), pp. 153–8.
31 WT, 20.25, pp. 946–8; A. Graboïs, 'La cité de Banyas et le château de Subeibeh pendant les croisades', *Cahiers de civilisation médiévale* 13 (1970), 43–62.
32 Chalandon, *Histoire de la domination normande*, vol. 2, pp. 395–6; Stanton, *Norman Naval Operations*, pp. 146–8.
33 Stanton, *Norman Naval Operations*, pp. 146–7.
34 *A History of the Ayyubid Sultans of Egypt Translated from the Arabic of al-Maqrīzī*, trans. R. J. C. Broadhurst (Boston, 1980), p. 47.
35 'A. R. 'Azzām, *Saladin* (Harlow, 2009), pp. 82–97.
36 WT, 20.27–8, pp. 950–2.
37 WT, 20.31, pp. 956–7.
38 *The Rare and Excellent History of Saladin, or al-Nawādir al-Sulṭāniyya wa'l-Maḥāsin al-Yūsfiyya by Bahā' al-Dīn Ibn Shaddād*, trans. D. S. Richards (Aldershot, 2002), p. 50.
39 *A History of the Ayyubid Sultans of Egypt*, pp. 48–9. One obvious inconsistency is the statement that a thousand horsemen were carried in the dromonds (*tarā'id*), but that 2,500 horsemen landed from them!
40 WT, 21.3, p. 963: 'Huius domini Balduini anno primo circa Augusti initium ducentarum navium classis, a domino Willemo Siculorum rege ad impugnandam Alexandriam missa, honestas tam equitum quam peditum copias deferens descendit in Egyptum. Ubi dum eius procuratores et primicerii incautius se habent, amissis ex utroque ordine quamplurius tam captivitatis quam peremptis gladio, post moram quinque aut sex dierum, quam circa urbem fecerant, confusi recesserunt.'
41 *Annales Pisani*, p. 61: 'Rex Guilielmus Sicilie misit exercitum magnum in Egiptum super Alexandriam, in principio Iulii, qui exercitus fuit CL galearum et L dermonum pro equis portandis, ubi fuerunt milites mille, et multi sagitarii et multi balisterii et multa edificia; qui cum applicuerunt ad portem Alexandrie in eodem portu invenerunt unam navem Pisanorum venientem de Venetia, quam pren[diderunt]' (but

dated to 1175). The *Annales Casinenses*, ed. G. Pertz, MGH SS 19 (Hanover, 1866), p. 312, gives only the laconic statement: 'Mense Augusti stolium regis ivit Alexandriam.'
42 J. H. Pryor, 'Transportation of horses by sea during the era of the crusades: Eighth century to 1285 A.D.', *Mariner's Mirror* 68 (1982), 9–27 and 103–25; J. H. Pryor, 'The naval architecture of crusader transport ships and horse transports revisited', *Mariner's Mirror* 76 (1990), 255–74; J. H. Pryor, 'A medieval Mediterranean maritime revolution: Crusading by sea, ca. 1096–1204', in D. N. Carlson, J. Leidwanger and S. M. Kampbell (eds), *Maritime Studies in the Wake of the Byzantine Shipwreck at Yassıada, Turkey* (College Station, 2015), pp. 174–88.
43 Bouriant, *Description topographique et historique de l'Égypte*, p. 516.
44 Bouriant, *Description topographique et historique de l'Égypte*, pp. 516–17.
45 Bouriant, *Description topographique et historique de l'Égypte*, p. 517. The realisation of what might be achieved by a small naval force may even have influenced the initiative of Reynald of Châtillon, lord of Transjordan, who in the winter of 1182–83 had a number of ships dismantled on the coast of Palestine, transported over the Sinai peninsula and reassembled in the Red Sea, where they preyed on Muslim commercial and pilgrim traffic until Saladin's brother al-'Ādil sent part of the Egyptian fleet from the Mediterranean to hunt them down. See W. Facey, 'Crusaders in the Red Sea: Renaud de Châtillon's raids of AD 1182–3', in J. C. M. Starkey (ed.), *People of the Red Sea: Proceedings of the Red Sea Project II* (Oxford, 2005), pp. 87–98.
46 Stanton, *Norman Naval Operations*, pp. 152–6.
47 *The Conquest of Jerusalem and the Third Crusade: Sources in Translation*, trans. P. W. Edbury (Aldershot, 1998), pp. 73–4. The text adds that William 'also detained pilgrims who were intending to sail from his kingdom's ports to the Holy Land'. The most likely explanation for this is that the king was requisitioning all available naval transport for his expedition; it is less likely that he hoped to enlist the pilgrims in it.

Bibliography

Unpublished archival sources

Benevento, Museo del Sannio, Fondo S. Sofia, XII, 16, 40, XXXIV, 1, 3, 4.
Frascati, Archivio Aldobrandini, Pergamene, I, 36.
Montecassino, Archive of Montecassino, aula III, ch. VI, 6.
Naples, Biblioteca Nazionale, XII.A.A. 1, 1.
Paris, Bibliothèque nationale de France, MS Lat. 11055, 11056.
Palermo, Archivio di Stato di Palermo, Fondo Miscellanea Archivistica Serie II, n. 5.

Published primary sources

'Abd al-Malik Ibn Hishām, *al-Sīra al-nabawīya*, ed. M. al-Saqqā, 2 vols (Cairo, 1955).
Acta passionis, et translationis sanctorum martyrum Mercurii, ac XII Fratrum, ed. V. Giovardi (Rome, 1730).
[*Les*] *Actes grecs de S. Maria di Messina*, ed. A. Guillou (Palermo, 1963).
[*Les*] *Actes latins de S. Maria di Messina (1103–1250)*, ed. L.-R. Ménager (Palermo, 1963).
Ahmed ibn Mohammed al-Makkari, *The History of the Mohammedan Dynasties in Spain*, trans. P. de Gayangos, 2 vols (New York, 1964).
Alexandri Telesini abbatis Ystoria Rogerii regis Sicilie, Calabrie atque Apulie, ed. L. de Nava, commentary by D. R. Clementi, FSI 112 (Rome, 1991).
Amatus of Montecassino, *Ystoire de li Normant. Édition du manuscript BnFfr. 688*, ed. M. Guéret-Laferté (Paris, 2011).
Annales Barenses, ed. G. Pertz, MGH SS 5 (Hanover, 1844).
Annales Casinenses, ed. G. Pertz, MGH SS 19 (Hanover, 1866).
Annales ordinis S. Benedicti occidentalium monachorum patriarchae, ed. J. Mabillon, 6 vols (Paris, 1703–39).

[*Gli*] *Annales Pisani di Bernardo Maragone*, ed. M. L. Gentile, RIS 6, 2 (Bologna, 1930–6).
Anonymi Barensis Chronicon, ed. L. Muratori, RIS 5 (Milan, 1726).
Antiqui chronologi quattuor, ed. A. Caracciolo (Naples, 1626).
Augustine, *De bono coniugali; de sancta virginitate*, ed. and trans. P. G. Walsh (Oxford, 2001).
Bonizonis episcopi Sutrini Liber ad amicum, ed. E. Dümmler, MGH Libelli de lite 1 (Hanover, 1941).
Borsari, S., 'Vita di San Giovanni Terista', *Archivio Storico per la Calabria et la Lucania* 22 (1953), 13–21, 136–51.
[*Die*] *Briefe des Petrus Damiani*, ed. K. Reindel, 4 vols, MGH Die Briefe der deutschen Kaiserzeit (Munich, 1983–93).
Brunonis episcopi Signini Libellus de symoniacis, ed. E. Sackur, MGH Libelli de lite 2 (Hanover, 1892).
Catalogus Baronum, ed. E. Jamison, FSI 101 (Rome, 1972).
'Chartes originales antérieures à 1121 conservées en France' (TELMA): www.cn-telma.fr//originaux/index/
Chronica magistri Rogeri de Houedene, ed. W. Stubbs, Rolls Series 51, 3 vols (London, 1868).
Chronica monasterii Casinensis, ed. H. Hoffmann, MGH SS 34 (Hanover, 1980).
[*The*] *Chronicle of Arnold of Lubeck*, trans. G. A. Loud (Abingdon, 2019).
[*The*] *Chronicle of Ibn al-Athīr for the Crusading Period from al-Kāmil fi'l-ta'rīkh, Part 2: The Years 541–589/1146–1193: The Age of Nur al-Dīn and Saladin*, trans. D. S. Richards (Aldershot, 2007).
Chronicle of the Third Crusade: A Translation of the Itinerarium Peregrinorum et gesta regis Ricardi, trans. H. J. Nicholson (Aldershot, 1997).
[*The*] *Chronicle of Richard of Devizes at the Time of King Richard the First*, ed. and trans. J. T. Appleby (London, 1963).
Chronicon Sanctae Sophiae (cod. Vat. Lat. 4939), ed. J.-M. Martin, with a study by G. Orofino, 2 vols, Fonti per la Storia dell'Italia Medievale, RIS 3 (Rome, 2000).
Chronicon Vulturnense del monaco Giovanni, ed. V. Federici, 3 vols, FSI 58–60 (Rome, 1925–38).
Clementi, D., 'Calendar of the diplomas of the Emperor Henry VI concerning the Kingdom of Sicily', *QF* 35 (1955), 86–225.
Codice diplomatico Barese, vol. 1, ed. G. B. Nitto de Rossi and F. Nitti di Vito (Bari, 1897).
Codice diplomatico longobardo, IV-2: I diplomi dei duchi di Benevento, ed. H. Zielinski, FSI 65 (Rome, 2003).
Codice diplomatico verginiano, ed. P. M. Tropeano, 13 vols (Montevergine, 1977–2000).

Collection des cartulaires de France: Cartulaire de l'abbaye de Saint-Père de Chartres, ed. M. Guérard, 2 vols (Paris, 1840).

[The] *Conquest of Jerusalem and the Third Crusade: Sources in Translation*, trans. P. W. Edbury (Aldershot, 1998).

Constitutiones regni Siciliae: ristampa anastatica dell'edizione di Napoli del 1786, ed. G. Carcani (Messina, 1992).

Corpus iuris canonici, ed. A. Friedberg, 2 vols (Leipzig, 1879–81).

Cronisti e scrittori sincroni napoletani I, ed. G. del Re (Naples, 1845).

[The] *Crusade of Frederick Barbarossa: The History of the Expedition of the Emperor Frederick and Related Texts*, trans. G. A. Loud (Abingdon, 2010).

Cuozzo, E. and Martin, J.-M., 'Documents inédits ou peu connus des archives du Mont-Cassin (VIIIe-Xe siècles)', *Mélanges de l'École française de Rome. Moyen Âge* 103 (1991), 115–210.

[The] *Damascus Chronicle of the Crusades Extracted and Translated from the Chronicle of Ibn al-Qalānisī*, trans. H. A. R. Gibb (London, 1932).

De rebus gestis Rogerii Calabriae et Siciliae comitis et Roberti Guiscardi ducis fratris eius auctore Gaufredo Malaterra, ed. E. Pontieri, RIS 2nd ser. 5:1 (Bologna, 1925–28).

[The] *Deeds of Count Roger of Calabria and Sicily and of his Brother Robert Guiscard by Geoffrey Malaterra*, trans. K. B. Wolf (Ann Arbor, 2005).

Dialogi de miraculis sancti Benedicti auctore Desiderio abbate Casinensi, ed. G. Schwartz and A. Hofmeister, MGH SS 30, 2 (Leipzig, 1934).

[I] diplomi greci ed arabi di Sicilia pubblicati nel testo originale, tradotti ed illustrate, ed. S. Cusa (Palermo, 1868–82, repr. Cologne–Vienna, 1983).

Documenti inediti dell'epoca normanni in Sicilia, ed. C.-A. Garufi (Palermo, 1899).

[The] *Ecclesiastical History of Orderic Vitalis*, ed. and trans. M. Chibnall, 6 vols (Oxford, 1969–80).

Epistolae pontificum Romanorum ineditae, ed. S. Loewenfeld (Leipzig, 1885).

Erchempert, *Historia Langobardorum Beneventanorum*, ed. G. H. Pertz and G. Waitz, MGH SS rerum Langobardicarum et Italicarum saec. VI-IX 1 (Hanover, 1878).

Falco of Benevento, *Chronicon Beneventanum*, ed. E. D'Angelo (Florence, 1998).

Filagato da Cerami, *Omelie per i vangeli domenicali e le feste di tutto l' anno*, vol. I: *Omelie per le feste fisse*, ed. G. R. Taibbi (Palermo, 1969).

Gautier Dalché, P. (ed.), *Du Yorkshire a l'Inde. Une'geographie urbaine et maritime de la fin du XII siècle (Roger de Howden)* (Geneva, 2005).

Geoffrey Malaterra, *Histoire du Grand Comte Roger et de son frère Robert Guiscard, Vol. 1: Livres I & II*, ed. M.-A. Lucas-Avenel (Caen, 2016).

[*The*] *Gesta Normannorum Ducum of William of Jumièges, Orderic Vitalis, and Robert of Torigni*, ed. and trans. E. M. C. van Houts, 2 vols (Oxford, 1992–95).

Gesta Philippi Augusti Rigordi Liber/Histoire de Philippe Auguste, ed. and trans. E. Carpentier, G. Pons and Y. Chauvin (Paris, 2006).

Gesta regis Henrici secundi et gesta regis Ricardi, ed. W. Stubbs, Rolls Series 49, 2 vols (London, 1867).

Girgensohn, D., 'Documenti beneventani inediti del secolo xii', *Samnium* 40 (1967), 262–317.

[*The*] *Great Roll of the Pipe for the Thirty First Year of the Reign of King Henry I Michaelmas 1130 (Pipe Roll 1)*, ed. and trans. J. A. Green, Publications of the Pipe Roll Society, vol. 95, n. s. vol. 57 (London, 2012).

Gregory the Great, *Registrum epistolarum*, 2 vols, ed. D. Norberg, Corpus Christianorum Series Latina 140 and 140a (Turnhout, 1982).

Gregory the Great, *Homiliae in evangelia*, ed. R. Etaix, Corpus Christianorum Series Latina 141 (Turnhout, 1999).

Guillaume de Pouille, La Geste de Robert Guiscard, ed. and trans. M. Mathieu (Palermo, 1961).

Guillelmi I Regis Diplomata, ed. H. Enzensberger, Codex Diplomaticus Regni Siciliae, Ser. I.iii (Cologne, 1996).

[*La*] *Historia o Liber de Regno Sicilie e la Epistola ad Petrum Panormitane Ecclesie Thesaurium di Ugo Falcando*, ed. G. B. Siragusa, FSI 22 (Rome, 1897).

Historia Rerum Anglicarum of William of Newburgh in *Chronicles of the Reigns of Stephen, Henry II, and Richard I*, ed. R. Howlett, Rolls Series 82, vol. 1 (1884).

[*A*] *History of the Ayyubid Sultans of Egypt Translated from the Arabic of al-Maqrīzī*, trans. R. J. C. Broadhurst (Boston, 1980).

[*A*] *History of Deeds Done beyond the Sea by William Archbishop of Tyre*, trans. E. A. Babcock and A. C. Krey, 2 vols (New York, 1943).

[*The*] *History of the Holy War: Ambroise's Estoire de la guerre sainte*, ed. and trans. M. Ailes and M. Barber, 2 vols: vol. 1 (Old French Text); vol. 2 (Translation) (Woodbridge, 2011).

[*The*] *History of the Normans by Amatus of Montecassino*, trans. P. N. Dunbar and rev. G. A. Loud (Woodbridge, 2004).

[*The*] *History of the Tyrants of Sicily by 'Hugo Falcandus' 1154–69*, trans. G. A. Loud and T. Wiedemann (Manchester, 1998).

Ibn al-Khaṭīb, *Al-Iḥāṭa fī akhbār Gharnaṭa*, ed. M. 'Abd Allāh 'Inān, 4 vols (Cairo, 1973).

Ibn Jubayr, *Riḥla*, 2nd rev. edn, ed. M. J. de Goeje and W. Wright (Leiden, 1907).

Ibn Jubayr, *Riḥlat Ibn Jubayr* (Beirut, 1964).

Ibn Manẓūr, *Lisān al-ʿArab*, 15 vols (Beirut, 1955–56).
Idrîsî, *La Première Géographie de l'Occident*, rev. trans. H. Bresc *et al.* (Paris, 1999).
Ignoti Monachi Cisterciensis Chronica Romanorum pontificum et imperatorum ac de rebus in Apulia gestis (ab an. 781 ad an. 1228), ed. A. Gaudenzi (Naples, 1888).
Innocentii II Concilium Pisanum, ed. L. Weiland, MGH Constitutiones 1 (Hanover, 1903).
Ioannis Saresberiensis Episcopi Carnotensis Policratici De nugis curialium et vestigiis philosophorum libri 8, ed. C. C. I. Webb, vol. 2 (Oxford, 1909).
Italia Pontificia, ed. P. F. Kehr, 10 vols [vol. 9, ed. W. Holtzmann (1963); vol. 10, ed. D. Girgensohn (1974)] (Berlin, 1905–74).
Italia sacra, ed. F. Ughelli, vol. 7 (Venice, 1721).
Itinerarium Peregrinorum et gesta regis Ricardi, ed. W. Stubbs, in *Chronicles and Memorials of the Reign of Richard I*, Rolls Series 38, vol. 1 (London, 1864).
[The] *Itinerary of Benjamin of Tudela*, trans. M. N. Adler (London, 1907).
Jansen, K. L., Drell, J. and Andrews F. (eds), *Medieval Italy: Texts in Translation* (Philadelphia, 2009).
[Die] *Konzilien Deutschlands und Reichsitaliens 1023–1059*, ed. D. Jasper, MGH Concilia 8 (Hanover, 2010).
[The] *Laws of the Kings of England from Edmund to Henry I*, ed. and trans. A. J. Robertson (Cambridge, 1925).
[Le] *leggi dei Longobardi. Storia, memoria e diritto di un popolo germanico*, ed. C. Azzara and S. Gasparri (Milan, 1992).
[The] *Liber Augustalis or Constitutions of Melfi Promulgated by the Emperor Frederick II for the Kingdom of Sicily in 1231*, trans. J. M. Powell (New York, 1971).
[Le] *Liber Censuum de l'Eglise Romaine*, ed. P. Fabre and L. Duchesne, 3 vols, Bibliothèque des Écoles Françaises d'Athènes et de Rome, 2, série 6 (Paris, 1889–1952).
[Le] *Liber Pontificalis. Texte, introduction et commentaire*, ed. L. Duchesne, vol. 2 (Paris, 1892).
Loud, G. A. (trans. and ed.), Medieval History Texts in Translation, University of Leeds [https://ims.leeds.ac.uk/online-resources/translations/] (includes several translations of important South Italian material by G. A. Loud).
Lupus Protospatharius, *Annales*, ed. G. Pertz, MGH SS 5 (Hanover, 1844).
Magna Carta, ed. and trans. D. Carpenter (London, 2015).
Monumenta ad Neapolitani ducatus historiam pertinentia, ed. B. Capasso, 2 tomes in 3 vols (Naples, 1881–92), reissued and edited by R. Pilone, 5 vols (Salerno, 2008).

Monumenta Corbeiensia, ed. P. Jaffé, Bibliotheca Rerum Germanicarum 1 (Berlin, 1864).
Novae Patrum Bibliothecae, ed. G. Cozza-Luzi, Tom. 10:2 (Rome, 1905).
Orderici Vitalis Historiae ecclesiasticae, libri tredecim, ed. A. Le Prévost, 5 vols (Paris, 1838–55).
Patrologia Latina, ed. J. P. Migne, 221 vols (Paris, 1844–64).
[*Le*] *pergamene greche esistenti nel Grande Archivio di Palermo*, ed. G. Spata (Palermo, 1862).
[*Le*] *più antiche carte del capitolo della cattedrale di Benevento (668–1200)*, ed. A Ciarelli, V. de Donato and V. Matera (Rome, 2002).
[*Il*] *Poema di Amato su S. Pietro Apostolo*, ed. A. Lentini, vol. 1 (Montecassino, 1958).
Pope Urban II, The Collectio Britannica, and the Council of Melfi (1089), ed. R. Somerville and S. Kuttner (Oxford, 1996).
[*The*] *Rare and Excellent History of Saladin, or al-Nawādir al-Sulṭāniyya wa'l-Maḥāsin al-Yūsfiyya by Bahā' al-Dīn Ibn Shaddād*, trans. D. S. Richards (Aldershot, 2002).
Rationes decimarum Italiae nei secoli XIII e XIV. Campania, ed. M. Inguanez, L. Mattei Cerasoli and P. Sella, Studi e Testi 97 (Vatican City, 1942).
Recueil des actes des ducs de Normandie de 911 à 1066, ed. M. Fauroux (Caen, 1961).
Recueil des actes des ducs normands d'Italie, 1046–1127, Vol 1: Les premiers ducs (1046–1087), ed. L.-R. Ménager (Bari, 1980).
Regesta Pontificum Romanorum, ed. P. Jaffé *et al.*, 2 vols, 2nd edn (Leipzig, 1885–88).
Regesta regum Anglo-Normannorum 1066–1154. Vol. III: Regesta regis Stephani ac Mathildis imperaticis et Gaufridi et Henrici ducum Normannorum, 1135–1154, ed. H. A. Cronne, R. H. C. Davis and H. W. C. Davis (Oxford, 1968).
Regesta regum Anglo-Normannorum: The Acta of William I, 1066–1087, ed. D. Bates (Oxford, 1998).
Regii Neapolitani Archivi Monumenta. Edita ac illustrata, vol. 5 (Naples, 1857).
[*Das*] *Register Gregors VII.*, ed. E. Caspar, MGH Epistolae selectae 2,2 (Berlin, 1923).
[*Die*] *Register Innocenz' III. 1. Pontifikatsjahr, 1198/99. Texte*, ed. O. Hageneder and A. Haidacher (Graz, 1964).
Registrum Petri Diaconi (Montecassino, archivio dell'abbazia, Reg. 3). Edizione e commento, ed. J.-M. Martin *et al.*, 4 vols, Sources et documents publiés par l'École française de Rome 4; Fonti per la storia dell'Italia medievale. Antiquitates 45 (Rome, 2015).

Rogerii II Regis Diplomata Latina, ed. C.-R. Brühl, Codex Diplomaticus Regni Siciliae, Ser. I.ii(1) (Cologne, 1987).
Roger II and the Creation of the Kingdom of Sicily, trans. and ed. G. A. Loud (Manchester, 2012).
Rollus rubeus: Privilegia ecclesie Cephaleditane, a diversis regibus et imperatoribus concessa, recollecta et in hoc volumine scripta, ed. C. Mirto (Palermo, 1972).
Saint-Jean-Théristès (1054–1265), ed. A. Guillou (Vatican City, 1980).
Schirò, G. (ed.), 'Vita inedita di S. Cipriano di Calamizzi dal cod. Sinaitico n. 522', *Bulletino della Badia greca di Grottaferrata* n.s. 4 (1950), 65–97.
Storia de' Normanni di Amato di Montecassino, ed. V. De Bartholomaeis, FSI 76 (Rome, 1935).
[*Die*] *Touler Vita Leos IX.*, ed. H.-G. Krause, MGH SS rerum Germanicarum in usum Scholarum 70 (Hanover, 2007)
[*The*] *Travels of Ibn Jubayr*, trans. R. J. C. Broadhurst (London, 1952).
Typicon du monastère du Saint-Sauveur à Messine, Codex Messinensis Gr 115 A.D. 1131, ed. M. Arranz (Rome, 1969).
[*The*] *Trotula: A Medieval Compendium of Women's Medicine*, ed. and trans. M. H. Green (Philadelphia, 2001).
Vita di S. Luca vescovo di Isola Capo Rizzuto, ed. and trans. G. Schirò (Palermo, 1954).
Widows, Heirs and Heiresses in the Late Twelfth Century: Rotuli de dominabus et pueris et puellis, ed. and trans. J. Walmesley (Tempe, 2006).
Willelmi Tyrensis Archiepiscopi Chronicon, ed. R. B. C. Huygens, Corpus Christianorum Continuatio Mediaevalis 63–63A (Turnhout, 1986).
Ymagines Historiarum of Ralph de Diceto in *Opera Historica*, Rolls Series 68, vol. 2 (1876).
Zaccagni, G., 'Il Bios di san Bartolomeo da Simeri (BHG 235)', *Rivista di studi bizantini e neoellenici* 33 (1996), 193–274.

Secondary sources

[Note: some works listed below also contain edited primary sources]
Abrams, L., 'Diaspora and identity in the Viking age', *Early Medieval Europe* 20 (2012), 17–38.
Abulafia, D., 'Pisan commercial colonies and consulates in twelfth-century Sicily', *EHR* 93 (1978), 68–81.
Abulafia, D., 'The Norman kingdom of Africa and the Norman expeditions to Majorca and the Muslim Mediterranean', *ANS* 7 (1985), 26–49.
Abulafia, D., 'Ethnic variety and its implications: Frederick II's relations with Jews and Muslims', in W. Tronzo (ed.), *Intellectual Life and the*

Court of Frederick II Hohenstaufen (Washington, DC, 1994), pp. 213–24.
Abulafia, D., 'Il Contesto mediterraneo e il primo disegno delle Due Italie', in G. Galasso (ed.), *Alle origini del dualismo italiano. Regno di Sicilia e Italia centro-settentrionale dagli Altavilla agli Angiò (1100–1350)* (Soveria Mannelli, 2014), pp. 11–28.
Abulafia, D., 'Evelyn Jamison, champion of southern Italy, champion of women's education', in J.-M. Martin and R. Alaggio (eds), *'Quei Maledetti Normanni': Studi offerti a Errico Cuozzo*, 2 vols (Ariano Irpino, 2016), vol. 1, pp. 1–12.
Acconcia Longo, A., 'S. Giovanni Terista nell'agiografia e nell'innografia', in A. Acconcia Longo, *Ricerche di Agiografia Italogreca* (Rome, 2003), pp. 121–43.
Albu, E., *The Normans in their Histories: Propaganda, Myth and Subversion* (Woodbridge, 2001).
Albu, E., 'Robert Guiscard', in C. Kleinhenz (ed.), *Medieval Italy: An Encyclopedia*, 2 vols, 2nd edn (New York, 2004), vol. 2, pp. 969–70.
Alexander, D., *Saints and Animals in the Middle Ages* (Woodbridge, 2008).
Althoff, G., 'Satisfaction: Peculiarities of the amicable settlement of conflicts in the Middle Ages', in B. Jussen (ed.), *Ordering Medieval Society: Perspectives on Intellectual and Practical Modes of Shaping Social Relations* (Philadelphia, 2001), pp. 270–84.
Althoff, G., 'The rules of conflict among the warrior aristocracy of the high middle ages', in K. Esmark *et al.* (eds), *Disputing Strategies in Medieval Scandinavia* (Leiden, 2013), pp. 313–32.
Althoff, G., 'Symbolic communication and medieval order: Strengths and weaknesses of ambiguous signs', in W. Jezierski *et al.* (eds), *Rituals, Performatives, and Political Order in Northern Europe, c.650–1350* (Turnhout, 2015), pp. 63–75.
Aubé, P., *Les Empires normands d'Orient* (Paris, 1991).
Aubrun, M., *L'ancien diocese de Limoges des origines au milieu du XI siècle* (Clermont-Ferrand, 1981).
'Azzām, 'A. R., *Saladin* (Harlow, 2009).
Bacharach, J. L., *A Middle East Studies Handbook* (Cambridge, 1984).
Bakirtzis, C., 'Le culte de saint Démétrius', in E. Dassmann and J. Engemann (eds), *Akten des XII. Internationalen Kongresses für christliche Archäologie*, 3 vols (Munster, 1995–97), vol. 1, pp. 58–68.
Balog, P., 'La monetazione della Sicilia araba e le sue imitazioni nell'Italia meridionale', in F. Gabrieli and U. Scerrato (eds), *Gli Arabi in Italia: cultura, contatti e tradizioni* (Milan, 1979), pp. 611–28.
Bates, D., *The Normans and Empire* (Oxford, 2013).
Bates, D., *William the Conqueror* (London, 2018).

Bates, D. and Bauduin, P. (eds), *911–2011: Penser les mondes normands médiévaux* (Caen, 2016).
Bauduin, P., 'Une famille châtelaine sur les confins normanno-manceaux: les Géré (Xe–XIIIe s.)', *Archéologie médiévale* 22 (1992), 309–56.
Bauduin, P., *La première Normandie (Xe–XIe siècles). Sur les frontières de la haute Normandie: Identité et construction d'une principauté* (Caen, 2004).
Bauduin, P., *Le monde franc et les Vikings, VIIIe–Xe siècle* (Paris, 2009).
Bauduin, P. and Musin, A. E. (eds), *Vers l'Orient et vers l'Occident: Regards croisés sur les dynamiques et les transferts culturels des Vikings à la Rous ancienne* (Caen, 2014).
Baumgärtner, I., Vagnoni, M. and Welton, M. (eds), *Representations of Power at the Mediterranean Borders of Europe (12th–14th Centuries)* (Florence, 2014).
Beck, F. and Henning, E. (eds), *Die archivalischen Quellen: Mit einer Einführung in die Historischen Hilfswissenschaften*, 5th edn (Cologne, 2012).
Becker, A., *Urban II*, vol. 3 (Hanover, 2012).
Becker, J., *Graf Roger I. von Sizilien: Wegbereiter des normannischen Königreichs* (Tübingen, 2008).
Becker, J., 'William of Apulia (Guglielmo di Puglia)', in G. Dunphy (ed.), *Encyclopedia of the Medieval Chronicle*, 2 vols (Leiden, 2010), vol. 2, pp. 1509–10.
Becker, J., 'Charters and chancery under Roger I and Roger II', in S. Burkhardt and T. Foerster (eds), *Norman Tradition and Transcultural Heritage: Exchange of Cultures in the 'Norman' Peripheries of Medieval Europe* (Farnham, 2013), pp. 79–95.
Becker, J., '… ut omnes habitatores Messane tam latini quam greci et hebrei habeant predictam libertatem … Vita cittadina e cittadinanza a Messina tra Normanni, Angioni er Aragonesi', in T. Jäckh and M. Kirsch (eds), *Urban Dynamics and Transcultural Communication in Medieval Sicily* (Paderborn, 2017), pp. 159–72.
Beckingham, C. F., 'The Riḥla: Fact or fiction?', in I. R. Netton (ed.), *Golden Roads: Migration, Pilgrimage and Travel in Medieval and Modern Islam* (Richmond, 1993), pp. 86–94.
Beech, G. T., 'The remarkable life of Ansger, a Breton monk and poet from the Loire Valley who became bishop of Catania in Sicily 1091–1124', *Viator* 45 (2014), 149–74.
Benveniste, H.-R., 'Crossing the frontier: Jewish converts to Catholicism in European history', in E. R. Dursteler *et al.* (eds), *From Florence to the Mediterranean and Beyond: Essays in Honour of Anthony Molho* (Florence, 2009), pp. 447–74.

Birk, J. C., *Norman Kings of Sicily and the Rise of the Anti-Islamic Critique: Baptized Sultans* (Cham, 2016).

Bisanti, A., 'Composizione, stile e tendenze dei *Gesta Roberti Wiscardi* di Guglielmo il Pugliese', *Archivio normanno-svevo* 1 (2008), 87–132.

Bloch, H., *Monte Cassino in the Middle Ages*, 3 vols (Rome, 1986).

Bloch, M., *The Historian's Craft*, trans. P. Putnam (New York, 1963).

Bloch, M., *Apologie pour l'histoire ou Métier d'historien*, 2nd edn (Paris, 1974).

Boccuzzi, M. and Cordasco, P. (eds), *Civiltà a contatto nel Mezzogiorno normanno-svevo: economia, società, istituzioni* (Bari, 2018).

Bouet, P., '1000–1100: La conquête', in P. Bouet and F. Neveux (eds), *Les Normands en Méditerranée dans le sillage des Tancrède* (Caen, 2nd edn, 2001), pp. 11–23.

Bouet, P., and Neveux, F. (eds), *Les Normands en Méditerranée dans le sillage des Tancrède* (Caen, 1994; 2nd edn 2001).

Bouriant, U., *Description topographique et historique de l'Égypte*, 2 vols [cont. pag.] (Paris, 1895–1900).

Breccia, G., 'Il *sigillion* nella prima età normanna. Documento pubblico e semipubblico nel Mezzogiorno ellenofono (1070–1127)', *QF* 79 (1999), 1–27.

Brett, M., 'Muslim justice under infidel rule: The Normans in Ifrīqiya, 517–555H/1123–1160 AD', *Cahiers de Tunisie* 43 (1995), 325–68.

Brett, M., *The Fatimid Empire* (Edinburgh, 2017).

Bruzelius, C. and Tronzo W., *Medieval Naples: An Architectural and Urban History 400–1400* (New York, 2011).

Bünemann, R., *Robert Guiskard 1015–1085: Ein Normanne erobert Süditalien* (Cologne, 1997).

Burgarella, F., 'Aspetti storici del *Bios* di san Bartolomeo da Simeri', in V. Ruggeri and L. Pieralli (eds), *EUKOSMIA. Studi miscellanei per il 75° di Vincenzo Poggi S.J.* (Soveria Mannelli, 2003), pp. 119–33.

Burkhardt, S. and Foerster, T. (eds), *Norman Tradition and Transcultural Heritage: Exchange of Cultures in the 'Norman' Peripheries of Medieval Europe* (Farnham, 2013).

Calasso, G., 'Les tâches du voyageur: décrire, mesurer, compter, chez Ibn Jubayr, Nāṣer-e Khosrow et Ibn Baṭṭūṭa', *Rivista degli Studi Orientali* 73 (1999), 69–104.

Canosa, R., *Etnogenesi normanne e identità variabili. Il retroterra culturale dei Normanni d'Italia fra Scandinavia e Normandia* (Turin, 2009).

Cantarella, G. M., *La Sicilia e i Normanni. Le fonti del mito* (Bologna, 1988).

Cantarella, G. M., 'La fondazione della storia nel regno normanno di Sicilia', in *L'Europa dei secoli XI e XII fra novità e tradizione: sviluppi di una cultura. Atti della decima Settimana internazionale di studio della Mendola* (Milan, 1989), pp. 171–96.

Cantarella, G. M., *Principi e corti: L'Europa del XII secolo* (Turin, 1997).
Cantarella, G. M., 'Liaisons dangereuses: il papato e i Normanni', in E. D'Angelo and C. Leonardi (eds), *Il Papato e i Normanni. Temporale e Spirituale in età normanna* (Florence, 2011), pp. 45–58.
Cantarella, G. M., *Ruggero II* (Rome, 2020).
Capitani, O., 'Specific motivations and continuing themes of the Norman chronicles of southern Italy: Eleventh and twelfth centuries', in *The Normans in Sicily and Southern Italy: The Lincei Lectures 1974* (Oxford, 1977), pp. 1–46.
Caracausi, G., *Lessico greco della Sicilia e dell'Italia meridionale (secoli X–XIV)* (Palermo, 1990).
Caracausi, G., *Dizionario onomastico della Sicilià: repertorio storico-etimologico di nomi di famiglia e di luogo*, 2 vols (Palermo, 1994).
Caravale, M., *Il Regno Normanno di Sicilia* (Milan, 1966).
Carocci, S., 'Le libertà dei servi. Reinterpretate il villanaggio medievale', *Storica* 37 (2007), 51–94.
Carocci, S., *Signorie di Mezzogiorno: società rurali, poteri aristocratici e monarcha (XII–XIII secolo)* (Rome, 2014).
Carocci, S., *Lordships of Southern Italy: Rural Societies, Aristocratic Powers, and Monarchy in the 12th and 13th Centuries*, trans. L. Byatt (Rome, 2018).
Caruso, S., 'Il santo, il re, la curia, l'impero. Sul processo per eresia contro Bartolomeo da Simeri (XI–XII sec.)', *Bizantinistica* 1 (1999), 51–72.
Caspar, E., *Ruggero II e la fondazione della monarchia normanna di Sicilia*, Ital. trans. (with an introductory essay from O. Zecchino) (Rome, 1999).
Catlos, B., *Muslims of Medieval Latin Christendom, c.1050–1614* (New York, 2014).
Chalandon, F., *Histoire de la Domination normande en Italie et en Sicile*, 2 vols (Paris, 1907).
Chevedden, P., ' "A crusade from the first": The Norman conquest of Islamic Sicily, 1060–1091', *Al-Masāq: Islam and the Medieval Mediterranean* 22 (2010), 191–225.
Chibnall, M., 'Le privilège de libre élection dans les chartes de Saint-Evroult', *Annales de Normandie* 28 (1978), 341–2.
Chibnall, M., *The World of Orderic Vitalis* (Oxford, 1984).
Chibnall, M., 'Les moines et les patrons de Saint-Évroult dans l'Italie du Sud au XIe siècle', in P. Bouet and F. Neveux (eds), *Les Normands en Méditerranée dans le sillage des Tancrède* (Caen, 1994), pp. 161–70.
Chibnall, M., *The Debate on the Norman Conquest* (Manchester, 1999).
Chibnall, M., *The Normans* (Oxford, 2000).
Churchill, W. J., 'The Annales Barenses and the Annali Lupi Protospatharii, Critical Edition and Commentary' (PhD dissertation, University of Toronto, 1979).

Cilento, A., *Potere e monachesimo. Ceti dirigenti e mondo monastico nella Calabria Bizantina, sec. IX–XI* (Florence, 2000).
Clementi, D., 'Notes on Norman Sicilian surveys', in V. H. Galbraith (ed.), *The Making of Domesday Book* (Oxford, 1961), pp. 55–8.
Cohen, R., *Global Diasporas: An Introduction* (London, 2008).
Contamine, P., *La Guerre au Moyen Âge* (Paris, 1980).
Cooper, J. P., '"Fear God, fear the Bogaze": The Nile mouths and the navigational landscape of the Nile delta, Egypt', *Al-Masāq: Islam and the Medieval Mediterranean* 24 (2012), 53–73.
Cooper, J. P., *The Medieval Nile: Route, Navigation, and Navigation and Landscape in Islamic Egypt* (Cairo, 2014).
Cordasco, P. and Siciliani, M. A. (eds), *Il Mezzogiorno normanno-svevo fra storia e storiografia* (Bari, 2014).
Corrao, P., 'Il servo', in G. Musca (ed.), *Condizione umana e ruoli sociali nel Mezzogiorno normanno-svevo. Atti delle none giornate normanno-sveve, Bari, 17–20 ottobre, 1989* (Bari, 1992), pp. 61–78.
Corriente, F., *Dictionary of Andalusi Arabic* (Leiden, 1997).
Cortese, E., 'Per la storia del mundio in Italia', *Rivista Italiana per le Scienze Giuridiche* 3rd ser. 8 (1955–56), 323–474.
Cowdrey, H. E. J., 'Simon Magus in south Italy', *ANS* 15 (1993), 77–90.
Cowdrey, H. E. J., *Lanfranc: Scholar, Monk, Archbishop* (Oxford, 2003).
Cuozzo, E., *Catalogus baronum. Commentario*, FSI 101 (b) (Rome, 1984).
Cuozzo, E., *'Quei maledetti Normanni'. Cavalieri e organizzazione militare nel Mezzogiorno normanno* (Naples, 1989).
Cuozzo, E., 'L'unificazione normanna e il regno normanno-svevo', in G. Galasso and R. Romeo (eds), *Storia del Mezzogiorno*, II/2, Il medioevo (Rome, 1989), pp. 593–825.
Cuozzo, E., 'Le feudalità del "Regnum" nell'età di Ruggero II', in O. Zecchino (ed.), *Le Assise di Ariano 1140–1990*, Centro Europeo di studi Normanni. Fonti e Studi 1 (Ariano Irpino, 1994), pp. 165–78.
Cuozzo, E., *Normanni: Feudi e feudatari* (Salerno, 1996).
Cuozzo, E., 'Intorno alla prima contea normanna nell'Italia meridionale', in E. Cuozzo and J.-M. Martin (eds), *Cavalieri alla conquista del Sud: Studi sull'Italia normanna in memoria di L.-R. Ménager* (Rome, 1998), pp. 171–93.
Curtis, E., *Roger of Sicily and the Normans in Lower Italy 1016–1154* (New York, 1912).
Curtis, E., *A History of Medieval Ireland from 1110 to 1513* (Dublin, 1923; 2nd edn 1938).
Cushing, K. G., *Reform and Papacy in the Eleventh Century: Spirituality and Social Change* (Manchester, 2005).

D'Alessandro, V., 'Roberto il Guiscardo nella storiografia medievale', in C. D. Fonseca (ed.), *Roberto il Guiscardo tra Europa, Oriente e Mezzogiorno* (Galatina, 1990), pp. 181–96.

D'Angelo, E., 'Studi sulla tradizione di Falcone Beneventano', *Filologia Mediolatina* 1 (1994), 129–81.

D'Angelo, E., *Storiografi e cronologi latini del Mezzogiorno normanno-svevo* (Naples, 2003).

D'Angelo, E. and Leonardi, C. (eds), *Il Papato e i Normanni: Temporale e spirituale in età normanna* (Florence, 2011).

Davis, R. H. C., *The Normans and their Myth* (London, 1976).

Davis, R. H. C., 'David Charles Douglas, 1898–1982', *Proceedings of the British Academy* 69 (1983), 513–42.

Davis-Secord, S., 'Muslims in Norman Sicily: The evidence of Imām al-Māzarī's fatwās', *Mediterranean Studies* 16 (2007), 46–66.

Davis-Secord, S., 'Medieval Sicily and southern Italy in recent historiographic perspective', *History Compass* 8 (2010), 61–87.

Davis-Secord, S., 'Bearers of Islam: Muslim women between assimilation and resistance in Christian Sicily', in M. Moore (ed.), *Gender in the Premodern Mediterranean* (Tempe, 2019), pp. 63–95.

d'Avray, D., *Medieval Marriage: Symbolism and Society* (Oxford, 2005).

de Biberstein Kazimirsky, A., *Dictionnaire arabe-français*, 2 vols (Paris, 1860).

Decaëns, J., 'Le patrimoine des Grentemesnil en Normandie, en Italie et en Angleterre aux XIe et XIIe siècles', in P. Bouet and F. Neveux (eds), *Les Normands en Méditerranée dans le sillage des Tancrède* (Caen, 1994), pp. 123–40.

Déer, J., *Das Papsttum und die süditalienischen Normannenstaaten, 1053–1212* (Göttingen, 1969).

Dejugnat, Y., 'À L'Ombre de la *fitna*, l'Émergence d'un Discourse du Voyage: À propos du *Tartîb al-rihla* d'Abû Bakr ibn al-'Arabî', *Médiévales* 60 (2011), 85–101.

Dejugnat, Y., 'Ibn Jubayr', in K. Fleet *et al.* (eds), *Encyclopedia of Islam*, 3rd edn (Leiden, 2017), pp. 130–2.

Delle Donne, F., 'Lupus Apulus Protospatharius (Protospata)', in G. Dunphy (ed.), *Encyclopedia of the Medieval Chronicle*, 2 vols (Leiden, 2010), vol. 2, p. 1051.

Diggelmann, L., 'Of Grifons and tyrants: Anglo-Norman views of the Mediterranean world during the Third Crusade', in L. Bailey, L. Diggelmann and K. M. Phillips (eds), *Old Worlds, New Worlds: European Cultural Encounters, c.1000–c.1750* (Turnhout, 2009), pp. 11–30.

D'Onofrio, M. (ed.), *I Normanni popolo d'Europa, 1030–1200* (Venice, 1994).

Douglas, D. C., *William the Conqueror* (London, 1964).
Douglas, D. C., *The Norman Achievement, 1050–1100* (London, 1969).
Dozy, R. P. A., *Supplément aux dictionnaires arabes*, 3rd edn, 2 vols (Leiden, 1877; Beirut, 1991).
Drehmann, J., *Papst Leo IX. und die Simonie. Ein Beitrag zur Vorgeschichte des Investiturstreits* (Leipzig, 1908).
Drell, J., 'Cultural syncretism and ethnic identity: The Norman "conquest" of southern Italy and Sicily', *JMH* 25 (1999), 187–202.
Drell, J., *Kinship and Conquest: Family Strategies in the Principality of Salerno during the Norman Period 1077–1194* (Ithaca, 2002).
Drell, J., 'From lemons to legislation: Welcoming foreigners in the medieval Regno', in J.-M. Martin and R. Alaggio (eds), *'Quei maledetti Normanni'. Studi offerti a Errico Cuozzo*, 2 vols (Ariano Irpino, 2016), vol. 1, pp. 371–84.
Du Cange, C. (ed.), *Glossarium mediae et infimae Latinitatis*, 10 vols (Niort, 1883–87).
Edbury, P. W. and Rowe, J. G., *William of Tyre: Historian of the Latin East* (Cambridge, 1988).
Efthymiades, S., 'Les saints d'Italie méridionale (IXe–XIIe s.) et leur rôle dans la société locale', in D. Sullivan, E. Fisher and S. Papaioannou (eds), *Byzantine Religious Culture: Studies in Honor of Alice-Mary Talbot* (Leiden, 2012), pp. 347–72.
Enzensberger, H., *Beiträge zum Kanzlei- und Urkundenwesen der normannischen Herrscher Unteritaliens und Siziliens* (Kallmünz, 1971).
Enzensberger, H., 'Bemerkungen zu Kanzlei und Diplomen Robert Guiskards', in *Roberto il Guiscardo e il suo tempo: Relazioni e comunicazioni nelle prime Giornate normanno-sveve* (Rome, 1975), pp. 107–13.
Enzensberger, H., 'Roberto il Guiscardo: documenti e cancellaria', in C. D. Fonseca (ed.), *Roberto il Guiscardo tra Europa, Oriente e Mezzogiorno* (Galatina, 1990), pp. 61–81.
Enzensberger, H., 'Messina e i re', in G. Fallico, A. Sparti and U. Balistreri (eds), *Messina: il Ritorno della memoria* (Palermo, 1994), pp. 331–6.
Enzensberger, H., 'Chanceries, charters and administration in Norman Italy', in G. A. Loud and A. Metcalfe (eds), *The Society of Norman Italy* (Leiden, 2002), pp. 117–50.
Facey, W., 'Crusaders in the Red Sea: Renaud de Châtillon's raids of AD 1182-3', in J. C. M. Starkey (ed.), *People of the Red Sea: Proceedings of the Red Sea Project II* (Oxford, 2005), pp. 87–98.
Fernández Aceves, H., 'The re-arrangement of the nobility under the Hauteville monarchy: The creation of the south-Italian counties', *Ex Historia* 8 (2016), 58–90.

Fernández Aceves, H., 'County and nobility in Norman Italy (1130–1189)' (PhD dissertation, University of Leeds, 2017).

Fisher, H. J., 'Text-centered research: *Fitna* as a case study and a way forward for guests in the house of African historiography', *Sudanic Africa* 5 (1994), 225–60.

Fodale, S., 'Il Gran Conte e la Sede apostolica', in *Ruggero il Gran Conte e l'inizio dello Stato normanno* (Rome, 1977), pp. 25–42.

Fodale, S., *L'Apostolica Legazia e altri studi su Stato e Chiesa* (Messina, 1991).

Follieri, E., 'I santi dell'Italia greca', in A. Jacob, J.-M. Martin and G. Noyé (eds), *Histoire et culture dans l'Italie byzantine. Acquis et nouvelles recherches* (Rome, 2006), pp. 103–26.

Forrai, R., 'Byzantine saints for Frankish warriors: Anastasius Bibliothecarius' Latin version of the Passion of Saint Demetrius of Thessaloniki', in S. Brodbeck *et al.* (eds), *L'Héritage byzantin en Italie (VIIIe–XIIe siècle)* (Rome, 2015), pp. 185–202.

France, J., 'The occasion of the coming of the Normans to Italy', *JMH* 17 (1991), 185–205.

France, J., *Western Warfare in the Age of the Crusades 1000–1300* (Ithaca, 1999).

Freed, J. B., *Frederick Barbarossa: The Prince and the Myth* (New Haven, 2016).

Freund, S., *Studien zur literarischen Wirksamkeit des Petrus Damiani* (Hanover, 1995).

Fuiano, M., 'La Battaglia di Civitate (1053)', *Archivio Storico Pugliese* 2 (1949), 125–33.

Gadet, L., 'Fitna', in B. Lewis *et al.* (eds), *Encyclopedia of Islam*, 2nd edn (Leiden, 1991), vol. 2, pp. 930–1.

Galasso, G. (ed.), *Alle origini del dualismo italiano. Regno di Sicilia e Italia centro-settentrionale dagli Altavilla agli Angiò (1100–1350)* (Soveria Mannelli, 2014).

Garbini, P., 'Lo stile della storia in Goffredo Malaterra', in F. Delle Donne (ed.), *In presenza dell'autore. L'autorappresentazione come evoluzione della storiografia professionale tra Basso Medioevo e Umanesimo* (Naples, 2018), pp. 13–34.

Garufi, C.-A., 'Censimento e catasto della popolazione servile: nuovi studi e ricerche sull'ordinamento amministrativo dei Normanni in Sicilia nei secoli 11 e 12', *Archivio storico siciliano* n.s. 49 (1928), 1–104.

Gazeau, V., *Normannia monastica (Xe–XIIe siècle): Princes normands et abbés bénédictins*, 2 vols (Caen, 2007).

Geltner, G., *Roads to Health: Infrastructure and Urban Wellbeing in Later Medieval Italy* (Philadelphia, 2019).

Getz, S., 'Permission to stay in "enemy" territory? Ḥanbalī juristic thinking on whether Muslims must emigrate from non-Muslim lands', *The Muslim World* 103 (2013), 94–106.

Gibbon, E., *History of the Decline and Fall of the Roman Empire*, 7 vols (London, 1853–55).

Gillingham, J., *Richard I* (New Haven, 1999).

Giuliani, P., *Memorie istoriche della città di Nicastro da' tempi più remoti fino al 1820* (Nicastro, 1867).

Glaze, F. E., 'Salerno's Lombard prince: Johannes "Abbas de Curte" as medical practitioner', *Early Science and Medicine* 23 (2018), 177–216.

Goullet, M., *Écriture et réécriture hagiographiques. Essai sur les réécritures de Vies de saints dans l'Occident latin médieval (VIIIe–XIIIe s.)* (Turnhout, 2005).

Graboïs, A., 'La cité de Banyas et le château de Subeibeh pendant les croisades', *Cahiers de civilisation médiévale* 13 (1970), 43–62.

Granara, W., *Narrating Muslim Sicily: War and Peace in the Medieval Mediterranean World* (London, 2019).

Green, J., 'Unity and disunity in the Anglo-Norman state', *Historical Research* 63 (1989), 115–34.

Greenway, D., 'Marjorie McCallum Chibnall, 1915–2012', *Biographical Memoirs of Fellows of the British Academy* 13 (2014), 43–62.

Grégoire, R., 'I dialoghi di Desiderio abate di Montecassino († 1087)', in F. Avagliano and O. Pecere (eds), *L'età dell'abate Desiderio III,1: Storia arte e cultura. Atti del IV convegno di studi sul medioevo meridionale (Montecassino – Cassino, 4–8 ottobre 1987)* (Montecassino, 1992), pp. 215–34.

Gresser, G., *Die Synoden und Konzilien in der Zeit des Reformpapsttums in Deutschland und Italien von Leo IX. bis Calixt II., 1049–1123* (Paderborn, 2006).

Grierson, P., 'The Salernitan coinage of Gisulf II (1052–77) and Robert Guiscard (1077–85)', *Papers of the British School at Rome* 24 (1956), 37–59.

Grierson, P., 'The role of silver in the early Byzantine economy', in S. A. Boyd and M. M. Mango (eds), *Ecclesiastical Silver Plate in Sixth-Century Byzantium* (Washington, DC, 1992), pp. 137–46.

Grierson, P., 'The coinages of Norman Apulia and Sicily in their international setting', *ANS* 15 (1993), 117–32.

Grierson, P., *Byzantine Coinage* (Washington, DC, 1999).

Grierson, P. and Travaini, L., *Medieval European Coinage Vol. 14: Italy III: South Italy, Sicily, Sardinia* (Cambridge, 1998).

Guéret-Laferté, M., 'L'identité normande dans l'Ystoire de li Normant d'Aimé du Mont-Cassin', in M. Guéret-Laferté and N. Lenoir (eds),

La Fabrique de la Normandie (CÉRÉdI, 2013) http://ceredi.labos.univ-rouen.fr/public/?l-identite-normande-dans-l-ystoire.html.

Hagger, M., 'Kinship and identity in eleventh-century Normandy: The case of Hugh de Grandmesnil, c.1040–1098', *JMH* 32 (2006), 212–30.

Hall, S., 'Who needs "identity"?', in S. Hall and P. du Gay (eds), *Questions of Cultural Identity* (London, 1996), pp. 1–17.

Haskins, C. H., *The Normans in European History* (Boston, 1915).

Haskins, C. H., *Norman Institutions* (Cambridge, MA, 1918).

Haye, T., *Päpste und Poeten. Die mittelalterliche Kurie als Objekt und Förderer panegyrischer Dichtung* (Berlin, 2009).

Hayes, D. M., 'The political significance of Roger II of Sicily's antiquated loros in the mosaic of Santa Maria dell'Ammiraglio, Palermo', *Allegorica* 29 (2013), 52–69.

Hayes, D. M., *Roger II of Sicily: Family, Faith, and Empire in the Medieval Mediterranean World* (Turnhout, 2020).

Head, T., *Hagiography and the Cult of Saints: The Diocese of Orléans, 800–1200* (Cambridge, 1990).

Hendy, M. F., *Coinage and Money in the Byzantine Empire, 1081–1261* (Washington, DC, 1969).

Hendy, M. F., *Studies in the Byzantine Monetary Economy c.300–1450* (Cambridge, 1985).

Hinschius, P., 'Über Pseudo-Isodor-Handschriften und Kanonessammlungen in spanischen Bibliotheken', *Zeitschrift für Kirchenrecht* 3 (1863), 122–46.

Houben, H., 'Una grande abbazia nel Mezzogiorno medioevale: la SS. Trinità di Venosa', in H. Houben, *Medioevo monastico meridionale* (Naples, 1987), pp. 85–108.

Houben, H., 'Roberto il Guiscardo e il monachesimo', in H. Houben, *Medioevo monastico meridionale* (Naples, 1987), pp. 109–27.

Houben, H., 'I benedettini e la latinizzazione della terra d'Otranto', in B. Vetere (ed.), *Ad Ovest di Bisanzio, il Salento medioevale* (Galatina, 1990), pp. 71–89.

Houben, H., *Die Abtei Venosa und das Mönchtum im normannisch-staufischen Süditalien* (Tübingen, 1995).

Houben, H., 'Adelaide "del Vasto" nella storia del regno normanno di Sicilia', in H. Houben, *Mezzogiorno normanno-svevo: Monasteri e castelli, ebrei e musulmani* (Naples, 1996), pp. 81–113.

Houben, H., *Ruggero II di Sicilia. Un sovrano tra Oriente e Occidente*, Italian trans. (Rome, 1999; orig. edn Darmstadt, 1997).

Houben, H., *Roger II of Sicily: A Ruler between East and West*, trans. G. A. Loud and D. Milburn (Cambridge, 2002).

Houben, H., *I Normanni*, Italian trans. (Bologna, 2013; orig. edn Munich, 2012).
Howe, J., 'Peter Damian and Montecassino', *Revue bénédictine* 107 (1997), 330–51.
Howe, J., 'St Berardus of Marsica (d.1130): "Model Gregorian bishop"', *Journal of Ecclesiastical History* 58 (2007), 400–16.
Hudson, J., *The Oxford History of the Laws of England: Volume II 871–1216* (Oxford, 2012).
Hüls, R., *Kardinäle, Klerus und Kirchen Roms 1049–1130* (Tübingen, 1977).
Hurlock, K. and Oldfield, P. (eds), *Crusading and Pilgrimage in the Norman World* (Woodbridge, 2015).
Jäckh, T. and Kirsch, M. (eds), *Urban Dynamics and Transcultural Communication in Medieval Sicily* (Paderborn, 2017).
Jamison, E., 'The Norman administration of Apulia and Capua more especially under Roger II and William I 1127–1166', *Papers of the British School at Rome* 6 (1913), 211–481.
Jamison, E., 'Pisan churches on the Via Traiana', *Journal of the British Archaeological Association* n.s. 35 (1929–30), 163–88.
Jamison, E., 'The Abbess Bethlem of S. Maria di Porta Somma and the barons of the Terra Beneventana', in *Oxford Essays in Medieval History Presented to Herbert Edward Salter* (Oxford, 1934), pp. 33–67 [reprinted in E. Jamison, *Studies on the History of Medieval Sicily and South Italy*, ed. D. Clementi and T. Kölzer (Aalen, 1992), pp. 123–57].
Jamison, E., 'Notes on Santa Maria della Strada at Matrice, its history and sculpture', *Papers of the British School at Rome* 14 (1938), 32–97.
Jamison, E., 'The Sicilian monarchy in the mind of Anglo-Norman contemporaries', *Proceedings of the British Academy* 24 (1938), 237–85.
Jamison, E., 'The alliance of England and Sicily in the second half of the twelfth century', *Journal of the Warburg and Courtauld Institutes* 6 (1943), 20–32.
Jamison, E., *Admiral Eugenius of Sicily: His Life and Work and the Authorship of the* Epistola ad Petrum *and the* Historia Hugonis Falcandi Siculi (London, 1957).
Jamison, E., 'Judex Tarentinus', *Proceedings of the British Academy* 53 (1968), 289–344.
Jamison, E., 'Additional work by E. Jamison on the *Catalogus Baronum*', *Bullettino dell'Istituto Italiano per il Medio Evo* 83 (1971), 1–63.
Jamison, E., *Studies on the History of Medieval Sicily and South Italy*, ed. D. Clementi and T. Kölzer (Aalen, 1992).
Jesch, J., *The Viking Diaspora* (London, 2015).

J. H., 'Edmund Curtis', *Analecta Hibernica* 16 (1946), 387–9.

Johns, J., 'The Greek church and the conversion of Muslims in Norman Sicily?', *Byzantinische Forschungen* 21 (1995), 133–57.

Johns, J., *Arabic Administration in Norman Sicily: The Royal Dīwān* (Cambridge, 2002).

Johns, J., 'The boys from Mezzoiuso: Muslim *jizya*-payers in Christian Sicily', in R. Hoyland and P. Kennedy (eds), *Islamic Reflections, Arabic Musings: Studies in Honor of Professor Alan Jones* (Cambridge, 2004), pp. 243–55.

Johns, J. and Jamil, N., 'Signs of the times: Arabic signatures as a measure of acculturation in Norman Sicily', *Muqarnas* 21 (2004), 181–92.

Johrendt, J., 'Die Reisen der frühen Reformpäpste. Ihre Ursachen und Funktionen', *Römische Quartalschrift für christliche Altertumskunde und Kirchengeschichte* 96 (2001), 57–94.

Kamp, H., *Friedensstifter und Vermittler im Mittelalter* (Darmstadt, 2001).

Kamp, N., *Kirche und Monarchie im staufischen Königreich Sizilien*, vol. 2 (Munich, 1975).

Kazhdan, A. P. and Wharton Epstein, A., *Change in Byzantine Culture in the Eleventh and Twelfth Centuries* (Berkeley, 1985).

Kedar, B. Z., 'The subjected Muslims of the Frankish Levant', in J. M. Powell (ed.), *Muslims under Latin Rules 1100–1300* (Princeton, 1990), pp. 135–74.

Kehr, P. F., 'Ergänzungen zu Falco von Benevent', *Neues Archiv der Gesellschaft für ältere deutsche Geschichtskunde* 27 (1902), 445–72.

Klewitz, H.-W., 'Studien über die Wiederherstellung der römischen Kirche in Süditalien durch das Reformpapsttum', *QF* 25 (1933/34), 105–57.

Korhonen, K., 'The role of onomastics for diachronic sociolinguistics: A case study on language shift in late medieval Sicily', *Journal of Historical Linguistics* 1/2 (2011), 147–74.

Kreiner, J., *The Social Life of Hagiography in the Merovingian Kingdom* (Cambridge, 2014).

Krumm, M., 'Streiten vor (und mit) dem Papst. Beobachtungen zur kurialen Gerichtspraxis anhand der Klosterchronik von Montecassino und des *Chronicon* Falcos von Benevent', in J. Nowak and G. Strack (eds), *Stilus – modus – usus. Regeln der Konflikt- und Verhandlungsführung am Papsthof des Mittelalters* [Rules of Negotiation and Conflict Resolution at the Papal Court in the Middle Ages] (Turnhout, 2019), pp. 67–95.

Krumm, M., *Herrschaftsumbruch und Historiographie. Zeitgeschichtsschreibung als Krisenbewältigung bei Alexander von Telese und Falco von Benevent* (Berlin/Boston, 2021).

Kuefler, M., *The Making and Unmaking of a Saint: Hagiography and Memory in the Cult of Gerald of Aurillac* (Philadelphia, 2014).

Kujawiński, J., 'Anonymi Barensis Chronicon', in G. Dunphy (ed.), *Encyclopedia of the Medieval Chronicle*, 2 vols (Leiden, 2010), vol. 1, p. 100.

Kujawiński, J., '*Ystoire de li Normant*, una testimonianza del secolo XI?', in G. M. Cantarella and A. Calzona (eds), *La Reliquia del Sangue di Cristo: Mantova, l'Italia e l'Europa al tempo di Leone IX* (Mantua, 2012), pp. 359–71.

Kümper, H., 'Annales Barenses (Annals of Bari)', in G. Dunphy (ed.), *Encyclopedia of the Medieval Chronicle*, 2 vols (Leiden, 2010), vol. 1, p. 55.

Kwakkel, E. and Newton, F., with an introduction by E. Glaze, *Medicine at Monte Cassino: Constantine the African and the Oldest Manuscript of his Pantegni* (Turnhout, 2019).

Kynsh, A., 'Ibn-Al Khaṭīb', in M. R. Menocal, R. P. Scheindlin and M. Sells (eds), *The Literature of Al-Andalus* (New York, 2000), pp. 358–71.

Lachaud, F., 'La simonie et les clercs simoniaques dans le Policraticus de Jean de Salisbury. Un aspect de la réforme morale et religieuse au milieu du XIIe siècle en Angleterre', in J. Barrow, F. Delivré and V. Gazeau (eds), *Autour de Lanfranc (1010–2010). Réforme et réformateurs dans l'Europe du Nord-Ouest (XIe – XIIe siècles)* (Caen, 2015), pp. 313–28.

Lane, E. W., *An Arabic–English Lexicon*, 8 parts (London and Edinburgh, 1863–93).

Lapina, E., 'St. Demetrius of Thessaloniki: Patron saint of crusaders', *Viator* 40 (2009), 93–112.

Lapina, E., *Warfare and the Miraculous in the Chronicles of the First Crusade* (University Park, 2015).

Lavarra, C., 'Coscienza civica e tensioni sociali nel Mezzogiorno normanno: Benevento nella prima metà del XII secolo', in C. Lavarra, *Mezzogiorno Normanno: Potere, spazio urbano, ritualità* (Galatina, 2005), pp. 97–140.

Lavarra, C., 'Rituali di accoglienza e spazio urbano nel Mezzogiorno normanno', in C. Lavarra, *Mezzogiorno normanno: potere, spazio urbano, ritualità* (Galatina, 2005), pp. 3–50.

Lefebvre, H., *The Production of Space*, trans. D. Nicholson-Smith (Oxford, 1991).

Lemarignier, J.-F., *Étude sur les privilèges d'exemption et de juridiction ecclésiastique des abbayes normandes depuis les origines jusqu'en 1140* (Paris, 1937).

Lemerle, P., 'Note sur les plus anciennes représentations de Saint Démétrius', Δελτίον ΧΑΕ 10 (1980–81), 1–10.

Le Patourel J., *The Norman Empire* (Oxford, 1976).

Lev, Y., *Saladin in Egypt* (Leiden, 1999).

Lévi-Provençal, E., 'Fatā', in *Encyclopaedia of Islam*, 2nd edn, 13 vols (Leiden, 1986), vol. 2, p. 837.

Licinio, R. and Violante, F. (eds), *I caratteri originari della conquista normanna. Diversità e identità nel Mezzogiorno (1030–1130)* (Bari, 2006).

Licinio, R. and Violante, F. (eds), *Nascita di un regno. Poteri signorili, istituzioni feudali e strutture sociali nel Mezzogiorno normanno (1130–1194)* (Bari, 2008).

Loud, G. A., 'Abbot Desiderius of Montecassino and the Gregorian papacy', *Journal of Ecclesiastical History* 30 (1979), 305–26.

Loud, G. A., 'The Norman counts of Caiazzo and the abbey of Montecassino', in *Monastica I. Scritti raccolti in memoria del XV centenario della nascita di S. Benedetto (480–1980)*, Miscellanea Cassinese 44 (Montecassino, 1981), pp. 199–217.

Loud, G. A., 'How "Norman" was the Norman conquest of southern Italy?', *Nottingham Medieval Studies* 25 (1981), 13–24.

Loud, G. A., 'The "Gens Normannorum": Myth or reality?', *ANS* 4 (1982), 104–16, 204–9.

Loud, G. A., *Church and Society in the Norman Principality of Capua, 1058–1197* (Oxford, 1985).

Loud, G. A., 'Byzantine Italy and the Normans', in J. D. Howard-Johnston (ed.), *Byzantium and the West c.850–c.1200* (Amsterdam, 1988), pp. 215–33.

Loud, G. A., 'Monarchy and monastery in the Mezzogiorno: The abbey of St. Sophia, Benevento and the Staufen', *Papers of the British School at Rome* 49 (1991), 283–318.

Loud, G. A., 'Norman Italy and the Holy Land', in B. Z. Kedar (ed.), *The Horns of Hattin* (Jerusalem, 1992), pp. 49–62.

Loud, G. A., 'Churches and churchmen in an age of conquest: Southern Italy, 1030–1130', *The Haskins Society Journal* 4 (1992), 37–53.

Loud, G. A., 'The genesis and the context of the Chronicle of Falco of Benevento', *ANS* 15 (1993), 177–98.

Loud, G. A., 'Continuity and change in Norman Italy: The Campania during the eleventh and twelfth centuries', *JMH* 22 (1996), 313–43.

Loud, G. A., 'A Lombard abbey in a Norman world: St Sophia, Benevento, 1050–1200', *ANS* 19 (1997), 273–305.

Loud, G. A., 'Politics, piety and ecclesiastical patronage in twelfth-century Benevento', in E. Cuozzo and J.-M. Martin (eds), *Cavalieri alla conquista del Sud. Studi sull'Italia normanna in memoria di Léon-Robert Ménager* (Rome, 1997), pp. 283–312.

Loud, G. A., 'Coinage, wealth and plunder in the age of Robert Guiscard', *EHR* 114 (1999), 815–43.

Loud, G. A., *Conquerors and Churchmen in Norman Italy* (Aldershot, 1999).
Loud, G. A., 'Il regno normanno-svevo visto dal regno d'Inghilterra', in G. Musca (ed.), *Il Mezzogiorno normanno-svevo visto dall'Europa e dal mondo mediterraneo* (Bari, 1999), pp. 175–95.
Loud, G. A., 'William the Bad or William the Unlucky? Kingship in Sicily 1154–1166', *Haskins Society Journal* 8 (1999), 99–113.
Loud, G. A., *The Age of Robert Guiscard: Southern Italy and the Norman Conquest* (Harlow, 2000).
Loud, G. A., *Montecassino and Benevento in the Middle Ages: Essays in South Italian Church History* (Aldershot, 2000).
Loud, G. A., 'A provisional list of the papal rectors of Benevento, 1101–1227', in G. A. Loud, *Montecassino and Benevento in the Middle Ages: Essays in South Italian Church History* (Aldershot, 2000), pp. 1–11.
Loud, G. A., 'The papacy and the rulers of southern Italy 1058–1198', in G. A. Loud and A. Metcalfe (eds), *The Society of Norman Italy* (Leiden, 2002), pp. 151–84.
Loud, G. A., 'The kingdom of Sicily and the kingdom of England, 1066–1266', *History* 88 (2003), 540–67.
Loud, G. A., 'Southern Italy in the eleventh century', in D. Luscombe and J. Riley-Smith (eds), *New Cambridge Medieval History*, vol. IV(2) (Cambridge, 2004), pp. 94–119.
Loud, G. A., 'Norman Sicily in the twelfth century', in D. Luscombe and J. Riley-Smith (eds), *New Cambridge Medieval History*, vol. IV(2) (Cambridge, 2004), pp. 442–74.
Loud, G. A., 'History writing in the twelfth-century kingdom of Sicily', in S. Dale, A. W. Lewin and D. J. Osheim (eds), *Chronicling History: Chroniclers and Historians in Medieval and Renaissance Italy* (University Park, 2007), pp. 29–54.
Loud, G. A., *The Latin Church in Norman Italy* (Cambridge, 2007).
Loud, G. A., 'The chancery and charters of the kings of Sicily (1130–1212)', *EHR* 124 (2009), 779–810.
Loud, G. A., 'Amatus of Montecassino (Amatus Casinensis)', in G. Dunphy (ed.), *Encyclopedia of the Medieval Chronicle*, 2 vols (Leiden, 2010), vol. 1, p. 34.
Loud, G. A., 'Southern Italy and the eastern and western empires, c.900–1050', *JMH* 38 (2012), 1–19.
Loud, G. A., 'Norman traditions in southern Italy', in S. Burkhardt and T. Foerster (eds), *Norman Tradition and Transcultural Heritage: Exchange of Cultures in the 'Norman' Peripheries of Medieval Europe* (Farnham, 2013), pp. 35–56.

Loud, G. A., 'Communities, cultures and conflict in southern Italy from the Byzantines to the Angevins', *Al-Masāq: Islam and the Medieval Mediterranean* 28 (2016), 132–52.
Loud, G. A., 'Innocent II and the kingdom of Sicily', in J. Doran and D. J. Smith (eds), *Pope Innocent II (1130–43): The World vs the City* (Abingdon, 2016), pp. 172–80.
Loud, G. A., 'A new document concerning the bishopric of Sebastea', *Crusades* 16 (2017), 21–31.
Loud, G. A. and Metcalfe A. (eds), *The Society of Norman Italy* (Leiden, 2002).
Loud, G. A. and Schenk, J. (eds), *The Origins of the German Principalities, 1100–1350: Essays by German Historians* (Abingdon, 2017).
Lucas-Avenel, M.-A., 'Le récit de Geoffroi Malaterra ou la légitimation de Roger, Grand Comte de Sicile', *ANS* 34 (2012), 169–92.
Luttrell, A., 'Gli ospedalieri nel mezzogiorno', in G. Musca (ed.), *Il mezzogiorno normanno-svevo e le crociate* (Bari, 2002), pp. 289–300.
Maillefer, J.-M., 'Une famille aristocratique aux confins de la Normandie: les Géré au XIe siècle', *Cahier des Annales de Normandie* 17 (1985), 175–206.
Mandalà, G., 'La sottoscrizione araba di ʿAbd al-Masīḥ (Palermo, 15 ottobre 1201)', *Quaderni di studi arabi* 3 (2008), 153–64.
Manselli, R., 'Epilogo', in *I Normanni e la loro espansione in Europa nell'Alto Medioevo*, Settimane di Studio del Centro Italiano di Studi sull'Alto Medioevo 16 (Spoleto, 1969).
Marcarelli, G., *L'oriente del Taburno. Storia dell'antica città di Tocco e dei suoi casali* (Benevento, 1915).
Marongiu, A., 'La forma religiosa del matrimonio nel diritto bizantino, normanno e svevo', *Archivio storico per la Calabria e la Lucania* 30 (1961), 1–30.
Marongiu, A., 'A model state in the middle ages: The Norman and Swabian kingdom of Sicily', *Comparative Studies in Society and History* 6 (1963–64), 307–20.
Marongiu, A., *Byzantine, Norman, Swabian and Later Institutions in Southern Italy* (London, 1972).
Marongiu, A., *Matrimonio e famiglia nell'Italia meridionale (sec. viii–xiii)* (Bari, 1976).
Martin, J.-M., 'Le monete d'argento nell'Italia meridionale del secolo XII secondo i documenti d'archivio', *Bolletino di numismatica* 6–7 (1986), 85–96.
Martin, J.-M., *La Pouille du VIe au XIIe siècle* (Rome, 1993).
Martin, J.-M., 'À propos d'un feuillet en écriture bénéventaine découvert à Rieti. Quelques considérations historiques', *Mélanges de l'École française de Rome. Moyen Âge* 114 (2002), 219–26.

Martin, J.-M., 'L'Italie méridionale', in *Città e campagna nei secoli altomedievali (Spoleto, 27 marzo-1 aprile 2008)*, 2 vols, Centro italiano di studi sull'alto medioevo. Atti delle Settimane 56 (Spoleto, 2009), vol. 2, pp. 733–74.
Martin, J.-M. and Alaggio, R. (eds), *'Quei Maledetti Normanni': Studi offerti a Errico Cuozzo*, 2 vols (Ariano Irpino, 2016).
Martino, F., 'Una ignota pagina del Vespro: la compilazione dei falsi privilegi Messinesi', *Archivio Storico Messinese* 57 (1991), 19–76.
Masud, M. K., 'The obligation to migrate: The doctrine of hijra in Islamic law', in D. F. Eickelman and J. Piscatori (eds), *Muslim Travellers: Pilgrimage, Migration, and the Religious Imagination* (Berkeley, 1990), pp. 29–49.
Matthew, D. J. A., *L'Europa normanna* (Rome, 1987).
Mattock, J. N., 'Ibn Baṭṭūta's use of Ibn Jubayr's *Riḥla*', in R. Peters (ed.), *Proceedings of the Ninth Congress of the Union Européenne des Arabisants et Islamisants* (Leiden, 1981), pp. 209–18.
Maume, P., 'Curtis, Edmund', *Dictionary of Irish Biography* (Cambridge, 2009).
Mauss, M., 'Essai sur le don. Forme et raison de l'échange dans les societies archaïque', *L'Année Sociologique*, 1 (1923–24), 30–186.
Mayer, H. E., 'Ein Deperditum Balduins III. von Jerusalem als Zeugnis seiner Pläne zur Eroberung Ägyptens', *Deutsches Archiv für Erforschung des Mittelalters* 36 (1980), 549–66.
Mayer, H. E., *Mélanges sur l'histoire du royaume latin de Jérusalem*, Mémoires de l'Académie des Inscriptions et Belles-Lettres, n.s. 5 (Paris, 1984).
Mayer, H. E., 'The beginnings of King Amalric of Jerusalem', in B. Z. Kedar (ed.), *The Horns of Hattin* (Jerusalem, 1992), pp. 121–35.
Mayer, H. E., *Geschichte der Kreuzzüge*, 10th edn (Stuttgart, 2005).
Mazzarese Fardella, E., *Aspetti dell'organizzazione amministrativa nel Regno normanno e svevo* (Milan, 1966).
Mazzarese Fardella, E., 'Il contributo di Evelyn Jamison agli studi sui Normanni d'Italia e di Sicilia', *Bulletino dell'Istituto Italiano per il Medio Evo* 83 (1971), 65–78.
Mazzarese Fardella, E., 'Problemi preliminari allo studio del ruolo delle contee nel regno di Sicilia', in *Società, potere e popolo nell'età di Ruggero II* (Bari, 1979), pp. 41–54.
McCready, W., 'Dating the dialogues of Abbot Desiderius of Montecassino', *Revue Bénédictine* 108 (1998), 145–68.
Melville, G., 'Aspekte zum Vergleich von Krisen und Reformen in mittelalterlichen Klöstern und Orden', in G. Melville and A. Müller (eds), *Mittelalterliche Orden und Klöster im Vergleich: methodische Ansätze und Perspektiven* (Berlin, 2007), pp. 139–60.

Ménager, L.-R., 'L'abbaye bénédictine de la Trinité de Mileto, en Calabre, à l'époque normande', *Bulletino dell'archivio paleografico italiano* 4–5 (1958–59), 9–94.

Ménager, L.-R., 'Les fondations monastiques de Robert Guiscard, duc de Pouille et de Calabre', *QF* 39 (1959), 1–116.

Ménager, L.-R., 'Inventaire des familles normandes et franques émigrées en Italie méridionale et en Sicilie (xie – xiie siècles)', in *Roberto il Guiscardo e il suo tempo: Relazioni e commuicazioni nelle Prime Giornate Normanno-Sveve del Centro di studi normanno-svevi* (Rome, 1975), pp. 260–390.

Ménager, L. R., *Hommes et institutions de l'Italie normande* (London, 1981).

Metcalfe, A., *Muslims and Christians in Norman Sicily: Arabic Speakers and the End of Islam* (London, 2003).

Metcalfe, A., *The Muslims of Medieval Italy* (Edinburgh, 2009).

Metcalfe, A., 'Before the Normans: Identity and societal formation in Muslim Sicily', in D. Booms and P. Higgs (eds), *Sicily, Heritage of the World* (London, 2019), pp. 102–19.

Möhring, H., *Saladin: The Sultan and his Times, 1138–1193*, trans. D. Bachrach (Baltimore, 2008).

Monti, G. M., 'Il testo e la storia esterna delle assise normanne', *Storia del diritto* 1 (1940), 295–348.

Monti, G. M., *Lo Stato Normanno Svevo. Lineamenti e ricerche* (Trani, 1945).

Moody, T. W., 'The writings of Edmund Curtis', *Irish Historical Studies* 12 (1943), 393–400.

Moody, T. W., 'Edmund Curtis (1881–1943)', *Hermathena* 63 (1944), 69–78.

Morrisson, C., 'Monnaie et prix à Byzance du Ve au VIIe siècle', in C. Morrisson, *Monnaie et finances à Byzance: analyses, techniques* (Aldershot, 1994), pp. 239–60.

Morrisson, C., 'Byzantine money: Its production and circulation', in E. Angeliki (ed.), *The Economic History of Byzantium: From the Seventh Through the Fifteenth Century*, vol. 3 (Washington, DC, 2002), pp. 909–66.

Mortensen, L. B., 'The glorious past: Entertainment, example or history? Levels of twelfth-century historical culture', *Culture and History* 13 (1994), 57–71.

Müller, M., *Die Lehre des hl. Augustinus von der Paradiesesehe und ihre Auswirkung in der Sexualethik des 12. und 13. Jahrhunderts bis Thomas von Aquin* (Regensburg, 1954).

Murray, A. V., 'Norman settlement in the Latin kingdom of Jerusalem, 1099–1131', *Archivio Normanno-Svevo* 1 (2009), 61–85.

Murray, A. V., 'The place of Egypt in the military strategy of the Crusades, 1099–1221', in E. J. Mylod *et al.* (eds), *The Fifth Crusade in Context: The Crusading Movement in the Early Thirteenth Century* (Abingdon, 2016), pp. 117–34.

Murray, A. V., 'The grand designs of Gilbert of Assailly: The Order of the Hospital in the projected conquest of Egypt by King Amalric of Jerusalem (1168–1169)', *Ordines Militares: Yearbook for the Study of the Military Orders* 20 (2016), 7–24.

Nef, A., 'Conquêtes et reconquêtes médiévales: la Sicile normande est-elle une terre de réduction en servitude généralisée?', *Mélanges de l'École française de Rome, Moyen-Âge* 112/2 (2000), 579–607.

Nef, A., *Conquérir et gouverner la Sicile islamique aux XIe et XIIe siècles* (Rome, 2011).

Nef, A., 'Imaginaire impérial, empire et oecuménisme religieux: quelques réflexions depuis la Sicile des Hauteville', *Cahiers de recherches médiévales et humanistes* 24 (2012), 227–49.

Nelson, J. L., 'Legislation and consensus in the time of Charles the Bald', in P. Wormald, D. Bullough and R. Collins (eds), *Ideal and Reality in Frankish and Anglo-Saxon Society: Studies Presented to J. M. Wallace-Hadrill* (Oxford, 1983), pp. 202–27.

Nelson, J. L., 'Kingship and empire', in J. H. Burns (ed.), *The Cambridge History of Medieval Political Thought c.350–c.1450* (Cambridge, 1988), pp. 211–51.

Netton, I. R., 'Basic structures and signs of alienation in the "*Riḥla* of Ibn Jubayr"', *Journal of Arabic Literature* 22 (1991), 21–37.

Netton, I. R., '*Riḥla*', in B. Lewis *et al.* (eds), *Encyclopedia of Islam*, 2nd edn (Leiden, 1995), vol. 8, p. 328.

Neveux, F., *L'Aventure des Normands (VIIIe–XIIIe siècle)* (Paris, 2006).

Newton, F., *The Scriptorium and Library at Monte Cassino, 1058–1105* (Cambridge, 1999).

Niermeyer, J. F. (ed.), *Mediae Latinitatis Lexicon Minus = Lexique latin médiéval = Medieval Latin dictionary = Mittellateinisches Wörterbuch* (Leiden, 2001).

Niermeyer, J. F. and van de Kieft, C. (eds), *Mediae Latinitatis Lexicon minus*, rev. edn, 2 vols (Leiden, 2002).

Noonan, J. T., 'Marriage in the Middle Ages I: Power to choose', *Viator* 4 (1973), 419–34.

[*I*] *Normanni e la loro espansione in Europa nell'Alto Medioevo*, Settimane di Studio del Centro Italiano di Studi sull'Alto Medioevo 16 (Spoleto, 1969).

Norwich, J. J., *The Normans in the South* (London, 1967) [published in the same year in New York under the title *The Other Conquest*].

Norwich, J. J., *The Kingdom in the Sun* (London, 1970).
Occhiato, G., 'Rapporti culturali e rispondenze architettoniche tra Calabria e Francia in età romantica: l'abbazia normanna di Sant'Eufemia', *Mélanges de l'Ecole française de Rome. Moyen Âge, temps moderne* 93 (1981), 565–603.
Occhiato, G., 'Robert de Grandmesnil: un abate "architetto" operante in Calabria nell'XI secolo', *Studi medievali* 28 (1987), 609–66.
Oexle, O. G., 'Peace through conspiracy', in B. Jussen (ed.), *Ordering Medieval Society: Perspectives on Intellectual and Practical Modes of Shaping Social Relations* (Philadelphia, 2001), pp. 285–322.
Oldfield, P., 'Urban government in southern Italy, c.1085–c.1127', *EHR* 122 (2007), 579–608.
Oldfield, P., 'The Iberian imprint on medieval southern Italy', *History* 93 (2008), 312–27.
Oldfield, P., *City and Community in Norman Italy* (Cambridge, 2009).
Oldfield, P., *Sanctity and Pilgrimage in Medieval Southern Italy, 1000–1200* (Cambridge, 2014).
Oldfield, P., *Urban Panegyric and the Transformation of the Medieval City, 1100–1300* (Oxford, 2019).
Panero, F., *Schiavi, servi, e villani nell'Italia medievale* (Turin, 1999).
Pennington, K., 'The birth of the *ius commune*: King Roger II's legislation', *Rivista internazionale di diritto comune* 17 (2006), 23–60
Pennington, K., 'The Normans in Palermo: King Roger II's legislation', *Haskins Society Journal* 18 (2006), 140–67.
Peri, I., *Villani e cavalieri nella Sicilia medievale* (Bari, 1993).
Pertusi, A., 'Monasteri e monaci italiani all'Athos nell'alto medioevo', in *Le Millénaire du Mont Athos 963–1963. Études et Mélanges*, 2 vols (Chevetogne/Venice, 1963–64), vol. 1, pp. 217–51.
Peters, A., 'Joannes Messor, seine Lebensbeschreibung und ihre Entstehung' (PhD dissertation, University of Bonn, 1955).
Peters-Custot, A., *Les Grecs de l'Italie méridionale post-byzantine (IXe–XIVe siècle). Une acculturation en douceur* (Rome, 2009).
Peters-Custot, A., 'Le monachisme italo-grec, entre Byzance et l'Occident (VIIIe-XIIIe siècles): autorité de l'higoumène, autorité du charisme, autorité de la règle', in J.-F. Cottier, D.-O. Hurel and B.-M. Tock (eds), *Les personnes d'autorité en milieu régulier. Des origines de la vie régulière au XVIIIe siècle* (Saint-Étienne, 2013), pp. 251–66.
Peters-Custot, A., '"Byzantine" versus "Imperial" kingdom: How "Byzantine" was the Hauteville king of Sicily?', in F. Daim *et al.* (eds), *Menschen, Bilder, Sprache, Dinge. Wege der Kommunikation zwischen Byzanz und dem Westen, 2. Menschen und Worte* (Mainz, 2018), pp. 235–48.

Petrizzo, F., 'Band of brothers: Kin dynamics of the Hautevilles and other Normans in southern Italy and Syria, c.1030–c.1140' (PhD dissertation, University of Leeds, 2018).

Petrukhin V. I., 'The Normans and the Khazars in the south of Rus (the formation of the "Russian land" in the Middle Dnepr area)', *Russian History* 19 (1992), 393–400.

Phillips, J., 'The travels of Ibn Jubayr and his view of Saladin', in K. V. Jensen, K. Salonen and H. Voght (eds) *Cultural Encounters During the Crusades* (Odense, 2013), pp. 75–90.

Piccitto, G., *Vocabolario Siciliano*, 5 vols (Catania–Palermo, 1977–2002).

Pispisa, E., 'Organizzazione urbana di Messina e i suoi rapporti con il territorio nel medioevo', in G. Fallico, A. Sparti and U. Balistreri (eds), *Messina: il Ritorno della memoria* (Palermo, 1994), pp. 337–41.

Pispisa, E., *Messina medievale* (Galatina, 1996).

Pohl, B., 'Schnittpunkt Süditalien: Päpste, Patriarchen und Normannen im späteren 11. Jahrhundert, 1054 und 1098', in M. Altripp (ed.), *Byzanz in Europa: Europas östliches Erbe* (Turnhout, 2012), pp. 97–113.

Pohl, B., 'What sort of man should the abbot be? Three voices from the Norman abbey of Mont-Saint-Michel', in S. Vanderputten (ed.), *Abbots and Abbesses as a Human Resource in the Ninth- to Twelfth-Century West* (Zurich, 2019), pp. 101–24.

Pohl, B., 'The problem of Cluniac exemption', in S. G. Bruce and S. Vanderputten (eds), *A Companion to the Abbey of Cluny in the Middle Ages* (Leiden, forthcoming).

Pohl, B. and Vanderputten, S., 'Fécamp, Cluny, and the invention of traditions in the later eleventh century', *Journal of Medieval Monastic Studies* 5 (2016), 1–41.

Pontieri, E., 'L'Abbazia benedettina di Sant'Eufemia in Calabria e l'abate Roberto di Grantmesnil', *Archivio storico per la Sicilia* 22 (1926), 92–115.

Porter, D., *Health, Civilization and the State: A History of Public Health from Ancient to Modern Times* (London, 1999).

Potts, C., *Monastic Revival and Regional Identity in Early Normandy* (Woodbridge, 1997).

Pratt, D., *The Political Thought of King Alfred the Great* (Cambridge, 2007).

Prutz, H., 'Studien über Wilhelm von Tyrus', *Neues Archiv der Gesellschaft für ältere deutsche Geschichtskunde* 8 (1883), 91–132.

Pryor, J. H., 'Transportation of horses by sea during the era of the crusades: Eighth century to 1285 A.D.', *Mariner's Mirror* 68 (1982), 9–27 and 103–25.

Pryor, J. H., 'The naval architecture of crusader transport ships and horse transports revisited', *Mariner's Mirror* 76 (1990), 255–74.

Pryor, J. H., 'A medieval Mediterranean maritime revolution: Crusading by sea, ca. 1096–1204', in D. N. Carlson, J. Leidwanger and S. M. Kampbell (eds), *Maritime Studies in the Wake of the Byzantine Shipwreck at Yassıada, Turkey* (College Station, 2015), pp. 174–88.

Rabbat, N., 'Who was al-Maqrizī? A biographical sketch', *Mamluk Studies Review* 7 (2003), 1–19.

Rachman, G., 'Rival historians trade blows over Brexit', *Financial Times* (13 May 2016).

Ramseyer, V., *The Transformation of a Religious Landscape: Medieval Southern Italy, 850–1150* (Ithaca, 2006).

Re, M., 'Il copista, la datazione e la genesi del *Messan. gr. 115* (*Typicon* de Messina)', *Bollettino della Badia Greca di Grottaferrata* 44 (1990), 145–56.

Reinhardt, H. J. F., *Die Ehelehre der Schule des Anselm von Laon. Eine theologie-und kirchenrechtsgeschichtliche Untersuchung zu den Ehetexten der frühen Pariser Schule des 12. Jahrhunderts*, Beiträge zur Geschichte der Philosophie und Theologie des Mittelalters, n.s. 14 (Münster, 1974).

Reuter, T., 'Gifts and simony', in E. Cohen and M. B. De Jong (eds), *Medieval Transformations: Texts, Power, and Gifts in Context* (Leiden, 2001), pp. 157–68.

Reynolds, P. L., *Marriage in the Western Church: The Christianisation of Marriage during the Patristic and Early Medieval Period* (Boston, 2001).

Roach, D., 'Saint-Évroul and southern Italy in Orderic's *Historia ecclesiastica*', in C. C. Rozier et al. (eds), *Orderic Vitalis: Life, Works and Interpretations* (Woodbridge, 2016), pp. 79–99.

Roche, T., 'Reading Orderic with charters in mind', in C. C. Rozier et al. (eds), *Orderic Vitalis: Life, Works and Interpretations* (Woodbridge, 2016), pp. 145–71.

Rouzati, N., *Trial and Tribulation in the Qur'an: A Mystical Theodicy* (Berlin, 2015).

Runciman, S., 'The visit of King Amalric I to Constantinople in 1171', in B. Z. Kedar, H. E. Mayer and R. C. Smail (eds), *Outremer: Studies in the History of the Crusading Kingdom of Jerusalem* (Jerusalem, 1982), pp. 153–8.

Russo, F., *Medici e veterinari calabresi (sec. VI–XV). Ricerche storico-bibliografiche* (Naples, 1962).

Russo, L., 'Oblio e memoria di Boemondo d'Altavilla nella storiografia normanna', *Bullettino dell'Istituto Storico per il Medio Evo* 106 (2004), 137–65.

Russo, L., *I Normanni del Mezzogiorno e il movimento crociato* (Bari, 2014).

Russo, L., 'The Norman Empire nella medievistica del XX secolo: una definizione problematica', *Schede Medievali* 54 (2016), 159–73.

Ryan, J. J., 'Letter of an anonymous French reformer to a Byzantine official in South Italy: De simoniaca heresi (Ms Vat. Lat. 3830)', *Mediaeval Studies* 15 (1953), 233–42.

Saad, R., 'War in the social memory of Egyptian peasants', in S. Heydemann (ed.), *War, Institutions, and Social Change in the Middle East* (Berkeley, 2000), pp. 240–57.

Safran, L., *The Medieval Salento: Art and Identity in Southern Italy* (Philadelphia, 2014).

Sambon, A., 'Monetazione di Ruggiero II Re di Sicilia (1130–1154)', *Rivista Italiana di Numismatica* 24 (1911), 437–75.

Scaduto, M., *Il monachesimo basiliano nella Sicilia medievale. Rinascità e Decadenza sec. XI–XIV* (Rome, 1982).

Schieffer, R., 'Motu proprio. Über die papstgeschichtliche Wende im 11. Jahrhundert', *Historisches Jahrbuch* 122 (2002), 27–41.

Schilling, B., *Guido von Vienne – Papst Calixt II* (Hanover, 1998).

Schlichte, A., *Der 'gute' König. Wilhelm II. von Sizilien (1166–1189)* (Tübingen, 2005).

Schlumberger, G., *Campagnes du roi Amaury Ier en Égypte, en XIIe siècle* (Paris, 1906).

Schmale, F.-J., 'Synoden Papst Alexanders II. (1061–1073). Anzahl, Termine, Entscheidungen', *Annuarium Historiae Conciliorum* 11 (1979), 307–38.

Sear, D. R., *Byzantine Coins and their Values*, 2nd edn (London, 1987).

Shopkow, L., *History and Community: Norman Historical Writing in the Eleventh and Twelfth Centuries* (Washington, DC, 1997).

Siegmund, D., *Die Stadt Benevent im Hochmittelalter* (Aachen, 2011).

Skinner, P., *Family Power in Southern Italy: The Duchy of Gaeta and its Neighbours 850–1139* (Cambridge, 1995).

Smail, R. C., *Crusading Warfare 1097–1193*, 2nd edn (New York, 1995).

Somerville, R., 'The councils of Gregory VII', *Studi Gregoriani per la storia della 'libertas ecclesiae'* 13 (1989), 33–53.

Souillet, G., 'Bécherel, Cocherel et Choisel', *Annales de Bretagne* 65 (1958), 547–50.

Spahr, R., *Le monete siciliane dai Bizantini a Carlo d'Angiò (582–1282)* (Zurich, 1976).

Spear, D. S., 'The Norman empire and the secular clergy, 1066–1204', *Journal of British Studies* 21 (1982), 1–10.

Spencer, S., '"Like a raging lion"': Richard the Lionheart's anger during the Third Crusade in medieval and modern historiography', *EHR* 132 (2017), 495–532.

Stafford, P., 'The laws of Cnut and the history of Anglo-Saxon royal promises', *Anglo-Saxon England* 10 (1981), 172–90.

Stanton, C. D., *Norman Naval Operations in the Mediterranean* (Woodbridge, 2011).

Stanton, C. D., 'The Battle of Civitate: A plausible account', *Journal of Medieval Military History* 11 (2013), 25–55.

Staunton, M., *The Historians of Angevin England* (Oxford, 2017).

Stephenson, Paul, *Byzantium's Balkan Frontier* (Cambridge, 2009).

Stiernon, D., 'Saint Cyprien de Calamizzi (+ vers 1210–1215). Notule chronologique', *Revue des Études Byzantines* 32 (1974), 247–52.

Strano, G., 'Echi storici nei testi agiografici italo-greci di età normanna. Le Vitae di San Luca, vescovo di Isola Capo Rizzuto, di San Bartolomeo da Simeri e di San Cipriano di Calamizzi', *Aiônos* 17 (2011–12), 101–41.

Stringer, K. J. and Jotischky, A. (eds), *Norman Expansion: Connections, Continuities, Contrasts* (Abingdon, 2013).

Stringer, K. J., and Jotischky, A. (eds), *The Normans and the 'Norman Edge': Peoples, Polities and Identities on the Frontiers of Medieval Europe* (London, 2019).

Stroll, M., *Calixtus II (1119–1124): A Pope Born to Rule* (Leiden, 2004).

Stürner, W., *Friedrich II*. Part 2: *Der Kaiser 1220–1250* (Darmstadt, 2003).

Szövérffy, J., 'Der Investiturstreit und die Petrus-Hymnen des Mittelalters', *Deutsches Archiv für Erforschung des Mittelalters* 13 (1957), 228–40.

Takayama, H., *The Administration of the Norman Kingdom of Sicily* (Leiden, 1993).

Takayama, H., *Sicily and the Mediterranean in the Middle Ages* (Abingdon, 2019).

Tangl, G., *Die Teilnehmer an den allgemeinen Konzilien des Mittelalters*, 2nd edn (Cologne, 1969).

Taviani-Carozzi, H., *La terreur du monde: Robert Guiscard et la conquête normande en Italie* (Paris, 1996).

Tayob, A., 'An analytical survey of al-Ṭabarī's exegesis of the cultural symbolic construct of *fitna*', in G. R. Hawting and A.-K. A. Shareef (eds), *Approaches to the Qurān* (New York, 1993), pp. 157–72.

Tescione, G., 'Roberto conte normanno di Alife, Caiazzo e S. Agata dei Goti', *Archivio storico di Terra di Lavoro* 4 (1975), 9–52.

Theotokis, G., *The Norman Campaigns in the Balkans, 1081–1108* (Woodbridge, 2014).

Touati, H., *Islam and Travel in the Middle Ages*, trans. L. G. Cochrane (Chicago, 2010).

Tounta, E., 'Saints, rulers and communities: The Vitae of the Italo-Greek saints (tenth to eleventh centuries) and their audiences', *JMH* 42 (2016), pp. 429–55.

Tounta, E., 'Conflicting sanctities and the construction of collective memories in Byzantine and Norman Italo-Greek Southern Calabria: Elias the Younger and Elias Speleotes', *Analecta Bollandiana* 135 (2017), 101–44.

Tramontana, S., 'I luoghi della produzione storiografica', in G. Musca (ed.), *Centri della produzione della cultura nel Mezzogiorno normanno-svevo* (Bari, 1997), pp. 21–40.

Travaini, L., 'La riforma monetaria di Ruggero II e la circolazione minuta in Italia meridionale tra X e XII secolo', *Rivista Italiana di Numismatica* 83 (1981), 133–53.

Travaini, L., *La monetazione nell'Italia normanna* (Rome, 1995).

Travaini, L., 'The monetary reforms of William II (1166–1189): Oriental and western patterns in Norman Sicilian coinage', *Schweizer Münzblätter* 46 (1996), 109–23.

Travaini, L., 'The Normans between Byzantium and the Islamic world', *Dumbarton Oaks Papers* 55 (2001), 179–96.

Treseler, W., 'Lothar III. und die Privilegien des Klosters Montecassino: symbolische Kommunikation während des Konfliktes zwischen Kaiser und Papst im Jahr 1137', *Frühmittelalterliche Studien* 35 (2001), 313–28.

Tronzo, W., *The Cultures of his Kingdom: Roger II and the Cappella Palatina in Palermo* (Princeton, 1997).

Vaccari, P., 'La celebrazione del matrimonio in una assisa di Ruggero II', in *VIII centenario della monte di Ruggero II. Atti del convegno internazionale di studi Ruggeriani (21–25 aprile 1954)*, 2 vols (Palermo, 1955), vol. 1, pp. 205–11.

Vagnoni, M., *Le rappresentazioni del potere. La sacralità regia dei Normanni di Sicilia: un mito?* (Bari, 2012).

van Houts, E., *Married Life in the Middle Ages, 900–1300* (Oxford, 2019).

Varvaro, A., 'Les Normands en Sicile aux XIe et XIIe siècles. Présence effective dans l'île des hommes d'origine normande ou gallo-romane', *Cahiers de Civilisation Médiévale* 23 (1980), 199–213.

Vehse, O., 'Benevent als Territorium des Kirchenstaates bis zum Beginn der avignonesischen Epoche. I', *QF* 22 (1930–31), 87–160.

Via, A. P., 'Tancred of Hauteville, sons of', in C. Kleinhenz (ed.), *Medieval Italy: An Encyclopedia*, 2 vols, 2nd edn (New York, 2004), vol. 2, pp. 1068–9.

Vigot, A.-S., 'Archaeological investigations at the Abbey of Saint-Évroult-Notre-Dame-du-Bois', in C. C. Rozier et al. (eds), *Orderic Vitalis: Life, Works and Interpretations* (Woodbridge, 2016), pp. 375–84.

Vigot, A.-S., 'La salle capitulaire de l'abbaye de Saint-Évroult-Notre-Dame-du-Bois: Rapport final d'opération archéologique' (2014) http://openarchive.eveha.fr/uploads/documents/280-rapport.pdf.

von Falkenhausen, V., 'Cristodulo', in *Dizionario Biografico degli Italiani* 31 (1985), pp. 49–51.
von Falkenhausen, V., 'L'Archimandritato del S. Salvatore in lingua phari di Messina e il monachesimo italo-greco nel regno normanno-svevo (secoli XI–XIII)', in G. Fallico, A. Sparti and U. Balistreri (eds), *Messina: il Ritorno della memoria* (Palermo, 1994), pp. 41–52.
von Falkenhausen, V., 'I rapporti con Bisanzio', in M. D'Onofrio (ed.), *I Normanni. Popolo d'Europa 1030–1200* (Venice, 1994), pp. 350–5.
von Falkenhausen, V., 'Friedrich II. und die Griechen im Königreich Sizilien', in A. Esch and N. Kamp (eds), *Friedrich II. Tagung des Deutschen Historischen Instituts in Rom im Gedenkjahr 1994* (Tübingen, 1996), pp. 235–62.
von Falkenhausen, V., 'The Greek presence in Norman Sicily: The contribution of archival material in Greek', in G. A. Loud and A. Metcalfe (eds), *The Society of Norman Italy* (Leiden, 2002), pp. 253–87.
von Falkenhausen, V., 'I logoteti greci nel regno normanno. Uno studio prosopografico', in P. Corrao and I. E. Mineo (eds), *Dentro e fuori la Sicilia: studi di storia per Vincenzo D'Alessandro* (Rome, 2009), pp. 101–24.
von Falkenhausen, V., 'Die griechischen Gemeinden in Messina und Palermo (11. bis 13. Jahrhundert)', in T. Jäckh and M. Kirsch (eds), *Urban Dynamics and Transcultural Communication in Medieval Sicily* (Paderborn, 2017), pp. 27–66.
Walter, C., *The Warrior Saints in Byzantine Art and Tradition* (Aldershot, 2003).
Wansbrough, J., *The Sectarian Milieu: Content and Composition of Islamic Salvation History* (New York, 1978).
Webber, E., 'Construction of identity in twelfth-century Andalusia: The case of travel writing', *The Journal of North African Studies* 5 (2000), 1–8.
Wedgwood, C. V., 'In memoriam: Evelyn Mary Jamison, 1877–1972', *The Brown Book: Lady Margaret Hall Oxford* (December, 1972), p. 35.
Wehr, H. and Cowan J. M. (eds), *A Dictionary of Modern Written Arabic: (Arabic-English*, 3rd edn (Wiesbaden, 1961; repr. Beirut, 1980).
West, C., 'Competing for the Holy Spirit: Humbert of Moyenmoutier and the question of simony', in F. Depreux, F. Bougard and R. Le Jan (eds), *Compétition et sacré au haut Moyen âge. Entre mediation et exclusion* (Turnhout, 2015), pp. 327–40.
White, Jr, L. T., *Latin Monasticism in Norman Sicily* (Cambridge, MA, 1938).
White, M., *Military Saints in Byzantium and Rus, 900–1200* (Cambridge, 2013).
Wieruszowski, H., 'Roger II of Sicily, *Rex-Tyrannus*, in twelfth-century political thought', *Speculum* 38 (1963), 46–78.

Wieruszowski, H., 'The Norman kingdom of Sicily and the crusades', in K. M. Setton *et al.* (eds), *A History of the Crusades*, 2nd edn, 6 vols (Madison, 1969–89), vol. 2, pp. 3–42.

Winkler E. A., Fitzgerald, L. and Small, A. (eds), *Designing Norman Sicily: Material Culture and Society* (Woodbridge, 2020).

Wolf, K. B, *Making History: The Normans and their Historians in Eleventh-Century Italy* (Philadelphia, 1995).

Wolter, H., *Ordericus Vitalis: ein Beitrag zur kluniazensischen Geschichtsschreibung* (Wiesbaden, 1955).

Zabbia, M., 'La cultura storiografica dell'Italia normanna riflessa nel *Chronicon* di Romualdo Salernitano', in I. Bonincontro (ed.), *Progetti di ricerca della Scuola storica nazionale: Contributi alla IV settimana di studi medievali* (Rome, 2009), pp. 5–16.

Zavarrone, A., *Note sopra la bolla di Godano arcivescovo dell'Acerenza* (Naples, 1755).

Zey, C., 'Die Augen des Papstes: zu Eigenschaften und Vollmachten päpstlicher Legaten', in J. Johrendt and H. Müller (eds), *Römisches Zentrum und kirchliche Peripherie. Das universale Papsttum als Bezugspunkt der Kirchen von den Reformpäpsten bis zu Innozenz III* (Berlin, 2008), pp. 77–108.

Additional websites

www.officiel-galeries-musees.com/musee/musee-de-normandie/exposition/russie-viking-vers-une-autre-normandie
www.unicaen.fr/craham/spip.php?article574&lang=fr

Index

For all individuals found within the Cefalù name-lists, and associated discussion of those names, see chapter 4 and the 'index of reconstructed names' in Table 4.1

'Abd al-Masīḥ, palace eunuch 126
Abelard, nephew of Robert
  Guiscard 269, 270
Abruzzi 2
Abulchares, Byzantine *catepan*
  269, 270
Accardus, baron 98
Acre 121, 122, 123, 124
Adelaide del Vasto, regent of Sicily
  221, 305, 306
Adeliza de Grandmesnil 195
Adelperga, daughter of Desiderius,
  king of the Lombards 247
al-'Aḍīd, caliph 312
Adriatic, sea 7, 265, 277, 317
Africa 19, 49, 278, 307, 308, 309
Agnes of Courtenay 310
Ailano 247, 251
Alberic, monk of
  Montecassino 233
Aleppo 119, 310, 317
Alexander, count of Conversano/
  Gravina 311, 312
Alexander II, pope 193, 229
Alexander III, pope 212, 252
Alexander of Telese, chronicler 3,
  22, 220, 294
Alexandria 115, 305, 308, 309,
  310, 313, 314, 315, 316, 318

Alexios Kontostephanos,
  commander 312
Alexius I Komnenos, emperor 157,
  288, 289, 290, 291, 292
Alfanus I, archbishop of
  Salerno 237
Alferada, abbess of St Mary of
  Capua 256
Alferius Draco, baron 98, 102, 103
Ali, son of Tamim ibn al Mu'izz of
  Mahdiyah 270
Alife 246, 252, 255, 256
Almohad empire 113, 115, 117,
  118, 309
Alo, archbishop of Siponto 194
Alps, mountain range 175,
  176, 197
Alta Irpinia 102
Amalfi 18
Amalric, king of Jerusalem 118,
  306, 307, 309–16, 318
Amato, river 193
Amatus of Montecassino,
  chronicler 2, 17, 35, 192,
  227, 228, 233, 234, 266,
  268, 272, 276
Ambroise, chronicler 172, 175,
  176, 177, 182
America 29

Amerino, knight/mercenary 275
Amicus, son-in-law of Jocelyn of Molfetta 269, 270
Anacletus II, (anti)pope 213, 216, 232, 233, 293
Anatolian Plateau 276
al-Andalus 60
  see also Spain
Angevin dynasty 23, 25
Anonymous, author of the Itinerarium Peregrinorum et Gesta Regis Ricardi 172, 175, 176, 177, 179, 181
Ansa, queen of the Lombards 248
Anselm of Laon, theologian 214
Anselperga, abbess of Holy Saviour (St Julia) of Brescia 248
Ansger, bishop of Catania 34
Ansketil of Maida 194
Anso, dominus of the Beneventans 254
Antioch 22, 23
  prinicipality of 313
  see also Bohemond, prince
Antony, prepositus of St Sophia (Benevento) 248
Apulia 18, 20, 191, 192, 197, 198, 218, 229, 255, 256, 257, 265, 267, 268, 269, 274, 275, 277, 284, 285, 292, 294, 295, 296, 309, 311, 318
Aquileia 94, 98
Arabia 117, 118
Aragonese dynasty 25
Argyritzos, of Bari 274, 275, 277
Argyros, catepan 271
Ariano Irpino 32, 100
'Assizes of Ariano' 158, 230, 284
Arichis II, duke/prince of Benevento 247, 248, 254
Arnold de Grandmesnil 195

Arnulf, archbishop of Cosenza 194
Arp Arslan, sultan 276
Ascalon 306, 307, 310, 317
Asia Minor 270
Atenulf I, prince 249
Augustine, saint 214
Autpertus, prepositus of St Sophia (Benevento) 248
Avartutele, Byzantine catepan 274, 275
Avellino 230
Aversa 231
Ayub, son of Tamim ibn al Mu'izz of Mahdiyah 270
Ayyūbid dynasty 313
  see also Saladin, sultan
al-'Azīz of Egypt 123

Baghdad 115
Bagnara 177
Baldwin I, king of Jerusalem 305, 306
Baldwin III, king of Jerusalem 306, 307, 310
Baldwin IV, king of Jerusalem 125, 311, 315
Baldwin V, count of Flanders 197
Balkans 265, 289, 290, 292, 295, 296
Banyas 313, 314
Barbatus, saint 232
Bari 7, 18, 32, 33, 219, 230, 257, 268, 269, 270–4
  see also Maio of Bari, admiral of admirals
Bartholomew di Pietrelcina, baron 98
Bartholomew of Simeri, saint 156–9, 164
Basilicata 229
Bassacius, abbot of Montecassino 248

Index

Belfast 16
Benedict, deacon and *prepositus* of St Sophia of Benevento 254
Benedict, saint 193, 247, 253
Benevento 6, 132–45, 228, 231, 232, 246, 247, 248, 249, 252, 254
　St Sophia, monastery 135, 143, 246, 247, 248, 249, 250, 253–5
　see also Falco of Benevento, chronicler
Benjamin of Tudela, traveller/author 173
Bernard, abbot of Montecassino 253
Bernay, monastery 203
Bizantius of Bari, *patrikios* 273, 274, 275
Bohemond, prince of Antioch 23, 257
Brescia 247, 248
Briatico 155
Brindisi 257, 268, 275, 277
British Isles 16, 22
Buonalbergo 100
Byzantium/Byzantine empire 4, 5, 7, 18, 21, 24, 25, 33, 36, 157, 179, 265, 268, 270, 285, 286, 293, 307, 310, 311, 317, 318
　see also Constantinople

Caen 30, 31
Caiazzo 231, 255
　monastery of Holy Spirit 231
Cairo 312
Calabria 6, 34, 152, 153–5, 156, 159, 160, 161, 164, 178, 191, 192, 197, 198, 218, 236, 250, 256, 267, 268, 269, 270, 273, 294
Calixtus II, pope 231, 232, 256
Calore, river 102
Cambridge 15
Campania 7
Cape Bon 309
Cappadocia 270
Capua 20, 35, 102, 218, 251, 254, 256, 294
　see also Jordan I, prince; Richard I, prince; Robert I, prince; Robert II, prince
Carda, abbess of St Mary of Capua 251
Caserta 247
Cassino 250
Castrogiovanni 268
Catania 80, 178, 278
Cava, monastery of Holy Trinity 3–4
Cefalù 5, 46–84, 269
　cathedral 46
　name-lists (for all individual names found within, and associated discussion of those names) 48–84
Celestine II, pope 100
Cephalonia 249
Ceprano 133
Cerami 268
Cerisy-La-Salle 31
Charlemagne, king/emperor 17, 247
Christodoulos, admiral 156, 157
Cilicia, kingdom of 313
Civitate 266, 267
Clement II, pope 229
Clement III, (anti)pope 234
　see also Guibert, archbishop of Ravenna
Cluny, monastery 196, 203

Cnut, king of Denmark/England/ Norway 216
Collesano 48
Constance, daughter of Philip I of France 257
Constance, empress and queen of Sicily 2
Constantine, bishop of Caiazzo 231
Constantine X Doukas, emperor 193
Constantinople 157, 171, 265, 269, 270, 273, 274, 275, 288, 291, 295, 311, 312, 318
Conversano 219, 231, 311
Cosenza 250, 268
Cotentin 6, 191, 266
  see also Normandy
County Donegal 16
Criscius, *medicus* and *prepositus* of St Sophia (Benevento) 248, 249
Crusader States 120–4, 126, 127
Cumberland 16
Cursano 159, 160
Cyprian of Calamizzi, saint and abbot 161–3, 164

Daddaeus, son of Landulf of Greca 136
Dalmatia 311
Damascus 115, 121, 307, 310, 313, 314, 317
Damietta 308, 309, 310, 312, 316
Dār al-Islām 6, 113, 117–20, 127
Darum 307, 312
David, abbot of Holy Trinity (Mileto) 48
Dead Sea 314
Demetrius, saint 289, 291, 292
Desiderius, abbot of Montecassino 35, 233
  see also Victor III, pope

Desiderius, king of the Lombards 247, 248
Deusdedit, abbot of St John (*de Porta Aurea*) of Benevento 246
Devon 16
Dirgham, vizier 310
Drogo of Hauteville 192
Dublin 17
Durazzo 276, 277
  see also Dyracchium
Durrës 290, 317
Dyrrachium 265, 290, 291, 317

Egypt 7, 115, 118, 123, 305–18
  see also Fatimid dynasty/empire
El 'Arish 307
Eleutherius, saint 249
Elvira of Castile 297
England 15, 17, 22, 23, 25, 30, 181, 216, 219
Enna *see* Castrogiovanni
Erchempert of Montecassino, chronicler 248
Eremburga of Hauteville 193
Ete, river 247, 249
Eternus, baron 98
Eudokia Makrembolitissa, imperial regent 270
Eugenius, admiral 21

Falco of Benevento, chronicler 3, 5, 19, 132–45, 231, 232, 284, 286
  see also Benevento
al-Farama 308
Faroaldus, *prepositus* of St Mary *in Cingla* 249
Fatimid dynasty/empire 115, 118, 307, 310, 312, 314
  see also al-'Aḍīd, caliph
Fico, port of 193, 194

Fitalie 86
France 31, 35, 172, 181, 193, 199
    see also Normandy
Frederick II, emperor and king
    of Sicily 2, 19, 162, 163,
    219, 220
Friuli 247
Fusṭāṭ 118

Gaeta 18
Gaitelgrima, daughter of Robert,
    count of Caiazzo 255
Gaitruda, abbess of St Mary in
    Cingla 249
Galilee 23, 313, 317
    sea of 313
Gariperga, nun of St Mary in
    Cingla 247
Gausani, abbess of St Mary in
    Cingla 247
Gaza 307, 312
Gemondus, baron 98
Geoffrey, count of Conversano
    269, 270
Geoffrey, of Taranto 268, 275
Geoffrey, son of Alexander of
    Conversano/Gravina 311
Geoffrey Malaterra, chronicler
    34–5, 36, 180, 192, 266,
    268, 270, 271, 272, 275,
    276, 277
George, saint 291
Gerace 268
Gerard, abbot of
    Montecassino 256
Gerard, cardinal of Santa
    Croce 94–6
Gerard, lord of Sidon 310
Gerard de Lanzulino, baron
    98, 103
German empire 21, 33, 94

Gibbertus, priest in the
    Dialogi 233
Gisepertus, *prepositus* of St Sophia
    (Benevento) 248
Gisulf, abbot of
    Montecassino 250
Gisulf II, duke of Benevento 246
Gizzeria 193
Granada 113, 115
Grandmesnil 195
Gratian, author of the
    Decretum 217
Gravina 311
Gregory, archbishop of
    Benevento 100
Gregory I (the Great), pope 229
Gregory VII, pope 232, 234, 235
Guibert, archbishop of Ravenna
    234
    see also Clement III, (anti)pope

Hattin 317
Hauteville dynasty 19, 23, 25, 33,
    35, 36, 94, 101, 153, 156,
    164, 191, 192, 204, 265,
    266, 311
Hawisa of Giroie 195
Hejaz 117, 118
Henry I, king of England 29, 220
Henry II, king of England 22,
    23, 220
Henry IV, emperor 193, 234
Henry VI, emperor 2, 22, 25, 174
Hohenstaufen dynasty 2, 25
    see also Frederick II, emperor
    and king of Sicily; Henry
    VI, emperor; Manfred, king
    of Sicily
Holy Cross on Monte Marsico,
    monastery 235
Holy Land 25, 30, 172, 175, 305,
    306, 318

Holy Saviour, monastery 250
Holy Saviour of Alife, monastery 246, 248, 251, 252, 255
Holy Saviour (St Julia) of Brescia, monastery 248
Honorius II, pope 293
Hugh, king of Italy 253
Hugh, signatory/witness 194
Hugh de Grandmesnil 195, 196, 199
Hugh of St Victor, theologian 214
Hugo, archdeacon of Mottola 231
'Hugo Falcandus', chronicler 3, 21, 174, 175, 176, 180
Humbert, cardinal-bishop of Silva Candida 236
Humphrey, baron 98
Humphrey of Hauteville 192, 267

Iberia 115
ibn al-'Arabī, jurist 117
Ibn al-Athīr, chronicler 116, 308, 309, 313
Ibn al-Khaṭīb, historian/scholar 114
Ibn al-Qalānisī, chronicler 307, 308
Ibn Baṭṭūṭa, traveller/scholar 115
Ibn Jubayr, traveller/pilgrim/scholar 6, 113–27, 173, 180
Ibn Shaddād, chronicler 314
Ibn Zur'ah, jurist 127
Iceland 25
Iconium 276
al-Idrīsī, Muḥammad, cartographer 19, 173
Ifriqiyah 278
Innocent II, pope 94, 95, 102, 213, 216, 230, 232, 253, 293, 294
Innocent III, pope 231
Iordanus Pinzzast (attested beginning of twelfth century) 253

Iraq 119
Ireland 16, 17
Isola Capo Rizzuto 153–5

Jerusalem 183, 314
  kingdom of 6, 7, 23, 114, 115, 116, 118, 120, 122, 124, 125, 127, 173, 305, 306, 307, 311, 312, 313, 314, 315, 316, 317, 318
  see also Amalric, king; Baldwin I, king; Baldwin III, king; Baldwin IV, king
Jesus Christ 193, 212, 214, 227, 286, 288, 289
Joanna, daughter of King Henry II of England 22
Jocelyn (lord?) of Molfetta 269, 270, 276
John, judge of Bevenento 134
John, king of England 219
John, *prepositus* of St Mary *in Cingla* (end of ninth century) 249
John, priest and *prepositus* of St Mary *in Cingla* (in 969) 249, 251
John II, bishop of Benevento 252
John VIII, pope 249, 250
John IX, pope 249, 250
John Theristis, saint 159–61, 164
Jordan, count of Ariano 135, 140
Jordan I, prince of Capua 217
Joseph, prophet 123
Judith of Evreux 196
Julius Caesar, ruler 17
Justinian I, Byzantine emperor 158

Kerak 313
Knights Hospitaller, order of 311
Konya *see* Iconium

Lake Manzala 307
Lamezia 193

Lancashire 16
Lancaster 15, 32
Lando, abbot of St Vincent in Capua 235
Landolf, bishop of Tertiveri 229
Landulf II, archbishop of Benevento 132–5, 136–45
Landulf of Greca, constable of Benevento 132–45
Laurence, deacon and *prepositus* of St Mary *in Cingla* 249
Lebanon 119
Lecce 257
Leeds 15
Leo, abbot of St Vincent on Volturno 252
Leo VI, emperor 217
Leo IX, pope 227, 228, 229, 233, 236, 267
Leo Marsicanus, chronicler and cardinal-bishop of Ostia 253, 254
Librizzi 86
Libya 307, 318
London 16, 21
Longobardia 249, 265
Lothar, king of Italy 253
Lothar III, emperor 94, 99, 103, 230, 232
Lucania 153
Lucca 286
Lucera 49
Luke, abbot of St Mary in Patire (Nea Hodegetria) and abbot of Holy Saviour, Messina 158, 159
Luke, saint and bishop of Isola Capo Rizzuto 153–5, 164
Lupus Protospatharius, author of annals 273, 275, 278

Macedonia 249
Madelfrid, count 136
Madelfrid, father of Landulf of Greca 135
Maghreb 118
Mahdiyah 267, 270
Maida 193
Maio of Bari, admiral of admirals 21, 257, 307, 309
  see also Bari
Malta 278
Mamlūk dynasty 308, 313
Manfred, king of Sicily 19, 25
Manuel I Komnenos, emperor 310, 312, 316, 317, 318
Manzikert 276
al-Maqrizī, chronicler 308, 309, 313, 315, 317
Maraldus, bishop-elect of Minervino 230
Maria Komnene, niece of Manuel I Komnenos 310, 311
Marinus II, pope 250, 251
Martorana (St Mary of the Admiral, church) 25, 217, 290, 295
Marturana 194
Mary, saint 194
  see also Virgin Mary
Massafra 231
Matera 311
Mathilda, sister of Roger II, king of Sicily 255
Mauger of Hauteville 192
Mecca 113, 114, 115, 117, 119, 121, 126
Mediterranean, sea 115, 173, 265, 278
Melfi 49, 162, 197, 219, 220, 228, 229, 267
Mercurius, saint 291
Messina 115, 124, 171–83, 267
  Holy Saviour, monastery 156–9, 174, 177
Mezzoiuso 86
Michael VII Doukas, emperor 291

Michael Maurex, naval
    commander 269, 275
Michael of Otranto,
    ambassador 311
Mignano 293
Mileto 153
Mileto, monastery of Holy Trinity
    48, 192, 199, 203
Misilmeri 270
Mleh, prince 313
Molfetta 269
Monopoli 275
Montecassino, monastery of
    St Benedict 35, 133, 232,
    233, 236, 246–51, 253–6
    see also Amatus of
    Montecassino, chronicler;
    Bassacius, abbot; Bernard,
    abbot; Desiderius, abbot;
    Erchempert of Montecassino,
    chronicler; Gerard,
    abbot; Gisulf, abbot; Leo
    Marsicanus, chronicler;
    Oderisius I, abbot; Peter the
    Deacon, chronicler; Petronax,
    abbot; Ragemprandus,
    abbot; Rainald I, abbot;
    Richerius, abbot
Montefusco 95, 98, 101, 102,
    136, 143
Montepeloso 270
Moses, prophet 122
Mosul 118, 121
Mottola 231
Mount Athos 157
Mount Lebanon 121
Muḥammad, prophet of Allāh 116,
    124, 127
Muḥammad b. Isḥāq, admiral 317

Naples 4, 7, 8, 20, 93, 102,
    245, 257

Naso 86
Nero, emperor 19, 234
Nicastro 193, 194, 204
Nicholas I, pope 249
Nicholas II, pope 197, 229, 267
Nile Delta 306, 307
Nile, river 115, 308, 309
Normandy 15, 18, 23, 30, 31, 33,
    192, 195, 196, 197, 199,
    203, 266
Nūr al-Dīn, ruler of Aleppo and
    Damascus 306, 310, 312,
    313, 314, 317, 318

Oderisius I, abbot of
    Montecassino 256
Orderic Vitalis, chronicler 22, 23,
    192, 195, 196, 199, 203
    see also St Évroult, monastery
Oria 231, 268
Orientano 193
Osbern, abbot of St Évroult
    196, 204
Otranto 265, 277, 311
Otto, archbishop of Capua 256
Outremer 305, 317, 318
Oxford 15, 17, 20, 21

Palermo 19, 33, 46, 126, 154, 159,
    164, 177, 180, 217, 267, 268,
    269, 270, 272, 273, 278, 294
Palestine 307, 312, 313, 318
Pancrituda, nun of St Mary *in
    Cingla* 247
Paris 199
Paschal II, pope 132–5, 137, 141,
    142, 143, 231
Paul, bishop of Caiazzo 231
Paul, saint 214
Pavia 286
Pays d'Ouche 195
Peloritani, mountain range 178

Perenos, duke of Durazzo 269
Pergolfus, *prepositus* of St Sophia (Benevento) 248
Persicus, judge of Benevento 134
Peter, cardinal bishop of Porto 138, 139
Peter, saint 133, 137, 140, 143, 233, 234, 293, 296
Peter Damian, cardinal-bishop of Ostia 236
Peter the Deacon, chronicler 230, 232
Petralia 269
Petronax, abbot of Montecassino 246, 247
Philagathos of Cerami, monk and preacher 159
Philip I, king of France 193
Philip II (Augustus), king of France 172, 176, 179, 180, 181, 182, 183
Pisa 232
Polignano 257
Pontecorvo 255

Rachisius, abbot of St Modestus (Benevento) 137
Ragempertus, *prepositus* of St Sophia (Benevento) 248
Ragemprandus, abbot of Montecassino 249
Rainald, archbishop of Bari 230
Rainald I, abbot of Montecassino 230, 232
Rainald Ridel, ruler of Gaeta 217
Rainer, prior of St Évroult 196
Rainulf I, count of Caiazzo 255, 256
Rainulf II of Alife, count of Caiazzo 94, 102, 103, 140, 255, 256

Ralph de Diceto, chronicler 172, 175
Rao de lo Tufo, baron 98, 103
Rashīd ad-Dīn Sinān, leader of the Nizari Ismaʿīlī 119
Ratchis, king of the Lombards 247
Red Sea 115
Reggio (Calabria) 161, 162, 267, 278
Richard I (Lionheart), king of England 171, 172, 176, 177, 179, 181, 182, 317
Richard I, prince of Capua 35, 196, 255, 266
Richard II, duke of Normandy 197
Richard II, prince of Capua 255
Richard of Devizes, chronicler 172, 175, 176, 177, 182, 183
Richerius, abbot of Montecassino 250
Rignano Garganica 102, 103
Rigord, chronicler 182
Robert, count of Caiazzo 135, 255
Robert I de Grandmesnil 195
Robert I, duke of Normandy 197
Robert I, prince of Capua 135
Robert II de Grandmesnil, abbot of St Euphemia 193–7, 198, 199–204
Robert II, prince of Capua 94
Robert de la Marca, baron 98, 102, 103
Robert FitzGiroie 195, 199
Robert Guiscard, duke of Apulia 8, 15, 18, 23, 24, 34, 35, 192, 194, 195, 197–8, 199, 203, 204, 255, 265–74, 285, 290, 291, 292, 293, 296
Robert of Bassunvilla, count of Conversano 311
Robert of Medania, count of Buonalbergo 100

Robert of Pietramaggiore, baron 102
Robert of Selby, chancellor 22, 99, 100, 230
Rocella 48
Rodelgarda, abbess of St Sophia of Benevento 253
Roffrid II, archbishop of Benevento 231
Roger, count of Ariano 93–7
Roger I, count of Sicily 18, 19, 24, 34–5, 153, 154, 192, 194, 199, 204, 265, 266, 267–70, 275, 276, 277, 278, 293, 305
Roger II, king of Sicily 2, 6, 7, 18, 19, 20, 21, 23, 25, 33, 34, 46, 48, 56, 89, 93–7, 154, 156, 157–9, 178, 212–21, 230, 232, 284–9, 305, 306, 307, 308, 311, 318
Roger III, duke of Apulia 285, 292, 296
Roger IV, duke of Apulia 297
Roger Borsa, duke of Apulia 34, 35, 266
Roger *de Boscione*, vassal of Robert, count of Caiazzo 256
Roger of Howden, chronicler 172, 174, 175, 176, 177, 182
Roger of Mistretta, scribe 46
Roger Toutebouve, lord of Monopoli(?) 269, 270
Rolpoto of Sant'Eustasio, constable of Benevento 94, 98
Romald, signatory/witness 194
Romanos IV Diogenes, emperor 270, 276
Rome 6, 20, 25, 30, 134, 137, 227, 230, 233, 235, 236, 293, 294
Romuald, cardinal deacon 138, 139
Romuald of Salerno, chronicler 3
Rosetta 308, 309
Rossano 156
  St Mary in Patire (Nea Hodegetria), monastery 156, 158
Rossemanus, archbishop of Benevento 102
Rottruda, founder of St Mary in Plumbariola and daughter of Ratchis, king of the Lombards 247
Russia 30

St Agatha of Catania, monastery 266
St Bartholomew of Taranto, monastery 257
St Benedict of Polignano, monastery 257
St Cassian, church 246
St Elia, monastery 193
St Euphemia (Campania), monastery 245
St Euphemia, monastery 6, 191–201
  town 191
  see also Calabria
St Évroult, monastery 192, 195, 196, 198, 199, 203, 204
  see also Normandy; Orderic Vitalis, chronicler
St Gregory, monastery 193
St John the Evangelist of Lecce, monastery 257
St Lawrence of Aversa, monastery 231
St Maria of Apeza 194
St Maria of Cipusa 193
St Martin, monastery 245

St Mary *de Canneto in finibus Beneventanis*, monastery 251
St Mary *in Cingla*, monastery 246–7, 248, 249, 250, 251, 252, 255, 256
St Mary *monialium* of Brindisi, monastery 257
St Mary of Capua, monastery 251, 255
St Mary of Cosenza, monastery 250, 251, 253
St Mary of Ferraria, monastery 93, 99
St Mary of Gallano, monastery 193
St Mary of Nicastro, church 194
St Mary of Piumarola, monastery 246, 247, 249, 250, 253
St Nicolas, monastery 193
St Nicholas of Calamizzi, monastery 161, 162, 163 *see also* Calabria; Cyprian of Calamizzi, saint and abbot
St Nicholas of Punta, church 158
St Peter of Episcopio, monastery 193
St Peter of Maida, monastery 194
St Peter on the Sabato, dependency of St Vincent on Volturno 251
St Petronilla, monastery 253
St Scholastica, monastery 250
St Scholastica of Bari, monastery 257
St Senator, port of 193
St Vesanatus, monastery 193
St Victorinus of Benevento, monastery 252
St Vincent on Volturno, monastery 248, 249, 251, 252
Sts Festus and Desiderius, monastery 245
Sts Gregory and Sebastian, monastery 245
Sts Marcellinus and Peter, monastery 246
Sts Nicander and Marcian, monastery 245
Saladin, sultan 115, 118, 119, 120, 121, 183, 306, 312, 313, 314, 315, 316, 317, 318
Salento peninsula 8, 268, 277
Salerno 4, 102, 227
San Germano 250
Sannio 102
Sant'Agata dei Goti 255
Sarolus de lo Tufo, baron 98, 102, 103
Sarracenus, *sculdahis* 246
Saxony 193
Seljuk dynasty 270, 276
Serlo of Hauteville 192
Shāwar, vizier 118, 310
Sheffield 16, 17
Shīrkūh, general/vizier 118, 310, 312
Sibylla, daughter of Amalric I 310
Sibylla of Burgundy 297
Sicily 2, 6, 21, 22, 24, 25, 34, 46–84, 100, 114, 115, 116, 123, 124–7, 152, 154, 156, 160, 164, 171–83, 191, 192, 197, 215, 236, 265, 267, 268, 269, 275, 276, 278, 285, 286, 293, 294, 307, 316, 317
Sigurð, king of Norway 25
Sikelgarda, daughter of Count Landulf 136
Simon Magus 233, 234
Sinai 317
Sousse 307
Soviet Union 30

Spain 22
Squillace 154
Stephen VII, pope 251
Stephen IX, pope 235
Stephan Pateranos, *praetor* 274, 275, 276, 277
Stilo 159, 161
Symbatikios, strategos of Macedonia, Thrace, Cephalonia and Longobardia 249
Syria 310, 317, 318

Tadeus de la Greca, baron 98
Tamim ibn al Mu'izz of Mahdiyah, emir 270
Tancred, brother of Alexander of Conversano/Gravina 311
Tancred, king of Sicily 2, 172, 177, 183
Tancred of Hauteville 18, 191, 192, 266
Tancred of Hauteville, prince of Galilee 23
Tarābulus *see* Tripoli (Libya)
Taranto 23, 257, 268
Tasia, founder of St Mary in Plumbariola and married to Ratchis, king of the Lombards 247
Telese 255
Templars, order of 307
Teopegisa, abbess of St Sophia of Benevento 254
Theodore, saint 291
Theodore Maurozoumes 312
Thessalonica 288, 289, 290, 291, 292, 295, 317
Thierry, abbot of St Évroult 196, 203
Thomas Brown, royal official 22

Thomas of Butera, bishop of Cefalù 46
Thomas of Fenucolo, baron 100
Thorald, donor of church of St Mary of Nicastro 194
Thrace 249
Tinnīs 305, 307–9, 317, 318
Transjordan 313, 314, 317
Trapani 126
Trigno, river 251
Tripoli (Libya) 307
Troia 228
Troina 268
Tunisia 307, 318
Twelve Martyr-Brothers, saints 247
Tyre 121, 122, 123, 310
Tyrrhenian, sea 204

Ufita, valley 101
United Kingdom 30
Urban II, pope 34, 35, 217, 228, 229, 231, 256
Ursus, abbot of St Sophia of Benevento 253
Ursus, *prepositus* of St Sophia (Benevento) 248
Uthmān, caliph 116

Val Demone 268, 269
Val Fortore 99, 101, 102, 103
Venice 24
Venosa, monastery of Holy Trinity 192, 199, 203
Victor III, pope 233
    see also Desiderius, abbot of Montecassino
Villa Santa Lucia 247
Virgin Mary 191, 193, 288
    see also Mary, saint
Volturno, river 247, 256

Index

William, bishop of Conversano 231
William, duke of Apulia 255
William I (the Conqueror), king of England 18, 23, 29, 30
  see also William II, duke of Normandy
William I, king of Sicily 19, 20, 21, 24, 160, 219, 220, 297, 307, 309, 318
William II, duke of Normandy 196, 197, 198
  see also William I (the Conqueror), king of England
William II, king of Sicily 19, 21, 22, 49, 114, 116, 124, 125, 126, 127, 178, 180, 219, 220, 230, 285, 309, 313, 314, 315, 316, 317, 318

William Capriolus, signatory/witness 194
William FitzGiroie 195, 199
William of Apulia, chronicler 2, 34, 35, 266, 271, 273, 275, 276, 277
William of Hauteville 192
William of Newburgh, chronicler 172, 179, 182
William of Tyre, chronicler 305, 306, 311, 315, 316, 318
William of Volpiano, abbot 203

Yemen 119

Zachary, pope 249
Zirid dynasty 267, 268, 270, 278